About the Author

David L. Hudson Jr. is the author or co-author of over two dozen books, including *The Handy Supreme Court Answer Book* (Visible Ink Press, 2007), *The Rehnquist Court: Understanding Its Impact and Legacy* (Praeger, 2006), and (as co-editor with John Vile and David Schultz) *The Encyclopedia of the First Amendment* (CQ Press, 2008). He works as First Amendment Scholar for the First Amendment Center and teaches classes at Vanderbilt Law School, Nashville School of Law, and Middle Tennessee State University. Hudson earned his undergraduate degree from Duke University and his law degree from Vanderbilt Law School. He resides in the Middle Tennessee area with his wife, Carla, and two dogs, Gloria and Gucci.

Also from Visible Ink Press

The Handy Anatomy Answer Book
by James Bobick and Naomi Balaban
ISBN: 978-1-57859-190-9

The Handy Answer Book for Kids (and Parents),
2nd edition
by Gina Misiroglu
ISBN: 978-1-57859-219-7

The Handy Astronomy Answer Book
by Charles Liu
ISBN: 978-1-57859-193-0

The Handy Biology Answer Book
by James Bobick, Naomi Balaban, Sandra
Bobick, and Laurel Roberts
ISBN: 978-1-57859-150-3

The Handy Dinosaur Answer Book, 2nd edition
by Patricia Barnes–Svarney and Thomas E.
Svarney
ISBN: 978-1-57859-218-0

The Handy Geography Answer Book, 2nd
edition
by Paul A. Tucci
ISBN: 978-1-57859-215-9

The Handy Geology Answer Book
by Patricia Barnes–Svarney and Thomas E.
Svarney
ISBN: 978-1-57859-156-5

The Handy History Answer Book, 2nd edition
by Rebecca Nelson Ferguson
ISBN: 978-1-57859-170-1

The Handy Math Answer Book
by Patricia Barnes–Svarney and Thomas E.
Svarney
ISBN: 978-1-57859-171-8

The Handy Ocean Answer Book
by Patricia Barnes–Svarney and Thomas E.
Svarney
ISBN: 978-1-57859-063-6

The Handy Philosophy Answer Book
by Naomi Zack
ISBN: 978-1-57859-226-5

The Handy Physics Answer Book
by P. Erik Gundersen
ISBN: 978-1-57859-058-2

The Handy Politics Answer Book
by Gina Misiroglu
ISBN: 978-1-57859-139-8

The Handy Religion Answer Book
by John Renard
ISBN: 978-1-57859-125-1

The Handy Science Answer Book®,
Centennial Edition
by The Science and Technology Department, Carnegie Library of Pittsburgh
ISBN: 978-1-57859-140-4

The Handy Sports Answer Book
by Kevin Hillstrom, Laurie Hillstrom, and
Roger Matuz
ISBN: 978-1-57859-075-9

The Handy Supreme Court Answer Book
by David L Hudson, Jr.
ISBN: 978-1-57859-196-1

The Handy Weather Answer Book, 2nd edition
by Kevin S. Hile
ISBN: 978-1-57859-215-9

Please visit the Handy series website at handyanswers.com

THE
HANDY
LAW
ANSWER
BOOK

THE

HANDY

LAW

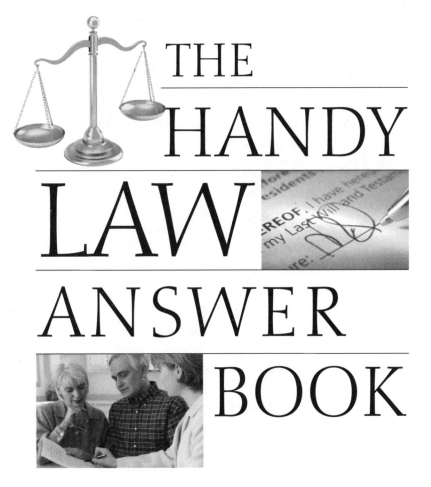

ANSWER

BOOK

David L. Hudson Jr.

Detroit

THE HANDY LAW ANSWER BOOK

Visible Ink Press®
43311 Joy Rd., #414
Canton, MI 48187-2075

Visible Ink Press is a registered trademark of Visible Ink Press LLC.

Most Visible Ink Press books are available at special quantity discounts when purchased in bulk by corporations, organizations, or groups. Customized printings, special imprints, messages, and excerpts can be produced to meet your needs. For more information, contact Special Markets Director, Visible Ink Press, www.visibleink.com, or 734-667-3211.

Managing Editor: Kevin S. Hile
Art Director: Mary Claire Krzewinski
Typesetting: Marco Di Vita
Proofreader: Sharon Malinowski
ISBN 978-1-57859-217-3

Cover images: iStock.com.

Library of Congress Cataloguing-in-Publication Data

Hudson, David L., 1969–
  The handy law answer book / by David L. Hudson Jr. — 1st ed.
      p. cm. — (Handy answer book series)
  Includes bibliographical references and index.
  ISBN 978-1-57859-217-3
  1. Law—United States—Outlines, syllabi, etc. I. Title.
  KF386.H82 2010
  349.73—dc22   2010000201

Printed in the United States of America

10 9 8 7 6 5 4 3 2 1

Contents

PERSONAL INJURY
LAW ... 307

Negligence ... Professional Negligence ...
Other Torts ... Product Liability

To three great lawyers:
Steve Waldron, Terry Fann, and
"King" Richard Sebastian.

Acknowledgments

I would like to thank Visible Ink Press publisher, Roger Jänecke, for his vision and for granting me another writing opportunity with the "Handy" series. I enjoyed writing the *Handy Law Answer Book* as much as my previous work in the series, *The Handy Supreme Court Answer Book*. I would also like to thank Managing Editor Kevin Hile for his superior editing abilities. Thanks to all of my students at Middle Tennessee State University, Nashville School of Law, and Vanderbilt Law School, who enrich my experience with teaching various legal subjects on a daily basis. Finally, I would like to thank my parents and my wife, Carla, for their constant love, support, and encouragement.

Introduction

Law in the United States is ubiquitous and unique. Pick up a newspaper or turn on the television and you will confront the law or the legal system. Recently, the leading stories in the news media involved the possibility of new federal healthcare legislation, a pending ruling by the U.S. Supreme Court on campaign finance, the implementation of behavioral profiles for would-be terrorists, and a gruesome murder. Obviously, all of these—pending legislation, a future court ruling, profiling possible terrorists, or criminals and a crime—directly trigger the legal system.

The American legal system is unique for many reasons, most notably its Constitution—the grand experiment created in secret at those fabled meetings during the summer of 1787 in Philadelphia, Pennsylvania. The founding fathers—a sizeable number of whom were lawyers—created a legal system that is the envy of the world. It separated power between three branches of government, divided authority between a central, federal government and various state governments, and even provided for measures of individual freedom, particularly after the addition of the first ten amendments known as the Bill of Rights.

Former U.S. Supreme Court Justice Oliver Wendell Holmes Jr., who is considered one of the country's great jurists, once wrote: "The rational study of law is still to a large extent the study of history." On another occasion, he wrote: "The law embodies the story of a nation's development through many centuries, and it cannot be dealt with as if it contained only the axioms and corollaries of a book of mathematics."

For this reason, *The Handy Law Answer Book* begins with an examination of the history and development of the Constitution—the fundamental blueprint of the legal system—and a discussion of constitutional law. The states passed the U.S. Constitution only upon the promise that Congress would pass certain provisions protecting individuals from the powers of the new central government. These first ten amendments to the U.S. Constitution are what James Madison called "the great rights of mankind"—the Bill of Rights. The next chapter of this book examines the various provisions of the Bill of Rights.

Chapter Three, The Court System, explains the structure of the judicial branch in both the federal and state systems. It examines not only the highest court—the so-called "Court of Last Resort"—but also various state courts. In Chapter Four, readers will learn more about lawsuits and lawyers, including how a lawsuit starts, how one becomes a lawyer, and how to choose a lawyer.

Many people are afraid of the legal system, baffled by its jargon, mystified by its complexity, or upset at its outcomes. But, the law often serves as the galvanizing force for social change. As Supreme Court Justice Robert Jackson once wrote: "Any legal doctrine which fails to enlist the support of well-regarded lawyers will have no real sway in this country."

The text then examines various substantive areas of law—not all areas of law, but those most commonly encountered by people in their everyday lives. These include criminal law, credit and bankruptcy, employment law, family law, and personal injury law. People often face criminal charges, encounter financial difficulty, suffer a job loss, endure a painful divorce, embark on a beautiful marriage, or suffer an injury in everyday life. These chapters will explain the legalities involved in all of these areas.

In the criminal field, readers will learn how a criminal case moves from arrest to arraignment to trial. You will learn about felonies and misdemeanors, bail, juvenile justice, and selecting juries. Regarding credit and bankruptcy, you will learn about credit records, credit cards, Chapters 7 and 13 bankruptcies, and the relatively new Bankruptcy Abuse Prevention and Consumer Protection Act of 2005. In employment law, you will read about employment contracts, the employment-at-will doctrine, just-cause clauses, discrimination lawsuits, and the Equal Employment Opportunity Commission. Finally, in tort law, you will discover various causes of action, the elements of a slip-and-fall case, the different type of damages in lawsuits, and the question of tort reform.

Recall the uniqueness of the American legal system. One of the more fascinating aspects of this system is its federalism—the allocation of power between the federal and state governments. Under our legal system, states are granted an impressive degree of discretion to develop their own laws and principles as long as they comport with the fundamental baselines of the U.S. Constitution. In other words, the workers compensation system in Tennessee can differ from the workers compensation system in Louisiana, as long as neither violates the U.S. Constitution. Similarly, personal injury law in California differs from personal injury law in Massachusetts. Different states have different grounds for divorce and different requirements for marriage.

The Handy Law Answer Book follows the format of the "Handy" series with its easily accessible question-and-answer format that provides an overview, a history, leading principles, seminal court rulings, and practical information.

In addition, the book features an array of sidebars titled "LegalSpeak" that seek to provide the actual language of laws and court rulings or to explain difficult legal concepts.

Unless otherwise indicated, the "LegalSpeak" quotes are taken from U.S. Supreme Court decisions.

The Handy Law Answer Book also includes three appendices that explain case and statute citations, provide a list of helpful online resources, and include the full text of the U.S. Constitution. You will also find a helpful glossary of legal terms and an index.

I hope readers enjoy the book as much as I did putting it together.

David L. Hudson, Jr.

CONSTITUTIONAL LAW

THE U.S. CONSTITUTION

What is the **primary source of law** in the **United States**?

The primary source of law is the U.S. Constitution, which serves as the blueprint for the country's legal system. It is the highest form of law. States also have their own constitutions, which serve as their highest forms of legal documents. If a law does not comport with the Constitution, the law is declared unconstitutional or void.

What this means is that other forms of law must comport with the Constitution. In other words, a common legal claim asserted by a party challenging a law is that the law is unconstitutional. This means that the law violates a provision of the Constitution and is unenforceable.

What exactly does the **U.S. Constitution do**?

This most fundamental of all legal documents defines and limits the powers of the federal government. It also separates and defines the powers of this federal government into three branches of government—the legislative, executive, and judicial branches. The Constitution also establishes the baseline between the federal government and various state governments.

How is the **U.S. Constitution composed**?

The U.S. Constitution is composed of seven articles. The first three articles are the longest and arguably the most important. These three articles explain the powers of the three branches of government—legislative, executive, and judicial. Article I of the Constitution outlines the powers of the U.S. Congress. Article II outlines the power of

1

The U.S. Constitution is the fundamental document that establishes a balance of power between the branches of the federal government, as well as for indicating what powers are under state or federal control (*iStock*).

the president—the chief officer of the executive branch. Article III outlines the powers of the judicial branch.

Article IV deals with the states and how the laws of one state are treated in other states. It also deals with how to admit a state to the union. Article V describes the amendment process. Article VI—a very short part of the Constitution—contains the Supremacy Clause, which ensures that federal law and the Constitution are the highest law of the land. Article VII consists of a single sentence explaining that it would take nine states to ratify the Constitution.

How many **constitutional amendments** have been enacted?

There have been only 27 amendments to the U.S. Constitution in over two centuries. The first ten amendments were added only four years after the ratification of the Constitution. These ten amendments are collectively known as "the Bill of Rights." The next amendments were added at various times in the nation's history.

The Amendments to the U.S. Constitution

Amendment	Issue Addressed
1st Amendment	Freedoms of religion, speech, press, assembly and petition
2nd Amendment	Right to bear arms

Amendment	Issue Addressed
3rd Amendment	No quartering of troops in private homes
4th Amendment	No unreasonable searches and seizures
5th Amendment	Right to grand jury, no double jeopardy, freedom from self-incrimination, due process and just compensation
6th Amendment	Speedy trial, public trial, notice of charges, compulsory process, confrontation clause and assistance of counsel
7th Amendment	Right to jury trials in civil cases
8th Amendment	No excessive bail, fines or cruel and unusual punishment
9th Amendment	Asserts unenumerated (nonlisted) rights; that is, that the Bill of Rights provides individual rights beyond those listed in the first eight amendments (e.g., right to privacy)
10th Amendment	Affirms a basic principle of federalism, that power is divided between federal and state governments; reserves powers to the states
11th Amendment	Asserts state sovereign immunity, which shields states from many lawsuits
12th Amendment	President and vice president must be from same political party
13th Amendment	Outlaws slavery and involuntary servitude
14th Amendment	Citizenship, rights of equal protection and due process
15th Amendment	Right to vote
16th Amendment	Income tax
17th Amendment	Popular election of senators
18th Amendment	Prohibition of alcohol
19th Amendment	Right of women to vote
20th Amendment	Date of presidential swearing-in; solves lame-duck problem
21st Amendment	Repeals the Eighteenth Amendment; no Prohibition
22nd Amendment	Limits presidents to two full terms (eight years)
23rd Amendment	District of Columbia; voting for president
24th Amendment	No poll tax
25th Amendment	Line of succession upon president's death
26th Amendment	Voting age becomes 18
27th Amendment	Congressional pay raises

What does the **Supremacy Clause** of the U.S. Constitution say?

The Supremacy Clause states: "This Constitution, and the laws of the United States which shall be made in pursuance thereof; and all treaties made, or which shall be made, under the authority of the United States, shall be the supreme law of the land; and the judges in every state shall be bound thereby, anything in the Constitution or laws of any State to the contrary notwithstanding."

HISTORY OF THE CONSTITUTION

What was the **pressing need** for the **Constitution**?

The previous constitution in the United States was called the Articles of Confederation. This confederation system of government did not provide sufficient power to the central government and allowed state governments too much power. Many leaders in the country saw that there was a pressing need for a stronger central government to regulate interactions (such as matters of commerce) between the states. This led to a series of meetings culminating in a meeting in Philadelphia, Pennsylvania. Representatives from every state except Rhode Island (a small, independently minded state) met in secret in Philadelphia to discuss how to improve and amend the Articles of Confederation. The Framers—as they came to be called—went far beyond their stated duty and formed an entirely new legal document called the U.S. Constitution.

What were the **problems** with the **Articles of Confederation**?

The primary problem with the Articles of Confederation was that the central government was too weak. It did not have the power to regulate different states' behavior. The commerce interests of the various states often were not aligned and the central government could not resolve these disputes. Under the Articles of Confederation, the Confederation Congress could not force state governments to raise monies for the federal government but had to depend on them to supply it voluntarily. The Confederation Congress could declare war but it could not raise an army. The states had to do that.

George Washington, who would later become the first president of the United States, was also one of the framers of the Constitution and a leader of the Philadelphia Convention (*iStock*).

New York political leader Alexander Hamilton wrote to colleague James Duane in 1780 about the problem with the Confederation Congress, which he described: "The fundamental defect is a want of power in Congress." Former United States Supreme Court Justice Warren Burger wrote, nearly two hundred years later, that the Articles "were barely more than a multinational treaty between thirteen independent, sovereign states."

Who were some of the **leaders** of the **Philadelphia Convention of 1787**?

The Philadelphia Convention included future Presidents George Washington and James Madison; future Supreme Court Justices Oliver Ellsworth, William Paterson, John Rutledge, and James Wilson; the first U.S. Attorney General, Edmund Randolph; and Roger Sherman, a principal draftsman of the Declaration of Independence.

Who were the 55 **Founding Framers** of the **Philadelphia Convention of 1787**

The following table lists who the Framers were and the states from which they hailed.

Founding Framers of the Philadelphia Convention of 1787

State	Framers
Connecticut	Oliver Ellsworth, William Samuel Johnson, Roger Sherman
Delaware	Richard Bassett, Gunning Bedford, Jacob Broom, John Dickinson, George Read
Georgia	Abraham Baldwin, William Few, William Houstoun, William Pierce
Maryland	Daniel Carroll, Luther Martin, James McHenry, John F. Mercer, Daniel of St. Thomas Jenifer
Massachusetts	Elbridge Gerry, Nathan Gorham, Rufus King, Caleb Strong
New Hampshire	Michael Gillman, John Langdon
New Jersey	David Brearley, Jonathan Dayton, William Houston, William Livingston, William Paterson
New York	Alexander Hamilton, Robert Lansing, Robert Yates
North Carolina	William Blount, William Richardson Davie, Alexander Martin, Richard Dobbs Spaight, Hugh Williamson
Pennsylvania	George Clymer, Thomas Fitzsimons, Benjamin Franklin, Jared Ingersoll, Thomas Mifflin, Gouverneur Morris, Robert Morris, James Wilson
South Carolina	Pierce Butler, Charles Cotesworth Pinckney, John Rutledge
Virginia	John Blair, James Madison, George Mason, James McClurg, Edmund Randolph, George Washington, George Wythe

Did **all** of the 55 **delegates sign** the final product of the **Philadelphia Convention**?

No, several delegates left before the Convention convened in September. These included: William Richardson Davie, Oliver Ellsworth, William Houston, William Houstoun, John Lansing, Jr., Alexander Martin, Luther Martin, James McClurg, John Francis Mercer, William Pierce, Caleb Strong, George Wythe, and Robert Yates.

Additionally, three members of the Convention stayed until the end but still refused to sign the document. These three were Elbridge Gerry, Edmund Randolph, and George Mason.

Why did Elbridge **Gerry**, Edmund **Randolph** and George **Mason refuse** to **sign** the Constitution?

Ironically, Randolph would later refuse to sign the Constitution at the end of the Convention in part because he believed his constituents in Virginia would disapprove of the Constitution. He argued that the people in the states, through their representatives, should have the "full opportunity" to propose amendments to the Constitution. However, during the ratification battle in his home state of Virginia, Randolph fought for its adoption.

Gerry and Mason, key contributors throughout the summer, refused to sign the Constitution in part because it lacked a Bill of Rights. Gerry, the Massachusetts delegate, later wrote: "There is no security in the proferred system, either for the rights of conscience or the liberty of the Press." For Mason's part, a few days earlier, he had said: "I would sooner chop off my right hand than put it to the Constitution."

Mason honestly believed that the system of government would produce either a "monarchy or a corrupt oppressive aristocracy." He also felt that the "Constitution has been formed without the knowledge or idea of the people." Mason believed that the delegates had exceeded their authority by secretly creating a powerful national government that would take away the powers of the states.

What were the **professions** of the **Founders**?

The majority (33) of the 55 Founding Framers were attorneys. They, as a class, were wealthy landowners who enjoyed strong political connections. They represented future presidents, Supreme Court justices, governors and similar high political positions. The future third president, Thomas Jefferson, who could not attend the Convention because he was serving as ambassador to France, called the men at the Convention "an assembly of demigods." Jefferson meant that the men participating at the Convention were among the best political leaders in the nation.

Why was **James Madison** a **key** person in the **Convention**?

James Madison of Virginia was a key person at the Convention, particularly for historical purposes. Madison kept the most detailed notes of anyone attending the Convention. Historians owe a huge debt of gratitude to Madison for this task alone. Madison also planned ahead of the Convention and introduced several key measures during the Convention.

What did the new **Constitution say** about **slavery**?

The new Constitution did not directly address the slavery problem, probably because many of the members knew that members—particularly from the more agrarian, southern states—would not be willing to compromise on the measure. However, the vast majority of the delegates did not want to dissolve the Union over slavery. Many members from the southern states would leave the Convention rather than agree to the abolition of slavery.

The issue of slavery was closely tied to the question of representation in Congress. The southern states wanted to count slaves in their population numbers because they would obtain more seats in the House of Representatives. The northern states did not want to count slaves for purposes of legislative representation since slaves would not vote or pay taxes. The northern states also did not want the southern states to obtain more power.

The delegates eventually agreed to tie taxation to representation and count slaves as 3/5ths of a person. Some historians contend that the Convention agreed to this compromise over slavery and representation in exchange for the exclusion of slavery in the Northwest Ordinance of 1787. The Northwest Ordinance dealt with the settlement of lands in the West north of the Ohio River.

The Northern and Southern delegates bargained over the issues of slavery and trade well into the month of August. On August 24, the Committee of Eleven issued a report that contained four provisions: (1) Congress could not prohibit the exportation of slaves until 1800; (2) Congress could tax imported slaves; (3) Exports could not be taxed; and (4) Congress could pass navigation acts by simple majority. The northern states, which depended on commerce, wanted Congress to pass laws regulating trade.

The Constitution would extend the date to allow the importation of slaves until 1808. The Constitution also contained a clause, called the Fugitive Slave Clause, which allowed Southerners to go into northern states to recover runaway slaves. Unfortunately, the fugitive slave clause enabled the capture of free blacks in northern territory by southern slave owners.

Thus, the Constitution approved of slavery—if somewhat less than enthusiastically—by counting slaves for the population of states for representative purposes. It also protected the African slave trade for 20 years and guaranteed that masters could recover their runaway slaves. Because of its approval of slavery, the renowned abolitionist William Lloyd Garrison famously burned a copy of the Constitution, calling it a "covenant with death and an agreement with Hell." However, not all members of the Convention approved of slavery. Gouvernour Morris famously referred to it as "the curse of Heaven on the states" that sanction it.

James Madison spoke about the Constitution and slavery at the Virginia ratification convention. Madison said: "The southern states would not have entered into the union of America, without the temporary possession of that trade." However, Madison pointed out that under the Articles of Confederation, the slave trade could have continued forever. At least under the new Constitution, the importation of slaves would end in 20 years.

Also, the Constitution never uses the words "slave" or "slavery."

Although the states in the North were technically free of slavery, before the U.S. Civil War the Fugitive Slave Clause allowed slave owners from the South to retrieve their "property" if the excapee fled north (*Library of Congress*).

What was the **Fugitive Slave Clause**?

The Fugitive Slave Clause in Article IV, Section 2 provided that masters could recover their fugitive slaves as property.

After the Constitution was signed, what happened during the **ratification process**?

Article VII of the Constitution provides: "The ratification of the conventions of nine states shall be sufficient for the establishment of the Constitution between the states so ratifying the same." This meant that the "real fight" did not come on the convention floor. It came in the states over whether to ratify the Constitution. Many merchants, manufacturers, and big plantation owners in the South favored the Constitution. They knew the new Constitution would help protect their business interests.

But, many small farmers did not want to sacrifice their individual freedom and become dependent on the business people. The battle over ratification became a great issue of the day. It captured the headlines and great space in the newspapers. Pamphlets were printed on each side. Congress directed the state legislatures to call ratification conventions to vote on the new document. Under the ratification process, the state legislatures would vote to call special conventions. Delegates, often the state legislators themselves, would vote at the conventions.

The ratification process was not easy. Political leaders were divided. Supporters of the new Constitution with its strong central government called themselves Federal-

8

ists. Opponents of the Constitution were called Anti-Federalists. Many of them opposed the Constitution because it failed to provide for a bill of rights and gave too much power to the federal government at the expense of the state governments.

What were the principal **objections** of the **Anti-Federalists** to the Constitution?

The Anti-Federalists were particularly concerned with the so-called "necessary and proper" clause of the new Constitution. Article I, Section 8 provided Congress with the power to "make all Laws which shall be necessary and proper" for executing its powers vested in the Constitution. Other Anti-Federalists were concerned with the supremacy clause in Article I. Many Anti-Federalists viewed this clause as wiping out the powers of state governments.

Many Anti-Federalists also argued that the Constitution gave too much power to the president. Some feared that the president and the Senate would unite to become similar to the King of England and the upper house of the English Parliament, the House of Lords. The King of England and the House of Lords represented aristocrats, the upper class of society, and tended to ignore the interests of regular people.

What were the *Federalist Papers* and what was their importance?

The *Federalist Papers* were a series of essays that galvanized much popular support for the Constitution during the ratification struggle. In the most populous states of New York and Virginia the Anti-Federalists fought hard. After the Philadelphia Convention, James Madison co-wrote a series of articles with Alexander Hamilton and John Jay that became known as *The Federalist Papers*. These 85 essays written under the pen name Publius are still considered the definitive work on the Constitution. Thomas Jefferson once called them "the best commentary on the principles of government which ever was written."

These articles discussed the framework of the Constitution, including the principles of checks and balances and separation of powers among three branches of government. Hamilton, Jay, and Madison sought to persuade the readers that the newly designed government was the best course of action for the young country. Hamilton wrote that the nation faced a "crisis." He wrote that if the country voted against the new Constitution, that decision would "deserve to be considered as the general misfortune of mankind."

In *Federalist 45* Madison argued that the state governments did not have much to fear from the federal government. Madison wrote: "The powers delegated by the proposed Constitution to the federal government are few and defined. Those which are to remain in the State governments are numerous and indefinite."

Did the **Anti-Federalists** have their own **published writings**?

Yes, the Anti-Federalists also relied on a series of anonymous essays. Several Anti-Federalists also wrote articles under pen names attacking various aspects of the Constitution. An Anti-Federalist who called himself the "Federal Farmer" critiqued the Constitution in a series of letters published in the *Poughkeepsie Country Journal* from November 1787 to January 1788. The letters also appeared in pamphlet form. For many years, it was assumed that Richard Henry Lee of Virginia was the author. Now, some historians believe the author was the New York Anti-Federalist Melancton Smith.

The "Letters from the Federal Farmer" criticized the new Constitution and its proponents as showing a "strong tendency to aristocracy." The Federal Farmer argued that the Constitution concentrated too much power in the central government. The Federal Farmer also made some accurate predictions about the future of our government. For example, the Federal Farmer wrote: "This system promises a large field of employment to military gentlemen and gentlemen of the law."

Robert Yates, a New York judge who served in the Convention, wrote a series of articles under the pen name "Brutus." Brutus was the Roman republican who helped assassinate Julius Caesar to prevent Caesar from overthrowing the Roman Republic. In one of his articles he criticized the powers granted to the judicial branch. He wrote that "the supreme court under this constitution would be exalted above all other power in the government, and subject to no control."

How did the **battle between** the **Federalists** and **Anti-Federalists** conclude?

The battle between the Federalists and Anti-Federalists was intense. However, the Federalists possessed advantages. They enjoyed most of the media support. The large newspapers from Boston, New York and Philadelphia took up the Federalist cause. They also seemed to have the best ammunition—the detailed document known as the Constitution. Though the Anti-Federalists made many arguments against provisions of the Constitution, they did not have their own document. The Anti-Federalists could only criticize the new document.

However, the Anti-Federalists seized upon the lack of a bill of rights as a prime weapon in the ratification battles. Delaware became the first state to ratify the Constitution and it did so unanimously on December 7, 1787. Then, an intense battle began in Pennsylvania. James Wilson took the lead in defending the Constitution in his home state.

In a well-known address delivered on October 6, 1787, Wilson argued that the inclusion of a bill of rights was "superfluous and absurd." The new Congress, Wilson argued, "possesses no influence whatever upon the press." Wilson pointed out that many Anti-Federalists were criticizing the new document because it provided for a standing army. Wilson responded: "Yet I do not know a nation in the world, which has not found it necessary and useful to maintain the appearance of strength in a season of the most profound tranquility."

The state assembly had to vote on a state convention. Many of the Anti-Federalists in the state legislature refused to attend the assembly. They did not want the Assembly to have a quorum, or a sufficient number of members to take a valid vote. Allegedly, a mob of people broke into a local home and dragged two Anti-Federalists to the Assembly floor in order to create a quorum. The delegates voted 45 to 2 in favor of a ratification convention. The state convention met for five weeks. Finally, on December 12, 1787, the delegates voted for ratification by a vote of 46 to 23. The vote upset some citizens with Anti-Federalists's sympathies. A mob of such people attacked James Wilson in Carlisle, Pennsylvania. The Pennsylvania delegates also considered fifteen amendments proposed by Anti-Federalist Robert Whitehill. These proposed amendments were similar to what would later become the U.S. Bill of Rights.

In what states was the **ratification debate** most **intense** and close?

Ratification was more difficult in the populous states of Massachusetts and New York. The debate in Massachusetts was particularly intense. Massachusetts voted 187 to 168 in favor of the Constitution on February 6, 1788, only after the Federalists agreed to recommend amending the Constitution to include protections for individual liberties.

Massachusetts became the first state officially to recommend amendments to the Constitution during the ratification process. Though the nine proposed amendments bear little resemblance to the final U.S. Bill of Rights, they were an important precursor to the Bill of Rights.

What **happened** in the large state of **Virginia** with respect to **ratification**?

Actually, New Hampshire became the required ninth state on June 21, 1788, voting 57 to 46 in favor of the Constitution. Although the Constitution was technically in effect after New Hampshire ratified it, Virginia was such a large and powerful state that it was crucial for it to ratify the Constitution. The large state of Virginia did not know that New Hampshire had become the necessary ninth state, so the debate continued there.

Virginia was the home of James Madison, George Washington, and Thomas Jefferson, all of whom supported the Constitution. However, the state was also the home of a group of well-known Anti-Federalists, including Patrick Henry and George Mason. The battle in Virginia was particularly difficult. After one debate, Madison fell ill and was bed-ridden for three straight days. Some great statesmen, such as the brilliant orator from Virginia, Patrick Henry, led the Anti-Federalists. During the debate on the ratification in his state, Henry asked: "What right had they [the Constitution delegates] to say, 'We the People?'"

One of the most prominent figures of the American Revolution and the country''s early history, Patrick Henry was an Anti-Federalist who opposed a U.S. Constitution that he feared would give government too much power over individuals (*Library of Congress*).

In arguing against the Constitution, George Mason wrote, "It is ascertained, by history, that there never was a government over a very extensive country without destroying the liberties of the people." However, state delegate Edmund Pendleton countered in the Virginia Ratification Convention: "In reviewing the history of the world, shall we find an instance where any society retained its liberty without government."

In June, Governor Edmund Randolph stood up and spoke in favor of the Constitution even though he had failed to sign it last September. Randolph explained that he did not sign because the document did not contain necessary amendments. However, he said that because other states had proposed amendments to be passed after ratification, he would vote in favor of ratification. He also pointed out that eight other states had already ratified.

Patrick Henry charged that Randolph had been persuaded to change positions by none other than George Washington. Though this charge cannot be proven beyond a shadow of a doubt, Washington did later name Randolph his first attorney general.

Madison managed to gather enough support for the Constitution in the Virginia state convention on June 25, 1788. The delegates narrowly approved the Constitution. Two days later, a committee at the convention proposed a bill of rights to be added to the Constitution. Virginia voted in favor of ratification by a narrow vote of 89 to 79. Virginia also attached proposed amendments as well, many of which would later be contained in the Bill of Rights. Some Anti-Federalists were very upset and wanted to resist the new Constitution. However, at a meeting in Richmond, Patrick Henry said that they must accept defeat. "As true and faithful republicans [honorable citizens] you had all better go home."

Many Anti-Federalists became supporters of the new government. For example, Anti-Federalist Elbridge Gerry, who refused to sign the Constitution, later became James Madison's vice president.

KEY CONCEPTS AND STRUCTURE
OF THE CONSTITUTION

What is **federalism**?

Federalism refers to a division of power between the federal government and the state governments. In federalism, some powers are delegated to the national, federal government and other powers are kept or reserved by the state governments.

What is **separation of powers**?

Separation of powers refers to the division of power among different parts of government. The U.S. Constitution reflects this principle by dividing power between the legislative, executive, and judicial branches. If one branch of government invades the province of another branch of government, then that branch has violated the separation of powers principle.

The Framers understood that dividing power among the different branches of government would ensure that no single branch would become too powerful. This concept is known as the separation of powers. Many of the Founding Fathers understood the importance of separating powers between the branches of government. Many of them had read the French philosopher the Baron de Montesquieu's *L'Esprit des Lois* ("The Spirit of the Laws"), which addressed this principle.

Madison in the *Federalist Papers* described Montesquieu as "the oracle who is always consulted and cited on this subject." Madison described the principle as: "The accumulation of all powers, legislative, executive and judiciary, in the same hands, whether of one, a few, or many, and whether hereditary, self-appointed, or elective, may justly be pronounced the very definition of tyranny." Separation of powers is a philosophy in which each branch has its own powers. U.S. Supreme Court Justice Anthony Kennedy explains: "Separation of powers was designed to implement a fundamental insight: Concentration of power in the hands of a single branch is a threat to liberty."

Our Constitution adheres to this principle. The powers of Congress are described in Article I. The powers of the executive branch are detailed in Article II, and the powers of the judicial branch are listed in Article III.

This principle is important in not only the federal government but also state governments. For example, state judicial branches traditionally have regulated lawyers. If a state legislature passes a law regulating the conduct of lawyers, such a law may violate the separation of powers principle. In this example, the legislative branch has invaded the province of the judicial branch.

The Constitution attempts to ensure separation of powers by instituting a system of checks and balances between the different branches of government. Each branch has a check on the other two branches. For example, the judicial branch has a check on Congress, because it can declare laws or bills passed by Congress unconstitutional. Similarly, the judicial branch has a check on the president because it can also declare executive acts unconstitutional.

What is an **example** of a **separation of powers problem**?

A prime example of a separation of powers problem presented itself in the Youngstown Steel case of *Youngstown Co. v. Sawyer* (1952). In that case, President Harry Truman seized control of the nation's steel mills by executive order after hearing of a nationwide steel strike. President Truman feared that such a strike could cripple the U.S. national defense.

The U.S. Supreme Court ruled that the president exceeded his powers as the head of the executive branch, as the government control of the steel mills could only be accomplished by a federal law passed by the U.S. Congress. Thus, the president infringed on the powers of the legislative branch, creating a separation-of-powers problem. The ruling stated in part:

> Nor can the seizure order be sustained because of the several constitutional provisions that grant executive power to the president. In the framework of our Constitution, the president's power to see that the laws are faithfully executed refutes the idea that he is to be a lawmaker. The Constitution limits his functions in the lawmaking process to the recommending of laws he thinks wise and the vetoing of laws he thinks bad. And the Constitution is neither silent nor equivocal about who shall make laws which the president is to execute. The first section of the first article says that "All legislative Powers herein granted shall be vested in a Congress of the United States"....

> The Founders of this Nation entrusted the lawmaking power to the Congress alone in both good and bad times. It would do no good to recall the historical events, the fears of power and the hopes for freedom that lay behind their choice. Such a review would but confirm our holding that this seizure order cannot stand.

LEGISLATIVE BRANCH

How did the U.S. **Constitution structure** the **legislative branch**?

The Constitution provides for a bicameral (two chamber) legislature—the House of Representatives and the United States Senate. The Founding Fathers found their inspiration for this bicameral model from the English Parliament, which had a House of Lords and a House of Commons. However, not all members of the Philadelphia

The Capitol Building houses the U.S. Congress and Senate. The United States has a bicameral system of representatives and senators inspired by the British model of government (*iStock*).

Convention supported a two-house Congress. Some members—particularly those from less populous states—favored a one-house Congress so that they would have the same power as the larger states.

What was the **Virginia Plan**?

The Virginia Plan, introduced on May 29, 1787, formed the basis of the Convention and was debated word by word. The plan contained 15 resolves. It was the first plan introduced in the convention and the one that most closely resembled the convention's final product. It proposed that the powers of the federal government should be expanded to accomplish three goals: "common defence, security of liberty and general welfare." Resolve number three provided for two houses of the Congress, or a bicameral legislature. Under the Virginia Plan, the people would elect the first branch. Then, the members of the first branch would elect the second branch of the "National Legislature."

Under the Virginia Plan, the U.S. Congress would possess great power. Resolve number six granted Congress the power to negate, or veto, any laws passed by state legislatures. Resolve number seven provided Congress with the power to appoint the "National Executive" or leader of the country. Thus, under this plan, Congress, not the people, would select the national leader. Resolve number nine provided for a "National Judiciary" or a set of judges that could hear cases throughout the country.

The Virginia Plan was, therefore, a plan for the structure of the new United States government under the new Constitution being discussed in the Philadelphia Convention. It established the three branches of government—the legislative, executive, and judicial branches; it called for a bicameral legislature; and it provided that each house would be selected based on the population of the respective states, meaning that the larger more populous states would have more representatives and senators. The Virginia Plan also called for a very strong national government.

With what plan did the **Virginia Plan compete**?

The other major plan for the structure of the new Constitution was the so-called New Jersey Plan, proposed by William Paterson of New Jersey. This plan called for a weaker national government, only one house of Congress, and equal representation in the legislative branch. It also called for an executive and judicial branch, but those branches would clearly be less powerful than the one-house legislature.

On June 15, 1787, Paterson introduced his plan. "Can we, as representatives of independent states, annihilate the essential powers of independency?" Paterson said when introducing his proposal. He wanted a weaker central government.

Under the New Jersey Plan, Congress could only act on certain matters. Congress would elect the members of the federal executive. Congress could remove the persons of the federal executive if a majority of state leaders voted such action necessary.

Interestingly, the New Jersey Plan proposed that the laws of the U.S. Congress "shall be the supreme law of the respective States." This formed the basis for the supremacy clause of the U.S. Constitution. The supremacy clause provides that the laws of the national, or federal, government are the supreme law of the land and trump the laws of the various states.

What was the **Great Compromise**?

The Great Compromise was a measure articulated by Roger Sherman of Connecticut that created the ultimate form of the United States Congress. It combined features of both the Virginia Plan and the New Jersey Plan. It allowed representatives from the larger states and the smaller states to agree on the composition of Congress. Under the Great Compromise, one house—the U.S. House of Representatives—is based on proportional representation. This meant that the larger states would have more representatives. The second house—the United States Senate—was based on equal representation, as each state would have two senators. Each side received something from the Great Compromise, in that the smaller states received proportional representation in the House and the larger states received equal representation in the Senate.

How **precarious** was the **Great Compromise** and its ultimate success?

It was a very precarious time and the Convention almost divided irreparably over this issue of legislative representation. Fortunately, delegate Roger Sherman of Connecticut proposed a measure that would eventually save the Constitution. Roger Sherman was an influential politician with a distinguished political career. Sherman has the distinction of signing several great American documents—the Declaration and Resolves of 1774 (a document in which the colonists declared their resolve to oppose British power), the Declaration of Independence, the Articles of Confederation, and finally the United States Constitution.

Sherman played an influential role in the Convention, but he is most remembered for his compromise that saved the Convention and the Constitution. Under this so-called "Great Compromise," the states would be represented equally in the Senate and the states would be represented proportionally in the House of Representatives based on population. This proposal reflects our current system.

However, Sherman's proposal was voted down 6 to 5 when it was first introduced. The delegates continued to argue over the issue of proportional versus equal representation. On July 2, the states voted 5 to 5 on the question of equal representation in the Senate. The states of Connecticut, New York, New Jersey, Delaware, and Maryland favored equal representation. The states of Massachusetts, Pennsylvania, Virginia, North Carolina, and South Carolina opposed equal representation. The state of Georgia could have broken the tie, but the two Georgia delegates present—William Houstoun and Abraham Baldwin—split.

Four delegates from Georgia were present at the Convention. However, two of the members, William Few and William Pierce, left the convention for New York to vote on pressing matters in Congress. Few and Pierce would have voted against equal representation. The Convention was hanging in the balance. The small states would have lost the question of equal representation this day if it had not been for the vote of Abraham Baldwin. Baldwin had lived in Connecticut virtually his whole life, having moved to Georgia only three years before the Convention. Some historians assert that Baldwin saved the Constitution because he split the Georgia votes and saved the small states from defeat. They argue that Baldwin voted the way he did because he knew the small states would collapse the Convention if they lost the equal representation question in the Senate.

The Convention then agreed to allow a committee of one person from each of the 11 states to be formed to explore the question of how to organize the Congress. The states voted 10 to 1 in favor of such a committee. The committee was composed primarily of individuals who were in favor of a senate chosen by equal representation. On July 5, 1787, the committee read its report to the entire delegation. The report called for proportional representation in the House and equal representation in the Senate. Many of the delegates who had wanted proportional representation in both houses had conceded this issue, realizing that the delegates from the small states might leave if they did not get their way.

What does the **Constitution say** about the **composition of Congress?**

The U.S. Constitution provides that Congress shall consist of two houses—a Senate and a U.S. House of Representatives. The Founders believed in a bicameral legislative body, meaning that the legislature consist of two bodies. This was based on the English Parliament, which consists of a House of Lords and a House of Commons.

What are the **requirements** for someone to **serve** in the **U.S. House of Representatives?**

A person must be at least 25 years of age to serve in the House of Representatives. He or she must have been a citizen of the United States for seven years and he or she must "be an Inhabitant of that State" in which he or she is chosen.

What are the **requirements** for someone to **serve** in the **U.S. Senate?**

A person must be at least 30 years of age to serve in the U.S. Senate. He or she must have been a U.S. citizen for at least nine years and also inhabit the state for which he or she has been elected to serve.

What are the **terms of office** for **representatives** and **senators?**

Members of the House of Representatives serve for two-year terms, while U.S. Senators serve for six-year terms.

How **many members** are there in the **House** and the **Senate?**

There are 435 members of the U.S House of Representatives and 100 members of the Senate. States have different numbers of representatives depending upon the population of that state. For example, Rhode Island has only two representatives, while California has 53 representatives.

What is the **speaker of the House?**

The speaker of the House is the technical leader of the House of Representatives. The speaker of the House calls the House to order, issues the oath of office to new members of the House, presides over House debates, calls on representatives to speak during debate, sets the legislative agenda, and leads the appointment process for various committees and committee chairs in the House.

The speaker of the House also is third in line to the presidency after the president and vice president.

The seat for the speaker of the House, as well as the Senate president. The speaker is third in line to the presidency (*iStock*).

Who was the **first speaker** of the **House**?

The first speaker of the House was Frederick Augustus Conrad Muhlenberg. Born in Trappe, Pennsylvania, in 1750, he was an ordained Lutheran minister, and he later served as a member of the Continental Congress, as a state representative for Pennsylvania, and speaker of the House for that state. A delegate to the 1787 Constitutional Convention, he was elected to the U.S. Congress and served as speaker for the First and Third Congresses. He died in 1801.

Who became the **first woman** to serve as **speaker of the House**?

The current speaker of the House, Nancy Pelosi, is the first woman to hold this office. She was elected to the position on January 4, 2007. A representative from San Francisco, California, Pelosi is the daughter of Thomas D'Alesandro, Jr., a former mayor of Baltimore and member of the House.

Who was the **only speaker of the House** also to **become president** of the United States?

James K. Polk, the eleventh president of the United States, first served as speaker of the House for the Twenty-fourth and Twenty-fifth Congresses from 1835 to 1839. He did not seek re-election in Congress but instead ran for governor of Tennessee. He

19

later served as president of the United States from 1845 to 1849. He did not seek re-election for president and died later in 1849.

How does the **Constitution give Congress** the **power** to impact law?

The early civics lesson taught in schools provides that the legislative branch creates laws, the executive branch enforces the laws, and the judicial branch interprets the laws. Article I, Section 7 of the Constitution explains that Congress has the power to pass laws by explaining how such laws can be passed. Article I, Section 8—the main source in the Constitution that explains Congress' various powers—states that Congress has the power to create courts lower than the United States Supreme Court.

The last clause in Article I, Section 8—the necessary and proper clause—gives Congress much power in the area of lawmaking by providing that it can pass all laws necessary and proper to carrying out its various powers and functions. The clause states:

> To make all laws which shall be necessary and proper for carrying into execution the foregoing powers, and all other powers vested by this Constitution in the government of the United States, or in any department or officer thereof.

How did the **necessary and proper clause affect** a famous case involving a **U.S. bank**?

Shortly after the Convention, Richard Henry Lee wrote in his *Letters of the Federal Farmer* that the necessary and proper clause granted broad authority to Congress. He stated that it was "impossible" to determine what "may be deemed necessary and proper." Lee turned out to be correct, because the necessary and proper clause has resulted in great congressional power.

Alexander Hamilton interpreted this clause broadly in 1791 when he argued for a first national bank. He argued that the necessary and proper clause gave Congress "implied powers." Implied powers refer to those that are not explicitly listed in the text of the Constitution. Chief Justice John Marshall also interpreted the necessary and proper clause broadly years later when he determined that Congress had the power to establish a second national bank. In his famous opinion of *McCullough v. Maryland* (1819), he wrote: "Let the end be legitimate, let it be within the scope of the Constitution, and all means which are appropriate, which are plainly adapted to that end, which are not prohibited, but consist with the letter and spirit of the constitution, are constitutional."

Marshall reasoned in this decision that Congress had the power to create a second national bank because it was a reasonably connected to Congress' power to "lay and collect taxes" and "to regulate commerce." Marshall determined that the term "necessary and proper" did not mean "absolutely necessary." If Congress had intended the clause to mean "absolutely necessary," it would have included that word in the clause, Marshall reasoned.

But the argument on which most reliance is placed is drawn from that peculiar language of this clause. Congress is not empowered by it to make all laws which may have relation to the powers conferred on the Government, but such only as may be "necessary and proper" for carrying them into execution. The word "necessary" is considered as controlling the whole sentence, and as limiting the right to pass laws for the execution of the granted powers to such as are indispensable, and without which the power would be nugatory. That it excludes the choice of means, and leaves to Congress in each case that only which is most direct and simple.

Is it true that this is the sense in which the word "necessary" is always used? Does it always import an absolute physical necessity so strong that one thing to which another may be termed necessary cannot exist without that other? We think it does not. If reference be had to its use in the common affairs of the world or in approved authors, we find that it frequently imports no more than that one thing is convenient, or useful, or essential to another. To employ the means necessary to an end is generally understood as employing any means calculated to produce the end, and not as being confined to those single means without which the end would be entirely unattainable. Such is the character of human language that no word conveys to the mind in all situations one single definite idea, and nothing is more common than to use words in a figurative sense. Almost all compositions contain words which, taken in their rigorous sense, would convey a meaning different from that which is obviously intended. It is essential to just construction that many words which import something excessive should be understood in a more mitigated sense—in that sense which common usage justifies. The word "necessary" is of this description. It has not a fixed character peculiar to itself. It admits of all degrees of comparison, and is often connected with other words which increase or diminish the impression the mind receives of the urgency it imports. A thing may be necessary, very necessary, absolutely or indispensably necessary. To no mind would the same idea be conveyed by these several phrases. The comment on the word is well illustrated by the passage cited at the bar from the 10th section of the 1st article of the Constitution. It is, we think, impossible to compare the sentence which prohibits a State from laying "imposts, or duties on imports or exports, except what may be absolutely necessary for executing its inspection laws," with that which authorizes Congress "to make all laws which shall be necessary and proper for carrying into execution" the powers of the General Government without feeling a conviction that the convention understood itself to change materially the meaning of the word "necessary," by prefixing the word "absolutely." This word, then, like others, is used in various senses, and, in its construction, the subject, the context, the intention of the person using them are all to be taken into view.

Let this be done in the case under consideration. The subject is the execution of those great powers on which the welfare of a Nation essentially depends. It must have been the intention of those who gave these powers to insure, so far as human prudence could insure, their beneficial execution. This could not be done by confiding the choice of means to such narrow limits as not to leave it in the power of Congress to adopt any which might be appropriate, and which were conducive to the end. This provision is made in a Constitution intended to endure for ages to come, and consequently to be adapted to the various crises of human affairs. To have prescribed the means by which Government should, in all future time, execute its powers would have been to change entirely the character of the instrument and give it the properties of a legal code. It would have been an unwise attempt to provide by immutable rules for exigencies which, if foreseen at all, must have been seen dimly, and which can be best provided for as they occur. To have declared that the best means shall not be used, but those alone without which the power given would be nugatory [of little significance], would have been to deprive the legislature of the capacity to avail itself of experience, to exercise its reason, and to accommodate its legislation to circumstances.

How is a **law created**?

Before a law can be passed, a member of Congress must introduce a bill, a joint resolution, or a concurrent resolution. The most common form of proposed legislation is a bill. A bill originating in the House is referred to by the abbreviation "H.R." for House of Representatives and then followed by a number. For example, H.R. 100 is the hundredth bill introduced in that particular session of the House of Representatives. A bill originating in the Senate is abbreviated "S." followed by a number.

Any member of Congress (the House or Senate) can introduce a bill when the body is in session. The bill must then pass both Houses of Congress in identical form. This can be a difficult process, as members of each House may have strong positions about particular language in a bill.

Once a bill has been passed with identical language in both Houses, it goes to the president for signing. If the president signs the bill, it becomes law. If the president refuses to sign the bill into law, he exercises his veto power. If the president vetoes the bill, then Congress can override the presidential veto by passing the measure with a two-thirds majority.

What happens **after** a **bill** is **introduced**?

After a member of Congress introduces a bill, the measure is often referred to a committee. The committee then will discuss the measure in a mark-up session. Many bills never make it out of the committee. The common saying is that the measure died in committee. However, if the bill makes it out of committee, it can reach the full House for an official vote.

Committees are often formed by Congress in order to study the merits of a bill before it goes up for a vote (*iStock*).

What are the various **House Committees**?

The House Committees include:

- Committee on Agriculture
- Committee on Appropriations
- Committee on Armed Services
- Committee on the Budget
- Committee on Education and Labor
- Committee on Energy and Commerce
- Committee on Financial Services
- Committee on Foreign Relations
- Committee on Homeland Security
- Committee on House Administration
- Committee on the Judiciary
- Committee on Natural Resources
- Committee on Oversight and Government Reform
- Committee on Rules
- Committee on Science and Technology
- Committee on Small Business
- Committee on Standards of Official Conduct
- Committee on Transportation and Infrastructure

- Committee on Veterans Affairs
- Committee on Ways and Means
- Joint Economic Committee
- Joint Congressional Committee on Inaugural Celebrations
- Joint Committee on Taxation
- House Permanent Select Committee on Intelligence
- House Select Committee on Energy Independence and Global Warming

What are **public hearings**?

If a bill is considered important enough, then the committee may hold a public hearing on the measure. The committee will hear testimony from experts who have specialized knowledge in the subject matter addressed in the bill.

What are some other **powers of Congress** mentioned in the U.S. Constitution?

Article I, Section 8 lists numerous powers of Congress. Among these powers, the Congress can:

- Set and collect taxes.
- Regulate commerce between the various states and with foreign nations, to coin money.
- Declare war.
- Provide and maintain a navy.
- Raise and support armies.
- Create post offices.
- Create courts lower than the U.S. Supreme Court.
- Establish uniform rules on naturalization and bankruptcy.

Why is the **Commerce Clause** so **important**?

The Commerce Clause is so important because it might be Congress' greatest control over what occurs in various states throughout the country. In other words, it is probably Congress' greatest power. Congress' ability to "regulate commerce" has proven to be a very important way in which the federal government regulates the states. Congress has used the power of the Commerce Clause, for example, to pass laws prohibiting racial discrimination in local restaurants, such as in the famous decision in *Katzenbach v. McClung* (1964; see LegalSpeak, p. 26). More recently the U.S. Supreme Court ruled in *Gonzalez v. Reich* (2005; see LegalSpeak, p. 28) that Congress validly exercised its Commerce Clause powers when it passed the Controlled Substances Act, which criminalized marijuana even in those states that had allowed medicinal uses of marijuana.

One of the powers of Congress is to regulate interstate commerce (*iStock*).

What are the categories of **Congress' powers** in **regulating interstate commerce**?

There are four major sources of congressional power to regulate interstate commerce under the Commerce Clause:

1. Regulate the channels of commerce.
2. Regulate the instrumentalities of commerce.
3. Regulate articles moving in commerce.
4. Regulate those activities that substantially affect interstate commerce.

What does the **Constitution say** about *ex post facto* laws?

Article I, Section 10 prohibits Congress from passing *ex post facto* laws, which essentially are laws that have a retroactive and detrimental impact on individuals. *Ex post facto* laws are those which make conduct a crime even if the conduct was legal when originally committed. The U.S. Supreme Court explained the types of *ex post facto* laws in *Calder v. Bull* (1798):

> I will state what laws I consider *ex post facto* laws, within the words and the intent of the prohibition. 1st. Every law that makes an action, done before the passing of the law, and which was innocent when done, criminal; and punishes such action. 2nd. Every law that aggravates a crime, or makes it greater than it was, when committed. 3rd. Every law that changes the punishment, and inflicts a greater punishment, than the law annexed to the crime, when

25

LegalSpeak: *Katzenbach v. McClung* (1964)

Moreover there was an impressive array of testimony that discrimination in restaurants had a direct and highly restrictive effect upon interstate travel by Negroes. This resulted, it was said, because discriminatory practices prevent Negroes from buying prepared food served on the premises while on a trip, except in isolated and unkempt restaurants and under most unsatisfactory and often unpleasant conditions. This obviously discourages travel and obstructs interstate commerce for one can hardly travel without eating. Likewise, it was said, that discrimination deterred professional, as well as skilled, people from moving into areas where such practices occurred and thereby caused industry to be reluctant to establish there.

We believe that this testimony afforded ample basis for the conclusion that established restaurants in such areas sold less interstate goods because of the discrimination, that interstate travel was obstructed directly by it, that business in general suffered and that many new businesses refrained from establishing there as a result of it. Hence the District Court was in error in concluding that there was no connection between discrimination and the movement of interstate commerce. The court's conclusion that such a connection is outside "common experience" flies in the face of stubborn fact.

It goes without saying that, viewed in isolation, the volume of food purchased by Ollie's Barbecue from sources supplied from out of state was insignificant when compared with the total foodstuffs moving in commerce. But, as our late Brother Jackson said for the Court in *Wickard v. Filburn* (1942): "That appellee's own contribution to the demand for wheat may be trivial by itself is not enough to remove him from the scope of federal regulation where, as here, his contribution, taken together with that of many others similarly situated, is far from trivial"....

This Court has held time and again that this power extends to activities of retail establishments, including restaurants, which directly or indirectly burden

committed. 4th. Every law that alters the legal rules of evidence, and receives less, or different, testimony, than the law required at the time of the commission of the offence, in order to convict the offender. All these, and similar laws, are manifestly unjust and oppressive.

What is the **full faith and credit** clause?

Article IV, Section 1 of the Constitution provides that "full faith and credit shall be given in each state to the public acts, records, and judicial proceedings of every other

or obstruct interstate commerce. We have detailed the cases in Heart of Atlanta Motel, and will not repeat them here.

The appellees contend that Congress has arbitrarily created a conclusive presumption that all restaurants meeting the criteria set out in the Act "affect commerce." Stated another way, they object to the omission of a provision for a case-by-case determination—judicial or administrative—that racial discrimination in a particular restaurant affects commerce.... Here, as there, Congress has determined for itself that refusals of service to Negroes have imposed burdens both upon the interstate flow of food and upon the movement of products generally. Of course, the mere fact that Congress has said when particular activity shall be deemed to affect commerce does not preclude further examination by this Court. But where we find that the legislators, in light of the facts and testimony before them, have a rational basis for finding a chosen regulatory scheme necessary to the protection of commerce, our investigation is at an end. The only remaining question—one answered in the affirmative by the court below—is whether the particular restaurant either serves or offers to serve interstate travelers or serves food a substantial portion of which has moved in interstate commerce.

Confronted as we are with the facts laid before Congress, we must conclude that it had a rational basis for finding that racial discrimination in restaurants had a direct and adverse effect on the free flow of interstate commerce....

The power of Congress in this field is broad and sweeping; where it keeps within its sphere and violates no express constitutional limitation it has been the rule of this Court, going back almost to the founding days of the Republic, not to interfere. The Civil Rights Act of 1964, as here applied, we find to be plainly appropriate in the resolution of what the Congress found to be a national commercial problem of the first magnitude. We find it in no violation of any express limitations of the Constitution and we therefore declare it valid.

state." This is the provision that provides that judgments in one state are generally respected by other states. It helped to create a single nation out of disparate states. The clause states:

> Full faith and credit shall be given in each State to the public acts, records, and judicial proceedings of every other state. And the Congress may by general laws prescribe the manner in which acts, records and proceedings shall be proved, and the effect thereof.

27

LegalSpeak: *Gonzalez v. Reich* (2005)

In assessing the validity of congressional regulation, none of our Commerce Clause cases can be viewed in isolation. As charted ... our understanding of the reach of the Commerce Clause, as well as Congress' assertion of authority thereunder, has evolved over time. The Commerce Clause emerged as the Framers' response to the central problem giving rise to the Constitution itself: the absence of any federal commerce power under the Articles of Confederation. For the first century of our history, the primary use of the Clause was to preclude the kind of discriminatory state legislation that had once been permissible. Then, in response to rapid industrial development and an increasingly interdependent national economy, Congress "ushered in a new era of federal regulation under the commerce power," beginning with the enactment of the Interstate Commerce Act in 1887, 24 Stat. 379, and the Sherman Antitrust Act in 1890, 26 Stat. 209, as amended, 15 U.S.C. § 2 et seq.

Cases decided during that "new era," which now spans more than a century, have identified three general categories of regulation in which Congress is authorized to engage under its commerce power. First, Congress can regulate the channels of interstate commerce. Second, Congress has authority to regulate and protect the instrumentalities of interstate commerce, and persons or things in interstate commerce. Third, Congress has the power to regulate activities that substantially affect interstate commerce. Only the third category is implicated in the case at hand.

Our case law firmly establishes Congress' power to regulate purely local activities that are part of an economic "class of activities" that have a substantial effect on interstate commerce. As we stated in *Wickard,* "even if appellee's activity be local and though it may not be regarded as commerce, it may still, whatever its nature, be reached by Congress if it exerts a substantial economic effect on interstate commerce." We have never required Congress to legislate with scientific exactitude....

One need not have a degree in economics to understand why a nationwide exemption for the vast quantity of marijuana (or other drugs) locally cultivated for personal use (which presumably would include use by friends, neighbors, and family members) may have a substantial impact on the interstate market for this extraordinarily popular substance. The congressional judgment that an exemption for such a significant segment of the total market would undermine the orderly enforcement of the entire regulatory scheme is entitled to a strong presumption of validity. Indeed, that judgment is not only rational, but "visible to the naked eye," under any commonsense appraisal of the probable consequences of such an open-ended exemption.

THE EXECUTIVE BRANCH

Were all the **Founders convinced** that the **executive branch** should consist of **one person**?

No, the Founders were divided on the composition of the executive. Much of the debate centered on whether the executive branch should consist of a single person or an executive committee. Some delegates feared that creating a single-person executive would be dangerous and lead to a monarch, such as George III. George III was the King of Great Britain who taxed the colonies and battled them during the Revolutionary War. Above all else, the majority of the Framers wished to avoid creating a king. Most of the delegates assumed that George Washington would become the country's chief executive.

For this reason, James Madison wrote to Thomas Jefferson that it was "peculiarly embarrassing" to have the delegates arguing about whether they could trust a single executive. It was "embarrassing," because Washington sat quietly while this discussion proceeded.

George Mason from Virginia proposed that there be a three-person executive branch. He said that one individual would come from the North, one from the South, and the other from the middle states.

The delegates disagreed about whether to create a strong independent executive or an executive that would be far less powerful than Congress. The delegates also changed their positions on the length of the president's term. A committee originally proposed that the president would be elected by the legislature for one seven-year term.

Finally, on August 31, another committee—the so-called Committee of Eleven—considered an earlier proposal by delegate James Wilson from Pennsylvania that a group of people called electors would choose the president. Under this system, each state would have the number of electors "equal to the whole

President Gerald R. Ford meets with AFL-CIO President George Meany in the Oval Office. The Founding Fathers decided that the executive branch would consist of just one person, the president (*iStock*).

number of senators and representatives of the House of Representatives." This proposal was another compromise measure between the larger and smaller states. In a direct popular election, the votes in the larger states would dominate. In an electoral college system, the larger states would have more electors but the smaller states would still have a significant role.

On September 6, the delegates approved of the electoral college as the way to select the president. The electors would meet in the various state capitals and vote for two persons. The person with the highest number of electoral votes would be president. The person with the second highest number of votes would be vice president. The House of Representatives would select the president in case of a tie.

The Founders did not foresee that the two highest vote getters might be political opposites. It would take the Twelfth Amendment to the Constitution to resolve this problem.

How are **presidents elected**?

Presidents are elected by the electoral college, a process that has faced intense scrutiny in recent years, particularly after the disputed 2000 election between George W. Bush and Al Gore. In that election, Gore carried the overall popular vote but lost in the electoral college.

The vote of the electors has become a formality because if a candidate wins the popular vote in a state, then that candidate receives that state's electoral votes. However, some critics argue that the electoral college system should be discarded. They point to the 2000 election as an example of the unfairness and undemocratic nature of the electoral college system. This has happened only a few times in American history when a candidate wins the popular vote and loses the election.

How does the **Constitution give** the **executive branch** a role in the **law**?

Article II, Section 2 provides that the president can nominate individuals to the courts, including the United States Supreme Court. Article II, Section 3 provides that the president "shall take care that the laws be faithfully executed." Article I, Section 7—the section that describes Congress' lawmaking powers—also explains that the president has the power to veto (deny) legislation.

What are the **powers** of the **president**?

The president, as the "Commander in Chief," can grant pardons, make treaties, appoint ministers and consuls, justices of the Supreme Court, and "all other Officers of the United States." The president also can fill vacancies that occur in the Senate by granting commissions. The president has the power to carry and enforce the laws

LegalSpeak: *Clinton v. City of New York* (1997)

The Line Item Veto Act authorizes the president himself to effect the repeal of laws, for his own policy reasons, without observing the procedures set out in Article I, Section 7. The fact that Congress intended such a result is of no moment. Although Congress presumably anticipated that the president might cancel some of the items in the Balanced Budget Act and in the Taxpayer Relief Act, Congress cannot alter the procedures set out in Article I, Section 7, without amending the Constitution.

Neither are we persuaded by the Government's contention that the president's authority to cancel new direct spending and tax benefit items is no greater than his traditional authority to decline to spend appropriated funds. The Government has reviewed in some detail the series of statutes in which Congress has given the Executive broad discretion over the expenditure of appropriated funds. For example, the First Congress appropriated "sum[s] not exceeding" specified amounts to be spent on various Government operations.... In those statutes, as in later years, the president was given wide discretion with respect to both the amounts to be spent and how the money would be allocated among different functions. It is argued that the Line Item Veto Act merely confers comparable discretionary authority over the expenditure of appropriated funds. The critical difference between this statute and all of its predecessors, however, is that unlike any of them, this Act gives the president the unilateral power to change the text of duly enacted statutes. None of the Act's predecessors could even arguably have been construed to authorize such a change....

If there is to be a new procedure in which the president will play a different role in determining the final text of what may "become a law," such change must come not by legislation but through the amendment procedures set forth in Article V of the Constitution.

made by Congress, has the power to veto or reject laws passed by Congress, and can issue executive orders that have the force of law.

What are some **famous executive orders** in American history?

Perhaps the most famous of all executive orders was the first numbered one issued by President Abraham Lincoln, the country's sixteenth president, in 1863—the Emancipation Proclamation (Executive Order #1). An example of a famous—or infamous—executive order was Executive Order 9066—which called for the removal of Japanese-American citizens during the time of World War II into internment camps. Another

U.S. President Andrew Johnson, who succeeded Abraham Lincoln, was the first president to be impeached when he was brought to trial in 1868, but he was acquitted (*Library of Congress*).

famous executive order was Executive Order 8022, called the Fair Employment Practice, which prohibited racial discrimination in the defense industry. Similarly, Executive Order 9981 prohibited discrimination on the basis of race, religion, or national origin in all of the armed forces.

Can the **president veto** only a **portion** of a **law** after it is passed by Congress?

No, the U.S. Supreme Court ruled in *Clinton v. City of New York* (1997; see LegalSpeak, p. 31) that the president did not have the constitutional authority to repeal, or nullify, a federal law once it becomes law. "There is no provision in the Constitution that authorizes the president to enact, amend, or to repeal statutes," the Court wrote in striking down the Line Item Veto Act of 1996. The Supreme Court made clear that there is a difference between a president vetoing a bill before it becomes law and a president canceling part of a law after it has already become law.

What is **"impeachment"**?

Impeachment refers to proceedings brought against certain federal public officials for offenses, abuse of office, or other misconduct while the official holds public office. The impeachment process involves both bodies of Congress—the House of Representatives and the Senate. Under Article I, Section 2 of the U.S. Constitution, the House has the "sole power of impeachment." This means that the House brings formal charges against an official. Article I, Section 3 of the Constitution provides that "the Senate shall have the sole power to try all impeachments."

Article 2, Section 4 of the Constitution provides that "The President, the vice president and all civil officers of the United States, shall be removed from office on impeachment for, and conviction of treason, bribery, or other high crimes and misdemeanors." Members of the House and Senate are not subject to impeachment. The House and Senate can expel their own members in a different process other than impeachment.

Can **presidents** be **impeached**?

Yes, Article II also says that a president can be impeached for "treason, bribery or other high crimes and misdemeanors."

What happened in the **Clinton impeachment hearings**?

This country debated the meaning of the phrase "high crimes and misdemeanors" when the House of Representatives voted to impeach President William J. Clinton for perjury and obstruction of justice. The controversy began after it was revealed Clinton concealed his relationship with former White House intern Monica Lewinsky during a deposition in a civil lawsuit filed by Paula Jones. Jones had alleged that Clinton sexually harassed her when he was governor of Arkansas.

Critics of the proceedings called them politically motivated prosecution about the private sexual life of the president. Proponents of the proceedings argued the proceedings were brought against the president because he lied and obstructed justice in the Paula Jones civil lawsuit. The House voted to impeach the president but he was acquitted in the Senate.

JUDICIAL BRANCH

How does the **Constitution give** the **judicial branch** a **role** in the **legal system**?

Article III, Section 2 speaks about the jurisdiction of the federal courts—specifically the United States Supreme Court. The Constitution does not specifically mention the power of the judiciary to review whether laws are constitutional. However, Chief Justice John Marshall—the fourth Chief Justice of the U.S. Supreme Court—wrote in a famous early Supreme Court decision *Marbury v. Madison* (1803): "It is emphatically the province and duty of the judicial department to say what the law is. Those who apply the rule to particular cases, must of necessity expound and interpret that rule. If two laws conflict with each other, the courts must decide on the operation of each." This is the power of judicial review.

Why is **judicial review celebrated** and **criticized** in the democracy?

This is a complex question, but judicial review allows judges to correct errors made by the legislative branch. If a law clearly violates constitutional rights, the court has the power to rectify the situation. A classic example of a celebrated use of judicial review was the U.S. Supreme Court's 1954 decision in *Brown v. Board of Education*. The U.S. Supreme Court determined that public schools must be desegregated because segregated public schools violated the Equal Protection Clause of the Fourteenth Amendment.

On the other hand, judicial review is criticized because it enables judges to thwart the will of the people as expressed in popular laws. For instance, the U.S. Supreme Court can strike down a law that Congress and the American people largely support. This to some is undemocratic and gives too much power to the judiciary.

What was the leading framer **James Madison's opinion** of **judicial review**?

Virginia delegate James Madison realized that too much power in any one branch could create problems when he wrote in the *Federalist 47*: "The accumulation of all powers, legislative, executive and judiciary, in the same hands, whether of one, a few or many, and where hereditary, self-appointed, or elective, may justly be pronounced the very definition of tyranny." Madison actually favored a system whereby the justices would join with members of the executive branch to form a council of revision that would review laws proposed by the U.S. Congress.

What were some important **precursors** to *Marbury v. Madison*?

Marbury v. Madison (1803) is rightfully considered the leading decision on judicial review since it was decided by the U.S. Supreme Court. However, it did not occur in a vacuum, as a few state courts had already assumed the power of judicial review to invalidate laws. These include *Rutgers v. Waddington* (1784), *Trevett v. Weeden* (1786), and *Bayard v. Singleton* (1787).

The *Rutgers* decision involved a British merchant named Waddington, who occupied the property of Rutgers under orders from the British military during the Revolutionary War. The legal issue concerned whether Waddington could be convicted of trespassing for invading the property of an American citizen. Alexander Hamilton defended Waddington, arguing that the New York trespass law must yield to a 1783 treaty between the United States and Great Britain that prohibited the punishment of British sympathizers (called Tories or Loyalists) for conduct during the war.

The *Trevett* decision concerned the prosecution of butcher James M. Varnum for violating a Rhode Island law that punished those who refused to accept paper money. The Rhode Island court struck down the state law, causing an outrage in the legislature. The legislature called the judges before it to question them for their act of striking down a state law. The legislature even refused to reappoint four of the five judges.

In *Bayard,* Elizabeth Bayard sought to recover property confiscated because her father was a Loyalist. The owner of the property, a Mr. Singleton, had purchased the property from the state of North Carolina. The North Carolina court ruled in favor of Bayard, striking down the Confiscation Act, passed by the North Carolina General Assembly during the American Revolution. The judges determined that the confiscation law violated the North Carolina Constitution's provision for trial by jury and determined that Bayard should have the opportunity to present her case before a jury.

These three decisions served as key precedents on the road to *Marbury v. Madison.*

Is **judicial review** an **American invention**?

No, judicial review clearly can be traced to the English system of common law. In 1610 English jurist Sir Edward Coke wrote: "when an act of Parliament is against common right and reason, or repugnant, or impossible to be performed, the Common Law will control it and adjudge such Act to be void." Several state-court jurists in early America also assumed the power of judicial review for the court.

What did Alexander **Hamilton** have to say about **judicial review**?

In his *Federalist 78*, Hamilton said:

> If then the courts of justice are to be considered as the bulwarks of a limited constitution against legislative encroachments, this consideration

Alexander Hamilton argued that court justices should have permanent tenure to afford them greater independence in making their judgments (*Library of Congress*).

will afford a strong argument for the permanent tenure of judicial offices, since nothing will contribute so much as this to that independent spirit of judges, which must be essential to the faithful performance of so arduous a duty.

This independence of the judges is equally requisite to guard the Constitution and the rights of individuals from the effects of those ill humors, which the arts of designing men, or the influence of particular conjunctures, sometimes disseminate among the people themselves, and which, though they speedily give place to better information, and more deliberate reflection, have a tendency, in the meantime, to occasion dangerous innovations in the government, and serious oppressions of the minor party in the community.

Why do **some consider** the **judicial branch** the **least powerful** branch of government?

The judicial branch—even though it has the power to interpret laws—is considered the weakest of the three branches by many because it cannot ensure that its decisions

35

are enforced. This dilemma was famously explained by President Andrew Jackson, who did not like two decisions by the U.S. Supreme Court that ruled in favor of the Cherokee Indians in a dispute with the State of Georgia. Jackson famously said: "John Marshall has made his decision, now let him enforce it."

However, federal judges have great power due in part to their longevity. Federal judges receive life appointments under the Constitution. This insulates them from the political pressures that state judges—most of whom serve for specific terms and face re-election or retention—encounter.

Does the **Constitution specify** the **number** of U.S. Supreme Court **justices**?

No, the Constitution does not mention how many justices must serve on the U.S. Supreme Court. The Judiciary Act of 1789, provided for a Chief Justice and five associate justices. In 1801, a new law provided that the Supreme Court would consist of one chief justice and four associate justices. In 1807, the number of associate justices was set at six. In 1837, there were eight associate justices. In 1864, Congress changed the number of associate justices to nine, meaning there were a total of ten Supreme Court justices (nine Associate Justices and the Chief Justice). In 1869, Congress passed a law setting the number of associate justices at eight. Since that time, there have been nine Supreme Court Justices.

STATE CONSTITUTIONS

Are **state constitutions based** on the **U.S. Constitution**?

Not necessarily, as many state constitutions were enacted before the 1787 U.S. Constitution. There are some similarities between the various constitutions but there are also distinct differences. For example, the Tennessee Constitution contains eleven articles instead of the seven contained by the U.S. Constitution.

Another difference between some state constitutions and the federal constitution concerns the number of amendments adopted. Some states have adopted hundreds and hundreds of amendments to their state constitution, as the amending process is much less rigorous than under the federal constitution. For example, the Alabama Constitution of 1901 has been amended approximately 800 times in its history.

Who determines the **meaning** of a **state constitution**?

A state high court—usually called a supreme court—is the final arbiter of the meaning of a state constitution. The only exception to that rule is that the state constitution cannot provide less protection than the protections offered by the U.S. Constitution.

THE BILL OF RIGHTS AND THE 14TH AMENDMENT

Why were the first ten amendments—the **Bill of Rights—added** to the **U.S. Constitution**?

The Bill of Rights were added to the Constitution in part because many people wanted them to ensure protection from this new, strong federal government created by the new Constitution. The two leading political parties of the time were the Federalists and the Anti-Federalists. The Federalists generally supported a very strong central government, while the Anti-Federalists showed more concern for the rights of individual state governments. The issue of the Bill of Rights was not a huge issue at the Philadelphia Convention in 1787 when the Constitution was created. Representative George Mason raised the issue, but it was quickly defeated.

However, the Bill of Rights became a huge political issue during the ratification debates in certain states. Eventually, supporters of the Constitution and ratification in a few states were able to secure ratification of the new Constitution only by promising that there would soon be the addition of a Bill of Rights.

Who was primarily responsible for **proposing** the **Bill of Rights**?

James Madison, the future fourth president of the United States, is often called the "Father of the Bill of Rights." In June 1789, he introduced the Bill of Rights in Congress, referring to it as the "great rights of mankind." Madison initially did not support the Bill of Rights, but he changed his mind in part because of persuasions by his fellow Virginian and friend Thomas Jefferson.

What did **James Madison** say in his **speech** to Congress on June **1789**, when he **argued for** the **Bill of Rights**?

Madison made the following speech before Congress concerning the Bill of Rights:

A statue of James Madison by Walker K. Hancock is on display at Memorial Hall in Washington, DC. Madison is often remembered as the Father of the Bill of Rights (*Library of Congress*).

It has been objected also against a bill of rights, that, by enumerating particular exceptions to the grant of power, it would disparage those rights which were not placed in that enumeration; and it might follow, by implication, that those rights which were not singled out, were intended to be assigned into the hands of the General Government, and were consequently insecure. This is one of the most plausible arguments I have ever heard urged against the admission of a bill of rights into this system; but, I conceive, that it may be guarded against. I have attempted it, as gentlemen may see by turning to the last clause of the fourth resolution.

It has been said, that it is unnecessary to load the constitution with this provision, because it was not found effectual in the constitution of the particular States. It is true, there are a few particular States in which some of the most valuable articles have not, at one time or other, been violated; but it does not follow but they may have, to a certain degree, a salutary effect against the abuse of power. If they are incorporated into the constitution, independent tribunals of justice will consider themselves in a peculiar manner the guardians of those rights; they will be an impenetrable bulwark against every assumption of power in the legislative or executive; they will be naturally led to resist every encroachment upon rights expressly stipulated for in the constitution by the declaration of rights. Besides this security, there is a great probability that such a declaration in the federal system would be enforced; because the State Legislatures will jealously and closely watch the operations of this Government, and be able to resist with more effect every assumption of power, than any other power on earth can do; and the greatest opponents to a Federal Government admit the State Legislatures to be sure guardians of the people's liberty. I conclude, from this view of the subject, that it will be proper in itself, and highly politic, for the tranquillity of the public mind, and the stability of the Government, that we should offer something, in the form I have proposed, to be incorporated in the system of Government, as a declaration of the rights of the people....

Having done what I conceived was my duty, in bringing before this House the subject of amendments, and also stated such as I wish for and approve, and offered the reasons which occurred to me in their support, I shall content myself, for the present, with moving "that a committee be appointed to consider of and report such amendments as ought to be proposed by Congress to the Legislatures of the States, to become, if ratified by three-fourths thereof, part of the constitution of the United States." By agreeing to this motion, the subject may be going on in the committee, while other important business is proceeding to a conclusion in the House. I should advocate greater despatch in the business of amendments, if I were not convinced of the absolute necessity there is of pursuing the organization of the Government; because I think we should obtain the confidence of our fellow citizens, in proportion as we fortify the rights of the people against the encroachments of the Government.

Where did James Madison look for possible proposals that eventually became included in the Bill of Rights?

Madison obtained most of his proposals from proposals in various state constitutions. Madison compiled a list of various proposals from the state constitutions. Many states had a section similar to the eventual bill of rights. Some of these sections were called declarations of rights.

Isn't it true that the original Constitution (before the Bill of Rights) was already a bill of rights of sorts?

There is some credence to the argument that the Constitution as it existed before the Bill of Rights already was a type of bill of rights. For example, the Constitution prohibits Congress or state legislatures from passing bills of attainder or *ex post facto* laws. Bills of attainders are laws that target a specific group of people, while *ex post facto* laws are laws that make something a crime after the fact. An *ex post facto* law makes conduct a crime retroactively.

Furthermore, the Constitution prohibits Congress from suspending the writ of *habeas corpus* except in very limited situations, such as war. Another provision of the Constitution prohibits individuals in political office from having to take religious tests to qualify for office. All of these provisions in the body of the Constitution do provide a measure of individual freedom—similar to what the Bill of Rights does.

Some have said James Madison used the Bill of Rights to save the Constitution. Is there truth to this?

Yes, James Madison avoided proposed amendments that would have altered the structure of the government and reduced the power of the federal government. Instead, he

39

James Madison felt that the Bill of Rights was needed in the U.S. Constitution, even though many of these rights were guaranteed by the states, to ensure that equal protections were granted to *all* U.S. citizens (*iStock*).

focused on proposed amendments that would add to individual liberty and garner popular support but would not lessen the power of the federal government.

What is an **example** of an *ex post facto* **law**?

A prime example of an *ex post facto* law is a law that punishes a defendant for conduct that was not criminal at the time it was committed. A recent example occurred in a federal district court in the Virgin Islands involving a convicted sex offender. The offender was convicted before the passage of a new federal law requiring increased reporting requirements for former sex offenders. The federal district court reasoned that applying the new federal registration requirement to a former sex offender whose crime of failing to register occurred prior to the passage of the new law. Thus, the court reasoned that retroactive application of the new federal sex offender law violated the prohibition against *ex post facto* laws.

Where are constitutional amendments placed in the **Constitution**?

Constitutional amendments are added on to the end of the legal document. This differs from many state constitutions, which simply amend language directly in the body of their constitutions. However, the process is different at the federal level, where all changes to the constitution take place by the state.

FIRST AMENDMENT

What freedoms does the **First Amendment protect**?

The First Amendment states that "Congress shall make no law respecting an establishment of religion or prohibiting the free exercise thereof; or abridging the freedom of speech, or of the press, or of the right of the people peaceably to assemble and to petition the government for a redress of grievances." It thus protects the freedoms of religion, speech, press, assembly and petition from interference by the government. The First Amendment also protects something known as the right of association—the right of groups and people to associate together for expressive purposes.

What does **freedom of religion** mean?

There are two clauses of the First Amendment dealing with religious freedom: the Establishment Clause and the Free Exercise Clause. The Establishment Clause— "Congress shall make no law respecting an establishment of religion"—means that there should be separation between church and state. Judges, scholars, politicians, and everybody else disagree over how much separation there should be between church and state. The Establishment Clause has led to interesting and controversial decisions impacting school-sponsored prayer in public schools, display of Ten Commandments monuments, and the constitutionality of the Pledge of Allegiance.

The Free Exercise Clause provides that the government cannot infringe upon a person's religious beliefs. People have the right to believe in whatever religious faith they wish or they have the right to believe in no religion at all. The controversies over the Free Exercise Clause arise when the government prohibits religious-based actions or conduct that people claim violate their religious faith. For example, the U.S. Supreme Court ruled in *Reynolds v. United States* (1878) that the government could prohibit George Reynolds from practicing polygamy even though that was a part of his religious faith.

How does the U.S. **Supreme Court determine** if something **violates** the **Establishment Clause**?

The U.S. Supreme Court employs several tests to determine whether something violates the Establishment Clause. The most prominent is the so-called "Lemon test" from the Court's 1971 decision *Lemon v. Kurtzman.* The Lemon test requires that the government have a secular purpose, that government regulation does not have a primary effect of advancing or inhibiting religion, and that it does not create an excessive entanglement between church and state.

Justice Sandra Day O'Connor introduced another test, which she called a "refinement" of the Lemon test. Her endorsement test asks whether a reasonable observer, familiar with the underlying circumstances, reasonably would believe that the government is endorsing religion.

When did Justice Sandra Day **O'Connor** introduce her **endorsement test**?

O'Connor introduced her endorsement test in a concurring opinion in *Lynch v. Donnelly* (1984). The case involved a Christmas display in Pawtucket, Rhode Island, that

41

featured a nativity scene alongside other more secular symbols, such as a Santa Clause, a reindeer, and as a holiday greeting banner.

The majority of the court, in an opinion by Chief Justice Warren Burger, applied the Lemon test to find the display permissible. O'Connor proposed what she termed a "clarification" of Lemon by applying an endorsement analysis. Justice O'Connor stated: "The second and more direct infringement is government endorsement or disapproval of religion. Endorsement sends a message to nonadherents that they are outsiders, not full members of the political community, and an accompanying message to adherents that they are insiders, favored members of the political community. Disapproval sends the opposite message."

Justice Stephen Breyer (concurring): "In certain contexts, a display of the tablets of the Ten Commandments can convey not simply a religious message but also a secular moral message (about proper standards of social conduct). And in certain contexts, a display of the tablets can also convey a historical message (about a historic relation between those standards and the law)—a fact that helps to explain the display of those tablets in dozens of courthouses throughout the Nation, including the Supreme Court of the United States. Here the tablets have been used as part of a display that communicates not simply a religious message, but a secular message as well. The circumstances surrounding the display's placement on the capitol grounds and its physical setting suggest that the State itself intended the latter, nonreligious aspects of the tablets' message to predominate. And the monument's 40-year history on the Texas state grounds indicates that that has been its effect."

Justice John Paul Stevens (dissenting): "The sole function of the monument on the grounds of Texas' State Capitol is to display the full text of one version of the Ten Commandments.... Viewed on its face, Texas' display has no purported connection to God's role in the formation of Texas or the founding of our Nation; nor does it provide the reasonable observer with any basis to guess that it was erected to honor any individual or organization. The message transmitted by Texas' chosen display is quite plain: This State endorses the divine code of the "Judeo-Christian" God."

Justice David Souter (dissenting): "A governmental display of an obviously religious text cannot be squared with neutrality, except in a setting that plausibly indicates that the statement is not placed in view with a predominant purpose on the part of government either to adopt the religious message or to urge its acceptance by others."

If the government places a **Ten Commandments monument** on **government property**, does that violate the Establishment Clause?

Maybe, but it would depend on the particular circumstances. In June 2005 the U.S. Supreme Court decided two Ten Commandments cases and reached opposite results in 5-to-4 decisions. In *Van Orden v. Perry* (2005; see LegalSpeak, p. 42), the Court ruled 5 to 4 that a Ten Commandments monument in a Texas public park that had been there for 40 years and was surrounded by other historical landmarks did not violate the Establishment Clause. However, in *McCreary County v. ACLU of Kentucky*, the U.S. Supreme Court ruled 5 to 4 that Ten Commandments displays in two Kentucky county courthouses did violate the Establishment Clause. The Court emphasized that the displays initially contained only the Ten Commandments and that they were challenged soon after their display.

In an earlier decision *Stone v. Graham* (1980), a divided Court struck down a Kentucky law that required the posting of the Ten Commandments in public school classrooms. The difficulty in these cases is that different justices have very different interpretations of the Establishment Clause. Lower courts now reach different results in Ten Commandments cases.

What explained the **difference** between the **two 2005 decisions** by the U.S. **Supreme Court**?

There were significant factual differences between the Texas park case and the Kentucky courthouse case. The monument in the Texas park had been there for nearly 40 years and it was surrounded by many other monuments. It also was located in a park where people did not have to visit on a daily basis. The displays in the Kentucky courthouses were there for a much shorter time, originally not surrounded by other displays and were located in a courthouse.

It is still an ongoing debate whether or not prayer in public schools violates the separation of Church and State (*iStock*).

However, these differences did not matter for eight of the nine U.S. Supreme Court justices. Four justices voted to uphold both displays and four justices voted to strike down both displays. It was only Justice Steven Breyer who voted to uphold the Texas monument and strike down the Kentucky display. This leaves this area of the law less than clear, which explains why there are so many Ten Commandment lawsuits in the country now.

Does **school prayer** violate the **Establishment Clause**?

School-sponsored prayer in public schools violates the Establishment Clause, but students praying on their own does not. In other words, teacher-led prayer constitutes an impermissible endorsement of religion, but student-led prayer very well may not pose an Establishment Clause problem. In the early 1960s the U.S. Supreme Court in *Engel v. Vitale* (1962) and *Abington School Dis-*

trict v. Schempp (1963) ruled that mandatory, teacher-led prayer and reading of Bible verses violated the Establishment Clause. The Court focused on the coercive pressure placed upon children who did not conform to the majority (Christian) religion.

What was the **prayer at issue** in the *Engel v. Vitale* case?

In *Engel v. Vitale* (1962) the issue concerned a prayer that the Board of Regents of the State of New York "recommended" different school districts adopt as a nondenominational prayer. A school board in North Hempstead, New York, adopted a resolution that "the Regents prayer be said daily in our schools." The prayer went as follows: "Almighty God, we acknowledge our dependence upon Thee, and we beg Thy blessings upon us, our parents, our teachers and our Country." The Supreme Court, however, decided that even this generic prayer violates the First Amendment.

Justice Hugo Black (majority): "It is a matter of history that this very practice of establishing governmentally composed prayers for religious services was one of the reasons which caused many of our early colonists to leave England and seek religious freedom in America.... The First Amendment was added to the Constitution to stand as a guarantee that neither the power nor the prestige of the Federal Government would be used to control, support or influence the kinds of prayer the American people can say that the people's religious must not be subjected to the pressures of government for change each time a new political administration is elected to office."

Justice Potter Stewart (dissenting): "With all respect, I think the Court has misapplied a great constitutional principle. I cannot see how an "official religion" is established by letting those who want to say a prayer say it. On the contrary, I think that to deny the wish of these school children to join in reciting this prayer is to deny them the opportunity of sharing in the spiritual heritage of our Nation."

Is a **moment of silence** law **constitutional**?

It depends. Moment of silence laws are constitutional if government officials had secular reasons for drafting them, rather than simply attempting to bring prayer back into public schools. In *Wallace v. Jaffree* (1985), the U.S. Supreme Court invalidated an Alabama moment of silence law that the sponsor of the measure bluntly stated was designed to bring prayer back into the public schools. Alabama legislators had amended an existing moment of silence law by adding the words "or voluntary prayer." The sponsor admitted that restoring prayer to schools was his only motivation. Under those facts, a majority of the Court found a clear religious purpose in violation of the *Lemon* test.

However, lower courts have upheld moment of silence laws in which legislators advanced for secular purposes. In *Croft v. Perry* (5th Cir. 2009), the 5th U.S. Circuit Court of Appeals upheld a Texas moment of silence law. The appeals court accepted the following secular purposes for the law: "fostering patriotism, providing a period for thoughtful contemplation, and protecting religious freedom." Other federal appeals court have upheld moment of silence laws in Georgia and Virginia in recent years.

In the case out of Georgia, the Georgia legislature referred to its measure as the "Moment of Quiet Reflection" law. The 11th U.S. Circuit Court of Appeals in *Bown v. Gwinnett County Schools* (11th Cir. 1997) reasoned that the valid secular purpose of this law was to give students the opportunity to reflect on the coming day.

What opinions were rendered by the U.S. Supreme Court concerning *Wallace v. Jaffree*.

The justices made the following statements concerning the moment of silence issue in *Wallace v. Jaffree* (1985).

Justice John Paul Stevens (majority): "The legislative intent to return prayer to the public schools is, of course, quite different from merely protecting every student's right to engage in voluntary prayer during an appropriate moment of silence during the schoolday…. The addition of 'or voluntary prayer' indicates that the State intended to characterize prayer as a favored practice. Such an endorsement is not consistent with the established principle that the government must pursue a course of complete neutrality toward religion."

Justice Lewis Powell (concurring): "The record before us, however, makes clear that Alabama's purpose was solely religious in character. Senator Donald Holmes, the sponsor of the bill that became Alabama Code 16-1-20.1 (Supp. 1984), freely acknowledged that the purpose of this statute was 'to return voluntary prayer' to the public schools."

Justice Sandra Day O'Connor (concurring): "A state-sponsored moment of silence in the public schools is different from state-sponsored vocal prayer or Bible reading. First, a moment of silence is not inherently religious. Silence, unlike prayer or Bible reading, need not be associated with a religious exercise. Second, a pupil who participates in a moment of silence need not compromise his or her beliefs. During a moment of silence, a student who objects to prayer is left to his or her own thoughts, and is not compelled to listen to the prayers or thoughts of others. For these simple reasons, a moment of silence statute does not stand or fall under the Establishment Clause according to how the Court regards vocal prayer or Bible reading. Scholars and at least one Member of this Court have recognized the distinction and suggested that a moment of silence in public schools would be constitutional."

Chief Justice Warren Burger (dissenting): "Some who trouble to read the opinions in these cases will find it ironic—perhaps even bizarre—that on the very day we heard arguments in the cases, the Court's session opened with an invocation for Divine protection."

Justice Byron White (dissenting): "Of course, I have been out of step with many of the Court's decisions dealing with this subject matter, and it is thus not surprising that I would support a basic reconsideration of our precedents."

Justice William Rehnquist (dissenting): "It is impossible to build sound constitutional doctrine upon a mistaken understanding of constitutional history, but unfortunately the Establishment Clause has been expressly freighted with Jefferson's misleading metaphor for nearly 40 years."

Does the **First Amendment** protect **graduation prayer**?

The U.S. Supreme Court ruled 5 to 4 in *Lee v. Weisman* (1992) that school-sponsored graduation prayer violates the First Amendment. The majority focused on the coercive pressure placed on students at graduation who did not adhere to the same religion as the religious figure giving the graduation prayer. The majority also noted that students at graduation were a captive audience who essentially had no choice as to whether to hear the prayer or not.

What was the *Santa Fe Independent School District v. Doe* case on school prayer and what did the U.S. Supreme Court decide?

The 2000 U.S. Supreme Court decision on school prayer was a case involving prayers announced over a loudspeaker at Texas high school football games. In *Santa Fe Independent School District v. Doe*, the Court ruled 6 to 3 that the practice violated the Establishment Clause in part because most observers would believe that the school was endorsing religion. Even though the student body voted on whether to have the prayers or not, the Court reasoned that the policy meant that majoritarian religious preferences would also trump those of the minority.

Justice John Paul Stevens (majority): "The actual or perceived endorsement of the message, moreover, is established by factors beyond just the text of the policy. Once the student speaker is selected and the message composed, the invocation is then delivered to a large audience assembled as part of a regularly scheduled, school-sponsored function conducted on school property. The message is broadcast over the school's public address system, which remains subject to the control of school officials. It is fair to assume that the pregame ceremony is clothed in the traditional indicia of school sporting events, which generally include not just the team, but also cheerleaders and band members dressed in uniforms sporting the school name and mascot."

Chief Justice William H. Rehnquist (dissenting): "The Court distorts existing precedent to conclude that the school district's student-message program is invalid on its face under the Establishment Clause. But even more disturbing than its holding is the tone of the Court's opinion; it bristles with hostility to all things religious in public life. Neither the holding nor the tone of the opinion is faithful to the meaning of the Establishment Clause."

What is obscentity and pornography, and what is art? Should the First Amendment protect *all* forms of speech? (*iStock*)

Does the **First Amendment** protect **all** forms of **free speech**?

No, the First Amendment does not protect all forms of speech even though the text of the amendment provides that "Congress shall make no law … abridging the freedom of speech." The First Amendment does not protect many forms of speech. Some examples include obscenity, child pornography, incitement to imminent lawless action, perjury, true threats, libel, and solicitation to commit murder.

What is **obscenity**?

Obscenity refers to hard-core pornography that goes beyond so-called contemporary community standards. Obscenity is judged by the so-called *"Miller* test" from the U.S. Supreme Court's 1973 decision *Miller v. California* (1973). The *Miller* test requires that material appeal predominately to the prurient (morbid or shameful) interest in sex, depict sexual material in a patently offensive way and have no serious literary, artistic, political, or scientific value.

For example, a federal district in Florida held that a rap music album filled with profanity and misogynistic language constituted obscenity. On appeal, the 11th U.S. Circuit Court of Appeal reversed and determined that the album *As Nasty as They Wanna Be* by the 2 Live Crew did not constitute obscenity, because the music (though profane) had some serious artistic value. Attorneys for the defendant produced several expert witnesses who testified as to the material's serious artistic value.

The U.S. Supreme Court in *Miller* stated:

The basic guidelines for the trier of fact must be: (a) whether "the average person, applying contemporary community standards" would find that the work, taken as a whole, appeals to the prurient interest, *Kois v. Wisconsin*, supra, at 230, quoting *Roth v. United States*, supra, at 489; (b) whether the work depicts or describes, in a patently offensive way, sexual conduct specifically defined by the applicable state law; and (c) whether the work, taken as a whole, lacks serious literary, artistic, political, or scientific value. We do not adopt as a constitutional standard the "utterly without redeeming social value" test of *Memoirs v. Massachusetts*, that concept has never commanded the adherence of more than three Justices at one time.... If a state law that regulates obscene material is thus limited, as written or construed, the First Amendment values applicable to the States through the Fourteenth Amendment are adequately protected by the ultimate power of appellate courts to conduct an independent review of constitutional claims when necessary....

We emphasize that it is not our function to propose regulatory schemes for the States. That must await their concrete legislative efforts. It is possible, however, to give a few plain examples of what a state statute could define for regulation under part (b) of the standard announced in this opinion, supra:

(a) Patently offensive representations or descriptions of ultimate sexual acts, normal or perverted, actual or simulated.

(b) Patently offensive representations or descriptions of masturbation, excretory functions, and lewd exhibition of the genitals.

How does the notion of **community standards affect obscenity cases**?

The first two prongs of the *Miller* test—prurient interest and patent offensiveness—are both judged by community standards. The applicable community could be a local or state standard. In a few states, there is a state-wide standard. In some states the community is county-by-county. There is no national standard or international standard in obscenity cases. This becomes a major issue in cases involving alleged obscenity on the Internet. Defendants—especially publishers or distributors of pornographic material—have alleged it is unfair for them to be subject to the community standards of a particularly restrictive locale when they for instance may have produced the material in a more tolerant community.

This occurred in a case *United States v. Thomas* (6th Cir. 1996) involving a California couple responsible for the creation of an online bulletin board full of sex materials. The California-based couple sold material to an undercover federal law enforcement agent in Memphis. The officer then charged the couple with obscenity and the case was prosecuted under the community standards of Tennessee, not California.

When does **speech cross the line** into **unprotected** incitement?

According to the U.S. Supreme Court's standard in *Brandenburg v. Ohio* (1969), even speech that advocates illegal conduct is protected speech under the First Amendment unless the speech incites imminent lawless action and is likely to cause such unlawful action. Brandenburg involved a Ku Klux Klan leader near Cincinnati, Ohio, area who gave a speech filled with racist comments about African-Americans and Jews. He also said that if the government kept up its course of action, there would have to be some "revengeance" taken. However, the Court unanimously determined that this fell far short of incitement to imminent lawless action.

49

The Court explained: "These later decisions have fashioned the principle that the constitutional guarantees of free speech and free press do not permit a State to forbid or proscribe advocacy of the use of force or of law violation except where such advocacy is directed to inciting or producing imminent lawless action and is likely to incite or produce such act."

When does **speech** cross the line and become a **true threat**?

True threats also are not protected by the First Amendment. Rhetorical hyperbole—even if the speaker uses harsh and colorful language—generally will not constitute a true threat because there is no serious intention to cause harm to another. The U.S. Supreme Court applied this principle in the case of *Watts v. United States* (1969), which involved a young African-American war protester. Speaking in a crowd, the young man said that if the government made him go with his "black brothers" to Vietnam that the first person he would put in the "scope of his rifle was L.B.J." referring to U.S. President Lyndon Baines Johnson. The Court determined that this was mere political hyperbole, rather than an actual threat.

In *Virginia v. Black* (2003), the Court offered a more concrete definition of a true threat in the context of a case involving cross burnings by Ku Klux Klan members. The Court determined that true threats "encompass those states where the speaker means to communicate a serious expression of an intent to commit an act of unlawful violence to a particular individual or group of individuals."

What was the U.S. Supreme Court's definition of a **true threat** in **Virginia v. Black** (2003).

"True threats" encompass those statements where the speaker means to communicate a serious expression of intent to commit an act of unlawful violence to a particular individual or group of individuals. The speaker need not actually intend to carry out the threat. Rather, a prohibition on true threats protects individuals from the fear of violence and from the disruption that fear engenders, in addition to protecting people "from the possibility that the threatened violence will occur. Intimidation in the constitutionally proscribable sense of the word is a type of true threat, where a speaker directs a threat to a person or group of persons with the intent of placing the victim in fear of bodily harm or death."

Does the **First Amendment** protect **advertising**?

Yes, in the mid 1970s the U.S Supreme Court ruled that advertising was a form of speech entitled to First Amendment protection. In an earlier ruling in *Valentine v. Chrestensen* (1942) the U.S. Supreme Court had ruled that the First Amendment does not protect "purely commercial advertising."

However, three decades later the Court realized that the "free flow of commercial information" was important in society and that people have a right to receive information and ideas in a commercial culture. The Court reached this conclusion in *Virginia Pharmacy Board v. Virginia Consumer Council* (1976; see LegalSpeak, p. 52), a case involving a challenge to a Virginia law that forbade pharmacists from advertising the prices of prescription drugs. The state pharmacy board argued that there should be no free-speech protection for purely commercial advertising. The board also contended that the state could prohibit pharmacists from advertising prices as a way to preserve professionalism.

The Supreme Court rejected these arguments and overruled *Valentine v. Chrestenson* in the process. The state pharmacy board wanted to prevent price advertising to protect the public. The Supreme Court said that there was another alternative to suppressing this information: "That alternative is to assume that this information is not in itself harmful, that people will perceive their own best interests if only they are well enough informed, and that the best means to that end is to open the channels of communication rather than to close them."

Is it okay to stretch the truth in an advertisement because you are exercising free speech under the First Amendment? Or should such ads be strictly regulated? (*iStock*)

Does the **status** of a speaker affect **First Amendment freedoms**?

Yes, context matters a great deal in First Amendment cases. Adult citizens have the full protection of the First Amendment when they are in society. However, adults do not have the same level of First Amendment rights when they work as public employees. Likewise, public school students—most of whom are minors—do not have the same level of First Amendment rights when they are in school as they do when they are out of school.

What is the **level** of **free speech protection** for **public employees**?

Public employees have First Amendment rights but they are limited by the employment relationship. In one decision, *Garcetti v. Ceballos* (2006; see LegalSpeak, p. 54), the U.S. Supreme Court ruled that public employees do not have free-speech protection for

51

LegalSpeak:
Virginia Pharmacy Board v. Virginia Consumer Citizens Council

The U.S. Supreme Court decision on *Virginia Pharmacy Board v. Virginia Consumer Citizens Council* (1976) read, in part, as follows:

> Here, in contrast, the question whether there is a First Amendment exception for "commercial speech" is squarely before us. Our pharmacist does not wish to editorialize on any subject, cultural, philosophical, or political. He does not wish to report any particularly newsworthy fact, or to make generalized observations even about commercial matters. The "idea" he wishes to communicate is simply this: "I will sell you the X prescription drug at the Y price." Our question, then, is whether this communication is wholly outside the protection of the First Amendment....

> As to the particular consumer's interest in the free flow of commercial information, that interest may be as keen, if not keener by far, than his interest in the day's most urgent political debate. Appellees' case in this respect is a convincing one. Those whom the suppression of prescription drug price information hits the hardest are the poor, the sick, and particularly the aged. A disproportionate amount of their income tends to be spent on prescription drugs; yet they are the least able to learn, by shopping from pharmacist to pharmacist, where their scarce dollars are best spent. When drug prices vary as strikingly as they do, information as to who is charging what becomes more than a convenience. It could mean the alleviation of physical pain or the enjoyment of basic necessities. Generalizing, society also may have a strong interest in the free flow of commercial information....

> There is, of course, an alternative to this highly paternalistic approach. That alternative is to assume that this information is not in itself harmful, that people will perceive their own best interests if only they are well enough informed, and that the best means to that end is to open the channels of communication rather than to close them. If they are truly open, nothing prevents the "professional" pharmacist from marketing his own assertedly superior product, and contrasting it with that of the low-cost, high-volume prescription drug retailer. But the choice among these alternative approaches is not ours to make or the Virginia General Assembly's. It is precisely this kind of choice, between the dangers of suppressing information, and the dangers of its misuse if it is freely available, that the First Amendment makes for us.

Do young students have the same rights to free speech as adults? Recent Supreme Court decisions have held that they do not (*iStock*).

speech made pursuant to their official job duties. However, if a citizen speaks more as a citizen than an employee, the courts will apply a two-part test from *Pickering v. Board of Education* (1968) and *Connick v. Myers* (1983). That test asks: (1) Did the employee's speech touch on matters of public concern or importance; and (2) does the employee's right to free speech trump the employer's right to an efficient, disruptive-free workplace.

A problem in this area is that it is unclear when an employee is speaking pursuant to their official job duties. Sometimes a public employee may speak both as an employee and as a concerned citizen. Many courts look to the "core functions" of an employee's job and try to determine whether the speech is required by the job.

What level of **First Amendment rights** do **students** possess?

Public school students possess First Amendment rights but they are limited by the school environment. Generally, public school officials can restrict student speech that they reasonably forecast would cause a substantial disruption or material interference with school activities. This is known as the *Tinker* standard from the U.S. Supreme Court decision in *Tinker v. Des Moines Independent Community School District* (1969; see LegalSpeak, p. 56).

In later decisions, the U.S. Supreme Court explained in *Bethel School District v. Fraser* (1986) that school officials can restrict student speech that is vulgar or lewd. The Court later ruled in *Hazelwood School District v. Kuhlmeier* (1988) that school

53

LegalSpeak: *Garcetti v. Ceballos* (2006)

Justice Anthony Kennedy (majority): "The controlling factor in Ceballos' case is that his expressions were made pursuant to his duties as a calendar deputy. See Brief for Respondent 4 ("Ceballos does not dispute that he prepared the memorandum 'pursuant to his duties as a prosecutor'"). That consideration—the fact that Ceballos spoke as a prosecutor fulfilling a responsibility to advise his supervisor about how best to proceed with a pending case—distinguishes Ceballos' case from those in which the First Amendment provides protection against discipline. We hold that when public employees make statements pursuant to their official duties, the employees are not speaking as citizens for First Amendment purposes, and the Constitution does not insulate their communications from employer discipline."

Justice John Paul Stevens (dissenting): "public employees are still citizens while they are in the office. The notion that there is a categorical difference between speaking as a citizen and speaking in the course of one's employment is quite wrong.... Moreover, it seems perverse to fashion a new rule that provides employees with an incentive to voice their concerns publicly before talking frankly to their superiors."

Justice David Souter (dissenting): "I agree with the majority that a government employer has substantial interests in effectuating its chosen policy and objectives, and in demanding competence, honesty, and judgment from employees who speak for it in doing their work. But I would hold that private and public interests in addressing official wrongdoing and threats to health and safety can outweigh the government's stake in the efficient implementation of policy, and when they do public employees who speak on these matters in the course of their duties should be eligible to claim First Amendment protection."

Justice Stephen Breyer (dissenting): "Where professional and special constitutional obligations are both present, the need to protect the employee's speech is augmented, the need for broad government authority to control that speech is likely diminished, and administrable standards are quite likely available. Hence, I would find that the Constitution mandates special protection of employee speech in such circumstances. Thus I would apply the *Pickering* (see p. 53) balancing test here."

officials have greater ability to restrict student speech that is school-sponsored, such as expression from most school newspapers, school plays and school mascots. More recently, the Court ruled in *Morse v. Frederick* (2007) that public school officials can restrict student speech that they reasonably believe advocates illegal drug use.

What happened in *Garcetti v. Ceballos*?

In this 2006 case, an assistant district attorney in Los Angeles, Richard Ceballos, learned from a defense attorney about possible perjured statements from a law enforcement officer in a search warrant affidavit. Ceballos conducted an independent investigation and agreed with the defense attorney that the officer's testimony was troubling. Ceballos, as calendar deputy which gave him some supervisory authority, wrote a memorandum to his superiors, recommending that the criminal charges in the case be dismissed. His superiors did not agree with Ceballos, who later testified at a suppression hearing in the criminal case. Ceballos was demoted and transferred to a less desirable office after this controversy. Ceballos sued Gil Garcetti, the district attorney, and others, contending that they retaliated against him for his protected speech.

The U.S. Supreme Court ruled 5 to 4 (see LegalSpeak, p. 54) against Ceballos, finding that his speech in his memorandum was part of his official job duties and not protected citizen speech.

What **expression** was involved in the *Tinker* case?

In *Tinker v. Des Moines Independent Community School District* (1969; see LegalSpeak, p. 56), several students wore black peace armbands to school to protest U.S. involvement in the Vietnam War. School officials had learned of the protest and quickly passed a no-armband rule. School officials believed the armbands were too controversial and could cause problems. The U.S. Supreme Court ruled 7 to 2 in favor of the students and against school officials. The Court reasoned that the school officials did not show that the armbands would be disruptive of school activities in any significant way.

SECOND AMENDMENT

What makes the **Second Amendment controversial**?

There are two very different interpretations of the Second Amendment, which provides: "A well regulated Militia, being necessary to the security of a free State, the right of the people to keep and bear Arms, shall not be infringed." The Second Amendment consists of two clauses—the prefatory clause speaking of a "well-regulated militia" and an operative clause speaking of the "the right of the people to keep and bear arms."

One interpretation of the Second Amendment focuses on the militia clause, emphasizing that the amendment was only designed to protect a collective right to bear arms through a militia. This collective-rights interpretation does not believe that the amendment was designed to give individuals a constitutional right to bear arms. The other interpretation of the Second Amendment—the individual-rights model—believes that the amendment gives individuals the right to bear arms.

LegalSpeak:
Tinker v. Des Moines Independent Community School District (1969)

Justice Abe Fortas (majority): "It can hardly be argued that either students or teachers shed their constitutional rights to freedom of speech or expression at the schoolhouse gate.... The District Court concluded that the action of the school authorities was reasonable because it was based upon their fear of a disturbance from the wearing of the armbands. But, in our system, undifferentiated fear or apprehension of disturbance is not enough to overcome the right to freedom of expression. Any departure from absolute regimentation may cause trouble. Any variation from the majority's opinion may inspire fear. Any word spoken, in class, in the lunchroom, or on the campus, that deviates from the views of another person may start an argument or cause a disturbance. But our Constitution says we must take this risk, and our history says that it is this sort of hazardous freedom—this kind of openness—that is the basis of our national strength and of the independence and vigor of Americans who grow up and live in this relatively permissive, often disputatious, society.

"In order for the State in the person of school officials to justify prohibition of a particular expression of opinion, it must be able to show that its action was caused by something more than a mere desire to avoid the discomfort and unpleasantness that always accompany an unpopular viewpoint. Certainly where there is no finding and no showing that engaging in the forbidden conduct would 'materially and substantially interfere with the requirements of appropriate discipline in the operation of the school,' the prohibition cannot be sustained."

Justice Hugo Black (dissenting): "Even a casual reading of the record shows that this armband did divert students' minds from their regular lessons, and that talk, comments, etc., made John Tinker 'self-conscious' in attending school with his armband. While the absence of obscene remarks or boisterous and loud disorder perhaps justifies the Court's statement that the few armband students did not actually 'disrupt' the classwork, I think the record overwhelmingly shows that the armbands did exactly what the elected school officials and principals foresaw they would, that is, took the students' minds off their classwork and diverted them to thoughts about the highly emotional subject of the Vietnam war. And I repeat that if the time has come when pupils of state-supported schools, kindergartens, grammar schools, or high schools, can defy and flout orders of school officials to keep their minds on their own schoolwork, it is the beginning of a new revolutionary era of permissiveness in this country fostered by the judiciary. The next logical step, it appears to me, would be to hold unconstitutional laws that bar pupils under 21 or 18 from voting, or from being elected members of the boards of education."

LegalSpeak: *District of Columbia v. Heller* (2008)

Justice Antonin Scalia (majority): "Putting all of these textual elements together, we find that they guarantee the individual right to possess and carry weapons in case of confrontation. This meaning is strongly confirmed by the historical background of the Second Amendment. We look to this because it has always been widely understood that the Second Amendment, like the First and Fourth Amendments, codified a *pre-existing* right. The very text of the Second Amendment implicitly recognizes the pre-existence of the right and declares only that it 'shall not be infringed.'"

Justice John Paul Stevens (dissenting): "The Second Amendment was adopted to protect the right of the people of each of the several States to maintain a well-regulated militia. It was a response to concerns raised during the ratification of the Constitution that the power of Congress to disarm the state militias and create a national standing army posed an intolerable threat to the sovereignty of the several States. Neither the text of the Amendment nor the arguments advanced by its proponents evidenced the slightest interest in limiting any legislature's authority to regulate private civilian uses of firearms. Specifically, there is no indication that the Framers of the Amendment intended to enshrine the common-law right of self-defense in the Constitution."

Which **interpretation—collective** or **individual**—has the U.S. Supreme Court adopted?

The U.S. Supreme Court interpreted the individual-rights model of interpreting the Second Amendment in *District of Columbia v. Heller* (2008). The Court ruled 5 to 4 that the prefatory clause about a "well-regulated militia" does not limit the operative clause that talks about "the right of the people."

What happened in the *Heller* case?

In *District of Columbia v. Heller* (2008) the U.S. Supreme Court struck down a District of Columbia law that forbade the private possession of handguns. Dick Heller, a D.C. special police officer who carried a gun in his work protecting the Federal Judicial Center, contended that he also should have a constitutional right to keep a handgun in his home for self-defense and home protection.

THIRD AND FOURTH AMENDMENTS

What was the **purpose** of the **Third Amendment**?

The Third Amendment arose out of the special conditions of the Revolutionary-War era when the government sometimes sought to require colonists to house British troops in their private homes. The amendment does not have much practical usage today, as the military has its own bases and quarters.

What is the **Fourth Amendment**?

The Fourth Amendment is the amendment that provides us with protection from "unreasonable searches and seizures" by law enforcement officials. It provides: "The right of the people to be secure in their persons, houses, papers, and effects, against unreasonable searches and seizures, shall not be violated, and no Warrants shall issue, but upon probable cause, supported by Oath or affirmation, and particularly describing the place to be searched, and the persons or things to be seized."

What is the fundamental **purpose** of the **Fourth Amendment**?

The Fourth Amendment serves to protect individuals from invasive searches and seizures conducted by government officials. The Framers worried that government officials could abuse individual liberty by engaging in roving, fishing-expedition searches pursuant to general warrants. The Fourth Amendment generally requires a law enforcement agent to have a warrant backed up by probable cause before being able to search a person and his or her belongings.

What is the meaning of **probable cause**?

The U.S. Supreme Court defined probable cause in *Brinegar v. United States* (1949) as: "a reasonable ground for belief of guilt … where the facts and circumstances within their [the officers'] knowledge and of which they had reasonably trustworthy information [are] sufficient in themselves to warrant a man of reasonable caution in the belief that an offense has been or is being committed."

Must government **officials always** obtain a **warrant** before conducting a search or a seizure?

No, there are several exceptions to the warrant requirement. Some of these include: searches of public school students, exigent circumstances, hot pursuit, plain view, plain feel, consent searches (where an individual has given consent to a government

LegalSpeak: *Redding v. Sanford Unified School District* (2009)

Justice David Souter (majority): "Savana's subjective expectation of privacy against such a search is inherent in her account of it as embarrassing, frightening, and humiliating. The reasonableness of her expectation (required by the Fourth Amendment standard) is indicated by the consistent experiences of other young people similarly searched, whose adolescent vulnerability intensifies the patent intrusiveness of the exposure…. In sum, what was missing from the suspected facts that pointed to Savana was any indication of danger to the students from the power of the drugs or their quantity, and any reason to suppose that Savana was carrying pills in her underwear. We think that the combination of these deficiencies was fatal to finding the search reasonable."

Justice John Paul Stevens (concurring in part, dissenting in part): "I disagree with its decision to extend qualified immunity to the school official who authorized this unconstitutional search."

Justice Ruth Bader Ginsburg (concurring in part, dissenting in part): "The Court's opinion in *T.L.O.* plainly stated the controlling Fourth Amendment law: A search ordered by a school official, even if 'justified at its inception,' crosses the constitutional boundary if it becomes 'excessively intrusive in light of the age and sex of the student and the nature of the infraction.'"

Justice Clarence Thomas (concurring in part, dissenting in part): "Unlike the majority, however, I would hold that the search of Savana Redding did not violate the Fourth Amendment. The majority imposes a vague and amorphous standard on school administrators. It also grants judges sweeping authority to second-guess the measures that these officials take to maintain discipline in their schools and ensure the health and safety of the students in their charge. This deep intrusion into the administration of public schools exemplifies why the Court should return to the common-law doctrine of *in loco parentis* under which 'the judiciary was reluctant to interfere in the routine business of school administration, allowing schools and teachers to set and enforce rules and to maintain order.'"

official to search), search incident to arrest, automobile exception, border-search exception, open fields, and stop and frisk.

Must **school officials** have **probable cause** before searching a student in a public school?

No, the U.S. Supreme Court in *New Jersey v. T.L.O.* (1985) ruled that the probable-cause requirement in public schools was too stringent and would hamper the mainte-

When is it okay to conduct a search of private property? Do the police always need a search warrant? (*iStock*)

nance of order and discipline in the schools. Instead, the Court articulated a "reasonableness standard," finding that the search must be justified at its inception and that it must be reasonably related in scope to the circumstances that justified the search in the first place.

New Jersey v. T.L.O. involved a search by an assistant school principal of a student's purse. The assistant principal originally suspected the juvenile girl of smoking in the bathroom, but later discovered that the girl may be involved in dealing marijuana after searching her entire purse.

Do **school officials** have unfettered authority to conduct **strip searches**?

No, strip searches are more invasive and there is a presumption that many strip searches would not pass the reasonableness inquiry under *New Jersey v. T.L.O.* (1985). In *Safford Unified School District v. Redding* (2009; see LegalSpeak, p. 59), the Court ruled that a strip search of a student for alleging possessing prescription drug pills was not reasonable under the specific facts of the case. The Court emphasized the intrusive nature of strip searches and the fact that there was little evidence that the student Savana Redding was carrying such pills.

However, the Court granted qualified immunity to the assistant school principal in part because the case law was so divided on the constitutionality of strip searches. Qualified immunity is a doctrine that shields government officials from liability unless they violate clearly established constitutional or statutory law.

What is **plain view**?

The plain view doctrine provides that if a law enforcement official comes across incriminating evidence that is in his or her plain view, the officer can conduct a search without having to first obtain a warrant. The Supreme Court has reasoned that the object or material must be in plain view of the officer and that the incriminating character of the material must be "immediately apparent." Also, the law enforcement official must lawfully be in the position from which he or she spots the incriminating material. It used to be the law that the plain view doctrine required that the officer's discovery of the incriminating material be inadvertent. However, the U.S. Supreme Court rejected that requirement in *Horton v. California* (1990).

The U.S. Supreme Court has expanded the plain view doctrine to also include the plain feel or plain touch exception to the Fourth Amendment.

How does a court determine if someone's **Fourth Amendment rights** have been **violated**?

Sometimes the Court will ask whether someone had a reasonable expectation of privacy to determine if there was a Fourth Amendment violation. Under this test, a person subjectively must exhibit an expectation of privacy. Also, the person's expectation must be one that society regards as objectively reasonable.

What is the **exclusionary rule**?

The exclusionary rule is a Fourth Amendment-based principle that provides that evidence seized as a result of a Fourth Amendment violation cannot be used as evidence. The classic phrase associated with this rule is that of Justice Benjamin Cardozo, who wrote when he was on the New York Court of Appeals, "the criminal goes free because the constable has blundered."

In what decision did the **Court extend** the **exclusionary rule** requirement to the states?

In *Mapp v. Ohio* (1961; see LegalSpeak, p. 63), the Court ruled 6 to 3 that the Fourth Amendment-based exclusionary rule, which holds that evidence illegally seized by law enforcement officials must be excluded from trial, applies to the states through the Fourteenth Amendment due-process clause. In 1949, the Court had ruled *Wolf v. Colorado* that in a prosecution in a State court for a State crime the Fourteenth Amendment does not forbid the admission of evidence obtained by an unreasonable search and seizure. The Court overruled that aspect of its *Wolf* decision 12 years later in *Mapp*. Justice Tom C. Clark, a former prosecutor, wrote: "We hold that all evidence obtained by searches and seizures in violation of the Constitution is, by that same authority, inadmissible in a state court."

61

Who was **Dollree Mapp**?

The defendant in *Mapp v. Ohio* (1961; see LegalSpeak, p. 63) was Dollree Mapp. The case began when at least seven Cleveland police officers searched for gambling paraphernalia in the home of Dollree Mapp. Instead, the officers found pornographic books, which they labeled obscene. Mapp was found not guilty of gambling charges but was convicted on the obscenity charges. The case eventually reached the U.S. Supreme Court, which reversed her conviction because the police officers failed to produce a search warrant before rummaging through Mapp's home.

Mapp was known in boxing circles. She was the ex-wife of former top-ranked light-heavyweight and heavyweight boxer Jimmy Bivins. Then, in 1956, Mapp filed a $750,000 lawsuit against world light-heavyweight champion Archie Moore. She claimed that Moore broke a promise to marry her and physically assaulted her. Mapp moved to Queens, New York. In 1970, police officers seized $250,000 in drugs and stolen property. Mapp was convicted and sentenced to a prison term of 20 years to life. Mapp claimed the charges were a vendetta against her after her famous case. In 1981, Governor Hugh Carey commuted Mapp's sentence. She had served more than nine years in a women's prison in New Bedford, New York.

Ironically, there was another soon-to-be famous person in the Mapp case who would later play a large role in the sport of boxing. Famed boxing promoter Don King used to be involved in gambling and numbers in Ohio. It was his phone call that led the police to believe there was gambling paraphernalia in Mapp's house.

FIFTH AMENDMENT

What **freedoms** does the **Fifth Amendment protect**?

The Fifth Amendment provides: "No person shall be held to answer for a capital, or otherwise infamous crime, unless on a presentment or indictment of a Grand Jury, except in cases arising in the land or naval forces, or in the Militia, when in actual service in time of War or public danger; nor shall any person be subject for the same offense to be twice put in jeopardy of life or limb; nor shall be compelled in any criminal case to be a witness against himself, nor be deprived of life, liberty, or property without due process of law; nor shall private property be taken for public use without just compensation."

The Fifth Amendment—the longest in the Bill of Rights—provides the following protections:

1. Right to a grand jury
2. Protection against double jeopardy
3. Protection against self-incrimination

> ## LegalSpeak: *Mapp v. Ohio* (1961)
>
> Justice Tom C. Clark: (majority): "The criminal goes free, if he must, but it is the law that sets him free. Nothing can destroy a government more quickly than its failure to observe its own laws, or worse, its disregard of the charter of its own existence.… [T]he ignoble shortcut to conviction left open to the State tends to destroy the entire system of constitutional restraints on which the liberties of the people rest. Having once recognized that the right to privacy embodied in the Fourth Amendment is enforceable against the States, and that the right to be secure against rude invasions of privacy by state officers is, therefore, constitutional in origin, we can no longer permit that right to remain an empty vessel."

4. Due process
5. Just compensation

What is **double jeopardy**?

The Fifth Amendment provides that "nor shall any person be subject for the same offence to be twice put in jeopardy of life or limb." Double jeopardy means that a person is placed in jeopardy of punishment for a crime twice. It prohibits a second prosecution after a person has been acquitted or convicted. It also prohibits multiple punishments for the same offense. The U.S. Supreme Court has declared that the double jeopardy clause is designed "to protect an individual from being subjected to the hazards of trial and possible conviction more than once for an alleged offense."

What is an **example** of the **double jeopardy clause** prohibiting multiple punishments for the same offense?

The U.S. Supreme Court's decision in *Brown v. Ohio* (1978) provides an excellent illustration of the Double Jeopardy Clause in action. County prosecutors initially charged Nathaniel Brown with joyriding. He pled guilty and served 30 days in jail. Upon his release, prosecutors charged him with the more serious crime of auto theft. Brown's lawyer contended that this subsequent charged violated his client's right to be free from double jeopardy.

The Supreme Court applied the *Blockburger* test—derived from *Blockburger v. United States* (1932): "The applicable rule is that where the same act or transaction constitutes a violation of two distinct statutory provisions, the test to be applied to determine whether there are two offenses or only one, is whether each provision requires proof of an additional fact which the other does not." Applying this test, the Court determined that joyriding and auto theft constituted the same offense.

63

When giving testimony, you are protected by the Fifth Amendment from self-incrimination, which means you cannot be forced to say anything that could make you look guilty (*iStock*).

What is the **protection** against **self-incrimination**?

This Fifth Amendment-based freedom means that the government cannot force an individual to the prosecution against him or her. In other words, it means that the government cannot force persons to incriminate themselves. A person can say "I take the Fifth," and the government cannot compel him or her to speak. We often think of the Fifth Amendment when someone takes the stand and a prosecutor asks them a question to which he or she responds: "I take the Fifth." But, the Fifth Amendment also applies when a person is subject to police interrogation and questioning.

In what **famous decision** did the U.S. Supreme Court establish **certain rights** to persons facing **interrogation** and questioning from police?

The U.S. Supreme Court ruled in four consolidated cases—*Miranda v. Arizona, Vignera v. New York, Westover v. United States,* and *California v. Stewart*—that law enforcement officials could not use statements obtained from a police interrogation unless they demonstrated the use of procedural safeguards effective to secure the privilege against self-incrimination. The Court held that police violate the Fifth Amendment if they do not inform a suspect prior to questioning that he or she has: (1) a right to remain silent; (2) that any statement he or she makes can be used against them in a court of law; (3) that he or she has the right to have an attorney present during questioning; and (4) that if he or she cannot afford an attorney, one will be provided to them. If law enforcement officials fail to provide these procedural safeguards, the Court said that evidence obtained during such interrogations cannot be used against the suspect.

Who was **Miranda** in the **famous case**?

Ernesto A. Miranda was a criminal defendant convicted of rape who challenged his conviction in a U.S. Supreme Court case that bears his name. Miranda was arrested on suspicion of robbery. During a two-hour interrogation at a Phoenix police station, Miranda not only confessed to the robbery, but also to sexually assaulting and raping a woman 11 days earlier. The police officers never informed Miranda that he had a right to have a lawyer present during questioning. A jury convicted Miranda of kidnapping and rape and sentenced him to 20 to 30 years for each offense. Miranda's lawyers argued that their client's Fifth Amendment right against self-incrimination was violated by the coercive interrogation. In *Miranda v. Arizona* (1966; see LegalSpeak, p. 66), the U.S. Supreme Court agreed.

What happened to Ernesto A. **Miranda after** the U.S. Supreme Court **decision**?

Prosecutors retried Miranda without evidence obtained from his confession. The prosecution presented the testimony of Miranda's common-law wife, who claimed that during a prison visit, Miranda confessed to her that he had raped the victim. A jury convicted him again on charges of kidnapping and rape in 1966. Miranda was paroled in 1972. However, in 1976, Miranda was stabbed to death in a bar fight. At the time of his death, he was carrying cards containing the text of the Miranda warnings.

What is **due process**?

Due process—a freedom also found in the Fourteenth Amendment— is one of the most important rights in the American legal system. It ensures a basic level of fundamental fairness before the state infringes on individual liberty.

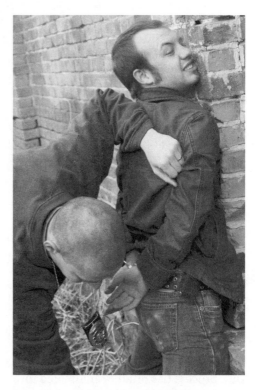

You must be read your Miranda rights if you are taken into custody. Named after the case involving Ernesto A. Miranda, this procedure informs you about, among other things, your right to legal council (*iStock*).

LegalSpeak: *Miranda v. Arizona* (1966)

The U.S. Supreme Court ruled:

In these cases, we might not find the defendants' statements to have been involuntary in traditional terms. Our concern for adequate safeguards to protect precious Fifth Amendment rights is, of course, not lessened in the slightest. In each of the cases, the defendant was thrust into an unfamiliar atmosphere and run through menacing police interrogation procedures. The potentiality for compulsion is forcefully apparent, for example, in Miranda, where the indigent Mexican defendant was a seriously disturbed individual with pronounced sexual fantasies....

Today, then, there can be no doubt that the Fifth Amendment privilege is available outside of criminal court proceedings and serves to protect persons in all settings in which their freedom of action is curtailed in any significant way from being compelled to incriminate themselves. We have concluded that without proper safeguards the process of in-custody interrogation of persons suspected or accused of crime contains inherently compelling pressures which work to undermine the individual's will to resist and to compel him to speak where he would not otherwise do so freely. In order to combat these pressures and to permit a full opportunity to exercise the privilege against self-incrimination, the accused must be adequately and effectively apprised of his rights and the exercise of those rights must be fully honored....

The warning of the right to remain silent must be accompanied by the explanation that anything said can and will be used against the individual in court. This warning is needed in order to make him aware not only of the privilege, but also of the consequences of forgoing it. It is only through an awareness of these consequences that there can be any assurance of real understanding and intelligent exercise of the privilege. Moreover, this warning may serve to make the individual more acutely aware that he is faced with a phase of the adversary system—that he is not in the presence of persons acting solely in his interest.

Due process has often been divided into two basic categories: procedural due process and substantive due process. Procedural due process means that the government must guarantee a fair process before taking away an individual's life, liberty, or property. The basic elements to procedural due process are notice and the right to a fair hearing. This prevents the government from arbitrarily taking away someone's job or freedom.

Substantive due process means that laws cannot be irrational and arbitrary. Instead laws must advance a legitimate, governmental objective. Normally, the government must have a rational basis for its laws.

What is **just compensation**?

Just compensation means that before the government takes away or infringes upon someone's private-property rights, that they must provide just compensation. The government does possess the power of eminent domain, or the right to take private property for public use. However, the Fifth Amendment requires that the government give "just compensation" before invoking this sovereign power.

What recent decision on **eminent domain** and **just compensation outraged** many?

The U.S. Supreme Court's decision in *Kelo v. City of New London* (2005) outraged many who believed that the Court overstepped its bounds. The city of New London, Connecticut, instituted its power of eminent domain to take property away from nine landowners to transfer the property to a private corporation as part of an economic development and revitalization plan. The landowners sued, contending that the city violated the Fifth Amendment, which provides in part: "Nor shall private property be taken for public use without just compensation."

The landowners contended that the forced transfer of property from themselves to another private owner was not a "public use." The Court majority determined that the city's decision to take the property for the purpose of economic development satisfied the "public use" requirement of the Fifth Amendment.

Justice O'Connor authored a strong dissent: "Under the banner of economic development, all private property is now vulnerable to being taken and transferred to another private owner, so long as it might be upgraded—i.e., given to an owner who will use it in a way that the legislature deems more beneficial to the public—in the process."

Justice Thomas also wrote a dissenting opinion, questioning the majority's wisdom: "If such "economic development' takings are for a 'public use,' any taking is, and the Court has erased the Public Use Clause from our Constitution."

SIXTH AMENDMENT

What **freedoms** does the **Sixth Amendment** protect?

The Sixth Amendment provides: "In all criminal prosecutions, the accused shall enjoy the right to a speedy and public trial, by an impartial jury of the State and district

Most people have no desire to see the inside of a courtroom, but if circumstances require it U.S. citizens all have right to a speedy trial with an impartial jury (*iStock*).

wherein the crime shall have been committed, which district shall have been previously ascertained by law, and to be informed of the nature and cause of the accusation; to be confronted with the witnesses against him; to have compulsory process for obtaining Witnesses in his favor, and to have the assistance of counsel for his defence."

It contains many protections to those charged with crimes. Sometimes people colloquially refer to the Sixth Amendment as the one that provides fair-trial rights to criminal defendants. It protects the rights to a speedy trial, a public trial, an impartial jury, information and notice of criminal charges, right to confront witnesses, right to have court compel witnesses to come to trial to testify and the right to the assistance of counsel.

What is the **right** to a **speedy trial**?

The right to a speedy trial means that the government must commence prosecution within a reasonable amount of time. The speedy-trial right means that the government cannot simply let a defendant have an indictment hang over his or her head without further action. The U.S. Supreme Court considers four factors in determining whether a defendant's speedy-trial rights have been infringed. They are: (1) whether delay before trial was uncommonly long; (2) whether the government or the criminal defendant is more to blame for that delay; (3) whether the defendant asserted his right to a speedy trial; and (4) and whether the defendant suffered prejudice from the delay.

What does it mean for a **trial** to be **public**?

A public trial means that generally a criminal defendant cannot be tried in a secret court proceeding, such as the Star Chamber in England in the sixteenth century. The rationale is that a public trial makes it less likely that a gross injustice will be perpetrated. The issue surfaces when a judge closes a courtroom and denies the press or others access to the courtroom.

Sometimes criminal defendants wish to deny the press access to their cases. Other times both parties agree that the case should be tried in private. The Sixth Amendment requires that the judge make specific findings as to why a case should be closed before engaging in such drastic measures. In *Richmond Newspapers v. Virginia* (1980), the U.S. Supreme Court explained the importance of conducting trials in open view: "People in an open society do not demand infallibility from their institutions, but it is difficult for them to accept what they are prohibited from observing. When a criminal trial is conducted in the open, there is at least an opportunity both for understanding the system in general and its workings in a particular case."

What is an **impartial jury**?

The Sixth Amendment right to an impartial jury means that a defendant must have a jury that is chosen in a process that represents a fair cross-section of the community. The U.S. Supreme Court explained in *Taylor v. Louisiana* (1975; see LegalSpeak, p. 70) that "selection of a petit [trial] jury from a representative cross section of the community is an essential component of the Sixth Amendment right to a jury trial."

What is the **Confrontation Clause**?

The Confrontation Clause provides that criminal defendants—through their attorneys—have the chance to confront their accusers face-to-face in the courtroom. It means that defense counsel can cross-examine those who make charges and give unfavorable testimony about defendants. In the words of the Supreme Court, the Confrontation Clause "aims to produce fairness by ensuring the reliability of testimony."

For example, police in the state of Washington charged Michael Crawford with assault and attempted murder after he stabbed a man who earlier had attempted to rape his wife. The wife later gave a tape-recorded statement to the police about the incident. However, at trial Crawford's wife refused to testify under a spousal exemption under state law that provides that spouses don't have to give evidence or testify against each other. The prosecution then tried to introduce the tape-recorded statement. Crawford countered that introducing that tape-recorded statement violated the Confrontation Clause, as he would not have an opportunity to cross-examine his wife.

The U.S. Supreme Court unanimously agreed in *Crawford v. Washington* (2004; see LegalSpeak, p. 71), reasoning that the lower court erred in allowing the wife's tes-

LegalSpeak: *Taylor v. Louisiana* (1975)

The U.S. Supreme Court ruled:

> We accept the fair-cross-section requirement as fundamental to the jury trial guaranteed by the Sixth Amendment and are convinced that the requirement has solid foundation. The purpose of a jury is to guard against the exercise of arbitrary power—to make available the common-sense judgment of the community as a hedge against the overzealous or mistaken prosecutor and in preference to the professional or perhaps overconditioned or biased response of a judge. This prophylactic vehicle is not provided if the jury pool is made up of only special segments of the populace or if large, distinctive groups are excluded from the pool. Community participation in the administration of the criminal law, moreover, is not only consistent with our democratic heritage but is also critical to public confidence in the fairness of the criminal justice system. Restricting jury service to only special groups or excluding identifiable segments playing major roles in the community cannot be squared with the constitutional concept of jury trial....
>
> We are also persuaded that the fair-cross-section requirement is violated by the systematic exclusion of women, who in the judicial district involved here amounted to 53% of the citizens eligible for jury service. This conclusion necessarily entails the judgment that women are sufficiently numerous and distinct from men and that if they are systematically eliminated from jury panels, the Sixth Amendment's fair-cross-section requirement cannot be satisfied.

timonial statement to be introduced when the husband did not have a chance at cross-examination.

What is the **importance** of **compulsory process**?

Compulsory process guarantees that a criminal defendant has the right "to have compulsory process for obtaining witnesses in his favor." Without compulsory process, defense attorneys could not produce many witnesses, as many people would rather not get involved in the court process.

What does **assistance of counsel** mean?

This last freedom mentioned in the Sixth Amendment ensures that those defendants facing prison time have a lawyer to assist them in their defense. The U.S. Supreme

LegalSpeak: *Crawford v. Washington* (2004)

First, the principal evil at which the Confrontation Clause was directed was the civil-law mode of criminal procedure, and particularly its use of *ex parte* examinations as evidence against the accused. It was these practices that the Crown deployed in notorious treason cases like Raleigh's; that the Marian statutes invited; that English law's assertion of a right to confrontation was meant to prohibit; and that the founding-era rhetoric decried. The Sixth Amendment must be interpreted with this focus in mind.

Accordingly, we once again reject the view that the Confrontation Clause applies of its own force only to in-court testimony, and that its application to out-of-court statements introduced at trial depends upon the law of Evidence for the time being.

Court in *Gideon v. Wainwright* (1963) recognized that attorneys in criminal cases are "necessities, not luxuries."

The Court explained:

Lawyers to prosecute are everywhere deemed essential to protect the public's interest in an orderly society. Similarly, there are few defendants charged with crime, few indeed, who fail to hire the best lawyers they can [542 U.S. 418] get to prepare and present their defenses. That government hires lawyers to prosecute and defendants who have the money hire lawyers to defend are the strongest indications of the widespread belief that lawyers in criminal courts are necessities, not luxuries. The right of one charged with crime to counsel may not be deemed fundamental and essential to fair trials in some countries, but it is in ours. From the very beginning, our state and national constitutions and laws have laid great emphasis on procedural and substantive safeguards designed to assure fair trials before impartial tribunals in which every defendant stands equal before the law. This noble ideal cannot be realized if the poor man charged with crime has to face his accusers without a lawyer to assist him.

Who was the **defendant** in *Gideon v. Wainwright*?

The defendant was Clarence Earl Gideon, who was charged with stealing money from a Florida pool hall. A jury convicted him of theft and a judge sentenced him to five years in jail. Gideon has asked for a lawyer to represent him, but the state of Florida at that time did not provide attorneys to those defendants who could not afford them. Gideon on his own wrote a five-page petition to the U.S. Supreme Court, asking them to hear his case. The U.S. Supreme Court appointed well-known D.C. lawyer Abe Fortas to represent Gideon at the Court.

How does the **court determine** if a **defendant** received **effective assistance** of counsel?

The Sixth Amendment provides as a basic freedom "the assistance of counsel." This means that a criminal defendant charged with a serious crime can receive an attorney appointed to represent him or her even if he or she cannot afford such counsel. But, the Sixth Amendment-based freedom means more than this. It also means that the defendant should receive competent counsel. Sometimes, criminal defendants challenge their underlying criminal conviction by asserting a so-called "ineffective assistance of counsel" claim either in state post-conviction proceedings or in federal *habeas corpus* proceedings. Both state post-conviction proceedings and federal *habeas corpus* proceedings take place after the trial and direct appeal in a criminal case.

In its 1984 decision *Strickland v. Washington,* the U.S. Supreme Court identified the standard for determining whether a defendant truly received "ineffective assistance of counsel." First, the defendant must show that his counsel was deficient and fell below an objective standard of reasonableness. This means that the attorney failed to perform as a reasonably competent attorney would under the circumstances. Then, the defendant must also show that the attorney's deficient performance actually prejudiced the defendant, meaning that it likely impacted the outcome of the criminal trial proceeding. Thus, there are two prongs to the *Strickland v. Washington* test: (1) a deficiency prong and (2) a prejudice prong.

It is very difficult to establish ineffective assistance of counsel, but some criminal defendants have been successful. One example is when a criminal defendant is able to show that his trial attorney failed to subpoena a key alibi witness crucial to the defense theory of the case. Another example would be if a criminal defendant could show that his trial counsel failed to advise him or her about a favorable plea bargain offer by the prosecution. Still another example would be where a criminal defense attorney failed to file a motion in court to suppress evidence that was seized unlawfully by the police.

SEVENTH AMENDMENT

What **freedom** does the **Seventh Amendment protect**?

The Seventh Amendment provides: "In Suits at common law, where the value in controversy shall exceed twenty dollars, the right of trial by jury shall be preserved, and no fact tried by a jury, shall be otherwise re-examined in any Court of the United States, than according to the rules of the common law."

The Seventh Amendment extends the right of jury trial in a civil, or non-criminal, case. The Seventh Amendment also guards against a judge second-guessing the jury's determination of the facts in a case. In our legal system, juries decide questions of fact, while judges decide questions of law.

EIGHTH AMENDMENT

How does the **Court determine** whether **punishment** is **cruel** and **unusual**?

Courts ask whether the punishment comports with what are called "contemporary, evolving standards of decency." They also examine whether the punishment for a crime is disproportionate to the offense. For example, a 20-year prison term for shoplifting a small amount of merchandise would appear to be quite disproportionate. The Courts also examine whether the punishment is directly related to legitimate penological objectives.

Is the **death penalty** considered cruel and unusual?

Currently, the death penalty *per se* is not considered cruel and unusual. Approximately 38 states still have the death penalty as an option in their criminal codes. The U.S. Supreme Court in *Furman v. Georgia* (1972; see LegalSpeak, p. 74) ruled 5 to 4 that Georgia's death penalty statute did violate the Eighth Amendment. That ruling led to the invalidation of the death penalty nationwide for four years until the Court in *Gregg v. Georgia* (1976; see LegalSpeak, p. 78) upheld some more narrowly drafted death penalty statutes.

Since 1976, the Court has never invalidated the death penalty on its face. Instead, it has prohibited application of the death penalty to certain types of defendants, including those who are insane in *Ford v. Wainwright* (1986), those who are mentally retarded in *Atkins v. Virginia* (2002), those who were juveniles when they committed murder in

Torture has been common through much of history and is still practiced in some countries today. The Eighth Amendment of the Constitution, however, prohibits cruel and unusual punishment (*iStock*).

73

Roper v. Simmons (2005), those who are rapists in *Coker v. Georgia* (1977), and child rapists when the rapes do not result in murder as in *Kennedy v. Louisiana* (2008).

What caused the U.S. **Supreme Court** to **change course** and uphold **death penalty** statutes only a few years after its Furman decision?

The Furman decision caused many states to pass new death penalty statutes that would provide more guidance to jurors on whether a defendant should be sentenced to death. Georgia's new statute required jurors to focus on aggravating and mitigating factors associated with the capital crime. In 1976, the U.S. Supreme Court ruled 7 to 2 that this Georgia law was constitutional in *Gregg v. Georgia*. Because it focused on these aggravating and mitigating factors, Justice Potter Stewart wrote: "No longer can a jury wantonly and freakishly impose the death sentence; it is always circumscribed by the legisla-

because it is morally unacceptable to the people of the United States at this time in their history."

Chief Justice Warren Burger (dissenting): "In the 181 years since the enactment of the Eighth Amendment, not a single decision of this Court has cast the slightest shadow of a doubt on the constitutionality of capital punishment. In rejecting Eighth Amendment attacks on particular modes of execution, the Court has more than once implicitly denied that capital punishment is impermissibly 'cruel' in the constitutional sense."

Justice Harry Blackmun (dissenting): "Although personally I may rejoice at the Court's result, I find it difficult to accept or to justify as a matter of history, of law, or of constitutional pronouncement. I fear the Court has overstepped. It has sought and has achieved an end."

Justice Lewis Powell (dissenting): "In terms of the constitutional role of this Court, the impact of the majority's ruling is all the greater because the decision encroaches upon an area squarely within the historic prerogative of the legislative branch—both state and federal—to protect the citizenry through the designation of penalties for prohibitable conduct. It is the very sort of judgment that the legislative branch is competent to make and for which the judiciary is ill-equipped.

Justice William Rehnquist (dissenting): "The task of judging constitutional cases imposed by Art. III cannot for this reason be avoided, but it must surely be approached with the deepest humility and genuine deference to legislative judgment. Today's decision to invalidate capital punishment is, I respectfully submit, significantly lacking in those attributes."

tive guidelines." Stewart wrote that the new statute focused the jury on "the particularized nature of the crime and the particularized characteristics of the individual defendant." Since *Gregg,* the U.S. Supreme Court has never ruled that the death penalty is *per se* unconstitutional. Only Justices William Brennan and Thurgood Marshall dissented.

What are some major **death penalty decisions** since *Furman v. Georgia* (1972)?

The following explains some of the most important Supreme Court rulings about the death penalty since 1972.

Furman v. Georgia (1972)

Decision: The U.S. Supreme Court rules 5 to 4 that Georgia's death penalty scheme violates the Eighth Amendment. Three justices in the majority attach the death penalty in general, while Justices Potter Stewart and Lewis Powell focus on the fact that the death penalty law does not give jurors sufficient guidance as to which capital defendants should receive the ultimate punishment. Stewart writes that "these death sentences are cruel and unusual in the same way that being struck by lightning is cruel and unusual." This ruling led to a halt on all executions in the country until 1977.

Gregg v. Georgia (1976)

Decision: The Court rules that some death penalty statutes are constitutional because they provide sufficient guidance to the jury in terms of aggravating and mitigating factors. The Court writes that "the concerns expressed in *Furman* that the penalty of death not be imposed in an arbitrary or capricious manner can be met by a carefully drafted statute that ensures that the sentencing authority is given adequate information and guidance."

Roberts v. Louisiana (1976)

Decision: The Court strikes down a Louisiana statute that required the death penalty for defendants who kill police officers and did not allow those defendants to offer any mitigating factors.

Woodson v. North Carolina (1976)

Decision: The Court strikes down a North Carolina statute that required the death penalty for all criminal defendants convicted of first-degree murder.

Gilmore v. Utah (1976)

Decision: The Court rejects the constitutional claims of Utah inmate Gary Gilmore. He becomes the first person executed in the United States since the *Furman* decision. His execution becomes memorialized in Norman Mailer's *The Executioner's Song.*

Coker v. Georgia (1977)

Decision: The Court rules that a sentence of death for rape is excessive punishment under the Eighth Amendment. The Court writes: "Rape is without doubt deserving of serious punishment; but in terms of moral depravity and of the injury to the person and to the public, it does not compare with murder."

Lockett v. Ohio (1978)

Decision: The Court invalidates Ohio's death penalty statute because it restricts mitigating evidence during the sentencing phase. The Court writes: "the Eighth and Fourteenth Amendments require that the sentencer, in all but the rarest kind of capital case, not be precluded from considering, as a mitigating factor, any aspect of a defendant's character or record and any of the circumstances of the offense that the defendant proffers as a basis for a sentence less than death."

Adams v. Texas (1980)

Decision: The Court invalidates a Texas inmate's death sentence because the trial judge dismissed prospective jurors who said they would be "affected" by the possibility of imposing the death penalty. The Court writes that "a juror may not be challenged for cause based on his views about capital punishment unless those views would prevent or substantially impair the performance of his duties as a juror in accordance with his instructions and his oath."

Edmund v. Florida (1982)

Decision: The Court rules that a defendant cannot be sentenced to death for participating in a felony that leads to murder if the defendant did not participate in the killing, attempt to kill or intend for killing to take place.

Eddings v. Oklahoma (1982)

Decision: The Court vacates the death sentence of inmate, who was 16 years old at the time of the murder, because the trial court refused to allow his attorney to introduce mitigating factors, such as his turbulent family history, beatings by his father and emotional problems.

California v. Ramos (1983)

Decision: The Court rules that a California trial judge did not violate the constitutional rights of a criminal defendant by instructing the jury that the governor could commute a defendant's life sentence to a sentence with the possibility of parole.

Barclay v. Florida (1983)

Decision: The Court rejects the claims of a Florida inmate who alleges his death sentence should be overturned because the trial judge allowed the jury to consider his criminal record as an aggravating factor.

Spaziano v. Florida (1984)

Decision: The Court rules that a trial judge may sentence a criminal defendant to death even though a jury has recommended a life sentence. The Court writes that "the purpose of the death penalty is not frustrated by, or inconsistent with, a scheme in which the imposition of the penalty in individual cases is determined by a judge."

Strickland v. Washington (1984)

Decision: The Court sets the standard for determining when a death sentence can be set aside for ineffective assistance of counsel. The Court writes that "the defendant must show that there is a reasonable probability that, but for counsel's unprofessional errors, the result of the proceeding would have been different."

Caldwell v. Mississippi (1985)

Decision: The Court sets aside a Mississippi inmate's death sentence after the prosecutor told the jury that an appeals court would review its determination of life or death. The Court writes "it is constitutionally impermissible to rest a death sentence on a determination made by a sentencer who has been led to believe that the responsibility for determining the appropriateness of the defendant's death rests elsewhere."

Ford v. Wainwright (1986)

Decision: The Court rules that the Eighth Amendment prohibits the execution of insane persons.

LegalSpeak: *Gregg v. Georgia* (1976)

Justice Potter Stewart (plurality): "The most marked indication of society's endorsement of the death penalty for murder is the legislative response to Furman. The legislatures of at least 35 States have enacted new statutes that provide for the death penalty for at least some crimes that result in the death of another person.... These recently adopted statutes have attempted to address the concerns expressed by the Court in *Furman* primarily (i) by specifying the factors to be weighed and the procedures to be followed in deciding when to impose

While instruments like the electric chair and guillotine are no longer used, some states still exercise the death penalty, usually by injecting lethal drugs into the condemned inmate (*iStock*).

Darden v. Wainwright (1986)

Decision: The Court rules that a prosecutor's improper comments during closing arguments in a death penalty case did not justify vacating the sentence. The Court wrote that a sentence should be set aside based on a prosecutor's comments only when the comments "so infected the trial with unfairness as to make the resulting conviction a denial of due process."

Skipper v. South Carolina (1986)

Decision: The Court sets aside a death sentence when the trial judge excluded as mitigating evidence the testimony of jailers regarding the good behavior of the defendant before his trial.

McCleskey v. Kemp (1987)

Decision: The Court ruled that a death penalty defendant cannot invalidate his death penalty based on a broad statistical study showing correlation between race and the

a capital sentence, or (ii) by making the death penalty mandatory for specified crimes. But all of the post-Furman statutes make clear that capital punishment itself has not been rejected by the elected representatives of the people."

Justice Byron White (concurring): "Imposition of the death penalty is surely an awesome responsibility for any system of justice and those who participate in it. Mistakes will be made and discriminations will occur which will be difficult to explain. However, one of society's most basic tasks is that of protecting the lives of its citizens and one of the most basic ways in which it achieves the task is through criminal laws against murder. I decline to interfere with the manner in which Georgia has chosen to enforce such laws on what is simply an assertion of lack of faith in the ability of the system of justice to operate in a fundamentally fair manner."

Justice William Brennan (dissenting): "Death is not only an unusually severe punishment, unusual in its pain, in its finality, and in its enormity, but it serves no penal purpose more effectively than a less severe punishment; therefore the principle inherent in the Clause that prohibits pointless infliction of excessive punishment when less severe punishment can adequately achieve the same purposes invalidates the punishment. The fatal constitutional infirmity in the punishment of death is that it treats 'members of the human race as nonhumans, as objects to be toyed with and discarded.'"

Justice Thurgood Marshall (dissenting): "The death penalty, unnecessary to promote the goal of deterrence or to further any legitimate notion of retribution, is an excessive penalty forbidden by the Eighth and Fourteenth Amendments."

death penalty. Rather, the majority rules that the defendant must show "that the decisionmakers in his case acted with discriminatory purpose."

Tison v. Arizona (1987)

Decision: The Court ruled that the Eighth Amendment does not prohibit the death penalty for a defendant who participates in a felony that leads to a murder.

Thompson v. Oklahoma (1988)

Decision: The Court ruled that it is unconstitutional for a state to execute a criminal defendant who was 15 years old when he committed murder.

Penry v. Lynaugh (1989)

Decision: The Court ruled that the Eighth Amendment does not prohibit the execution of a mentally retarded inmate.

Stanford v. Kentucky (1989)

Decision: The Court ruled that the Eighth Amendment does not prohibit the execution of a criminal defendant who was 16 or 17 when he or she committed murder. This decision was overruled by the Court in its 2005 decision *Roper v. Simmons*.

Coleman v. Thompson (1991)

Decision: In a controversial ruling, the Court ruled that a federal court could not review a death sentence issued by state courts when the defendant's lawyer in his *habeas corpus* appeal missed the appeal deadline by one day. The case is controversial because some believe the inmate in question, Roger Coleman, was innocent of the convicted crime.

Payne v. Tennessee (1991)

Decision: The Court ruled that a death-penalty jury can hear evidence from the victim's family during the sentencing phase. This case effectively overruled *Booth v. Maryland* (1987).

Herrera v. California (1993)

Decision: The Court ruled that "actual innocence" is not a constitutional claim in and of itself in a federal *habeas corpus* claim. This means that a defendant is not entitled to federal court review of his death sentence unless he or she can show an independent constitutional violation that occurred during the original state court trial proceedings.

Romano v. Oklahoma (1994)

Decision: The Court ruled that it was not a constitutional violation for a capital jury to hear evidence that the defendant had received a prior death sentence for another murder.

Buchanan v. Angellone (1998)

Decision: The Court ruled that a capital defendant was not entitled to jury instructions on specific mitigating factors.

Atkins v. Virginia (2002)

Decision: The Court ruled that a state cannot execute a mentally retarded inmate. This decision overruled the Court's 1989 decision in *Penry v. Lynaugh*.

Ring v. Arizona (2002)

Decision: The Court ruled that a jury, not a trial judge, should make the factual determinations necessary of the presence of aggravating factors in determining whether a defendant should receive a life in prison or death sentence. This decision overruled the Court's 1990 decision in *Walton v. Arizona*.

Wiggins v. Smith (2003)

Decision: The Court ruled that a capital defendant's Sixth Amendment right to counsel was violated when his attorney failed to put forth any evidence of mitigating factors during his sentencing phase.

Roper v. Simmons (2005)

Decision: The Court ruled that a state cannot execute an inmate who committed his capital crime when he was a juvenile. The Court overruled its 1989 decision in *Stanford v. Kentucky*.

Kennedy v. Louisiana (2008)

Decision: The Court struck down a Louisiana statute that provided that child rapists could be executed.

What did the Court decide with respect to criminal **three-strikes laws**?

The U.S. Supreme Court upheld California's Career Criminal Punishment Act (also known as the "three strikes" law) sentencing law in *Ewing v. California* (2003) and *Lockyer v. Andrade* (2003). Under the California law, if a criminal defendant is convicted of at least three felonies, he is subject to the three-strikes law which carries a penalty of 25 years to life.

The cases involved Gary Ewing who stole three golf clubs and Leandro Andrade, who stole $150 worth of videotapes. However, both defendants had multiple criminal convictions in their past, including burglaries, that made them eligible as recidivist offenders under the state law. They challenged their sentences and the three-strikes law as a violation of the Eighth Amendment's cruel and unusual punishment clause.

The Court rejected the argument that the defendants' sentences violated the Eighth Amendment's prohibition against cruel and unusual punishment. "The gross disproportionality principle reserves a constitutional violation for only the extraordinary case," Justice Sandra Day O'Connor wrote for the Court in *Andrade*. In her *Ewing* opinion, Justice O'Connor explained that states have the right to pass laws protecting the public from career criminals: "When the California Legislature enacted the three strikes law, it made a judgment that protecting the public safety requires incapacitating criminals who have already been convicted of at least one serious or violent crime. Nothing in the Eighth

In *Roper v. Simmons* the Supreme Court ruled that inmates who committed their crimes while they were legally juveniles cannot be executed for said crimes (*iStock*).

81

Amendment prohibits California from making that choice." She also cited statistics showing that a disturbing number of inmates committed repeat offenses upon release from incarceration.

NINTH AND TENTH AMENDMENTS

What rights does the **Ninth Amendment protect**?

The Ninth Amendment provides: "The enumeration in the Constitution, of certain rights, shall not be construed to deny or disparage others retained by the people." It means that there are other rights retained by the people even though they are not specifically listed, or enumerated, in the Bill of Rights.

One common objection to the Bill of Rights was that listing, or enumerating, certain rights in the Bill of Rights would mean that those were the only rights the people possessed. To answer this concern, James Madison adopted the Ninth Amendment which implies that people retain other rights not specifically listed in the Bill of Rights. For 175 years, the Ninth Amendment was, in the words of one Supreme Court Justice, a "constitutional curiosity." However, in the 1965 case involving marital privacy, *Griswold v. Connecticut* (see LegalSpeak, p. 82), Justice Arthur Goldberg revived the amendment and said that it protected a right to privacy.

What is the **Tenth Amendment**?

The Tenth Amendment provides: "The powers not delegated to the United States by the Constitution, nor prohibited by it to the States, are reserved to the States respectively, or to the people." It is the only amendment in the Bill of Rights that does not focus solely on protecting an individual right. Rather it limits the power of the federal government vis-à-vis the state governments. It ensures that the federal government does not operate like a super-state government and supersede all state powers. In other words, the Tenth Amendment seeks to "reserve" some powers for the states and reaffirms the basic notion that the federal government is a government of enumerated (listed) powers, not unlimited powers.

Courts often refer to the concept of "dual sovereignty" when mentioning the Tenth Amendment, because it is a key provision in creating a federal system of government in which power is often shared between the federal and state governments.

Periodically, the news media, political pundits, and others refer to "states' rights" usually as a claim that the federal government is encroaching upon the states' domain. The constitutional hammer for those who advocate for states' rights is the Tenth Amendment.

What type of **law** creates a **Tenth Amendment issue**?

Any time that the federal government passes a law or regulation that requires state or local government officials to administer a federal program, there is an argument that the Tenth Amendment comes into play. The U.S. Supreme Court explained the principle quite bluntly in *New York v. United States* (1992) that dealt with a federal law imposing requirements on states with respect to the disposal and cost for disposing of radioactive waste: "The Federal Government may not compel the States to enact or administer a federal regulatory program."

What is an **example** of power that should be **"reserved" to the states** under the Tenth Amendment?

The U.S. Supreme Court has ruled that much legislation dealing with the regulation of guns is a power properly reserved to the states. In *Printz v. United States* (1997), the Court struck down parts of a federal law that required local officials to conduct background checks on individuals purchasing handguns. The Court ruled that, under the Tenth Amendment, the federal government could not force the states to administer this federal program because it infringed on an area "reserved" for the states under the Tenth Amendment.

83

The U.S. Supreme Court has determined that gun laws for citizens should be mostly regulated at the state level (*iStock*).

What does the **Tenth Amendment** have to do with the concept of **federalism**?

Federalism refers to the division of power between the federal and state governments. Members of the United States Supreme Court vehemently disagree over the proper conception of federalism. The Tenth Amendment plays a large role in federalism by specifically referring to the principle that certain powers not given to the national, federal government are "reserved" to the states.

FOURTEENTH AMENDMENT

Why is the **Fourteenth Amendment** sometimes called a **Second Bill of Rights**?

The Bill of Rights—the first ten amendments of the Constitution—only protects individuals from the federal government. The beginning of the Bill of Rights refers only to "Congress shall make no law." This refers to the U.S. Congress, which was quickly interpreted by the U.S. Court to mean all three branches of the federal government—not just Congress.

However, in the 1833 decision on *Barron v. Baltimore*, Chief Justice John Marshall for a unanimous Court wrote that the Bill of Rights only limited the federal government, not the state governments. This meant that individuals harmed by their

> ## LegalSpeak: Sections 1 and 5 of the Fourteenth Amendment
>
> Section. 1. All persons born or naturalized in the United States and subject to the jurisdiction thereof, are citizens of the United States and of the State wherein they reside. No State shall make or enforce any law which shall abridge the privileges or immunities of citizens of the United States; nor shall any State deprive any person of life, liberty, or property, without due process of law; nor deny to any person within its jurisdiction the equal protection of the laws.
>
> Section. 5. The Congress shall have power to enforce, by appropriate legislation, the provisions of this article.
>
> For full text of the Fourteenth Amendment, see Appendix.

state or local governments could not state a claim under the U.S. Constitution's Bill of Rights. Rather they had to assert a claim under their own state constitution.

However, members of the 39th Congress in the aftermath of the Civil War created three amendments during the period of Reconstruction. Included among those three was the Fourteenth Amendment. The primary sponsor of the Fourteenth Amendment—Rep. John Bingham from Ohio—wanted the Fourteenth Amendment to extend the reach of the U.S. Bill of Rights to the states.

Eventually, the United States Supreme Court—nearly exclusively in the twentieth century—began to incorporate various provisions of the U.S. Bill of Rights to the states. The vehicle of this incorporation process was the "due process" clause of the Fourteenth Amendment.

Section 1 of the Fourteenth Amendment contains a due-process clause—"nor shall any State deprive any person of life, liberty, or property, without due process of law." The U.S. Supreme Court has used this due process clause to extend the Bill of Rights to the states.

What exactly is **incorporation** and **how** does this **work**?

This is a difficult concept that troubles even law school students when they take and study constitutional law. However, it is a vitally important concept to understanding the U.S. system of constitutional law.

Let's use the example of the First Amendment freedom of speech to explain how this works. The First Amendment prohibits the federal government from punishing individuals' freedom of speech under many circumstances. However, in the nineteenth century the U.S. Supreme Court determined that the entire Bill of Rights only protected individuals from the federal government. This meant that the First Amendment freedom of speech only protected individuals from invasions by federal officials. If a state or local police officer violated an individual's free-speech rights, he or she had to assert a constitutional claim under the state constitution.

That changed with the U.S. Supreme Court's interpretation of the First and Fourteenth Amendments in the early twentieth century. Remember that the due-process clause provides: "nor shall any state deprive any person of life, liberty or property without due process of law." The U.S. Supreme Court determined that "freedom of speech" was part of the "liberty" mentioned in the due-process clause of the Fourteenth Amendment.

In other words, the due-process clause provides that no state shall deprive any person of liberty, which includes freedom of speech. Throughout most of the twentieth century, the U.S. Supreme Court, through the process of selective incorporation and the due-process clause, extended the bulk of the Bill of Rights to the states.

Are all **freedoms** in the **Bill of Rights** extended to the **states**?

No, there are a few freedoms in the Bill of Rights that have not been extended to the states through the process of selective incorporation. The Fifth Amendment requirement of a grand jury has not been extended to the states. This means that a state criminal court defendant does not have a federal constitutional right to have his case screened by a grand jury before indictment. The Second Amendment "right to bear arms" has not yet been extended to the states. In the October 2010 term, the Court will hear a case out of the city of Chicago that may change that—*McDonald v. City of Chicago*.

Other provisions not incorporated are the Third Amendment quartering of troops and the Seventh Amendment right to a jury trial in a civil case.

What are the **two core clauses** of the **Fourteenth Amendment**?

The two most important clauses of the Fourteenth Amendment are the due-process clause and the equal protection clause. The due-process clause ensures that the government acts with a certain level of fundamental fairness before infringing on an individual's "life, liberty or property" interests. The equal-protection clause ensures that similarly situated individuals or classes of people are treated similarly.

What are the **two types** of **due process**?

The two types of due process are procedural due process and substantive due process. Procedural due process means that before the government can take away a life, liberty, or property interest of a person—such as a public employee's job—the government must provide certain procedures, such as notice and a hearing to challenge to the governmental action. Substantive due process means that a law must on its substance be reasonable and rational rather than arbitrary or irrational. In other words, some laws are said to be so unreasonable as to violate due process.

What is an **example** of an **equal protection violation**?

A prime example of an equal protection violation is to treat people differently based on their race or gender. The most famous equal-protection case in all of constitutional law is probably *Brown v. Board of Education* (1954) where the U.S. Supreme Court unanimously ruled that segregated public schools were "inherently unequal" under the Equal Protection Clause. Another example was the Supreme Court unanimously striking down a Virginia law that prohibited interracial marriages in *Loving v. Virginia* (1967).

Racial and gender classifications are subject to increased scrutiny by Courts. In fact, the U.S. Supreme Court has said that racial classifications—even racial classifications for a benign (non-discriminatory) purpose—are "inherently suspect." The court has also looked very searchingly at gender classifications.

THE COURT SYSTEM

What does the U.S. **Constitution say** about the U.S. **Supreme Court**?

Article III, Section I of the Constitution provides: "The judicial Power of the United States, shall be vested in one supreme Court, and in such inferior Courts as the Congress may from time to time ordain and establish." In another part of the Constitution, it refers to a "Chief Justice" of the Court, as the person who shall preside over impeachment proceedings of the president. Article I, Section III—the part of Article I that describes the powers of the Senate—provides: "When the President of the United States is tried, the Chief Justice shall preside."

The Chief Justices in U.S. Supreme Court History

Chief Justice	Years as Chief
John Jay	1789–1795
John Rutledge	1795
Oliver Ellsworth	1796–1800
John Marshall	1801–1835
Roger Taney	1836–1864
Salmon P. Chase	1864–1873
Morrison Waite	1874–1888
Melville W. Fuller	1888–1910
Edward White	1910–1921
William Howard Taft	1921–1930
Charles Evans Hughes	1930–1941
Harlan Fiske Stone	1941–1946
Fred Vinson	1946–1953

Chief Justice	Years as Chief
Earl Warren	1953–1969
Warren Burger	1969–1986
William Rehnquist	1986–2005
John G. Roberts Jr.	2005–

Where did the U.S. Supreme Court first meet?

The U.S. Supreme Court first met in the Royal Exchange Building on Broad Street in New York City on February 2, 1790. The Court met on the second floor of the building in the afternoons, as the New York state legislature met in the room during the morning hours. The Court met in New York for only one year, meeting in Philadelphia the next year.

When did the U.S. Supreme Court get its own building?

Surprisingly, the U.S. Supreme Court did not receive its own building until 1935. The Court had met for more than 145 years before it moved into the Supreme Court Building, located at First and East Capitol Streets NE, in Washington. In 1929, Chief Justice William Howard Taft (a former president of the United States) managed to convince Congress to fund a building for the U.S. Supreme Court.

What is the nickname of the Supreme Court Building?

The nickname of the building is the Marble Palace, because white marble represents the primary material used in the building. According to the Supreme Court's Web site, $3 million worth of marble was used in its construction. Famous attorney and scholar John Paul Frank published a book about the U.S. Supreme Court in 1958 entitled *Marble Palace: The Supreme Court in American Life.*

How long do justices serve on the Supreme Court?

U.S. Supreme Court justices—and all other federal judges—serve for life. Article III, Section I provides: "The Judges, both of the supreme and inferior Courts, shall hold their Offices during good Behavior, and shall, at stated Times,

The first U.S. Supreme Court Chief Justice was John Jay, who served on the bench from 1789 to 1795 (*Library of Congress*).

receive for their Services a Compensation which shall not be diminished during their Continuance in Office."

Many times through the years, members of Congress have introduced measures to limit the tenure of justices—to 10-year terms, 20-year terms, and other time allotments—but none of these measures has been enacted.

Which justices have served the longest in history?

Justice William O. Douglas served more than 36 years on the Court from 1949–1975. However, many other justices have served more than 30 years, including: Stephen J. Field (34 years), John Marshall (34 years), Joseph Story (34 years), John Marshall Harlan (34 years), Hugo Black (34 years), William Brennan (33 years), William Rehnquist (33 years), John McLean (32 years), James Wayne (32 years), and William Johnson (30 years). Current U.S. Supreme Court Justice John Paul Stevens could break the record for longevity if he serves until July 2012. However, as of this printing, speculation has indicated that Stevens will retire in 2010.

How many women have served as Supreme Court justices?

There have been only three women to serve as U.S. Supreme Court justices in the history of the Court: Justice Sandra Day O'Connor, Ruth Bader Ginsburg, and Sonia Sotomayor. President Ronald Reagan nominated O'Connor in 1981 in part to fulfill a campaign promise to nominate the first woman on the Court. President Bill Clinton nominated Ruth Bader Ginsburg in 1993 and she still serves on the Court at the time of this writing. President Barack Obama nominated Sotomayor to the Court in 2009 to replace the retiring David Souter.

Did any of the recent justices on the Supreme Court previously serve as a judge in some capacity?

Yes, all of the current justices have previously served as federal judges in some capacity before they were elevated to the high court. None of the justices has previously had experience as a state court judge. Only Justice Sotomayor has ever served as a trial court judge, having served many years as a federal district court judge.

Previous Judgeships of the Current U.S. Supreme Court

Justice	Previous Judgeships
John G. Roberts Jr.	U.S. Court of Appeals for the District of Columbia
John Paul Stevens	U.S. Court of Appeals for the 7th Circuit
Anthony Kennedy	U.S. Court of Appeals for the Ninth Circuit
Antonin Scalia	U.S. Court of Appeals for the District of Columbia

Justice	Previous Judgeships
Clarence Thomas	U.S. Court of Appeals for the D.C. Circuit
Ruth Bader Ginsburg	U.S. Court of Appeals for the D.C. Circuit
Stephen Breyer	U.S. Court of Appeals for the First Circuit
Samuel Alito	U.S. Court of Appeals for the Third Circuit
Sonia Sotomayor	U.S. Court of Appeals for the 2nd Circuit and federal district court judge in New York

Is it a **requirement** for a Supreme Court justice to have **prior judicial experience**?

No. Some of the most famous and prominent justices in American history never had prior judicial experience before their elevation to the U.S. Supreme Court. For example, Chief Justice Earl Warren and Chief Justice William Rehnquist never had prior judicial experience before they assumed the mantle of not only justice but also Chief Justice.

Can U.S. Supreme court **justices** be **removed from office**?

Yes, U.S. Supreme Court Justices and all other federal judges can be impeached for "treason, Bribery or other high crimes and misdemeanors." The U.S. Constitution gives the U.S. House of Representatives the "sole power of impeachment" and the U.S. Senate "the sole Power to try all impeachments." It takes a two-thirds majority vote in the Senate for a justice to be impeached.

Have any U.S. Supreme Court **justices** been **impeached**?

Yes, Samuel Chase, an associate justice on the U.S. Supreme Court from 1796 to 1811, was impeached by the House in 1804, but he was acquitted in the Senate in 1805.

What happened with the **Chase impeachment proceedings**?

Samuel Chase had a distinguished political history. He had signed the Declaration of Independence. He had served as the chief judge of Maryland's highest state court. However, Chase landed into trouble when he became a Supreme Court justice. His troubles occurred when he rode circuit and served as presiding judge in some key cases. For example, Chase apparently conducted himself in a very partisan manner during the sedition trial of James Callender. He also attacked President Thomas Jefferson, saying the president had engaged in "seditious attacks on the principles of the Constitution."

The House of Representatives impeached Chase 72 to 32 on eight charges in March 1804. However, the Senate acquitted Chase in 1805. On one charge, the Senate voted 19 to 15 to convict Chase. But Chase was acquitted on even this charge because there needed to be a two-thirds vote for conviction (or 24 votes). Many view the acquittal of Justice Chase as essential to the principle of an independent judiciary.

Which **federal judges** have been **impeached**?

The following judges have been impeached as of 2010.

1803: John Pickering, U.S. District Court for the District of New Hampshire (impeached by House and convicted by the Senate).

1804–1805: Samuel Chase, Associate Justice of the U.S. Supreme Court (impeached by the House in 1804 and acquitted by the Senate in 1805).

1830: James H. Peck, U.S. District Court for the District of Missouri (impeached by the House and acquitted by the Senate).

1862: West H. Humphreys, U.S. District Court for the Middle, Eastern and Western Districts of Tennessee (impeached by House and convicted in the Senate).

1873: Mark H. Delahay, U.S. District Court for the District of Kansas (impeached by the House and resigned before trial in the Senate).

1904: Charles Swayne, U.S. District Court for the Northern District of Florida (impeached by the House and acquitted in the Senate).

1912: Robert W. Archbald, U.S. Commerce Court (impeached by the House and convicted by the Senate).

1926: George W. English, U.S. District Court for the Eastern District of Illinois (impeached by the House and resigned from office).

1933: Harold Louderback, U.S. District Court for the Northern District of California (impeached by the House and acquitted by the Senate).

1936: Halsted L. Ritter, U.S. District Court for the Southern District of Florida (impeached by the House and convicted by the Senate).

1986: Harry E. Claiborne, U.S. District Court for the District of Nevada (impeached by the House and convicted in the Senate).

1988: Alcee L. Hastings, U.S. District Court for the Southern District of Florida (impeached by the House and convicted in the Senate).

1989: Walter L. Nixon, U.S. District Court for the Southern District of Mississippi (impeached by the House and convicted by the Senate).

THE SUPREME COURT TERM

When does the U.S. **Supreme Court meet**?

The U.S. Supreme Court convenes the first Monday of October for the start of its new term. The Court's term usually ends at the end of June. Federal law, codified at 28

U.S.C. section 2 provides: "The Supreme Court shall hold at the seat of government a term of court commencing on the first Monday in October of each year and may hold such adjourned or special terms as may be necessary."

When did the **Court originally begin** its new **terms**?

The Judiciary Act of 1789 provided that the Court's terms shall begin the first Monday of February and the first Monday of August. The first meeting of the Court occurred on February 2, 1790.

Does the Court ever **meet outside** of its **traditional term** time?

Yes, the Court sometimes holds special sessions in important cases. For example, the Court held a special session on July 19, 1942, to hear the case of *Ex Parte Quirin* to determine whether alleged German saboteurs were entitled to a federal *habeas corpus* review of their military commission convictions. More recently, the Court called a special session to hear the case of *McConnell v. Federal Election Commission* in September 2003. The case involved a major First Amendment challenge to the Bipartisan Campaign Reform Act, a federal law restricting soft money spending and other funding restrictions in political elections.

How do **justices get on** the U.S. **Supreme Court**?

The president of the United States nominates or appoints U.S. Supreme Court justices. However, the U.S. Senate confirms the nominees or appointees by majority vote. In recent years, most persons nominated for service on the U.S. Supreme Court have served as lower federal court judges. However, nothing requires a person to have had prior judicial experience before serving on the U.S. Supreme Court. For example, former Associate Justice and later Chief Justice William H. Rehnquist had never served on the Court before his appointment by President Richard Nixon as associate justice in 1972.

Who was the **greatest Supreme Court justice**?

There perhaps is no clear answer to this question, just as there is no clear answer to the question of who is the greatest president. But, many believe that the greatest Supreme Court justice in history was the nation's fourth chief justice, John Marshall, who headed the Court from 1801 to 1834. Marshall wrote several seminal opinions that increased the power of the judicial branch, solidified the power of judicial review, and garnered greater respect for the Court. Supreme Court Justice Sandra Day O'Connor wrote of him in her book *The Majesty of the Law*: "It is no overstatement to claim that Chief Justice Marshall fulfilled the Constitution's promise of an independent federal judiciary."

Construction on the U.S. Supreme Court Building in Washington, D.C., was completed in 1935 (*iStock*).

Others say that Earl Warren, who led the Court from 1954 to 1969 was the Court's greatest chief justice. The Warren Court desegregated the public schools, revolutionized criminal procedure, struck down school-sponsored prayer (receiving much public criticism) and extended various provisions of the Bill of Rights to the states. Warren wrote the Court's unanimous opinion in *Brown v. Board of Education* (1954) that is considered one of the great achievements in American history. He wrote: "We conclude that, in the field of public education, the doctrine of 'separate but equal' has no place. Separate educational facilities are inherently unequal. Therefore, we hold that the plaintiffs and others similarly situated for whom the actions have been brought are, by reason of the segregation complained of, deprived of the equal protection of the laws guaranteed by the Fourteenth Amendment."

What type of **jurisdiction** does the U.S. **Supreme Court** have?

The U.S. Supreme Court has appellate—not original—jurisdiction over most cases that it hears. This means that the vast majority of cases that come before the high court are heard in various lower courts in the federal and state court systems. These cases are then appealed to the U.S. Supreme Court. The U.S. Supreme Court has original jurisdiction in only certain types of cases—those in which states sue each other or in cases involving foreign diplomats. For example, the U.S. Supreme Court exercised its original jurisdiction to hear a border dispute between two states in the case of *Virginia v. Tennessee* (1893).

95

LegalSpeak: Extending Criminal Procedure Rights in the Bill of Rights to the States

The Warren Court extended many constitutional freedoms to the states in several of its rulings. These include:

Court Case: *Mapp v. Ohio* (1961)

Extended Freedoms: Fourth Amendment exclusionary rule; the exclusionary rule provides that evidence seized in violation of the Fourth Amendment is excluded from evidence and must be suppressed. Justice Benjamin Cardozo referred to it as "the criminal goes free because the constable has blundered."

Court Case: *Robinson v. California* (1962)

Extended Freedoms: Eighth Amendment ban on cruel and unusual punishment, which provides that punishment cannot be too disproportionate and excessive in proportion to the crime committed. For example, a 30 year sentence for simple assault would be "cruel and unusual" under the Eighth Amendment.

Court Case: *Gideon v. Wainwright* (1963)

Extended Freedoms: Sixth Amendment right to counsel; this means that criminal defendants charged with serious crimes in state court have a right to an attorney. In this case, the Court said that criminal defense attorneys were "necessities, not luxuries."

Court Case: *Malloy v. Hogan* (1964)

Extended Freedoms: Fifth Amendment right against self-incrimination; this means that the state cannot force a criminal defendant or suspect to speak against his or her will.

Appellate jurisdiction means that a higher court has the power to review a lower court ruling. The U.S. Supreme Court normally hears cases from state high courts, the federal circuit court of appeals and sometimes from special rulings by three-judge federal district court rulings.

How **often** does the **Supreme Court** hear **cases**?

The U.S. Supreme Court hears only a tiny fraction of cases that are appealed to it. More than 8,000 cases are appealed to the Court every year and the Court only hears

Court Case: *Pointer v. Texas* (1965)

Extended Freedoms: Sixth Amendment right to confront witnesses; the Confrontation Clause enables criminal defendants (or their lawyers) to challenge the testimony and accuracy of witness's statements and accusations.

Court Case: *Parker v. Gladden* (1966)

Extended Freedoms: Sixth Amendment right to an impartial jury; this means that a jury must be selected from a fair-cross section of the community and not exclude certain groups based on race for instance.

Court Case: *Klopfer v. North Carolina* (1967)

Extended Freedoms: Sixth Amendment right to a speedy trial; this means that the government must institute legal proceedings and not simply keep a person in jail without proceeding with the case against the defendant.

Court Case: *Washington v. Texas* (1967)

Extended Freedoms: Sixth Amendment right to compulsory process; the compulsory process clause means that a defendant has the right to have the court issue subpoenas to witnesses to help in his or her defense.

Court Case: *Duncan v. Louisiana* (1968)

Extended Freedoms: Sixth Amendment right to a jury trial in criminal cases; this means that criminal defendants have a right to present their defense before a jury of their peers.

Court Case: *Benton v. Maryland* (1969)

Extended Freedoms: Fifth Amendment right to be free from double jeopardy; the double jeopardy clause means that the government cannot bring a subsequent prosecution if the person was already found innocent or guilty of the crime.

about 70 to 75 cases per year. The current Court—led by Chief Justice John G. Roberts Jr.—has heard fewer cases than at any time since the early 1950s.

What **determines** when the U.S. **Supreme Court** will **hear** a **case**?

The Court hears a case when four justices agree to review a lower court decision. This unwritten rule is called "the rule of four." Often the Court will hear a case when the justices believe that they must settle a conflict in the lower courts—sometimes referred to as a split in the circuits or split in the different state high courts.

The Justices of the 1894 U.S. Supreme Court (from left to right): Horace Gray, Howell E. Jackson, Stephen J. Field, Henry B. Brown, Melville W. Fuller (Chief Justice), George Shiras Jr., John M. Harlan, Edward D. White (who would succeed Fuller as Chief Justice), and David J. Brewer. The number of justices has been set at nine since the Judiciary Act of 1869 (*Library of Congress*).

What **types of attorneys argue** cases before the U.S. **Supreme Court**?

Most lawyers never argue a case before the U.S. Supreme Court. Some attorneys practice regularly before the U.S. Supreme Court as members of the Supreme Court Bar. Other attorneys have argued an almost unbelievable number of cases. Walter Jones argued a record 317 cases before the high court from 1801 to 1850. The great Daniel Webster, a U.S. congressman and attorney from Massachusetts who lived from 1782 to 1852, argued nearly 250 cases before the U.S. Supreme Court. He was involved in many landmark decisions, such as *Dartmouth College v. Woodward* (1819), *Gibbons v. Ogden* (1824), and *Charles River Bridge v. Warren Bridge* (1837).

William Wirt, who served as the country's U.S. attorney general from 1817 to 1829, argued more than 170 cases before the U.S. Supreme Court, including *McCullough v. Maryland* (1819), *Cherokee Nation v. Georgia* (1832).

Another U.S. attorney general, William Pinckney, argued numerous cases before the U.S. Supreme Court. Current Supreme Court litigator Steven M. Shapiro called Pinckney the "Supreme Court's greatest advocate."

In the twentieth century, Hayden Covington—longtime counsel to the Jehovah Witnesses, won 37 of the 44 cases he argued before the high court in the U.S. Supreme Court, including a victory for boxer Cassius Clay (better known as Muhammad Ali).

John William Davis, who lived from 1873 to 1955, argued 140 cases before the U.S. Supreme Court, including *Youngstown Sheet and Tube Co. v. Sawyer* (1952), and *Brown v. Board of Education* (1954).

In the present day, Tom Goldstein of Akin Gump Strauss Hauer and Feld has argued 21 cases before the U.S. Supreme Court, and he is only 40 years old. His practice consists nearly entirely of U.S. Supreme Court cases. Other lawyers may argue one case before the U.S. Supreme Court, while representing a the litigant from the beginning of a case.

Those who serve as solicitor general, a position appointed by the president to argue for the United States, naturally argue many more cases than even those members of the Supreme Court Bar who regular argue cases. Seth Waxman, now a law professor, previously served as solicitor general and argued 31 cases before the high court.

One of the greatest attorneys to have argued cases before the U.S. Supreme Court was John William Davis, whose career also included time served in the House of Representatives, as a diplomat to Great Britain, and founder of the law firm Davis, Polk & Wardell (*Library of Congress*).

JUDICIARY ACT OF 1789

When did **Congress establish** the **lower federal courts**?

Article III of the U.S. Constitution simply says that there will be "one supreme court" and such "inferior courts" as Congress deemed necessary. Congress addressed this with the Judiciary Act of 1789, which created a three-tiered system of federal courts (a system that still exists today). In this law, Congress created a supreme court composed of six justices, federal circuit court of appeals, and federal district courts.

The circuit courts did not have separate judges during this time. Each circuit court consisted of panels of three judges—a local district court and two U.S. Supreme Court justices. The justices did not enjoy the experience of riding the circuits because the travel schedule was too burdensome.

LegalSpeak: What is Rule 10 of the Supreme Court?

Review on a writ of certiorari is not a matter of right, but of judicial discretion. A petition for a writ of certiorari will be granted only for compelling reasons. The following, although neither controlling nor fully measuring the Court's discretion, indicate the character of the reasons the Court considers:

(a) a United States court of appeals has entered a decision in conflict with the decision of another United States court of appeals on the same important matter; has decided an important federal question in a way that conflicts with a decision by a state court of last resort; or has so far departed from the accepted and usual course of judicial proceedings, or sanctioned such a departure by a lower court, as to call for an exercise of this Court's supervisory power;

(b) a state court of last resort has decided an important federal question in a way that conflicts with the decision of another state court of last resort or of a United States court of appeals;

(c) a state court or a United States court of appeals has decided an important question of federal law that has not been, but should be, settled by this Court, or has decided an important federal question in a way that conflicts with relevant decisions of this Court.

A petition for a writ of certiorari is rarely granted when the asserted error consists of erroneous factual findings or the misapplication of a properly stated rule of law.

Who was the **principal author** of the **Judiciary Act of 1789**?

Oliver Ellsworth of Connecticut was the principal author of the Judiciary Act of 1789. A member of the Philadelphia Convention of 1787, Ellsworth became a U.S. senator when the Senate first convened in 1789. He was elected chair of the committee designed to follow the dictates of Article III of the new Constitution to create a federal judicial system. William Paterson from New Jersey, another member of the 1787 Convention and an original U.S. senator, also assisted in the drafting of the Judiciary Act of 1789. Both Ellsworth and Paterson later became justices on the U.S. Supreme Court. They were classmates at Princeton College before they entered politics.

What **type of federal court system** did Congress create in the **Judiciary Act of 1789**?

Congress passed the Federal Judiciary Act of 1789, which filled in many of the blanks in Article III of the Constitution. For example, Article III simply stated that there would be "one supreme court" and "such inferior courts" as Congress deemed necessary.

The Judiciary Act created a three-tiered system of federal courts, which still exists into the twenty-first century. The Act created a U.S. Supreme Court (of six justices), federal circuit courts, and federal district courts. There were 13 district courts, consisting of the districts of Maine, New Hampshire, Massachusetts, Connecticut, New York, New Jersey, Pennsylvania, Delaware, Maryland, Virginia, Kentucky, South Carolina, and Georgia. In each district, there would be a district court and a district judge that would hold four annual sessions.

The Judiciary Act also called for three circuit courts—the Eastern, Middle and Southern Circuits. The Eastern Circuit consists of the districts of Connecticut, Maine, Massachusetts, New Hampshire, and New York. The Middle Circuit consists of the districts of Delaware, Kentucky, Maryland, New Jersey, Pennsylvania, and Virginia. The Southern Circuit consists of the districts of Georgia and South Carolina. Each circuit court would consist of panels of three judges—a local district court judge and two U.S. Supreme Court justices.

Who were the **original federal district court judges** in these thirteen districts?

The thirteen original federal district court judges were:

- Richard Law (District of Connecticut)
- David Sewall (District of Maine)
- John Lowell (District of Massachusetts)
- John Sullivan (District of New Hampshire)
- James Duane (District of New York)
- Gunning Bedford (District of Delaware)
- Harry Innes (District of Kentucky)
- William Paca (District of Maryland)
- David Brearley (District of New Jersey)
- Francis Hopkinson (District of Pennsylvania)
- Cyrus Griffin (District of Virginia)
- Nathaniel Pendleton (District of Georgia)
- William Drayton (District of South Carolina)

What **three additional federal district courts** were created within two years of the Judiciary Act of 1789?

Congress added federal district courts in the states of North Carolina, Rhode Island, and Vermont. President George Washington nominated John Stokes for the District of North Carolina; Harry Marchant for the District of Rhode Island; and Nathaniel Chipman for the District of Vermont.

What **part** of the **Judiciary Act of 1789** gives the Supreme Court the power to **review state laws**?

Section 25 of the Judiciary Act of 1789 provides that the U.S. Supreme Court can review state laws to determine whether they comport with the Constitution. The section reads that where "the validity of a state law is questioned on the ground of being repugnant to the constitution, treaties or laws of the United States," the U.S. Supreme Court has jurisdiction. This section originally caused great controversy, as many believed that the rights of the states were being invaded by the federal government and its courts. Section 25 reads:

> And be it further enacted, That a final judgment or decree in any suit, in the highest court of law or equity of a State in which a decision in the suit could be had, where is drawn in question the validity of a treaty or statute of, or an authority exercised under the United States, and the decision is against their validity; or where is drawn in question the validity of a statute of, or an authority exercised under any State, on the ground of their being repugnant to the constitution, treaties or laws of the United States, and the decision is in favour of such their validity, or where is drawn in question the construction of any clause of the constitution, or of a treaty, or statute of, or commission held under the United States, and the decision is against the title, right, privilege or exemption specially set up or claimed by either party, under such clause of the said Constitution, treaty, statute or commission, may be re-examined and reversed or affirmed in the Supreme Court of the United States upon a writ of error.

What was **circuit duty**?

The Judiciary Act of 1789 created 13 lower federal courts called district courts. These district courts were divided into three circuits: the Eastern, the Middle, and the Southern. The circuit courts were composed of a district court judge and two justices of the U.S. Supreme Court. "Circuit duty" or "riding circuit" meant that U.S. Supreme Court justices had to travel across the country to hear cases across the country. An early U.S. Supreme Court justice, Thomas Johnson of Maryland, resigned after a little more than a year because of the difficulties caused by traveling to different circuit courts. In 1793, Congress passed a law that required circuit courts to consist of only one U.S. Supreme Court justice. Supreme Court justices rode circuit until 1891.

When did Congress create **separate judges** for the **circuit courts**?

Congress established 16 judgeships in six circuit courts in the Judiciary Act of 1801. The first five circuits would receive three judges each, while a single judge would preside over the Sixth Circuit. The outgoing administration of Federalist president John Adams wanted to strengthen the federal judicial system, particularly before the Demo-

The U.S. Circuit Court judges gather for a photo at a conference, accompanied by then-U.S. Supreme Court Justice William Howard Taft (fourth from right) in an undated 1920s photo (*Library of Congress*).

cratic-Republican administration of incoming president Thomas Jefferson and a new Congress dominated by Jefferson's party took office. The Democratic-Republicans repealed the Judiciary Act of 1801 in the Judiciary Act of 1802. This new law kept the structure of the six circuits but abolished the separate judgeships.

Which **federal judges lost** their **jobs** because of the **Judiciary Act of 1802**?

The Judiciary Act of 1802 abolished the new judgeships created by the Judiciary Act of 1801. The following judges lost their jobs: First Circuit: Benjamin Bourne and Jeremiah Smith; Second Circuit: Egbert Benson, Samuel Hitchcock, and Oliver Wolcott; Third Circuit: Richard Bassett, William Griffith, and William Tilghman; Fourth Circuit: Philip Barton Key, Charles Magill, and George Keith Taylor; Fifth Circuit: Joseph Clay, Dominic Augustin Hall, and Edward Harris; and Sixth Circuit: William McClung.

How **many federal district courts** and federal **appeals courts** are there?

The federal district courts are the trial courts in the federal system. There are 94 federal judicial districts in the United States. There are multiple judicial districts in most states, one in the District of Columbia, Puerto Rico, the Virgin Islands, Guam, and the Marinara Islands. Federal district courts hear both civil and criminal cases before juries. Federal district courts also have separate bankruptcy courts. The vast majority of cases before a federal district court are held before a single judge.

The federal appeals courts are divided into 13 circuits—11 numbered circuits, the D.C. Circuit, and the Federal Circuit. Most cases at the federal appellate court level are heard by panels of three judges. The Circuit Courts are organized as follows:

1st Circuit   federal cases from the states of Maine, Massachusetts, New Hampshire, Rhode Island, and Puerto Rico

2nd Circuit   federal cases from the states of New York, Vermont, and Connecticut

3rd Circuit   federal cases from the states of Pennsylvania, New Jersey, and Delaware

4th Circuit   federal cases from the states of Maryland, Virginia, West Virginia, North Carolina, and South Carolina

5th Circuit   federal cases from the states of Texas, Louisiana, and Mississippi

6th Circuit   federal cases from the states of Tennessee, Kentucky, Ohio, and Michigan

7th Circuit   federal cases from the states of Illinois, Indiana, and Wisconsin

8th Circuit   federal cases from the states of Arkansas, Iowa, Missouri, Minnesota, North Dakota, South Dakota, and Nebraska

9th Circuit   federal cases from the states of Alaska, Arizona, California, Hawaii, Idaho, Montana, Nevada, Oregon, and Washington

10th Circuit   federal cases from the states of Colorado, Kansas, Oklahoma, Utah, and Wyoming

11th Circuit   federal cases from the states of Alabama, Georgia, and Florida

When did Congress create the circuit courts in their present form?

Congress created the modern circuit court judgeships in the Judiciary Act of 1891, which created nine circuit courts composed of three judges each. In 1893, Congress created the D.C. Circuit. Then in 1929 Congress created the 10th Circuit. In 1980, Congress created the 11th Circuit by dividing the existing 5th Circuit into two parts. Two years later in 1982 Congress created the federal circuit, which hears specialized appeals in patent and civil personnel cases.

What was the Evarts Act?

Congress created nine circuit courts of appeals by the Judiciary Act of 1891, also called the Evarts Act, named after U.S. senator William Evarts of New York. These new circuit court of appeals featured three judges each. A court of appeals for the D.C. Circuit was added in 1893; a court of appeals for the 10th Circuit was added in 1929; and the 11th Circuit was added in 1980 by dividing the existing 5th Circuit into two parts. In 1982, the Court created the federal circuit, which hears specialized appeals in patent and civil personnel cases among others. The Evarts Act essentially established the basic model for the modern-day federal judicial system.

Who was **William Evarts**?

William Maxwell Evarts was one of the nation's leading lawyers. He also served in the U.S. Senate and sponsored the Judiciary Act of 1891. Evarts served as counsel for President Andrew Johnson during his impeachment proceedings. He also served as U.S. attorney for President Abraham Lincoln and as secretary of state for President Rutherford B. Hayes.

How does the federal **court system created** by the **Founding Fathers compare** and contrast with the **current** federal court **system**?

The Judiciary Act of 1789 created the same three-tiered court system of federal district courts, federal circuits, and U.S. Supreme Court that exists today. The Evarts Act modernized the system by actually placing new judges on the circuit court appellate level, as opposed to staffing the circuit courts with district judges and U.S. Supreme Court justices. Now, there are 94 federal district courts, 13 federal circuit courts of appeals, and one U.S. Supreme Court composed of nine justices. One major difference in the current system from the 1789 system is that now there are separate judges on the federal circuit courts of appeals. Another major difference is that the circuit courts of appeals are appellate courts; they no longer function as trial courts.

How do **circuit courts of appeal** hear **cases**?

Most cases come to the federal circuits after first having been heard before a federal district court. Most cases are heard by a circuit court panel of three judges. The panel normally consists of three judges from the actual circuit, but sometimes the panels consist of two judges from the circuit and a federal district court judge sitting by designation.

How many **judges** serve on the **circuit courts**?

It varies depending on the respective circuit court. For example, there are current 24 judges on the Sixth Circuit—eight senior judges and 16 judges. The Ninth Circuit—the largest circuit court in the country—has 48 judges; 21 of those judges are senior judges.

Has there been recent movement in Congress to **change** the **circuit court structure**?

Yes, there have been several bills introduced in Congress over the last several years to create an additional circuit court of appeals because the 9th Circuit is so large. In 2009, Rep. Mike Simpson introduced the Ninth Circuit Court of Appeals Judgeship and Reorganization Act of 2009. This proposed measure would create an additional federal appeals court—the 12th Circuit—that would consist of the states of Alaska, Arizona, Idaho, Montana, Nevada, Oregon, and Washington.

Who are some of the nation's **leading federal appeals court judges**?

Without a doubt one of the country's most respected federal appeals court judges is Richard Posner of the 7th U.S. Circuit Court of Appeals. Widely recognized as a genius, Posner has authored numerous books and articles on a wide variety of legal subjects. After graduating from Harvard Law School, Posner clerked for U.S. Supreme Court Justice William Brennan in 1962 and later ascended to the 7th Circuit in 1981. He also teaches as a "Senior Lecturer in Law" at the University of Chicago Law School. Bruce Selya is the senior judge on the 1st U.S. Circuit Court of Appeals. Known for his distinctive writing style and impressive vocabulary, Selya has been on the 1st Circuit since President Ronald Reagan appointed him in 1986. Like Posner, Selya earned his law degree from Harvard.

Frank Easterbrook, the current chief judge of the 7th Circuit, is another highly respected federal appeals court jurist. Easterbrook used to work in the Solicitor General's Office in the 1970s where he argued more than 20 cases before the United States Supreme Court. President Reagan nominated him to the 7th Circuit in 1984. Like Posner, Easterbrook teaches at the University of Chicago Law School.

Another star at the federal appellate level is 1st Circuit Judge Sandra L. Lynch of the First Circuit, who made history as the first female judge on the 1st Circuit in 1995. Lynch's opinions have been cited by many other courts.

Who was the **most famous federal appeals court judge** to never make it to the U.S. Supreme Court?

Many experts consider Billings Learned Hand to be the greatest federal judge to never serve on the U.S. Supreme Court. Hand served on the U.S. Court of Appeals for the 2nd Circuit for many years from 1924 until 1961. Before that, Hand served as a federal district court judge from 1909 until 1924. The U.S. Supreme Court regularly cited his opinions. In fact, legal scholars and the Supreme Court have cited Learned Hand more than any other lower court judge in history. Hand served many years on the court with his first cousin, Augustus Noble Hand, a respected jurist in his own right.

What are some famous **quotes** by **Learned Hand**?

Hand on the freedom of speech: "In each case (courts) must ask whether the gravity of the evil, discounted by its improbability, justifies such invasion of free speech as is necessary to avoid the danger."

On incitement and freedom of speech: "To assimilate agitation, legitimate as such, with direct incitement to violent resistance, is to disregard the tolerance of all methods of political agitation which in normal times is a safeguard of free government."

On tort law and determining the duty of care: "Since there are occasions when every vessel will break from her moorings, and since, if she does, she becomes a menace to those about her; the owner's duty, as in other similar situations, to provide against resulting injuries is a function of three variables: (1) The probability that she will break away; (2) the gravity of the resulting injury, if she does; (3) the burden of adequate precautions. Possibly it serves to bring this notion into relief to state it in algebraic terms: if the probability be called P; the injury, L; and the burden, B; liability depends upon whether B is less than L multiplied by P: i.e., whether $B < PL$."

Hand's "Lessons of Liberty" speech in 1944:

Billings Learned Hand was considered one of the best judges to ever serve on a federal court bench, but he was never named a Supreme Court justice (*Library of Congress*).

Liberty lies in the hearts of men and women; when it dies there, no constitution, no law, no court can even do much to help it. While it lies there it needs no constitution, no law, no court to save it. And what is this liberty which must lie in the hearts of men and women? It is not the ruthless, the unbridled will; it is not freedom to do as one likes. That is the denial of liberty, and leads straight to its overthrow.

A society in which men recognize no check upon their freedom soon becomes a society where freedom is the possession of only a savage few; as we have learned to our sorrow. The spirit of liberty is the spirit which is not too sure that it is right; the spirit of liberty is the spirit which seeks to understand the mind of other men and women; the spirit of liberty is the spirit which weighs their interests alongside its own without bias; the spirit of liberty remembers that not even a sparrow falls to earth unheeded; the spirit of liberty is the spirit of Him who, near two thousand years ago, taught mankind that lesson it has never learned but never quite forgotten; that there may be a kingdom where the least shall be heard and considered side by side with the greatest.

107

How many different districts are there?

There are 94 different judicial districts in the United States and its territories. Many states have multiple federal judicial districts. For example, Tennessee has an Eastern, Middle and Western district. South Dakota only has one judicial district, though its one district has four divisions.

What Is the main difference between a federal district court and the other federal courts?

Federal district courts are trial courts, while the federal circuit courts and the U.S. Supreme Court are appellate courts. Federal district courts are headed by one judge, while the federal appellate courts hear cases before multiple judges or justices.

When can a federal judge become a senior judge?

At the federal district court and federal circuit court level, judges may elect to take senior status upon reaching age 65. These judges still hear cases when asked to do so by the chief justice of the district or circuit.

What does the Federal Magistrates Act do?

Federal district court judges often assign much of their work to federal judges called magistrates. In 1968, Congress passed a law known as the Federal Magistrates Act, which empowered federal district court judges to hire magistrate judges to assist in the control of their caseloads. Magistrate judges do not hold their offices for life, but serve at the discretion of the federal district court. They initially serve eight-year terms. 28 U.S.C. § 631 reads:

> The judges of each United States district court and the district courts of the Virgin Islands, Guam, and the Northern Mariana Islands shall appoint United States magistrate judges in such numbers and to serve at such locations within the judicial districts as the Judicial Conference may determine under this chapter. In the case of a magistrate judge appointed by the district court of the Virgin Islands, Guam, or the Northern Mariana Islands, this chapter shall apply as though the court appointing such a magistrate judge were a United States district court. Where there is more than one judge of a district court, the appointment, whether an original appointment or a reappointment, shall be by the concurrence of a majority of all the judges of such district court, and when there is no such concurrence, then by the chief judge. Where the conference deems it desirable, a magistrate judge may be designated to serve in one or more districts adjoining the district for which he is appointed. Such a designation shall be made by the concurrence of a majority of the judges of

each of the district courts involved and shall specify the duties to be performed by the magistrate judge in the adjoining district or districts.

Are there **other federal courts** that are **not Article III** courts?

Yes, there are other federal courts not called for in Article III, but that are in Article I, which spells out the powers of the legislative branch. Examples of these Article I courts are the U.S. Court of Military Appeals and the U.S. Tax Court.

What is the **work product** of judges and courts?

Judges, particularly federal judges, express their work product through judicial opinions. When people colloquially refer to a case, they are often referring to the judicial opinion authored by the judge or the court. These judicial opinions are written resolutions of legal issues. Oftentimes these judicial opinions divide Court members. For example, on many important constitutional law issues, the U.S. Supreme Court will divide 5 to 4 on the questions. The types of opinions are:

- *Majority opinion:* This opinion, which must have five votes, is the ruling of the Court. It stands as precedent for future cases. If all justices vote with the majority, the opinion is said to be a unanimous opinion.
- *Plurality opinion:* The main opinion of the Court but one that fails to command a majority of the justices. For instance, a case may have four justices agreeing with one opinion, two justices who file concurring opinions but not joining the other four, and three justices in dissent. In this 4-2-3 split, there is no majority opinion.
- *Concurring opinion:* An opinion that agrees with the result but not the reasoning of the majority or main opinion of the Court. A justice who writes a concurring opinion may want to emphasize particular points of law or simply indicate that the main opinion reached the right result by taking the wrong path.
- *Dissenting opinion:* An opinion that disagrees with the result of the majority opinion.
- *Per curiam opinion:* An opinion rendered by the Court, or a majority of the Court, collectively instead of a single justice.

If the majority opinion becomes the law of the land, are **concurring** and **dissenting opinions important**?

Yes, concurring and even dissenting opinions can be important. Sometimes, the law will develop such that a concurring opinion will actually become the guidepost for future decisions in the area. A classic example was Justice John Marshall Harlan's concurring opinion in the Fourth Amendment case *Katz v. United States* (1967). While

Justice Potter Stewart wrote the Court's majority opinion, Harlan's concurring opinion and "reasonable expectation of privacy" test has become the opinion relied on by the majority of lower courts.

Similarly, dissenting opinions can be important, particularly if the U.S. Supreme Court overrules itself in a particular area of the law. A classic example of a dissenting opinion that became the law of the land was Justice Hugo Black's dissenting opinion in the Sixth Amendment right to counsel case of *Betts v. Brady* (1942). The majority in Betts ruled that state courts did not have to provide an attorney to all indigent defendants charged with felonies in non-death penalty cases. However, the Court overruled that decision 21years later in *Gideon v. Wainwright* (1963) and, in a remarkable irony, Justice Hugo Black had the honor of writing the unanimous opinion for the Court, taking the same position that he took in dissent in *Betts*.

Justices can express either a majority, plurality, concurring, or dissenting opinion in Supreme Court cases (*iStock*).

What opinions have **precedential value**?

It is majority opinions or the main opinion of the Court that has precedential value, because those opinions establish precedents for other courts to follow. Courts follow the principle of stare decisis, which is Latin for "let the decision stand." This means that courts generally will follow past decisions unless there are compelling reasons not to follow the past decision.

Also, in our legal system, the decisions of higher courts are mandatory authority or precedent for lower courts in that jurisdiction. For example, lower federal courts have to follow U.S. Supreme Court decisions. Likewise, a federal district court in North Carolina would have to follow a decision by the 4th U.S. Circuit Court of Appeals. A federal district court in Florida would have to follow a decision by the 11th U.S. Circuit Court of Appeals.

Is there a difference between **mandatory authority** and **persuasive authority**?

Yes, there is a very important difference between mandatory authority and persuasive authority for courts and judges in the American legal system. If a decision is mandatory authority, it means that a lower court has to follow that decision. If a decision is persuasive authority, it means that a lower court can follow that higher court decision but does not have to do so.

The basic rule is that lower courts must follow the decisions of higher courts in their jurisdiction, while they do not have to follow higher courts not in their jurisdiction. Take the example of a federal district court in Tennessee, which is located in the purview of the 6th U.S. Circuit Court of Appeals. This means that for the federal district court in Tennessee, Sixth Circuit decisions are mandatory authority, while decisions from the other circuits are persuasive authority.

Do **courts always follow** their past **decisions**?

No, sometimes courts will overrule their past decisions. The law evolves and changes over time due to changes in societal attitudes, the composition of the court and other factors. The most classic example was when the U.S. Supreme Court in *Brown v. Board of Education* (1954) overruled the "separate but equal" doctrine in *Plessy v. Ferguson* (1896). The Court in *Brown* determined that segregated public schools violated the Equal Protection Clause, while the Court in *Plessy* had upheld a Louisiana law mandating separate railroad travel for different races.

More recently, the U.S. Supreme Court in *Roper v. Simmons* (2005) ruled that juvenile murders cannot be executed, because that would violate the Eighth Amendment against cruel and unusual punishment. The Court focused on the fact that juveniles have less appreciation and cannot control their behavior as much as adults. The Court overruled its prior decision in *Stanford v. Kentucky* (1989).

Perhaps the quickest reversal occurred in the 1943 decision *West Virginia Board of Education v. Barnette* (1943) where the justices reversed the decision in *Minersville School District v. Gobitis* (1940). In *Barnette*, the Court invalidated a West Virginia flag salute law that forced public school students to stand, recite the Pledge of Allegiance and salute the flag. In *Gobitis,* the Court had upheld a similar Pennsylvania law.

STATE COURTS

How are **state court systems established**?

State court systems are created by state constitutions. Many states have three-tiered systems of courts—trial courts, intermediate appellate courts, and supreme courts. Many state trial courts are called circuit or district courts. Intermediate appellate courts are called courts of appeal. Most state final appellate courts are state supreme courts.

Many states also have separate courts for juvenile cases, probate matters (wills and trusts), and family law. Most states also recognize certain smaller courts of limited jurisdiction—often called general sessions courts or common pleas courts.

How are **state court** judges **picked**?

In most states, the bulk of judges are elected. Nearly 40 states hold judicial elections for certain judges. In many states, trial judges are selected or elected differently than appellate court judges. Some states like Utah fill most of their judges through a merit selection process. In other states, such as Alabama and Washington, hold elections for all types of judges.

For more information on how state judges are selected, visit the American Judicature's site at http://www.judicialselection.us/.

Which **states do not** have **elections** for any type of **judges**?

The following states do not hold elections for their judges: Colorado, Connecticut, Delaware, Hawaii, Iowa, Maine, Massachusetts, Nebraska, New Hampshire, and New Jersey.

Are all state **high courts** called **supreme courts**?

No, most—but not all—state high courts are called supreme courts. In New York the Supreme Courts are trial courts, not final appellate courts. Maryland and Nebraska's high courts are called Courts of Appeals, not Supreme Courts.

Do all **state high courts** have the same **number of justices** or judges?

No, the state high courts are varied in how many justices serve on their courts. All states either have five, seven, or nine members. Only the states of Alabama, Mississippi, Oklahoma, and Texas have nine justices. The majority of states have seven justices, while a sizeable minority have five justices.

Number of Justices on State High Courts

Court	Number of Justices
Alabama Supreme Court	9
Alaska Supreme Court	5
Arizona Supreme Court	5
Arkansas Supreme Court	7
California Supreme Court	7
Colorado Supreme Court	7

The New York State Supreme Courthouse. While U.S. Supreme Court justics are appointed, in most states they have to run for election (*iStock*).

Court	Number of Justices
Connecticut Supreme Court	7
Delaware Supreme Court	5
Florida Supreme Court	7
Georgia Supreme Court	7
Hawaii Supreme Court	5
Idaho Supreme Court	5
Illinois Supreme Court	7
Indiana Supreme Court	5
Iowa Supreme Court	7
Kansas Supreme Court	7
Kentucky Supreme Court	7
Louisiana Supreme Court	7
Maine Supreme Judicial Court	7
Maryland Court of Appeals	7
Massachusetts Supreme Judicial Court	7
Michigan Supreme Court	7
Minnesota Supreme Court	7
Mississippi Supreme Court	9

Court	Number of Justices
Missouri Supreme Court	7*
Montana Supreme Court	7
Nebraska Supreme Court	7
Nevada Supreme Court	7
New Hampshire Supreme Court	5
New Jersey Supreme Court	7
New Mexico Supreme Court	5
New York Court of Appeals	7
North Carolina Supreme Court	7
North Dakota Supreme Court	5
Ohio Supreme Court	7
Oklahoma Supreme Court	9
Oregon Supreme Court	7
Pennsylvania Supreme Court	7
Rhode Island Supreme Court	5
South Carolina Supreme Court	5
South Dakota Supreme Court	5
Tennessee Supreme Court	5
Texas Supreme Court	9
Utah Supreme Court	5
Vermont Supreme Court	5
Virginia Supreme Court	7
Washington Supreme Court	9
West Virginia Supreme Court of Appeals	5
Wisconsin Supreme Court	7
Wyoming Supreme Court	5

*Only the chief justice is called a "justice."

Are all state court systems based on the **three-tiered model** of trial court, intermediate appellate court, and final appellate court?

Most states do follow this three-tiered model of trial courts, intermediate appellate courts, and final appellate courts. But, a few states do not. For example, South Dakota's state court system is a two-tiered model of circuit courts and one supreme court.

What is the **relationship** between state **high courts** and state **constitutions**?

State constitutions created the state high courts. The other relationship is that state high courts, not the U.S. Supreme Court, are the ultimate arbiters and interpreters of the meaning of state constitutions. State supreme courts are free to interpret their state constitutions to provide greater protection under the state constitution than the U.S. Supreme Court has done under the U.S. Bill of Rights.

Do many states have **family courts**?

Some states have specific courts that solely address family law cases. In other states, some circuit courts address family law and other types of cases. This varies dramatically from state to state. New York has a New York City Family Court, which has jurisdiction over cases involving abused or neglected children, adoption, custody and visitation, domestic violence, foster care approval and review, guardianship, juvenile delinquency, paternity, persons in need of supervision, and support. See http://www .nycourts.gov/courts/nyc/family/index.shtml.

Hawaii adopted family courts by statute in 1965. Delaware had its first statewide family court in 1971. The movement is on the rise for the creation of more family courts. Maine had its first family court in 1998. The North Carolina Legislature created some family courts in 1999.

LAWYERS AND LAWSUITS

BECOMING A LAWYER

What does it take to **become a lawyer**?

Lawyers must possess a degree from a law school and then pass a difficult test known as the bar exam to receive authorization to practice law in the state in which they pass the exam. Most law schools are either three or four year programs. Virtually everyone entering law school must have a college diploma and take a pre-entrance test called the Law School Aptitude Test (LSAT).

After graduating from law school, applicants must then take the bar exam, which is a two-day test in most states (in some states it is three days). Most aspiring applicants take a preparation course, as the bar exam tests person's knowledge in at least 20 different areas of the law. The test features a difficult 200-question multiple choice exam known as the Multistate exam. This exam—national in scope—tests knowledge of six core areas: (1) contracts; (2) torts; (3) property; (4) constitutional law; (5) criminal law; and (6) evidence. Most states also feature an essay portion of the exam, which focuses more on state law.

What is the **American Bar Association**?

The American Bar Association (ABA) is the largest voluntary professional association of lawyers (or any group of professionals) in the world with more than 400,000 members. It provides law school accreditation (approval), provides continuing legal education services, programs to assist lawyers and judges in their work and a variety of other legal services. The ABA's stated mission is "to serve equally our members, our profession and the public by defending liberty and delivering justice as the national representative of the legal profession."

After they graduate from law school, students must study for and pass the bar exam administered by the American Bar Association before they can practice (*iStock*).

Can all law school **graduates take** the **bar exam**?

Most law school graduates take the bar exam, but there are exceptions. Every bar school applicant must fill out a detailed form. Most state supreme courts have rules that require bar applicants to show that they have the character, fitness, and moral qualifications to practice law. The vast majority of graduates are able to successfully apply to sit for the bar (take the bar exam). However, some graduates—because of past criminal histories, serious credit issues, or character problems—do not receive approval to take the bar exam. For example, if a student commits plagiarism in law school, that may raise a red flag to those who interview the applicant for bar admission—even if the student received punishment in law school and went on to graduate.

If a person **passes** the **bar exam**, is he or she automatically entitled to **practice law**?

No, in many states a person can pass the bar exam but still not pass a character and fitness examination, which may occur after the bar test. Passing the bar exam is simply one part of the applicant's responsibility. He or she must also demonstrate to an interviewer—usually a practicing attorney in his or her locale—that he or she is fit to practice law.

A well-known case in Illinois involved an admitted white supremacist named Matthew Hale, who graduated from Southern Illinois law school and passed the bar

LegalSpeak: Ohio Supreme Court Governing
Bar Rule 1. Admission to the Practice of Law

Section 1. General Requirements.

To be admitted to the practice of law in Ohio, an applicant shall satisfy all of the following requirements:

(A) Be at least twenty-one years of age;

(B) Have earned a bachelor's degree from an accredited college or university in accordance with any of the following:

   (1) Prior to admission to law school;

   (2) Subsequent to admission to law school, through completion of courses and credits other than those received in law school, if the applicant has made a record of academic achievement that is satisfactory to the Court and receives Court approval;

   (3) From participation in a joint bachelor's/law degree program that has been reviewed and approved by the Court, requires at least seven years of full-time study, and results in the award of both a bachelor's degree and a law degree;

(C) Have earned a J.D. or an L.L.B. degree from a law school that was approved by the American Bar Association at the time the degree was earned or, if not located in the United States, from a law school evaluated and approved in accordance with Section 2(C) or Section 9(C)(13) of this rule; to the practice of law and have been approved as to character, fitness, and moral qualifications under procedures provided in this rule; ...

(D) Prior to taking the Ohio bar examination or being admitted without examination pursuant to Section 9 of this rule, have demonstrated that the applicant possesses the requisite character, fitness, and moral qualifications for admission;

(E) Have passed both the Ohio bar examination and the Multistate Professional Responsibility Examination, or have been approved for admission without examination pursuant to Section 9 of this rule;

(F) Have taken the oath of office pursuant to Section 8(A) of this rule....

exam. However, an Illinois Committee on Character and Fitness refused to allow him to practice law.

What can **disqualify** a person from sitting for a **bar exam**?

If there are serious red flags raised during the application process or from evaluations from the student's law school, there could be problems. Serious criminal law issues could present a problem, as could allegations of sexual harassment or other bad behavior. If the bar examiners in a state believe that a lawyer has been untruthful or lacked candor in the application process, then there could be problems for that candidate. If a person had an issue with plagiarism or other form of academic dishonesty, that could be cause for concern. It is hard to generalize because these issues vary from state to state.

How **many bar exams** are there?

There are two bar exams every year. The first is given in February and the second is given in July.

What is **tested** on the **bar exam**?

Bar exams are given in every state and consist of two parts. The first part is the called the Multistate, which is given nationwide to applicants in every state except for Washington and Louisiana. The Multistate part of the bar exam consists of 200 multiple-choice questions covering the subjects of contracts, criminal law, constitutional law, property, torts, and evidence. While it may sound easy, it is very difficult. Many of the questions appear to have two correct answers and the applicant must select the better of the two answers.

The second part of the exam is an essay exam, which requires applicants to answer essay questions covering a much broader array of legal subjects. For instance, a state essay exam requires applicants often to be familiar with wills and estates, domestic relations, state constitutional law, secured transactions, and other areas simply not tested on the multistate exam.

Do all states **require** individuals to take a **bar exam** to practice law?

All states require applicants to take the bar exam except for the state of Wisconsin, which provides that students who graduate from law school in Wisconsin are automatically licensed to practice law in the state. This benefit for Wisconsin school grad is called the state diploma privilege. It means that law graduates from Wisconsin Law School and Marquette University do not have to take the Wisconsin Bar Exam.

However, there is a currently a federal lawsuit that is challenging the constitutionality of this diploma privilege. It was filed by a lawyer who took the Wisconsin Bar Exam but was not entitled to the diploma privilege because he graduated from a law school in Oklahoma.

If a lawyer **passes** a **state bar** exam can he or she then **practice** in **any state**?

No, becoming licensed in one state does not entitle a lawyer to practice in another state. Many states do have what is known as reciprocity, which means that after a lawyer has practiced for a period of time (usually five years), he or she can apply to practice in another state without taking another bar exam. The lawyer must receive approval from the new state's highest court to receive admission.

A key exception in most states is that lawyers can apply for what is known as *pro hac vice* status, which is Latin for "this one occasion or event." This means that a lawyer is applying to practice in a different state for one case.

What is **continuing legal education**?

Continuing legal education (CLE) is a requirement imposed on lawyers in nearly every state that requires them to take a certain number of hours in legal study to ensure continuing competence and professionalism. Various bar associations and other groups offer CLE courses, which usually consist of presentations by experts, panels debating current legal topics, and various other teaching methods. Many states now allow attorneys to take online CLE courses. Attorneys can also obtain CLE credit for publishing legal articles and teaching law courses to undergraduates, paralegals, or law students.

FINDING A LAWYER

Where does a person go to **find a lawyer**?

There are many avenues of finding a lawyer. There are many online directories, such as Martindale-Hubbell at http://www.martindale.com, that are helpful. Under Martindale-Hubbell, you can search for an attorney by location, by name, by practice areas, and by zip code.

Findlaw.com (http://www.findlaw.com) also has a section on its website for locating attorneys by practice areas and location. Local and state bar associations have helpful information on locating attorneys. Many attorneys advertise in a variety of media—from the yellow book to Internet websites. On this site you can look for attorney by location and by practice area.

What are the **lawyer ratings** provided for by **Martindale-Hubbell**?

Martindale-Hubbell offers a peer review rating system in which attorneys are rated by their peers in the legal profession. There are three ratings—AV, BV, and CV. AV is the highest rating available, though none of the ratings reflect poor lawyering. CV is the highest rating attainable for a lawyer who has been practicing only three to four

121

Picking a good lawyer who will represent you well is a decision that must be carefully made. There are websites that include rating systems that can help (*iStock*).

years. BV is the highest rating available for a lawyer who has been practicing for five to nine years.

What should you look for in an attorney?

A person would want to select an attorney who is proficient and competent in that particular area of the law. For example, if you have been involved in a personal injury, you would want to select an attorney who has some experience and training in that area of law. Law is very specialized and many attorneys specialize in a few areas of law.

Some attorneys specialize in intellectual property (copyright, trademarks, patents), family law, employment law, personal injury, medical malpractice defense, or criminal law. If you are facing criminal charges, you need the services of an attorney well versed in criminal law. Likewise if you are looking to trademark a business slogan, you need the services of someone who is knowledgeable in intellectual property law.

A famous celebrity endorsed a lawyer, but does that mean this is a superior lawyer?

Not necessarily—all that means is that the lawyer had enough money to hire the celebrity to give what is called a testimonial. Most states allow attorneys to advertise with testimonials, but in a few states testimonials are viewed with great skepticism if not prohibited.

LegalSpeak: *Ohralik v. Ohio* (1978)

Unlike a public advertisement, which simply provides information and leaves the recipient free to act upon it or not, in-person solicitation may exert pressure and often demands an immediate response, without providing an opportunity for comparison or reflection. The aim and effect of in-person solicitation may be to provide a one-sided presentation and to encourage speedy and perhaps uninformed decisionmaking; there is no opportunity for intervention or counter-education by agencies of the Bar, supervisory authorities, or persons close to the solicited individual....

The substantive evils of solicitation have been stated over the years in sweeping terms: stirring up litigation, assertion of fraudulent claims, debasing the legal profession, and potential harm to the solicited client in the form of overreaching, overcharging, underrepresentation, and misrepresentation....

The Rules prohibiting solicitation are prophylactic measures whose objective is the prevention of harm before it occurs. The Rules were applied in this case to discipline a lawyer for soliciting employment for pecuniary gain under circumstances likely to result in the adverse consequences the State seeks to avert. In such a situation, which is inherently conducive to overreaching and other forms of misconduct, the State has a strong interest in adopting and enforcing rules of conduct designed to protect the public from harmful solicitation by lawyers whom it has licensed.

The State's perception of the potential for harm in circumstances such as those presented in this case is well founded. The detrimental aspects of face-to-face selling even of ordinary consumer products have been recognized and addressed by the Federal Trade Commission, and it hardly need be said that the potential for overreaching is significantly greater when a lawyer, a professional trained in the art of persuasion, personally solicits an unsophisticated, injured, or distressed lay person. Such an individual may place his trust in a lawyer, regardless of the latter's qualifications or the individual's actual need for legal representation, simply in response to persuasion under circumstances conducive to uninformed acquiescence. Although it is argued that personal solicitation is valuable because it may apprise a victim of misfortune of his legal rights, the very plight of that person not only makes him more vulnerable to influence but also may make advice all the more intrusive. Thus, under these adverse conditions the overtures of an uninvited lawyer may distress the solicited individual simply because of their obtrusiveness and the invasion of the individual's privacy, even when no other harm materializes. Under such circumstances, it is not unreasonable for the State to presume that in-person solicitation by lawyers more often than not will be injurious to the person solicited.

Can **attorneys advertise** in any way they want?

No, attorneys cannot engage in advertising that is false or misleading. A few states have rules that prohibit "self-laudatory" advertising and many states prohibit advertising that creates unjustified expectations on the part of potential clients. For example, if an attorney advertised, "I guarantee you will receive a six-figure settlement offer from the insurance company," then that advertisement could land the attorney in trouble with the state disciplinary bar for improper advertising.

Lawyers also cannot engage in direct, face-to-face solicitation with people in order to obtain their business *Ohralik v. Ohio* (1978; see LegalSpeak, p. 123). This means that a lawyer cannot go into a hospital room to an injured person and try to become that person's lawyer. Believe it or not, that happened in that went all the way to the U.S. Supreme Court.

How much can you expect to **pay a lawyer**?

This varies quite dramatically depending on the type of the case, the particular lawyer you select, the arrangement you work out with the lawyer, the geographic location in which you reside, and other factors. Most importantly, it may depend on the complexity of the case and the number of hours required for the lawyer to provide his or her professional skills.

Many attorneys will provide an initial consultation for free. This will give you the opportunity to meet the attorney and see if you like their attitude and comportment, and generally feel comfortable with that person handling an important aspect of your life.

How is a **lawyer paid**?

This depends on what type of agreement you sign and often what type of case is involved. Sometimes lawyers are paid on an hourly basis, by a flat fee or by contingency fee. In an hourly fee arrangement, the client pays the lawyer an hourly rate. Lawyers' prices vary quite dramatically geographically.

For less complex legal matters an attorney and client can work out a flat-fee arrangement. Uncontested divorces, simple wills, and other more routine legal work are ideal for flat-fee agreements.

Contingency fee arrangements are typical of lawyers who represent plaintiffs (remember the plaintiff is the person or company who sues) in personal injury tort and employment discrimination cases. In a contingency fee arrangement, a lawyer is paid only if (contingent on) the plaintiff prevails in the lawsuit. In other words, if your lawyer takes your case on a 30 percent contingency fee arrangement, you will not pay your lawyer directly. Rather, the lawyer receives 30 percent of your recovery or award

Paying your lawyer can be done in a number of ways, including on an hourly basis, a flat rate, or through a contingency fee arrangement (*iStock*).

in the case. Contingency fee cases are common in personal injury and employment discrimination suits. Contingency fees are disfavored in other types of cases.

Are **contingency fees** available for **all types** of **cases**?

No, contingency fees are not available for criminal cases and are frowned upon for family law cases as well.

Do some lawyers work on **retainer**?

Yes, some attorneys work on retainer, but a retainer is usually for a business or a person who has many legal issues for which they need regular legal work. This business or individual will pay an attorney (or usually a law firm) to work on retainer. This means that the law firm will be on call to provide a variety of legal services for that client.

Sometimes the word "retainer" is used for the term down payment. In other words, some high-profile family law attorneys will require a $5,000 retainer to handle a complex divorce. This means that the client has to put up $5,000 initially out of which the lawyer's fees are drawn in the beginning. This will likely not be the total cost of the case but simply the initial monies that are paid to the lawyer to get the attorney–client relationship started.

125

What **types of jobs** do **lawyers** have?

Most lawyers in this country are in private practice, meaning that they do not work for the government. Many lawyers work together with other lawyers in groups known as law firms. These firms provide a range of services with different attorneys specializing in different areas of the law. Many of the larger law firms have multiple offices—often in large cities in the United States and sometimes an office overseas as well.

Some attorneys work for themselves and are called solo practitioners. This means that the lawyer does not officially work for or with any other attorneys, though many attorneys will share office space with other attorneys or may have friendly relationships with other attorneys.

Other attorneys work for the government in a variety of settings—a federal or state agency, a district attorney's office, a defender's office, or some other type of job.

What is a **public interest law firm**?

A public interest law firm is a private association of attorneys whose principal goal is to assist clients in a particular area of law and advance certain ideological goals rather than to make money. The primary goal of private law firms is to make money practicing law. Public interest law firms usually have a different agenda. There are many public interest law firms that defend civil liberties, advance guns-rights and libertarian points of view, advocate on behalf of religious causes, and defend certain types of cases. Some well known public interest law firms include: National Legal Aid and Defenders Association, Alliance Defense Fund, Legal Services Corporation, American Civil Liberties Union, National Center on Poverty Law, Public Justice, the Rutherford Institute, and the American Center for Law and Justice.

What **advantage** is it for a person to have representation from a **public interest law firm**?

The advantage is that often the person has to pay little or no legal fees. The public interest law firms take cases on a *pro bono* (for free) basis. Given the rising and often high cost of legal services, the value of public interest law firms is immense.

Do **private attorneys** take cases *pro bono*?

Pro bono publico ("for the public good") is recommended by the American Bar Association and state bar associations. The ABA recommends that attorneys devote 50 hours a year in *pro bono* legal services.

Are there **limitations** on the amount of **attorney's fees**?

Yes, most states' ethical codes prohibit lawyers from charging exorbitant or unreasonable fees. That begs the question of when is a lawyer's fee unreasonable. The ABA

LegalSpeak: ABA Model Rule 6.1. Voluntary Pro Bono Public Service

Every lawyer has a professional responsibility to provide legal services to those unable to pay. A lawyer should aspire to render at least (50) hours of *pro bono* publico legal services per year. In fulfilling this responsibility, the lawyer should:

(a) provide a substantial majority of the (50) hours of legal services without fee or expectation of fee to:
(1) persons of limited means or
(2) charitable, religious, civic, community, governmental and educational organizations in matters which are designed primarily to address the needs of persons of limited means; and
(b) provide any additional services through:
(1) delivery of legal services at no fee or substantially reduced fee to individuals, groups or organizations seeking to secure or protect civil rights, civil liberties or public rights, or charitable, religious, civic, community, governmental and educational organizations in matters in furtherance of their organizational purposes, where the payment of standard legal fees would significantly deplete the organization's economic resources or would be otherwise inappropriate;
(2) delivery of legal services at a substantially reduced fee to persons of limited means; or
(3) participation in activities for improving the law, the legal system or the legal profession.

In addition, a lawyer should voluntarily contribute financial support to organizations that provide legal services to persons of limited means.

Comment (1): Comment

[1] Every lawyer, regardless of professional prominence or professional workload, has a responsibility to provide legal services to those unable to pay, and personal involvement in the problems of the disadvantaged can be one of the most rewarding experiences in the life of a lawyer. The American Bar Association urges all lawyers to provide a minimum of 50 hours of *pro bono* services annually. States, however, may decide to choose a higher or lower number of hours of annual service (which may be expressed as a percentage of a lawyer's professional time) depending upon local needs and local conditions. It is recognized that in some years a lawyer may render greater or fewer hours than the annual standard specified, but during the course of his or her legal career, each lawyer should render on average per year, the number of hours set forth in this Rule. Services can be performed in civil matters or in criminal or quasi-criminal matters for which there is no government obligation to provide funds for legal representation, such as post-conviction death penalty appeal cases.

If you don't have enough money for an attorney, one will be appointed for you (*iStock*).

Model Rules of Professional Conduct list numerous factors that should be considered. These factors include the time and labor involved, the customary fee charged for such services in the area and the experience, reputation and ability of the lawyer who charges the fees.

What if you are charged with a crime and **don't have** enough **money** for an **attorney**?

If a person is indigent (poor) and cannot afford an attorney, he or she may qualify for representation from a public defender's office. There are federal public defender's offices for those charged with federal crimes and local public defender offices for those charged with state or local crimes.

When a person is taken into custody, the authorities may make them fill out a form that describes their assets and financial condition. If a person qualifies, then the public defender's office will apply to represent them or the court will appoint the public defender's office to represent them.

If your lawyer does a lousy job on your case, for **what reasons** can you **sue for malpractice**?

You may be able to pursue a claim of legal malpractice against your lawyer if he or she caused harm to your case and that, absent the legal malpractice, there is a reasonable probability that you would have had a good case and prevailed. Legal malpractice claims are sometimes based on contract law, breach of fiduciary duty, and negligence. If your lawyer violates the attorney-client agreement, then he or she may have breached the contract and may be liable for liquated damages under contract law.

The lawyer–client relationship is one that creates a special relationship and special duties of care placed upon the professional—the lawyer. In some circumstances, the lawyer may be liable for breaching a fiduciary duty if he or she did not provide loyalty and confidentiality to his client.

Most legal malpractice claims are pursued under a theory of tort law and this makes sense because another name for malpractice is professional negligence. In a legal malpractice case based on negligence, the client asserts that the lawyer failed to exercise the level of care, skill, and knowledge normally provided by a lawyer. Legal malpractice cases are very difficult to prove, as generally the plaintiff must show that he or she would have prevailed in the underlying legal matter without the lawyer's negligence.

It is even harder to prevail in a legal malpractice case arising out of a criminal matter because courts require a plaintiff to present a colorable claim (appearance of plausibility but actually deceptive) of innocence before prevailing.

Are **public defenders good** lawyers?

Yes, there is a public misconception that public defenders are less than stellar attorneys or inferior to private attorneys. For most public defenders this is an inaccurate or false characterization. The difference is that sometimes wealthy defendants have greater financial resources to challenge the government and hire more expert witnesses and, perhaps, have a better chance sometimes at an acquittal.

Can a **judge appoint attorneys** to represent someone?

Yes, sometimes a public defender's office may have a conflict and cannot represent a particular individual. For example, if three defendants are charged with a crime, the public defender may be representing one of those three defendants and cannot represent the other two, because all three individuals may testify against each other and try to obtain the best deals possible. Other times the public defender's office may have an overwhelming caseload. In this situation, a judge may appoint a lawyer in private practice to represent a defendant.

Are **all** lawyers **litigators**?

No, most lawyers are not purely litigators. Litigators refer to those attorneys who regularly appear in court and try (or litigate) cases. Sometimes these attorneys are called trial attorneys, because they have jury trials. Many attorneys work in areas of practice where litigation does not occur that frequently. These attorneys negotiate deals, file motions and do other work that does not require frequent courtroom appearances.

Other attorneys focus on settling cases rather than taking them to trial. These attorneys may be well versed in an area of law, but simply prefer to settle cases rather than try cases before a jury.

Still other attorneys may be appellate attorneys, which mean that they do not practice in trial courts. These attorneys specialize in appearing before appellate courts, reviewing lower court decisions and trying to identify errors of law committed. Some attorneys, in fact, specialize almost entirely in U.S. Supreme Court litigation.

Can your **attorney settle** a case **without your approval**?

No, attorneys are supposed to consult with clients before making a decision about whether to settle a case. Attorneys have a duty to communicate settlement offers to clients so that clients can give informed consent and make a reasoned decision.

The Comment to Rule 1.4 of the ABA Model Rules of Professional Conduct provides:

> For example, a lawyer who receives from opposing counsel an offer of settlement in a civil controversy or a proffered plea bargain in a criminal case must promptly inform the client of its substance unless the client has previously

indicated that the proposal will be acceptable or unacceptable or has authorized the lawyer to accept or to reject the offer.

What can people do when they feel their **lawyers** have been **unethical or unprofessional**?

The person can file a complaint with the department or agency established by a state high court to monitor and regulate the legal professional. In Tennessee, complaints can be filed with the so-called Board of Professional Responsibility. In Illinois, complaints can be filed with the Attorney Registration and Disciplinary Commission. New Mexico has a body called the Commission on Client Protection. These groups or commissions have websites and usually have online forms in which to file a complaint or at least explain how a complaint can be filed. Some states require complaints to be mailed. An example is the form to file a claim against a New Mexico-based attorney can be accessed at http://www.nmbar.org/Attorneys/CPF/CPFClaimForm.pdf.

Can you **find out** if a **lawyer** has faced **discipline**?

Yes, some states allow you to do a search online to determine if an attorney has faced discipline. For example, the Tennessee Board of Professional Responsibility has a section entitled "Online Attorney Directory" at http://www.tbpr.org/Consumers/AttorneySearch/ at which you can search attorneys by their names and bar license numbers. If the lawyer has had discipline it will reveal whether a petition for discipline has been filed and whether there was any punishment (such as a public censure) against an attorney.

How are **lawyers punished** for misconduct?

State supreme courts can punish lawyers in a number of ways. The worst form of lawyer sanction in the legal profession is disbarment, which means that the lawyer is no longer capable of practicing law, as he or she has lost his or her law license. Stealing money from a client, committing a serious crime, or lying to the court on important matters could result in disbarment proceedings.

In many states, lawyers could face a suspension for a period of several years if they commit serious breaches of the lawyer ethical rules. They also could

Punishments for attorney misconduct can range from a mere reprimand all the way up to disbarment from practice (*iStock*).

131

receive a public censure or a private reprimand. All states do not have the same level of punishment for attorneys.

The ABA's Standards for Imposing Legal Discipline—adopted in 1986 to serve as a guide and provide some much-needed uniformity in the area of lawyer discipline—provide for several types of lawyer discipline. These include disbarment, suspension, interim suspension, reprimand, admonition, and probation.

What are some common **grounds** for **attorney discipline**?

A major ethical breach occurs when attorneys fail to deliver money to clients or commit some type of fraud upon their own clients. Attorneys even are prohibited from commingling (mixing) their funds with that of their clients. The fear is that the attorneys will not return the necessary monies to the clients.

2.4 Interim Suspension

Interim suspension is the temporary suspension of a lawyer from the practice of law pending imposition of final discipline. Interim suspension includes:

(a) suspension upon conviction of a serious crime or,

(b) suspension when the lawyer's continuing conduct is or is likely to cause immediate and serious injury to a client or the public.

2.5 Reprimand

Reprimand, also known as censure or public censure, is a form of public discipline which declares the conduct of the lawyer improper, but does not limit the lawyer's right to practice.

2.6 Admonition

Admonition, also known as private reprimand, is a form of non-public discipline which declares the conduct of the lawyer improper, but does not limit the lawyer's right to practice.

2.7 Probation

Probation is a sanction that allows a lawyer to practice law under specified conditions.

Probation can be imposed alone or in conjunction with a reprimand, an admonition or immediately following a suspension. Probation can also be imposed as a condition of readmission or reinstatement.

Another common problem is that attorneys fail to manage a case properly by not responding to court demands in a case or not filing the proper pleadings in a case. Another problem occurs when attorneys fail to file a lawsuit within the necessary time period—called a statute of limitations. If a lawyer fails to file a lawsuit within the necessary time period, then the client loses his or her right to recover even if the suit is meritorious.

LAWSUITS

What is the **document** called that **starts a lawsuit**?

The complaint is the initial charging document that begins a lawsuit. The plaintiff is the person suing and the defendant is the person being sued. The complaint lays out

A lawsuit document that begins legal action is called a "complaint" (*iStock*).

the parties' names and addresses, the jurisdiction of the court, underlying facts of why there is a suit, the legal claims asserted in the suit and the relief sought by the plaintiff. Each statement in a complaint is given a number. Thus, a complaint is written in number form in different sections. This document is then served on the defendant. This is called service of process.

When **served** with a complaint, what is the **legal responsibility** of a **defendant**?

A defendant must file a response to the complaint—usually within 30 days—called an answer. The answer responds to each and every allegation contained in a complaint. The defendant must admit, deny, or respond that he or she does not have sufficient knowledge to answer the allegation. Many times defendants will admit basic information in a complaint like the parties' names, the court's jurisdiction (sometimes) and a few of the underlying facts (such as plaintiff worked for the defendant) but deny the substance of the allegations and the legal claims.

What types of **relief** do **plaintiffs seek**?

Most lawsuits seek some type of monetary relief or damages. Plaintiffs often ask for what are known as compensatory damages—to compensate them for the harm that they have suffered. Often plaintiffs will seek attorneys' fees. This means that the plaintiff wants the court to order the defendant to pay the plaintiff's attorney fees.

Many statutes (such as civil rights, employment discrimination statutes) are fee-shifting statutes in that they allow a prevailing plaintiff (the plaintiff-litigant who wins the case) to have the defendant pay his or her attorney fees. In cases involving alleged egregious or very bad conduct, a plaintiff may also seek what are known as punitive damages.

In other cases, a plaintiff may seek injunctive or declaratory relief. Injunctive relief means that the plaintiff petitions the court to enjoin (or prohibit) the defendant from engaging in certain conduct. Declaratory relief means that the plaintiff asks the court to declare a certain law, regulation, or policy unconstitutional or void. The key point, however, is that the plaintiff must declare the relief he or she is seeking in the complaint.

What happens **after** a plaintiff files a complaint and a **defendant files** the **answer**?

The case then proceeds to what is known as the discovery phase of a case. In discovery, each side uses certain tools—such as interrogatories or depositions—to discover more about the case. If the plaintiff's case is weak, the defense might file a motion to dismiss. Sometimes motions to dismiss are filed in conjunction with an answer or shortly after the answer. Some motions to dismiss are called motions to dismiss for failure to state a claim. This motion asserts that the plaintiff's claim does not advance a recognizable legal claim for recovery.

What are the common **tools of discovery**?

After the basic pleadings—the complaint and answer—have been filed, each side enters the discovery process. The common tools of discovery are: interrogatories, depositions, requests for production of documents, requests for admissions and requests for examinations.

Interrogatories are written questions about a case submitted by one party to the other. Interrogatories must be answered under oath by the other party. Commonly asked interrogatories inquire about witnesses that are likely to be called by the other side, questions about persons familiar with the allegations and the existence of any documents that might prove or disprove part of a case. Other interrogatories may inquire about the financial status of a party and the names and addresses of all witnesses to key events in the lawsuit.

Depositions are live questionings of a party or potential witness under oath, usually in one of the attorney's offices. The attorney asks questions and the party or prospective witnesses answer questions. If a plaintiff or defendant is deposed, he or she will have his or her attorney present to object to certain questions. Deposition testimony is important for many reasons. First of all, most of it (unless there is an objection) is admissible at trial. Attorneys often try to show a disconnect between a party's deposition testimony and his or her trial testimony. If a person testifies differently at trial than he or she did at her deposition, then the opposing attorney will show that difference to the jury and try to weaken that person's credibility.

Requests for production of documents are another key discovery tool. Parties can use this tool to attempt to gain access to the premises of the other party in order to inspect, take photographs and copy key materials. Other times this request forces the other side to turn over key reports or documents.

What happens if a **party** will **not respond** to **discovery requests**?

The other side can then file a motion to compel discovery with the court. This motion asks the court to force the other side to honor the discovery requests. If a party refuses to obey the court and still refuses discovery, the court can then impose sanctions.

LegalSpeak: Federal Rule of Civil Procedure, Rule 56

(a) By a Claiming Party.

A party claiming relief may move, with or without supporting affidavits, for summary judgment on all or part of the claim. The motion may be filed at any time after:

(1) 20 days have passed from commencement of the action; or

(2) the opposing party serves a motion for summary judgment.

(b) By a Defending Party.

A party against whom relief is sought may move at any time, with or without supporting affidavits, for summary judgment on all or part of the claim.

(c) Serving the Motion; Proceedings.

The motion must be served at least 10 days before the day set for the hearing. An opposing party may serve opposing affidavits before the hearing day. The judgment sought should be rendered if the pleadings, the discovery and disclosure materials on file, and any affidavits show that there is no genuine issue as to any material fact and that the movant [one who makes a motion before a court] is entitled to judgment as a matter of law.

(d) Case Not Fully Adjudicated on the Motion.

(1) Establishing Facts.

If summary judgment is not rendered on the whole action, the court should, to the extent practicable, determine what material facts are not genuinely at issue. The court should so determine by examining the pleadings and evidence before it and by interrogating the attorneys. It should then issue an order specifying what facts—including items of damages or other relief—are not genuinely at issue. The facts so specified must be treated as established in the action.

(2) Establishing Liability.

An interlocutory summary judgment may be rendered on liability alone, even if there is a genuine issue on the amount of damages.

What is **summary judgment**?

Summary judgment is a motion filed by a party, requesting that the court grant that party a judgment before the matter ever reaches trial. In a summary judgment motion, a party explains to the court why it should prevail as a matter of law and that

(e) Affidavits; Further Testimony.

(1) In General.

A supporting or opposing affidavit must be made on personal knowledge, set out facts that would be admissible in evidence, and show that the affiant is competent to testify on the matters stated. If a paper or part of a paper is referred to in an affidavit, a sworn or certified copy must be attached to or served with the affidavit. The court may permit an affidavit to be supplemented or opposed by depositions, answers to interrogatories, or additional affidavits.

(2) Opposing Party's Obligation to Respond.

When a motion for summary judgment is properly made and supported, an opposing party may not rely merely on allegations or denials in its own pleading; rather, its response must—by affidavits or as otherwise provided in this rule—set out specific facts showing a genuine issue for trial. If the opposing party does not so respond, summary judgment should, if appropriate, be entered against that party.

(f) When Affidavits Are Unavailable.

If a party opposing the motion shows by affidavit that, for specified reasons, it cannot present facts essential to justify its opposition, the court may:

(1) deny the motion;

(2) order a continuance to enable affidavits to be obtained, depositions to be taken, or other discovery to be undertaken; or

(3) issue any other just order.

(g) Affidavits Submitted in Bad Faith.

If satisfied that an affidavit under this rule is submitted in bad faith or solely for delay, the court must order the submitting party to pay the other party the reasonable expenses, including attorney's fees, it incurred as a result. An offending party or attorney may also be held in contempt.

there are no disputed issues of material fact that need to be decided by a jury. Remember that juries decide questions of fact and judges decide questions of law.

Throughout discovery, a party can establish facts and then explain why he or she should prevail. Most often defendants attempt to win cases on summary judgment, while plaintiffs hope to settle a case or take it to trial. In other words, plaintiffs hope to avoid summary judgment, while defendants attempt to win on summary judgment. This is not always the case, as sometimes plaintiffs will file summary judgment motions as well.

What are the **rules** of **civil procedure**?

The rules of civil procedure govern civil cases. There are separate rules of criminal procedure for federal cases. There are federal rules of civil procedure and rules of procedure in every state. They are similar but there are a few differences. These rules of civil procedure govern the requirements of pleadings, motions, the discovery process, and even the trial process.

What is a **pre-trial conference**?

A pre-trial conference is a meeting of the attorneys with the judge in the case to discuss the case. There are different purposes of pre-trial conferences. Sometimes judges use them to facilitate discovery, to expedite the case, to discourage certain pre-trial activities, to settle certain evidentiary disputes, and to facilitate a settlement of the case. Sometimes at a pre-trial conference, parties will agree to certain stipulations. If the parties stipulate to a fact, that fact is presumed valid and does not have to be covered or disputed at trial.

Some jurisdictions require the attorneys in a case to attend a settlement conference, in which each side discusses certain strengths and weaknesses of their case.

What happens at the **trial process**?

An initial step is that the court must empanel or sit a jury. In most locales, juries are composed of 12 members. But, the 12 must be selected from a much larger body of persons. Collectively, all prospective jurors comprise the jury pool.

The process of selecting a jury is known as *voir dire*. Attorneys ask questions of prospective jurors to determine if they have certain biases or outlooks that would be beneficial or detrimental to their client's case.

Can **attorneys challenge** certain **jurors**?

Yes, there are two basic types of challenges: (1) challenges for cause and (2) peremptory challenges. Challenges for cause occur when it is clear that a juror is too biased or predisposed in a case and could not decide the case impartially. There is no limit to for-cause challenges but usually it has to be pretty clear that the prospective juror is biased.

Peremptory challenges are those in which an attorney has a gut feeling that someone would not make a good juror for his side. The court sets the number of peremptory challenges in a case or the number may be established by a state's rules of civil procedure.

The court must select a jury before trial. This can be a long process, as the attorneys for each side have the right to challenge whether someone can be a juror (*iStock*).

Are there other **limits** on who can be **dismissed** and not **selected as jurors**?

Yes, many states have laws that limit the dismissal of blind persons as jurors. Texas law provides that a person's blindness cannot be the "sole reason" for their dismissal.

Are there any **limitations** on **peremptory challenges**?

Yes, attorneys may not dismiss jurors in a discriminatory way based on race, gender, or religion. The U.S. Supreme Court ruled in *Batson v. Kentucky* (1986) that it violates the equal protection clause of the Fourteenth Amendment to dismiss jurors based on race.

What **happens** during a **trial**?

The attorneys in the case begin with opening statements. In an opening statement, the attorney attempts to establish his or her client's basic theory of the case. Sometimes attorneys will reference upcoming evidence that the jury will hear.

After the opening statements, the plaintiff presents his or her "case in chief." The plaintiff calls his or her witnesses—in the order that the attorney wishes—and conducts direct examinations. Direct examination of a witness consists of a series of questions designed to elicit testimony favorable to the client and the client's theory of the case. During direct examination, the attorney is not supposed to ask leading questions, which essentially tell the witness how to answer or put words into the witness' mouth.

139

62.104. Disqualification for Legal Blindness

(a) A person who is legally blind is not disqualified to serve as a juror in a civil case solely because of his legal blindness except as provided by this section.

(b) A legally blind person is disqualified to serve as a juror in a civil case if, in the opinion of the court, his blindness renders him unfit to serve as a juror in that particular case.

(c) In this section, "legally blind" means having:

(1) no more than 20/200 of visual acuity in the better eye with correcting lenses; or

(2) visual acuity greater than 20/200, but with a limitation in the field of vision such that the widest diameter of the visual field subtends an angle no greater than 20 degrees.

However, after the plaintiff finishes with his direct examination, opposing counsel (for the defense) gets to cross-examine the witness. The cross-examination process is often more heated, as often the defense counsel and the plaintiff's witness are on opposite sides and there can be some antagonism displayed though the judge will maintain fairly tight control in most circumstances. During the examinations, opposing counsel will often make objections to certain questions. The attorneys then argue briefly why the questioning was admissible or not and the judge will make the final decision.

After cross-examination, a party can re-call their witness for redirect examination. Attorneys often use redirect examination to rehabilitate their witness who may have not fared well during the cross examination process.

At the conclusion of the plaintiff's case-in-chief, the defense often makes a motion for a directed verdict, or immediate judgment, contending that the plaintiff did not prove their case.

If the motion for a directed verdict is granted, the case is over. If the motion is not granted, then the defense presents his case-in-chief. The defense case proceeds like the plaintiff's case in terms of witnesses followed by direct examination, cross examination, and redirect examination.

What are **expert witnesses**?

Expert witnesses are those who have specialized knowledge in a particular field from education or personal experience that qualifies them to answer opinion questions.

Examples of expert witnesses are those who testify on accident reconstruction, ballistics, casino security, traffic engineering, and vocational rehabilitation. In some cases—such as medical malpractice—a person alleging negligence must come forward with expert proof that the medical provided failed to adhere to the proper standard of care.

What are **briefs**?

Briefs are one of the great misnomers in our legal system. The saying goes that "only a lawyer could write a 50-page document and call it a brief." Lawyers—particularly appellate lawyers—have to file a brief, explaining the legal arguments and explaining why the court should rule in their client's favor. Most courts have very specific rules on the length and style of briefs.

What are **jury instructions**?

One of the most important aspects of a case are when the judge instructs the jury. The judge reads a long document created by the judge with input from attorneys on each side that explains the various legal concepts in the case, the jurors' obligations and other issues.

The judge will have a standard jury instructions form for a particular type of case (auto accident case) but then will ask the attorneys if they want to submit proposed jury instructions. The judge then decides whether to accept the attorney's proposed jury instructions.

What are **closing arguments**?

Closing arguments are the last statements or speeches made by the attorneys to the jury before the jury goes back to deliberate. Closing arguments enable the attorney to sum up the evidence and make a last persuasive appeal to the jury.

If a party **loses**, what are his or her **legal options**?

A litigant can petition the court for a judgment notwithstanding the verdict, asking the judge to find that the jury's

The closing argument is when an attorney makes his last arguments before the jury deliberates on the case (*iStock*).

141

verdict clearly was against the weight of the evidence. A litigant can also petition the court for a new trial.

Realistically, the only option may be to appeal the verdict to a higher court. Appellate courts often deal mainly with questions of law but can also overrule a lower court if there is a clear factual error. Many legal errors are reviewed *de novo*, meaning that the higher court will give a fresh view to those issues.

Often a client will keep the same lawyer, but sometimes the client may want to hire an attorney who specializes in appellate advocacy—the art of arguing before appellate courts.

Why is **legal language** sometimes **hard to understand**?

The reason is that many lawyers still use much legal jargon, called legalese. Since the mid-1980s there has been a push among some in the legal profession for the so-called "Plain English" movement, which would attempt to make more legal product (statutes, judicial opinions, legal forms, etc.) more accessible and readable to the general public. The movement still has work to do to accomplish its goal.

CRIMINAL PROCEDURES

What is a **crime**?

A crime is a wrongful act that violates the norms or laws of society in which the perpetrator (if found guilty) receives some type of punishment. The word comes from the Latin word "crimen," which means accusation or guilt.

What **distinguishes criminal** law from **civil law**?

In criminal law, society—in the form of a government—brings an action against an individual for wrongful conduct. The purpose of a criminal action is punishment or societal retribution against those who have violated laws. In civil law, one party sues another for monetary damages or some other form of noncriminal relief. The purpose behind most civil law actions is compensation.

An individual's liberty is at stake in a criminal action brought by a government. In civil law, one party sues another, seeking not confinement but usually monetary damages. For example, *State v. Hudson* is a hypothetical criminal case where the state brings criminal charges against Hudson. *Jones v. Hudson* is a hypothetical civil case in which the party named Jones sues the party named Hudson. Criminal law cases are governed by rules of criminal procedure, while civil law cases are governed by the rules of civil procedure.

Perhaps the most important difference between criminal and civil law concerns the different burdens of proof. In a criminal case the prosecution has to prove that the defendant committed the crime beyond a reasonable doubt—a very high standard. In a civil case the normal standard is simply preponderance of the evidence, which means more likely than not.

What exactly does **"beyond a reasonable doubt"** mean?

Beyond a reasonable doubt is hard to quantify, but it basically means that the prosecution has removed nearly all doubts as to whether the defendant committed the crime. Many states define reasonable doubt in their codes or in their common law (in their judicial opinions). For example, an Ohio law defines "reasonable doubt" as follows:

> "Reasonable doubt" is present when the jurors, after they have carefully considered and compared all the evidence, cannot say they are firmly convinced of the truth of the charge. It is a doubt based on reason and common sense. Reasonable doubt is not mere possible doubt, because everything relating to human affairs or depending on moral evidence is open to some possible or imaginary doubt. "Proof beyond a reasonable doubt" is proof of such character that an ordinary person would be willing to rely and act upon it in the most important of the person's own affairs.

Is a **trial judge required** to give a **definition** of **beyond** a **reasonable doubt**?

The trial judge must explain the concept of beyond a reasonable doubt to jurors. This is a basic requirement of due process. The U.S. Supreme Court explained in *Victor v. Nebraska* (1994) that "so long as the court instructs the jury on the necessity that the defendant's guilt be proved beyond a reasonable doubt, the Constitution does not require that any particular form of words be used in advising the jury of the government's burden of proof."

What are the basic types of crimes?

Crimes are divided into three basic categories: (1) felonies, (2) misdemeanors, and (3) infractions. Felonies are the most serious offenses that lead to longer-term confinement. The basic rule is that any crime from which a person can serve a year or more in jail is a felony. Misde-

Murder, the most heinous of crimes, is categorized as a felony (*iStock*).

meanors are less serious criminal offenses for which the person usually receives a fine or a jail term of less than a year. Finally, infractions are very petty crimes—generally at the local level—for which a person usually only has to pay a fine and not serve any jail time.

Many states further subdivide felonies and misdemeanors into different classes.

Who determines whether conduct constitutes a **felony** or a **misdemeanor**?

Legislative, executive, and judicial branches all have a role to play in this important determination. The primary responsibility falls with the legislative branch, as the legislature classifies certain offenses as either felonies or misdemeanors. The legislature—at the federal, state or local level—may set penalties for certain offenses. Thus, the crime of murder is a felony established by law. However, a law may provide a range of penalties for certain conduct—such as possession of marijuana—that may constitute either a felony or a misdemeanor.

However, the executive and judicial branches still have a role in what offense a person is charged and/or convicted. For example, a prosecutor—a member of the executive branch—often has the discretion to determine whether certain conduct should be prosecuted as a felony or misdemeanor. This is referred to as prosecutorial discretion. Oftentimes, a criminal defendant's attorney may bargain with the prosecutor's office—a process called plea bargaining—in an attempt to have the defendant plead guilty to a misdemeanor rather than a felony.

The judicial branch also has a role to play in whether a defendant is sentenced to a felony or misdemeanor. The jury will decide whether a defendant's conduct fits into one crime or another, while the judge often will impose a sentence pursuant to the jury's findings.

What are **examples** of **crimes** that constitute **felonies**?

The more serious crimes are felonies. These include murder, kidnapping, rape, arson, sexual assault, and burglary. Generally speaking, serious crimes that involve harm to persons will be classified as felonies.

What are the legal **results** of a **felony conviction**?

Obviously, a person convicted of a felony will be imprisoned for a certain amount of time. Furthermore, some states have so-called "three strikes laws" where a third felony conviction could lead to a life sentence even if the specific crime in question in isolation called for a much shorter sentence.

But, there are collateral consequences of a felony conviction that attach to a person after he or she has served his or her sentence. These collateral consequences vary from state to state. In many states, a person convicted of a felony cannot vote, cannot serve on juries, or own a firearm. They may not be able to hold down certain jobs or engage in certain professions. As a practical reality, it is much more difficult for a person convicted of a felony to obtain a job than for someone who does not have such a serious criminal record.

All of these are reasons why if a person is charged with a crime, he or she should consider any agreement with the prosecution that would require them to plead guilty only to a misdemeanor.

What is a **wobbler**?

A wobbler is a hybrid crime that can constitute either a felony or misdemeanor under state law. The U.S. Supreme Court explained in *Ewing v. California* (1998) that "under California law, a 'wobbler' is presumptively a felony and remains a felony except when the discretion is actually exercised to make the crime a misdemeanor." The designation is vitally important in criminal law, as multiple felony convictions can lead to a much longer sentence than multiple misdemeanor convictions.

LegalSpeak:
What are some examples of how states define first degree murder?

In the state of Tennessee, the statute (39-13-202) is as follows:

(a) First degree murder is:

(1) A premeditated and intentional killing of another;

(2) A killing of another committed in the perpetration of or attempt to perpetrate any first degree murder, act of terrorism, arson, rape, robbery, burglary, theft, kidnapping, aggravated child abuse, aggravated child neglect, rape of a child, aggravated rape of a child or aircraft piracy; or

(3) A killing of another committed as the result of the unlawful throwing, placing or discharging of a destructive device or bomb.

(b) No culpable mental state is required for conviction under subdivision (a)(2) or (a)(3), except the intent to commit the enumerated offenses or acts in those subdivisions.

(c) A person convicted of first degree murder shall be punished by:

(1) Death;

(2) Imprisonment for life without possibility of parole; or

(3) Imprisonment for life.

(d) As used in subdivision (a)(1), "premeditation" is an act done after the exercise of reflection and judgment. "Premeditation" means that the intent to kill must have been formed prior to the act itself. It is not necessary that the purpose to kill pre-exist in the mind of the accused for any definite period of time. The mental state of the accused at the time the accused allegedly decided to kill must be carefully considered in order to determine whether the accused was sufficiently free from excitement and passion as to be capable of premeditation.

The Missouri statute (565.020), which does not apply to persons under 16 years of age, reads:

1. A person commits the crime of murder in the first degree if he knowingly causes the death of another person after deliberation upon the matter.

2. Murder in the first degree is a class A felony, and the punishment shall be either death or imprisonment for life without eligibility for probation or parole, or release except by act of the governor; except that, if a person has not reached his sixteenth birthday at the time of the commission of the crime, the punishment shall be imprisonment for life without eligibility for probation or parole, or release except by act of the governor.

What **felonies** can lead to the **death penalty**?

Murder is the crime that can lead to the death penalty. It used to be that other very serious felonies—such as rape—could lead to the ultimate punishment, but the U.S. Supreme Court ruled that rape that did not result in death could not be punishable by death. There are, however, different classifications of murder.

There is first-degree murder, second-degree murder, voluntary manslaughter, involuntary manslaughter, criminally negligent homicide, and vehicular homicide. Different states will have differences in their classifications.

The most serious charge is first-degree murder, which in most states can be punishable by death. Other common sentences for first-degree murder are life in prison without the possibility of parole and life with parole. In some states, such as Missouri, the only penalties for first-degree murder are death and life imprisonment without the possibility of parole.

THE CRIMINAL PROCESS

How does the **criminal process begin**?

That is a difficult question to answer, as the process begins differently depending on the situation. Generally, the process begins with law enforcement officials (the police) investigating a person for suspicion of committing a crime or crimes. However, sometimes the process may begin when the police actually see a person committing a crime.

What is an **arrest**?

An arrest is a process in which the police detain or seize a person or deprive them of their liberty for committing a criminal offense. Often when police officers arrest people, they take them into custody.

What **warnings must** the **police give** you when they **arrest** you and place you in **custody**?

The police must give you so-called Miranda warnings, which consist of you telling you several things: (1) that you have the right to remain silent and that anything you say can be used against you in court; (2) that you have the right to an attorney even if you cannot afford an attorney. The police must "Mirandize" you before they interrogate you, meaning that they must inform of the right to remain silent and the right to an attorney.

Oftentimes, if the police fail to give a suspect his or her Miranda warnings, then any subsequent confession cannot be used against the suspect.

Being arrested means you are being detained, not necessarily that you are guilty. Police must read you your Miranda warnings, which explain your rights to legal representation and that anything you say can be used against you in court (*iStock*).

When a person is arrested and **taken into custody**, what happens **next**?

After a person is arrested and taken into custody, they are taken through the booking process. This process consists of providing information to a desk clerk (such as name, social security number, and driver's license information), the taking of a photograph called a mug shot, the collection of the suspect's personal property, and fingerprinting. Often times the police will then search a person. This consists of an invasive search, called a body cavity search, to make sure there are no hidden weapons or drugs. Finally, oftentimes jail officials will do a quick health screen of the person.

Is a **person entitled** to an **attorney** during the **booking process**?

No, the booking process is considered an administrative, rather than adjudicative, proceeding. The booking process is a routine process where officials obtain identification information. However, suspects must be careful not to reveal incriminating information to police officers. Statements to police made during the booking process can later be used at trial.

After a person is **booked**, what happens **next**?

Shortly after the booking process, the suspect is brought before a magistrate or judge—sometimes in person and sometimes via closed circuit television. At this procedure—called an initial appearance or first appearance—the magistrate determines if the police had probable cause to arrest the suspect (if there was no arrest warrant), sets bail, and assigns legal counsel if the defendant cannot afford counsel and the charge is serious enough to warrant jail time. This appearance usually takes place within 24 hours or 48 hours of the initial arrest. Other states provide different time limits for when this appearance must take place.

Is there a **difference** between the **initial appearance** and the **arraignment**?

There is at the federal level. In a federal criminal case the federal rules of criminal procedure require "a person making an arrest within the United States must take the defendant without unnecessary delay before a magistrate judge or before a state or local judicial officer." This must take place very soon after the arrest. The arraignment then takes place later.

Federal Requirements at Arraignment: Federal Rule of Criminal Procedure 10(a) states the following:

(a) In General.

An arraignment must be conducted in open court and must consist of:

(1) ensuring that the defendant has a copy of the indictment or information;

(2) reading the indictment or information to the defendant or stating to the defendant the substance of the charge; and then

(3) asking the defendant to plead to the indictment or information.

What is **bail**?

Bail refers to money or security paid to the court in order to secure the temporary release of a defendant charged with a crime. The defendant—or the friend or family of the defendant—pays money to the court in the promise that the defendant will reappear for the next court hearing in the case. Historically, bail did not require the delivery of money, but a person would serve as a surety and promise that the defendant would appear for later court dates.

What are the **purposes** or reasons for **bail**?

Bail lessens or reduces the chances that innocent persons will be detained in jail. It also reduces hardship on the defendant and the defendant's family members. Bail also gives a defendant the opportunity to get his or her affairs in order, hire a lawyer, and mount an effective defense. Bail also serves institutional purposes in that it can help to reduce crowding of jails.

Except for the most serious crimes, accused people who are put in jail have the option of paying bail in many cases so that they can more easily prepare their cases and get their affairs in order before the trial (*iStock*).

Are **all persons** charged with crimes **entitled** to **bail**?

No, if a crime is serious enough or the defendant is considered to be a flight risk, a judge does not have to provide bail. This means that the defendant will stay detained pending the outcome of the criminal process. Some states also have laws that provide for a list of non-bailable offenses.

What **factors** do courts use to determine whether someone is **entitled to bail** and what **amount**?

States vary in the factors they consider in determining the availability and amount of bail. Some commonly considered factors include: the length of time the defendant has resided in the community, the defendant's employment status in the community, the financial history and resources of the defendant, whether the defendant has ever skipped a court hearing before, the defendant's reputation and character, the criminal history of the defendant, whether the defendant poses a risk to the community, and the seriousness of the underlying offense.

Are there **constitutional limitations** to **bail**?

Yes, the Eighth Amendment of the U.S. Constitution provides in part that "excessive bail shall not be required."

LegalSpeak: Non-Bailable Offenses in Arizona

A.R.S. § 13-3961 (2008)

Offenses not bailable; purpose; preconviction; exceptions:

A. A person who is in custody shall not be admitted to bail if the proof is evident or the presumption great that the person is guilty of the offense charged and the offense charged is one of the following:

   1. A capital offense.

   2. Sexual assault.

   3. Sexual conduct with a minor who is under fifteen years of age.

   4. Molestation of a child who is under fifteen years of age.

   5. A serious felony offense if there is probable cause to believe that the person has entered or remained in the United States illegally.

How does a court determine if **bail** is **excessive**?

A court examines whether the bail amount is much higher than the state interests involved in setting bail in the first place. As a practical matter, constitutional-based challenges to bail (arguing that the bail violates the "Excessive Bail" clause of the Eighth Amendment) are not very successful. The more successful challenges are that a court did not follow the state or federal statute providing for bail. Under the federal law known as the Bail Reform Act of 2004, a judge "shall order the pretrial release of the person on personal recognizance, or upon execution of an unsecured appearance bond in an amount specified by the court … unless the judicial officer determines that such release will not reasonably assure the appearance of the person as required or will endanger the safety of any other person or the community."

What is a **bail bondsman**?

A bail bondsman is a private individual who issues a bond to the court, ensuring that the defendant will appear in court even if released on bond. The defendant then has to pay the bail bondsman a fee—typically 10% of the bond—and agrees to appear in court for the court hearings. The 10% fee paid to the bail bondsman is generally nonrefundable.

Who appoints an **attorney** for a criminal **defendant**?

The court appoints attorneys for those criminal defendants who do not have sufficient funds to pay for their own attorney. Individuals always have the option to pay for their own attorney who will represent them. However, many individuals charged with crimes do not have the resources to pay for legal representation. Many attorneys make

LegalSpeak: *Stack v. Boyle* (1951)

Unless this right to bail before trial is preserved, the presumption of innocence, secured only after centuries of struggle, would lose its meaning.

The right to release before trial is conditioned upon the accused's giving adequate assurance that he will stand trial and submit to sentence if found guilty. Like the ancient practice of securing the oaths of responsible persons to stand as sureties for the accused, the modern practice of requiring a bail bond or the deposit of a sum of money subject to forfeiture serves as additional assurance of the presence of an accused. Bail set at a figure higher than an amount reasonably calculated to fulfill this purpose is "excessive" under the Eighth Amendment.

Since the function of bail is limited, the fixing of bail for any individual defendant must be based upon standards relevant to the purpose of assuring the presence of that defendant.

at least a part of their living off of appointed cases. Many jurisdictions have appointment lists from which judges will select attorneys for representation.

Who was **Gideon** and who eventually was his **appointed counsel**?

Clarence Earl Gideon was the criminal defendant in the famous case *Gideon v. Wainwright* (1963). Gideon allegedly broke into a Florida pool hall to steal money. This criminal act earned him felony charges and later a conviction in Florida state court. In the beginning of the case, Gideon asked the court for a lawyer. The trial judge responded that under Florida law the only criminal defendants entitled to a court-appointed lawyer were those defendants facing capital (death-penalty) charges. Gideon insisted that "the United States Supreme Court says I am entitled to be represented by Counsel."

Gideon appealed his case all the way to the United States Supreme Court. The Court accepted his case for review and appointed him a Washington, D.C.-based attorney named Abe Fortas to represent Gideon before the Court. Ironically, Fortas later became a United States Supreme Court Justice.

As alluded to earlier, Gideon's case spurred action by the U.S. Congress which required in every federal judicial district a system to create proper legal representation for criminal defendants.

What is the **right to counsel**?

The "right to counsel" means that a criminal defendant who faces imprisonment is entitled to an attorney whether he or she can afford an attorney. This right is constitutionally based in the Sixth Amendment's "assistance of counsel." (See chapter two on the Bill of Rights, especially the Sixth Amendment.) The U.S. Supreme Court provided that this Sixth Amendment-based right was extended to state court defendants charged with felonies in the case *Gideon v. Wainwright* (1963; see LegalSpeak above). In that decision, Justice Hugo Black explained that attorneys in criminal cases were "necessities, not luxuries."

Are all **criminal defendants entitled** to a **court-appointed attorney**?

No, not all criminal defendants are entitled to an attorney. A person has to face jail or prison time in order to qualify for an attorney. This means that if you receive a traffic ticket or some other citation or infraction (the terminology varies from state to state) that does have the possibility of leading to jail time, then the court does not have to appoint you an attorney. In basic terms, if you are charged with a felony or most misdemeanors, then you are entitled to an attorney. If you face only a fine, then you are not entitled to a court-appointed attorney.

How do you **qualify** for a **court-appointed attorney**?

You must be facing possible imprisonment for your alleged crime. But, you also must be indigent as defined by applicable state rules. In other words, the court must deem you to be financially unable to afford your own attorney. Most states define indigency in their rules of criminal procedure. For example, Florida Rule of Criminal Procedure

American citizens have the right to legal counsel, even if they cannot afford to pay for their own defense. This right is guaranteed under the Sixth Amendment (*iStock*).

defines an indigent as "a person who is unable to pay for the services of an attorney, including costs of investigation, without substantial hardship to the person or the person's family." Some states, like Florida, also provide that individuals who are "partially indigent" can also receive a court-appointed attorney.

In many states the court will require a criminal defendant to take an oath and fill out an "affidavit of indigency" showing that he or she does not have the financial means to hire his or her own private attorney. The judge may ask the defendant questions to determine if he or she answered the questions truthfully in the affidavit.

Why does a **criminal defendant** need an **attorney**?

Justice Black expressed it best in *Gideon v. Wainwright* (1963; see LegalSpeak p. 154) when he wrote that an attorney in a criminal case is a necessity. A criminal defense attorney will be able to investigate a case, often hiring a trained investigator who is essential to establishing a proper defense or attacking the prosecution's theory of the case. A criminal defense attorney also knows the lawyers in the prosecutor's or district attorney's office and likely would be able to negotiate a much better plea agreement than a self-represented defendant. Also, criminal defense attorneys will know the law better and be able to make constitutional-based or statutory-based arguments that a layperson would simply now know. Simply stated, a criminal defense attorney knows the ins and outs of the criminal law far better than a layperson.

Can a person choose to **waive or decline counsel** and represent himself or herself?

Yes, a criminal defendant can decide to waive or decline counsel and represent himself in a criminal case. Federal law has provided for the right of self-representation since the Judiciary Act of 1789. The right of self-representation also applies to state court defendants. Most state constitutions explicitly provide for this right of self-representation. Even in those states that do not provide so in the state constitution, it is a right recognized either by a statute or in the common law (case law).

The U.S. Supreme Court recognized this right for a state-court defendant charged with grand auto theft in *Farretta v. California* (1975). The Court reasoned that historically the colonies had protected the right of self-representation and the Court reasoned that the Sixth Amendment right to counsel should be interpreted to have the right not to have unwanted counsel foisted upon a defendant.

What else takes place at the arraignment?

At the initial appearance or arraignment, the judge will inform the defendant of the charges and then ask the defendant if he or she has a plea. The defendant often will then enter a plea of guilty or not guilty or *nolo contendere*. If the defendant enters a plea of not guilty, then the court will set a date for the next court appearance, which could be a preliminary hearing in the case of felony charges.

Does the **defendant** have to **physically appear** before a judge at the **initial appearance** and the **arraignment**?

It depends on the individual state. Many states have laws that allow the use of "two-way electronic audio-video communication" between the defendant and the judge. Mississippi law provides that a defendant can appear via "closed circuit television or Web cam." Other states, such as Montana, have a provision that allows a judge to order the defendant to be physically present for the initial appearance.

What happens if the **defendant pleads guilty**?

If the defendant pleads guilty, then the judge will set a date for sentencing. At the sentencing date, the judge will then impose the time period that the defendant will have to serve or whatever other form of punishment the judge deems appropriate. In other cases, particularly those that involve less serious and less violent crimes, the judge will go ahead and impose the sentence at the initial appearance.

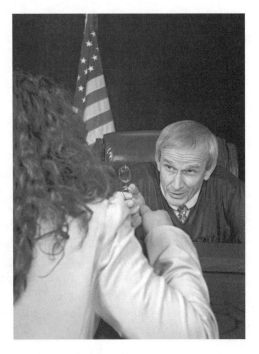

In most cases, a defendant must appear in person before a judge, but some states allow the use of electronic audio-video communications to get the job done (*iStock*).

What is the process of **plea bargaining**?

Plea bargaining is a process in which the prosecuting attorney and the defense attorney bargain over the sentence to be imposed on the defendant. This process can occur at the time of the initial appearance all the way up to the time that the trial is supposed to take place. Usually, the plea bargaining process results in a defendant pleading guilty to a lesser charge. In other words, a defendant takes a plea to ensure a lesser sentence than if the case goes to trial and the jury issues a guilty verdict, which could lead to a much longer sentence. Thus, plea bargaining normally results in a reduced sentence for the defendant.

What **role** does a **judge** have with respect to **plea bargaining**?

The judge has the option of approving the plea agreement. Many states have laws that provide that the judge must determine that there is a factual basis for the plea. The judge must also determine that the defendant voluntarily accepts the plea agreement. The U.S. Supreme Court made it a constitutional requirement in

LegalSpeak: *Boykin v. Alabama* (1969)

It was error, plain on the face of the record, for the trial judge to accept petitioner's guilty plea without an affirmative showing that it was intelligent and voluntary. That error, under Alabama procedure, was properly before the court below and considered explicitly by a majority of the justices and is properly before us on review.

A plea of guilty is more than a confession which admits that the accused did various acts; it is itself a conviction; nothing remains but to give judgment and determine punishment.. Admissibility of a confession must be based on a "reliable determination on the voluntariness issue which satisfies the constitutional rights of the defendant." The requirement that the prosecution spread on the record the prerequisites of a valid waiver is no constitutional innovation. In *Carnley v. Cochran*, 369 U.S. 506, 516, we dealt with a problem of waiver of the right to counsel, a Sixth Amendment right. We held: "Presuming waiver from a silent record is impermissible. The record must show, or there must be an allegation and evidence which show, that an accused was offered counsel but intelligently and understandingly rejected the offer. Anything less is not waiver.

We think that the same standard must be applied to determining whether a guilty plea is voluntarily made. For, as we have said, a plea of guilty is more than an admission of conduct; it is a conviction. Ignorance, incomprehension, coercion, terror, inducements, subtle or blatant threats might be a perfect cover-up of unconstitutionality. The question of an effective waiver of a federal constitutional right in a proceeding is of course governed by federal standards.

Several federal constitutional rights are involved in a waiver that takes place when a plea of guilty is entered in a state criminal trial. First, is the privilege against compulsory self-incrimination guaranteed by the Fifth Amendment and applicable to the States by reason of the Fourteenth. Second, is the right to trial by jury. Third, is the right to confront one's accusers. We cannot presume a waiver of these three important federal rights from a silent record.

What is at stake for an accused facing death or imprisonment demands the utmost solicitude of which courts are capable in canvassing the matter with the accused to make sure he has a full understanding of what the plea connotes and of its consequence. When the judge discharges that function, he leaves a record adequate for any review that may be later sought, and forestalls the spin-off of collateral proceedings that seek to probe murky memories.

Defendants can sometimes plea bargain down to a more lenient sentence. By doing so, courts can save time and money (*iStock*).

Boykin v. Alabama (1969) for judges to ensure that a defendant's plea of guilty was truly voluntary.

What are the **benefits** of **plea bargaining**?

The primary benefit of plea bargaining from the defendant's perspective is the opportunity to receive a much shorter sentence. Another benefit of plea bargaining is that it saves resources. The criminal courts are often crowded, prosecutors' workloads are demanding, and it also saves the time of police officers, who do not have to make it to as many court appearances.

What are **possible disadvantages** of **plea bargaining**?

The disadvantages of plea bargaining include abandoning the traditional system of adversary justice in a courtroom trial, the possibility of manipulation of defendants by prosecutors, and great disparity in sentences. Some critics charge that the plea bargaining process also leads to criminal defendants receiving overly lenient sentences.

Once a prosecutor offers a **plea bargain** can he or she **renege** on the deal?

No, the U.S. Supreme Court made clear in *Santobello v. New York* (1971; see Legal-Speak p. 160) that a prosecutor cannot renege on a plea agreement once the agree-

LegalSpeak: *Santobello v. New York* (1971)

The disposition of criminal charges by agreement between the prosecutor and the accused, sometimes loosely called "plea bargaining," is an essential component of the administration of justice. Properly administered, it is to be encouraged. If every criminal charge were subjected to a full-scale trial, the States and the Federal Government would need to multiply by many times the number of judges and court facilities.

Disposition of charges after plea discussions is not only an essential part of the process but a highly desirable part for many reasons. It leads to prompt and largely final disposition of most criminal cases; it avoids much of the corrosive impact of enforced idleness during pretrial confinement for those who are denied release pending trial; it protects the public from those accused persons who are prone to continue criminal conduct even while on pretrial release; and, by shortening the time between charge and disposition, it enhances whatever may be the rehabilitative prospects of the guilty when they are ultimately imprisoned.

ment has been reached. The Court explained that a prosecutor must fulfill the promises made to a defendant, writing that: "a constant factor is that when a plea rests in any significant degree on a promise or agreement of the prosecutor, so that it can be said to be part of the inducement or consideration, such promise must be fulfilled."

Does a **judge have** to **accept** a **plea bargain** and give the defendant the sentence offered by the prosecution?

No, a judge does not have to accept a plea bargain reached between the prosecution and the defense. The U.S. Supreme Court wrote in *Santobello v. New York* (1971; see LegalSpeak p. 160) that: "There is, of course, no absolute right to have a guilty plea accepted." The Nevada Supreme Court explained in a recent case: "Judicial power to reject plea bargains serves to modify and condition the absolute power of the prosecutor, consistent with the doctrine of separation of powers, by establishing a check on the abuse of prosecutorial (executive) prerogatives." However, as a matter of course, judges most of the time accept plea bargains. Courts ordinarily do not second-guess prosecutorial decisions in the plea-bargaining process.

What is **an information**?

An information is a document which includes an accusation of formal charges of criminal conduct against a defendant. It is a common method of introducing criminal charges against defendants in many states. The prosecution files the information and a

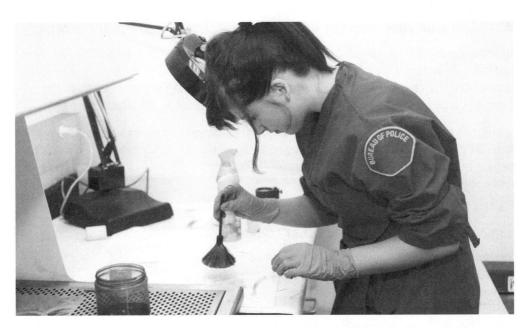

A forensic scientist tests for fingerprints. A possible lack of evidence tying the accused to a crime is one preliminary hearings are held to decide if a case should go to trial (*iStock*).

judge considers the information at a preliminary hearing. This is the most common method of proceeding with the prosecution of criminal cases in many states and differs greatly from the grand jury process. In many states a prosecutor has the option of proceeding with an information or with a grand jury indictment.

What is a **preliminary hearing**?

A preliminary hearing is a court hearing conducted before trial in which a defendant can challenge whether the prosecution has probable cause that the defendant committed the crime in question. The preliminary hearing serves as a screening mechanism to ensure that the proper cases go forward to trial. At the end of the preliminary hearing, the judge decides whether there is enough evidence for the case to go forward.

Does a defendant have a **right** to a **preliminary hearing** in **state court**?

It depends on individual state law. Some states require preliminary hearings in most all cases. Other states require preliminary hearings in certain felony cases. For example, Colorado provides that all defendants charged with a class 1, 2, or 3 felony have a right to demand a preliminary hearing. In South Dakota, a defendant has a right to a preliminary hearing if charged with a felony or the most serious type of misdemeanor charge. The South Dakota law provides: "No defendant is entitled to a preliminary hearing unless charged with an offense punishable as a felony or class 1 misdemeanor."

What does a **defense attorney** hope to accomplish at a **preliminary hearing**?

In some cases, the defense attorney may hope to dismiss the case altogether by showing that the prosecution does not have probable cause to believe that the defendant committed the crime. In other words, sometimes the goal for the defense at the preliminary hearing is victory—getting the charges dismissed by a judge.

Other times, however, the defense might use the preliminary hearing to see what types of witnesses and/or evidence the prosecution has. In other words, defense attorneys sometimes use the preliminary hearing as a strategic testing ground to find out more about the prosecution's case.

Can a defendant **waive** a **preliminary hearing**?

Yes, a defendant can waive a preliminary hearing. In some cases, the defendant may intend to plead guilty and does not wish to attract any more publicity or attention to a case.

What is a **grand jury**?

A grand jury is a body of citizens, usually in groups of 16 to 23, who decide whether a prosecutor has presented enough evidence to obtain an indictment of an individual. Grand juries are designed to serve as a type of buffer between the prosecution and the defendant. Critics charge that grand juries—more often than not—do not serve this ideal buffering function and instead serve as a rubber stamp for the prosecution. There is a famous saying about grand juries that reflects this sentiment—"a grand jury will indict a ham sandwich."

Grand jurors take an oath of secrecy because grand jury proceedings are not public (*iStock*).

Grand juries are distinct from trial juries—or petit or trial juries—which usually consist of 12 people. Sometimes prosecutors use the grand jury method of initiating criminal charges against individuals, rather than filing what an accusatory document—called an information—and proceeding with a preliminary hearing. The grand jury serves as a screening mechanism to determine whether the prosecutor has enough evidence to obtain what is known as a true bill. If the grand jury decides there is no evidence, it would issue what is called a no bill. Grand juries are used in federal court and in some states. Most states explain the operational workings and functions of the grand jury in their rules of criminal procedure.

What are **other** distinguishing **features** of a **grand jury**?

Perhaps the most distinguishing feature of a grand jury is its secrecy. Grand jury proceedings are not public and grand jurors are required to take an oath about secrecy. Another distinguishing feature is that traditional rules of evidence do not apply in the grand jury setting. Prosecutors are able to present evidence that might be excluded at trial for being hearsay. Grand juries also have the power to compel witnesses to testify.

The grand jury usually is composed of more citizens than the petit jury. In Texas, however, grand jurors are composed of 12 jurors. Second, the grand jury only hears from the prosecutor, not the defense. The prosecutor decides what witnesses to call and which individuals receive immunity for their grand jury testimony. The subject or target of a grand jury is not allowed to bring an attorney and present evidence. The grand jury has broad powers to subpoena witnesses, including the defendant. The defendant can assert his Fifth Amendment right against self-incrimination at the grand jury proceeding.

If the grand jury **refuses to indict** can the **prosecutor re-file**?

Yes, in most states a prosecutor can seek an indictment with another grand jury if the first grand jury refuses to issue a true bill for an indictment. In some states the prosecutor must come forward with new evidence in order to pursue another indictment.

TRIAL PROCESS

If the case **proceeds to trial** what happens next?

If the case proceeds to trial, there will be pre-trial hearings in which the court will decide questions related to trial management and also decide motions *in limine*—which are pre-trial motions to exclude certain evidence.

Is a defendant **entitled** to a **jury trial**?

Yes, if a case goes to trial and the defendant faces imprisonment, the Sixth Amendment guarantees that criminal defendants have a right to trial by jury. The exception is for so-called petty crimes that cannot result in imprisonment for very long.

Can a defendant **waive** his or her **right** to a **jury**?

Yes, a criminal defendant can waive his or her right to a trial by jury and proceed with a bench (trial only by a judge) trial. This usually is not advisable, as the defendant probably has a better chance before a jury. The vast majority of jurisdictions require that juries be unanimous, which holds out the possibility that a few jurors will not go along with other jury members and vote to convict. Furthermore, defense attorneys have a large role in selecting the jury, which can be to the advantage of their clients.

What is **voir dire**?

Voir dire is the process of selecting a jury. This process occurs in those cases in which there is the need for a jury, as opposed to a bench trial where the judge serves as the jury. In the voir dire process, prosecutors and defense attorneys ask members of the

or affection, or for any reward, or the promise or hope thereof, but that you will present the truth, the whole truth, and nothing but the truth, according to the best of your skill and understanding. So help you God.

(5) Charge to the Grand Jury.

After the grand jury has been impaneled and sworn, the judge shall instruct it concerning its powers and duties and the relevant law....

(d) Powers of the Grand Jury.

The grand jury has inquisitorial powers over-and has the authority to return a presentment-of all indictable or presentable offenses found to have been committed or to be triable within the county. At all proper hours, the grand jurors are entitled to free access to all county offices and buildings and to examine, without charge, all records and other papers of any county officers in any way connected with the grand jurors' duties.

(e) Duties of the Grand Jury.

It is the duty of the grand jury to:

(1) inquire into, consider, and act on all criminal cases submitted to it by the district attorney general;

(2) inquire into any report of a criminal offense brought to its attention by a member of the grand jury;

(3) inquire into the condition and management of prisons and other county buildings and institutions within the county;

(4) inquire into the condition of the county treasury;

(5) inquire into the correctness and sufficiency of county officers' bonds;

(6) inquire into any state or local officers' abuse of office;and

(7) report the results of its actions to the court.

jury pool questions to determine whether or not they want those jurors to remain on the jury pool. In federal court, the judge often asks most of the questions. For example, if a prospective juror clearly indicates that they are biased either for or against law enforcement officials that would send a clear signal to the attorneys as to whether they would want that juror to serve.

What types of **challenges** are available to **strike jurors**?

There are two types of challenges to remove prospective jurors. The first is a for-cause challenge. These are used to remove those people who clearly evince an

These principles support our conclusion that a defendant may establish a *prima facie* case of purposeful discrimination in selection of the petit jury solely on evidence concerning the prosecutor's exercise of peremptory challenges at the defendant's trial. To establish such a case, the defendant first must show that he is a member of a cognizable racial group, and that the prosecutor has exercised peremptory challenges to remove from the venire members of the defendant's race. Second, the defendant is entitled to rely on the fact, as to which there can be no dispute, that peremptory challenges constitute a jury selection practice that permits "those to discriminate who are of a mind to discriminate." Finally, the defendant must show that these facts and any other relevant circumstances raise an inference that the prosecutor used that practice to exclude the veniremen from the petit jury on account of their race. This combination of factors in the empaneling of the petit jury, as in the selection of the venire, raises the necessary inference of purposeful discrimination.

In deciding whether the defendant has made the requisite showing, the trial court should consider all relevant circumstances. For example, a "pattern" of strikes against black jurors included in the particular venire might give rise to an inference of discrimination. Similarly, the prosecutor's questions and statements during voir dire examination and in exercising his challenges may support or refute an inference of discriminatory purpose. These examples are merely illustrative. We have confidence that trial judges, experienced in supervising voir dire, will

obvious bias and cannot decide a case impartially. If there was an auto accident case involving an insurance company and a prospective juror exclaimed during voir dire—"I hate insurance companies." That might be enough for the presiding judge to find that the person could not decide the case impartially and could be dismissed for cause.

The other type of challenge is a peremptory challenge. This means that an attorney can strike the juror peremptorily for any reason, such as simply a hunch that the person would not be a good juror for their side. While lawyers have broad leeway with their peremptory challenges, they do have unfettered discretion. The U.S. Supreme Court ruled in *Batson v. Kentucky* (1986; see LegalSpeak, above)—a burglary case involving defendant James Batson—that prosecutors violated the Equal Protection Clause of the Fourteenth Amendment by striking jurors based on race. Later, in *J.E.B. v. Alabama* (1994) the Court also ruled that attorneys could not exercise their peremptory challenges in a gender discriminatory way.

be able to decide if the circumstances concerning the prosecutor's use of peremptory challenges creates a *prima facie* case of discrimination against black jurors.

Once the defendant makes a *prima facie* showing, the burden shifts to the State to come forward with a neutral explanation for challenging black jurors. Though this requirement imposes a limitation in some cases on the full peremptory character of the historic challenge, we emphasize that the prosecutor's explanation need not rise to the level justifying exercise of a challenge for cause.... Just as the Equal Protection Clause forbids the States to exclude black persons from the venire on the assumption that blacks as a group are unqualified to serve as jurors, so it forbids the States to strike black veniremen on the assumption that they will be biased in a particular case simply because the defendant is black. The core guarantee of equal protection, ensuring citizens that their State will not discriminate on account of race, would be meaningless were we to approve the exclusion of jurors on the basis of such assumptions, which arise solely from the jurors' race. Nor may the prosecutor rebut the defendant's case merely by denying that he had a discriminatory motive or "affirm[ing] [his] good faith in making individual selections." If these general assertions were accepted as rebutting a defendant's *prima facie* case, the Equal Protection Clause "would be but a vain and illusory requirement." The prosecutor therefore must articulate a neutral explanation related to the particular case to be tried. The trial court then will have the duty to determine if the defendant has established purposeful discrimination.

What is a **Batson challenge**?

A Batson challenge is a challenge filed by a defense attorney that the prosecution has struck jurors in a racially discriminatory manner. When a Batson challenge is made and the defense is able to show that jurors were struck apparently on race, the prosecutor must then offer a race-neutral explanation for the decision. For example, if the prosecutor struck the lone African-American juror from the panel, the prosecutor might respond that he or she struck that juror because the person refused to make eye contact. Refusal to make eye contact likely would suffice as a sufficient, race-neutral explanation.

Are there an **unlimited number** of **peremptory challenges**?

No, there are a certain number of peremptory challenges according to various state laws and the type of case. Federal Rule of Criminal Procedure provides that each side

LegalSpeak: *Ballew v. Georgia* (1978)

First, recent empirical data suggest that progressively smaller juries are less likely to foster effective group deliberation. At some point, this decline leads to inaccurate fact-finding and incorrect application of the common sense of the community to the facts. Generally, a positive correlation exists between group size and the quality of both group performance and group productivity. A variety of explanations have been offered for this conclusion. Several are particularly applicable in the jury setting. The smaller the group, the less likely are members to make critical contributions necessary for the solution of a given problem. Because most juries are not permitted to take notes, memory is important for accurate jury deliberations. As juries decrease in size, then, they are less likely to have members who remember each of the important pieces of evidence or argument. Furthermore, the smaller the group, the less likely it is to overcome the biases of its members to obtain an accurate result. When individual and group decisionmaking were compared, it was seen that groups performed better because prejudices of individuals were frequently counterbalanced, and objectivity resulted. Groups also exhibited increased motivation and self-criticism. All these advantages, except, perhaps, self-motivation, tend to diminish as the size of the group diminishes. Because juries frequently face complex problems laden with value choices, the benefits are important and should be retained. In particular, the counterbalancing of various biases is critical to the accurate application of the common sense of the community to the facts of any given case.

Second, the data now raise doubts about the accuracy of the results achieved by smaller and smaller panels. Statistical studies suggest that the risk of convicting an innocent person rises as the size of the jury diminishes....

Third, the data suggest that the verdicts of jury deliberation in criminal cases will vary as juries become smaller, and that the variance amounts to an imbalance to the detriment of one side, the defense.

receives only three peremptory challenges in misdemeanor cases. There are usually more peremptory challenges available in a capital case for instance.

Do trial juries have to be composed of **12 jurors**?

In federal criminal cases, the number of jurors must be 12. Federal Rule of Criminal Procedure Rule 23 provides: "A jury consists of 12 persons unless this rule provides otherwise." This is in contrast to federal civil cases, where there often are only six jurors. State criminal cases range from between 6 to 12 jurors.

Jury verdicts must be unanimous in most cases, although a few states allow criminal cases to have dissenting votes (*iStock*).

Can a state conduct a criminal trial with **only five jurors**?

No, the United States Supreme Court ruled in *Ballew v. Georgia* (1978; see Legal-Speak, p. 168) that a state could not conduct a criminal trial with less than six jurors, because a five-member jury would violate a criminal defendant's right to a jury trial guaranteed by the Sixth Amendment. The court cited empirical research showing a correlation between jury size and good results. "As juries decrease in size, then, they are less likely to have members who remember each of the important pieces of evidence or argument," Justice Harry Blackmun wrote the Court.

Who was the **defendant Ballew**?

Claude Davis Ballew was the manager of an adult movie theater in Atlanta, Georgia, who faced obscenity charges for showing the pornographic movie *Behind the Green Door.*

Do jury **verdicts** have to be **unanimous**?

Yes, jury verdicts in federal criminal cases must be unanimous. Federal Rule of Criminal Procedure Rule 31(a) provides: "The jury must return its verdict to a judge in open court. The verdict must be unanimous."

However, a few states do allow non-unanimous verdicts in criminal cases. The United States Supreme Court upheld a Louisiana law that allowed individuals to be convicted if at least 9 of 12 jurors voted for conviction. In *Johnson v. Louisiana* (1972), the Court reasoned that "disagreement of three jurors does not alone establish reasonable doubt, particularly when such a heavy majority of the jury, after having considered the dissenters' views, remains convinced of guilt."

Can judges **sequester juries**?

Yes, trial judges—particularly in criminal cases—have the option of sequestering jurors to prohibit outside influences from contacting jurors. This can help to ensure that criminal defendants receive a fair trial and also to protect jurors.

Can a court use an **anonymous jury**?

Some courts have ruled that anonymous juries are permissible in the appropriate case where juror safety is an issue. These courts reason that protecting jurors from harm is a compelling or very strong governmental interest that justifies the extraordinary use of an anonymous jury. A Minnesota appeals court reasoned in *State v. Ferguson* (Minn.App. 2007) that an anonymous jury could be used if the following two factors were met: (1) there was strong reason to believe that the jury needs protection and (2) the court takes precautions to minimize any possible prejudice to the defendant that the jurors' anonymity might present.

How do **criminal trials proceed**?

Criminal trials proceed like civil trials in the sense that there are opening statements by both attorneys. The prosecution then presents its case-in-chief with the defense being able to cross-examine witnesses. After the prosecution finishes its case or rests, the defense has the opportunity to ask for a directed verdict of acquittal or motion to dismiss. Often, this is not granted. The defense then presents its case. After the conclusion of the case-in-chief, the parties then make closing arguments to the jury. Then, the judge will read jury instructions to help the jurors understand their duty and apply the law properly.

Must a criminal **defendant testify** on behalf of himself or herself?

No, the Fifth Amendment of the U.S. Constitution provides that a defendant does not have to incriminate himself by testifying on his or her own behalf. This amendment means that the defendant can sit quietly at trial and require the prosecutor to prove that he or she committed the crime beyond a reasonable doubt—a formidable legal standard.

Can a **judge** declare a **mistrial**?

Yes, a judge can declare a mistrial if there is legal error committed during the trial or if something happens that the judge believes substantially prejudices the case. For

LegalSpeak: *Johnson v. Louisiana* (1972)

Of course, the State's proof could perhaps be regarded as more certain if it had convinced all 12 jurors instead of only nine; it would have been even more compelling if it had been required to convince and had, in fact, convinced 24 or 36 jurors. But the fact remains that nine jurors—a substantial majority of the jury— were convinced by the evidence. In our view disagreement of three jurors does not alone establish reasonable doubt, particularly when such a heavy majority of the jury, after having considered the dissenters' views, remains convinced of guilt. That rational men disagree is not in itself equivalent to a failure of proof by the State, nor does it indicate infidelity to the reasonable-doubt standard. Jury verdicts finding guilt beyond a reasonable doubt are regularly sustained even though the evidence was such that the jury would have been justified in having a reasonable doubt; even though the trial judge might not have reached the same conclusion as the jury, and even though appellate judges are closely divided on the issue whether there was sufficient evidence to support a conviction. That want of jury unanimity is not to be equated with the existence of a reasonable doubt emerges even more clearly from the fact that when a jury in a federal court, which operates under the unanimity rule and is instructed to acquit a defendant if it has a reasonable doubt about his guilt.... If the doubt of a minority of jurors indicates the existence of a reasonable doubt, it would appear that a defendant should receive a directed verdict of acquittal rather than a retrial. We conclude, therefore, that verdicts rendered by nine out of 12 jurors are not automatically invalidated by the disagreement of the dissenting three. Appellant was not deprived of due process of law.

example, Idaho Rule of Criminal Procedure, Rule 29.1 provides: "A mistrial may be declared upon motion of the defendant, when there occurs during the trial an error or legal defect in the proceedings, or conduct inside or outside the courtroom, which is prejudicial to the defendant and deprives the defendant of a fair trial."

What are **jury consultants**?

Jury consultants are individuals who have specialized knowledge and expertise in reading people's tendencies. They are hired by litigants in order to help empanel a jury most helpful to the defendant's cause.

What happens at the **start** of a **criminal trial**?

Just as in a typical civil case, the attorneys begin with opening statements. The prosecution goes first and then the defense attorney follows. The opening statements do not

171

LegalSpeak: N.M. Dist. Ct. R.Cr.P. 5-607

5-607 Order of trial

The order of trial shall be as follows:

A. a qualified jury shall be selected and sworn to try the case;

B. initial instructions as provided in UJI Criminal shall be given by the court;

C. the state may make an opening statement. The defense may then make an opening statement or may reserve such opening statement until after the conclusion of the state's case;

D. the state shall submit its evidence;

E. out of the presence of the jury, the court shall determine the sufficiency of the evidence, whether or not a motion for directed verdict is made;

F. the defense may then make an opening statement, if reserved;

G. the defense may submit its evidence;

H. the state may submit evidence in rebuttal;

I. the defense may submit evidence in surrebuttal;

J. at any time before submission of the case to the jury, the court may for good cause shown permit the state or defense to submit additional evidence;

K. out of the presence of the jury, the court shall determine the sufficiency of the evidence, whether or not a motion for directed verdict is made;

L. the instructions to be given shall be determined in accordance with Rule 5–608. The court shall then instruct the jury;

M. the state may make the opening argument;

N. the defense may make its argument;

O. the state may make rebuttal argument only.

contain evidence, as the introduction of evidence is not allowed. A good opening statement attracts the attention of the jury members and sets the stage for the attorneys' case-in-chief.

After the prosecution makes their opening statement, the defense usually makes their opening statement. However, many jurisdictions' court rules allow a defense attorney to choose whether to make their opening statement right after the prosecution's opening statement or to delay their opening statement until after the prosecution has presented its case.

> ## LegalSpeak: Rhode Island Superior Court Rules of Criminal Procedure, Rule 26.2, Opening statements
>
> **B**efore any evidence is offered at trial, the State may make an opening statement. If a defendant chooses to make an opening statement, he or she may do so just prior to the introduction of evidence by the State, or just prior to presenting his case.

During the **prosecution's case**, is there a chance at **cross-examination**?

Yes, each side in a criminal case—just as in a civil case—has the chance to cross-examine the other side's witnesses. In a criminal case, this is guaranteed by the Confrontation Clause in the Sixth Amendment, which ensures that defendants have the right to confront those who accuse them of wrongdoing.

After the **prosecution finishes** its case, can the **defense** immediately file for **dismissal**?

Yes, defense attorneys can ask the court to dismiss the case after the conclusion of the prosecution's case-in-chief. The defense attorneys argue that the prosecution simply has not proven its case—that the defendant committed the crime and met the rigorous beyond a reasonable doubt standard.

What happens in the **closing argument** phase?

Each side presents a closing argument in which they attempt to persuade the jury as to why the jury should vote guilty or not guilty. Attorneys usually attempt to summarize the evidence from their side's perspective.

What does **each side** hope to **accomplish** with **closing arguments**?

Each side hopes to win its case and leave a lasting, positive impression on the jury during closing arguments. Usually, the prosecution will emphasize the strength of the evidence and that the evidence points to the defendant's guilt. The defense often emphasizes that the prosecution failed to meet the "beyond a reasonable doubt" standard and that the defense witnesses established that the defendant did not commit the crime.

What is the **order of argument** with respect to closing arguments?

Often, the prosecutor first makes a closing argument, followed by the defense. Some states allow the trial judge the discretion to determine the order of the final argu-

Each side in a criminal case has the opportunity to cross-examine a witness, a procedure guaranteed by the Sixth Amendment (*iStock*).

ments. For example, Vermont Rule of Criminal Procedure, Rule 29.1, provides that "closing argument, and the order of such argument, shall be governed by the sound discretion of the trial judge."

Other jurisdictions allow the prosecutor the choice of whether to argue first or second. Still other jurisdictions—such as Tennessee and Florida—allow the prosecution to argue first followed by the defense, but then give the prosecution a second closing argument to rebut the defense's final argument. This final argument by the prosecution is called the "rebuttal argument."

Is there a **set time** for **closing arguments**?

In most states, court rules—either state-wide, federal or local—grant trial judges the discretion to regulate the time of closing arguments as they see fit.

What happens in the **jury instruction phase** of the trial?

Attorneys for each side—the prosecution and the defense—submit proposed jury instructions to the judge for consideration. The judge may have pattern jury instructions for a particular type of case that serves as the default. The judge then determines to accept the parties' proposed jury instructions.

Where do attorneys obtain proposed jury instructions?

Many proposed jury instructions come from appellate court decisions. An attorney may find a particular important point expressed in a particular way that he or she wants to submit as a proposed jury instruction. There are also books that give standard jury instructions in particularly types of cases.

What happens with the attorneys' proposed jury instructions?

Many court rules provide for a "instruction conference," which takes place in the courtroom without the jury present. At this conference, the attorneys can argue for the inclusion and exclusion of certain proposed jury instructions. The trial judge then makes the decisions as to which instructions are included in the final version that the judge reads to the jury.

Can the jury receive written copies of the judge's instructions?

In many jurisdictions, jurors can receive a written copy of the judge's instructions to the jury. For example, Arkansas Rule of Criminal Procedure, Rule 33.6 provides that upon request of an attorney in the case or any juror, a written copy of the jury instructions shall be provided to the jury. Utah Rule of Criminal Procedure, Rule 19 provides: "Final instructions shall be in writing and at least one copy provided to the jury. The court shall provide a copy to any juror who requests one and may, in its discretion, provide a copy to all jurors."

Why are jury instructions important?

Jury instructions are important because most jurors take their civic responsibility very seriously and genuinely desire to follow the law. These jurors often pay particular attention to what the trial judge says. Furthermore, jury instructions are often a focus of defendants' appeals, and appellate courts do pay close attention to jury instructions. For example, if a trial judge refuses to grant a defense attorney's proposed jury instruction, that could be a good basis for an error of law committed by the trial judge.

Can jury members discuss the case before deliberations?

No, jury members are admonished by trial judges not to discuss the case with

Sometimes, no matter how much time they are given, a jury becomes deadlocked. A judge cannot force a jury to reach a verdict. (*iStock*).

each other or with anybody else until the case is concluded and the case is submitted for formal jury deliberations. If a trial judge finds out that a juror has violated this provision, the trial judge will remove the juror.

If the **jury** cannot agree and is **deadlocked**, what does a court do?

If a jury deadlocks, the trial judge may call the jury back into the courtroom and ask them to continue deliberating. However, rules prohibit a judge from actually forcing a jury to reach a verdict. For instance, Kentucky Rule of Criminal Procedure, Rule 9.57 provides: "no juror should surrender his or her honest conviction as to the weight or

closing argument or the state has waived all argument or its final argument.

(2) Scope of State's Final Closing Argument.

The state's final closing argument is limited to the subject matter covered in the state's first closing argument and the defendant's intervening argument.

(d) Court's Discretion to Control Closing Arguments.

(1) Discretion to Regulate Arguments.

The court has discretion to set:

(A) the number of closing arguments permitted on behalf of the state beyond the first and final closing arguments;

(B) the number of closing arguments in excess of one permitted each defendant; and

(C) the order and length of closing arguments.

(2) Policies.

The court shall allow adequate but not excessive time for closing arguments to make a full presentation of the theory of the case. If more than two arguments are made for the state, the court shall ensure that no defendant is deprived of the opportunity to answer a new argument made by the state against that defendant. It is the purpose of this rule to ensure that all argument be waived only with the consent of both sides; that the defendant shall be permitted to waive all remaining argument after the state's first closing argument; and that while the state, having the burden of proof, has the right to open and close the argument, this right shall not be exercised in such way as to deprive the defendant of the opportunity to fully answer all state argument. The court, on motion, shall enforce this purpose.

effect of the evidence solely because of the opinion of other jurors, or for the mere purpose of returning a verdict."

Can **juror misconduct** lead to a **mistrial**?

Yes, it can. If juror misconduct substantially prejudices the defendant's rights and the defense makes a motion for a new trial, a trial judge may grant the defendant's motion for a new trial. For example, Ohio Rule of Criminal Procedure, Rule 33 provides: "A new trial may be granted on motion of the defendant for any of the following causes affecting materially his substantial rights ... misconduct of the jury, prosecuting attorney, or the witnesses for the state."

What happens if a **jury cannot** reach a **decision**?

Under Federal Rule of Criminal Procedure, Rule 31(d), if a jury cannot reach a decision, the trial judge can order the jury to deliberate some more or may declare a mistrial and dismiss the jury.

If the **jury convicts** the defendant, what are the **defendant's options**?

The defendant can ask the judge to overrule the jury's determination, finding that the jury's decision was against the weight of the evidence. The defendant can file a motion for a new trial or the defendant can appeal the adverse verdict.

When can a **judge reverse** a **jury verdict**?

Usually, trial judges do not overturn jury's guilty verdicts. However, in most jurisdictions trial judges do have the power to do so when they feel that the verdict is in clear error.

> **LegalSpeak: How to Deal with Drunk Jurors**
>
> Miss. Code Ann. § 13-5-83. Intoxicated jurors; jurors under the control of the court:
>
> If any juror summoned to appear at court, should render himself unfit for service by intoxication before his name is called in court, he shall be fined in a sum not exceeding one hundred dollars, and be imprisoned for a term not exceeding twenty-four hours. After grand and petit jurors are impaneled they shall be under the control of the court, and, for any breach of duty or contempt of court, may be fined and imprisoned.

Some states provide that if a defendant has filed a motion for a judgment of acquittal, the judge can reserve judgment on that motion until after the jury reaches its decision.

For example, Virginia law provides: "If the jury returns a verdict of guilty, the court may, on motion of the accused made not later than 21 days after entry of a final order, set aside the verdict for error committed during the trial or if the evidence is insufficient as a matter of law to sustain a conviction." Tennessee court rules provide that a trial judge can grant a new trial if the judge finds that the jury's verdict is against the weight of evidence.

SENTENCING

What happens **after** a person is **convicted**?

The part of a criminal trial is the guilt/innocence phase. In this part, the jury determines whether a person is guilty or not guilty. The next phase is sentencing where the judge determines the amount of time the person must serve. Most crimes carry a range of sentences, such as between five and 15 years. The judge then determines exactly what the sentence will be.

Does it **matter** if a person has **prior convictions**?

Yes, a person's prior criminal convictions can influence a judge's sentencing decision. In some states, prior convictions can cause someone to be classified as a career offender and career offenders receive longer sentences than those who are first-time offenders. In addition, some states—such as Florida—require those classified as "career offenders" to register with authorities once they have been released from prison.

What is a **suspended sentence**?

A suspended sentence is one where the judge suspends the serving of prison time and places the defendant on probation. The defendant who receives a suspended sentence must not engage in conduct that would violate probation or the court may impose the original sentence (that was suspended). Generally, first-time offenders who commit a misdemeanor or a non-violent felony can be eligible for a suspended sentence. Often, defendants will plead guilty in exchange for receiving a suspended sentence recommendation from the prosecution to the judge.

If a **defendant** is **sentenced** to three years, how much time will the defendant **actually serve**?

This varies greatly from the federal system and from state to state. Generally, defendants sentenced in federal court serve at least 80 to 85 of their prison terms. State court defendants could serve a much lower percentage of their actually imprisonment, such as 20% to 30% of their actual sentence.

What is **time served**?

"Time served" refers to the time period in which a defendant is incarcerated before trial. Sometimes for more minor offenses, a defendant will receive only a "time served" sentence, because the defendant has already spent a significant time behind bars before the conclusion of his or her trial. In more serious cases, a defendant's actual time of imprisonment will be reduced by "time served."

What is the difference between serving **sentences concurrently** or **consecutively**?

The difference is huge, because a defendant who serves offenses concurrently serves time for the different crimes at the same time. In other words, if a defendant was convicted of two crimes, he or she would not have to serve one sentence and then another—the sentences would both run as soon as the defendant was in prison.

On the other hand, a defendant who serves sentences consecutively must serve one sentence before the next sentence begins. This means that consecutive sentencing keeps the defendant in prison for much longer than concurrent sentencing.

How does a **judge determine** whether sentencing is **concurrent** or **consecutive**?

Generally sentencing judges in states have broad discretion to impose either concurrent or consecutive sentencing. However, some states have laws that provide when a judge can impose concurrent or consecutive sentencing. Some of these laws provide discretion to the judges to decide this important issue. In some states, if a defendant is convicted of a violent felony and another offense, the judge must sentence the defendant consecu-

A judge can vary a guilty party's sentence, depending on circumstances, such as if the defendant has a prior record or if the party has already served time (*iStock*).

tively. The rationale is that the defendant deserves a longer sentence and the public needs protection from this violent felony offender.

What **factors** does a **judge consider in determining sentencing?**

Judges often consider so-called aggravating or mitigating factors in determining the sentence of a criminal defense. Aggravating factors are those which increase a sentence, while mitigating factors are those which may lessen a sentence. Typical aggravating factors include: whether the defendant is a repeat offender, whether the offense was violent, whether the defendant held public office and trust, whether the defendant's victim was older, whether the defendant received compensation for the crime, whether the defendant selected his victim because of disability or race, whether the sentence is necessary to deter others from committing the same crime, and whether the defendant committed the crime as part of an organized gang.

Typical mitigating factors include that the defendant was not the leader of the offense and showed concern for the physical well-being for the victim, the defendant was much younger than the leader of the criminal conspiracy, the defendant was pro-

LegalSpeak: Illinois State Law on Consecutive Sentencing

730 ILCS 5/5-8-4 CONCURRENT AND CONSECUTIVE TERMS OF IMPRISONMENT

(d) CONSECUTIVE TERMS; MANDATORY. The court shall impose consecutive sentences in each of the following circumstances:

(1) One of the offenses for which the defendant was convicted was first degree murder or a Class X or Class 1 felony and the defendant inflicted severe bodily injury.

(2) The defendant was convicted of a violation of Section 12-13 (criminal sexual assault), 12-14 (aggravated criminal sexual assault), or 12-14.1 (predatory criminal sexual assault of a child) of the Criminal Code of 1961.

(3) The defendant was convicted of armed violence based upon the predicate offense of any of the following: solicitation of murder, solicitation of murder for hire, heinous battery, aggravated battery of a senior citizen, criminal sexual assault, a violation of subsection (g) of Section 5 of the Cannabis Control Act, cannabis trafficking, a violation of subsection (a) of Section 401 of the Illinois Controlled Substances Act, controlled substance trafficking involving a Class X felony amount of controlled substance under Section 401 of the Illinois Controlled Substances Act, a violation of the Methamphetamine Control and Community Protection Act (720 ILCS 646/), calculated criminal drug conspiracy, or streetgang criminal drug conspiracy....

(5) The defendant was convicted of a violation of Section 9-3.1 (concealment of homicidal death) or Section 12-20.5 (dismembering a human body) of the Criminal Code of 1961.

(6) If the defendant was in the custody of the Department of Corrections at the time of the commission of the offense, the sentence shall be served consecutive to the sentence under which the defendant is held by the Department of Corrections. If, however, the defendant is sentenced to punishment by death, the sentence shall be executed at such time as the court may fix without regard to the sentence under which the defendant may be held by the Department.

(7) A sentence under Section 3-6-4 for escape or attempted escape shall be served consecutive to the terms under which the offender is held by the Department of Corrections....

voked by the victim, the defendant has compensated or will compensate the victim for the harm, the defendant is likely to respond to probationary treatment, and the willingness of the defendant to cooperate with law enforcement.

APPEALS

What **further legal options** are available to a person once **convicted**?

A defendant has a constitutional right to appeal his conviction and/or his sentence to an appeals court. The defendant's attorney petitions the appellate court to overturn the defendant's sentence because of error committed during the trial court process.

What are some **commonly alleged errors** in criminal trials?

Some errors that are used concern a trial judge's exclusion or admission of certain evidence, failure to give a particular jury instruction, or failure to consider mitigating factors when imposing a sentence. Other arguments often advanced are that the prosecutor made improper statements during his closing argument, that the trial court failed to adequately protect the defendant's constitutional rights by failing to exclude certain evidence, and that the jury's verdict was against the weight of evidence.

Is there a **time limit** on **appeals**?

Yes, there is a strict time limit for appeals. The time period begins to run (or toll) when the trial court enters a final judgment. Often the time period is 45 days or 90 days depending upon the jurisdiction.

What is **the record**?

"The record" refers to the trial court proceedings that are gathered together and filed before the appellate court. "The record" will usually consist of a transcription of the trial record, exhibits in the trial court, and various pre-trial and post-trial motions filed in the case. There must be a sufficient "record" before the appellate court so that the appellate court can determine whether the lower committed error during its proceedings.

What is an **appellate brief**?

If the defendant appeals his or her sentence, he is called the appellant (the person who appeals). The government then becomes the appellee (the person defending the original conviction or sentence). The defendant-appellant must file a brief that explains why the lower court erred during the trial process. The government-appellee will then file a brief that rebuts the defendant's arguments and defends the rulings of the trial court.

A convicted person can appeal the decision made in his or her case if the appellant feels adequate representation was not provided, or that the court made some sort of error (*iStock*).

Note that the word "brief" in this context is a misnomer, as briefs are often many pages long. Appellate courts have strict rules on the content of briefs, which is why many trial attorneys refer appeals to appellate lawyers—those lawyers who have special expertise in the appellate process.

What is the **direct appeal**?

Direct appeal refers to the appealing of the underlying criminal conviction or sentence in a higher court. The direct appeal process consists of appealing to all higher courts of the original conviction or sentence. Once the highest court has affirmed the conviction or sentence, then the direct appeal process has finished. Then, the defendant's only option is to file a petition for post-conviction relief.

If an **appellate court reverses** a trial court, what happens **next**?

This depends on the ruling of the appellate court. An appellate court could find that a trial court erred in admitting certain evidence that was prejudicial to the defendant. The trial court would then order that the prosecution afford the defendant a new trial. If the appellate court determines that the trial court erred in the sentencing phase of the trial, it might send the case back down to the trial for re-sentencing.

LegalSpeak: *Strickland v. Washington* (1984)

The Court has not elaborated on the meaning of the constitutional requirement of effective assistance in the latter class of cases—that is, those presenting claims of "actual ineffectiveness." In giving meaning to the requirement, however, we must take its purpose—to ensure a fair trial—as the guide. The benchmark for judging any claim of ineffectiveness must be whether counsel's conduct so undermined the proper functioning of the adversarial process that the trial cannot be relied on as having produced a just result....

A convicted defendant's claim that counsel's assistance was so defective as to require reversal of a conviction or death sentence has two components. First, the defendant must show that counsel's performance was deficient. This requires showing that counsel made errors so serious that counsel was not functioning as the "counsel" guaranteed the defendant by the Sixth Amendment. Second, the defendant must show that the deficient performance prejudiced the defense. This requires showing that counsel's errors were so serious as to deprive the defendant of a fair trial, a trial whose result is reliable. Unless a defendant makes both showings, it cannot be said that the conviction or death sentence resulted from a breakdown in the adversary process that renders the result unreliable.

What is a **post-conviction proceeding**?

A post-conviction proceeding is a proceeding provided for in state court that enables a defendant to challenge the constitutionality or legality of some aspect of the trial court proceeding. It is called a post-conviction proceeding because it occurs after the conviction and after the direct appeal process. In many states, it is a statutory, not a constitutional, right. There are generally time limits on when a defendant may file a state post-conviction proceeding.

If a **direct appeal** process and the state **post-conviction** process both **fail**, are there any **other legal avenues**?

Yes, there is another important legal avenue and that is seeking a writ of *habeas corpus* in federal court. "Habeas corpus" is a Latin term literally meaning "you have the body." In a writ of *habeas corpus*, a defendant collaterally challenges his underlying conviction (often in state court), alleging that there were constitutional violations committed during his trial.

For example, a defendant may allege that his underlying conviction should be overturned because his Sixth Amendment right to receive assistance of counsel was denied. This is often called an "ineffective assistance of counsel" claim. Or the defendant may show that the prosecution unlawfully refused to disclose exculpatory evidence over to the defendant's attorney. Or the defendant may contend that the trial judge violated the defendant's due-process rights by holding the proceedings in a manner fundamentally unfair to the defendant.

What is **ineffective assistance** of **counsel**?

Ineffective assistance of counsel is a constitutionally based claim under the Sixth Amendment in which a defendant asserts that his legal representation was so poor that he did not receive "assistance of counsel" within the meaning of the Sixth Amendment. This is a difficult burden to meet.

JUVENILE DEFENDANTS

If you're **convicted** of a crime as a **juvenile** can you be **tried** as an **adult**?

It depends on your specific age and the nature of the crime. For most crimes, juveniles are not transferred to adult criminal court. However, if a juvenile is at least 14 years old and commits a violent felony—such as murder or armed robbery—then the states have mechanisms in place to provide for the transfer of such juvenile defendants to adult court. Often, if the juvenile meets these conditions (be at least 14 and believed to have committed a violent felony), a juvenile court judge will hold a transfer hearing to determine whether or not to send the juvenile defendant to adult criminal court or to keep them in the juvenile court system.

Do **juveniles** in juvenile court receive all of the **same rights** as **adults** charged in criminal court?

Juveniles have most, but not all, of the same rights as adults in the criminal system. For example, juveniles do not have the right to a jury trial. Instead, juveniles are tried before a single juvenile court judge. However, juveniles have many of the same rights, including: right to counsel, right to be informed of criminal charges, right to a speedy trial, right to confront witnesses, right to have compulsory process to have witnesses subpoenaed, to decide not to testify and others.

What is a **status offense**?

A status offense is an offense that is reserved for minors. Common examples of status offenses include truancy (missing school), violating a curfew, or the use of tobacco by a minor. The juvenile court has the power to impose sanctions upon a juvenile who commits status offenses. The thinking is that the juvenile court judge can bring a

LegalSpeak: Juvenile Transfer Law in Virginia

Va. Code Ann.

In determining whether a juvenile is a proper person to remain within the jurisdiction of the juvenile court, the court shall consider, but not be limited to, the following factors:

a. The juvenile's age;

b. The seriousness and number of alleged offenses, including (i) whether the alleged offense was committed in an aggressive, violent, premeditated, or willful manner; (ii) whether the alleged offense was against persons or property, with greater weight being given to offenses against persons, especially if death or bodily injury resulted; (iii) whether the maximum punishment for such an offense is greater than twenty years confinement if committed by an adult; (iv) whether the alleged offense involved the use of a firearm or other dangerous weapon by brandishing, threatening, displaying or otherwise employing such weapon; and (v) the nature of the juvenile's participation in the alleged offense;

c. Whether the juvenile can be retained in the juvenile justice system long enough for effective treatment and rehabilitation;

d. The appropriateness and availability of the services and dispositional alternatives in both the criminal justice and juvenile justice systems for dealing with the juvenile's problems;

e. The record and previous history of the juvenile in this or other jurisdictions, including (i) the number and nature of previous contacts with juvenile or circuit courts, (ii) the number and nature of prior periods of probation, (iii) the number and nature of prior commitments to juvenile correctional centers, (iv) the number and nature of previous residential and community-based treatments, (v) whether previous adjudications and commitments were for delinquent acts that involved the infliction of serious bodily injury, and (vi) whether the alleged offense is part of a repetitive pattern of similar adjudicated offenses;

f. Whether the juvenile has previously absconded from the legal custody of a juvenile correctional entity in this or any other jurisdiction;

g. The extent, if any, of the juvenile's degree of mental retardation or mental illness;

h. The juvenile's school record and education;

i. The juvenile's mental and emotional maturity; and

j. The juvenile's physical condition and physical maturity.

LegalSpeak: *Roper v. Simmons* (2005)

Minors are given special consideration under the law, even when they commit serious crimes, because it is generally understood that juveniles do not possess the same reasoning abilities and self-control that adults do (*iStock*).

Justice Anthony Kennedy (majority): "Respondent and his *amici* have submitted, and petitioner does not contest, that only seven countries other than the United States have executed juvenile offenders since 1990: Iran, Pakistan, Saudi Arabia, Yemen, Nigeria, the Democratic Republic of Congo, and China. Since then each of these countries has either abolished capital punishment for juveniles or made public disavowal of the practice. Brief for Respondent 49 to 50. In sum, it is fair to say that the United States now stands alone in a world that has turned its face against the juvenile death penalty....

"It is proper that we acknowledge the overwhelming weight of international opinion against the juvenile death penalty, resting in large part on the understanding that the instability and emotional imbalance of young people may often be a factor in the crime.... The opinion of the world community, while not controlling our outcome, does provide respected and significant confirmation for our own conclusions.

"Over time, from one generation to the next, the Constitution has come to earn the high respect and even, as Madison dared to hope, the veneration of the

juvenile under control and hopefully get them rehabilitation so that the juvenile will not regress into more serious criminal offenses.

Can a **juvenile** defendant receive the **death penalty** or **life** in prison without the possibility of parole?

Juveniles cannot receive the death penalty. The U.S. Supreme Court ruled in *Roper v. Simmons* (2005) that it constitutes "cruel and unusual punishment" under the Eighth Amendment to execute juveniles in part because juveniles are less mature and less able to appreciate the gravity of their actions than adults.

American people. See The Federalist No. 49, p. 314 (C. Rossiter ed. 1961). The document sets forth, and rests upon, innovative principles original to the American experience, such as federalism; a proven balance in political mechanisms through separation of powers; specific guarantees for the accused in criminal cases; and broad provisions to secure individual freedom and preserve human dignity. These doctrines and guarantees are central to the American experience and remain essential to our present-day self-definition and national identity. Not the least of the reasons we honor the Constitution, then, is because we know it to be our own. It does not lessen our fidelity to the Constitution or our pride in its origins to acknowledge that the express affirmation of certain fundamental rights by other nations and peoples simply underscores the centrality of those same rights within our own heritage of freedom."

Justice Antonin Scalia (dissent): "The Court thus proclaims itself sole arbiter of our Nation's moral standards—and in the course of discharging that awesome responsibility purports to take guidance from the views of foreign courts and legislatures. Because I do not believe that the meaning of our Eighth Amendment, any more than the meaning of other provisions of our Constitution, should be determined by the subjective views of five Members of this Court and like-minded foreigners, I dissent....

More fundamentally, however, the basic premise of the Court's argument—that American law should conform to the laws of the rest of the world—ought to be rejected out of hand. In fact the Court itself does not believe it. In many significant respects the laws of most other countries differ from our law—including not only such explicit provisions of our Constitution as the right to jury trial and grand jury indictment, but even many interpretations of the Constitution prescribed by this Court itself. The Court-pronounced exclusionary rule, for example, is distinctively American."

As of this writing, it is uncertain whether juveniles can receive the second toughest criminal sentence—life in prison without the possibility of parole. On November 9, 2009, the U.S. Supreme Court heard oral arguments in two cases from Florida—*Sullivan v. Florida* and *Graham v. Florida* that will decide the question.

Did the U.S. **Supreme Court** rely on **international law** in reaching its decision against the **death penalty** for **juvenile** offenders?

Yes, the majority of the Court relied in part on international law—or the law of other countries—in reaching its decision that executing juvenile murderers would violate

189

the Eighth Amendment. The Court noted that at least for 50 years it has referred to the laws of other countries and to international authorities as instructive for its interpretation of the Eighth Amendment's prohibition of "cruel and unusual punishments." The majority noted that the United Nations' Convention on the Rights of Children prohibited the death as did "several other significant international covenants." The majority later added: "The opinion of the world community, while not controlling our outcome, does provide respected and significant confirmation for our own conclusions."

CREDIT AND BANKRUPTCY LAW

What is **credit** and why is it so **important**?

Credit refers to your ability to borrow money and then pay it back over a period of time. It also refers to how trustworthy a person is considered to be in terms of whether he or she will be eligible for loans and be able to pay off loans. Credit is important because most people cannot afford to pay cash for large purchases, such as houses and cars. You need good credit in order to receive financing in order to obtain a loan to make large purchases.

Why is **credit expensive**?

Credit can be expensive because lenders or creditors do not lend $5,000 and then simply ask for $5,000 back in return. Rather, they charge you—the debtor—for the extension of credit. You have to pay interest—often called finance charges—as you pay back the loan amount. If you miss payments, then you will have to pay even more money in order to pay off your debt. Consumer credit has risen to nearly $3 trillion dollars, as many people regularly spend beyond their means.

What is **APR**?

APR stands for annual percentage rate and constitutes the yearly cost of credit expressed in terms of interest. APRs are important when considering a credit card application. APRs can range from six percent to as high as 30 percent or more, so you must be sure to make payments in a timely fashion or the creditors will raise the APR.

Are there different **types** of **credit**?

Yes, sometimes a loan agreement requires that the debtor pay off the full balance within a certain amount of time. Other credit arrangements are referred to as open-end credit, which is a revolving door type of credit. The debtor must make regular payments and has a credit limit, but must make payments in a timely fashion or risk additional charges. Most credit cards involve this type of revolving credit.

How do you know if you have **too much debt**?

If you only can make minimum payments on credit cards, that is a sign that you have more debt than you can handle. If you have to use your credit cards regularly for items—such as groceries and meals—that you used to pay in cash, that could be another telltale sign that you are carrying too much debt. If you have exhausted your savings to pay for normal living expenses, that is another possible warning sign that you have too much debt. Another warning sign is if you are regularly making late payments. Those will be reported and result in a lower credit score.

What **should you do** if you have too much **debt**?

First, you might try to lower your use of credit cards and cut down all luxury or nonnecessity purchases. You then should consider developing a budget. Most people do not realize that they live beyond their means or how much they currently live beyond their means. A good budget plan can be a real eye-opener.

Additionally, you might consider contacting several of your creditors to see if you can reduce the annual percentage rates (APR) that are burdening you with excess interest. You might also consider speaking with an attorney well-versed in credit, debt, and bankruptcy law to see what are your available options.

Medical bills, credit cards, school loans and more have increasingly burdened American consumers. If you can only manage paying the minimum on your bills, or not even that much, you may have a serious debt problem (*iStock*).

Didn't the **U.S. Congress** just pass a new **law** on **credit cards**?

Yes, Congress passed, and President Barack Obama signed into law, the Credit Card Act of 2009, which is designed to curb abuses in the credit industry and protect consumers. The new law requires credit card companies to give consumers 45 days advance notice about interest rate increases. It also requires consumers to apply payments to the highest-interest rate balances first before applying the payment to a lower-interest rate, balance-interest-free loan.

The new law also requires consumers to "opt-in" in order to be able to make charges that exceed your credit card limit. This change will enable consumers to learn when they are approaching their credit limits.

What **factors** determine whether you will **receive credit**?

Creditors consider several factors in determining whether you receive credit. These factors include your income and ability to repay debt, your creditworthiness and credit history, your job stability, and your assets. The higher your income level, the more likely that someone will take a chance and extend you credit. If you have a history of missing payments or making late payments, that reflects poorly on your credit history and makes you less a creditworthy individual. Likewise, if you have worked at the same job for a period of time, that stability could be factored into the credit loan decision. Also, if you have assets (a car, a house and other property), those could be considered in the credit process.

How can you build **good credit**?

A good way to build a good credit history is to open a bank account and use it responsibly. Another good way is to open up some other type of account—perhaps a single credit card—and make payments in a timely fashion and keep the balance much lower than the actual credit limit. Maintaining steady employment and owning a home can also help increase your credit score and make you more creditworthy.

Where do you go to select the **right credit card**?

Good question; this is an important decision. Remember that a federal law known as the Truth in Lending Act requires credit card companies to disclose the basis terms of the card to you in their solicitations. There are several places to go to find information about credit cards. Some of the most common include: Cardweb.com, Bankrate.com and CreditcardSearchEngine.com.

What is a **variable rate**?

Variable rate is tied to the annual percentage rate described above. Many credit card companies will offer a variable rate as opposed to a pure fixed rate. They often will say that the APR on the card will vary with the corresponding prime rate in the market. Also, credit card companies may something like three different percentages for an APR (9.99%, 11.99%, or 14.99% depending on your credit).

Do credit cards always have **annual fees**?

Some credit cards do and some credit cards do not. This is one factor you may want to weigh in determining whether or not you want to apply for and/or accept a particular card.

What can you do if there is an **error** on your **credit card bill**?

Fortunately, there is a federal law known as the Fair Credit Billing Act which provides an avenue for relief for those who are charged wrongly, incorrectly, or unfairly. Under the Fair Credit Billing Act, you must notify the credit of the error promptly—within 60 days of first receiving notice. You may wish to contact the creditor in writing and explain the error so as to ensure the triggering of the protections of this law.

Your letter (which you should send by certified mail) should contain your name and the account number on which the error took place, your belief as to the specific billing error and the amount of the error, and the reasons why this is in error (never charged, wrong amount charged, double billing, etc.)

The good news is that a creditor cannot harm or threaten to harm your credit rating during the pendency of the particular dispute.

What is a **credit report**?

A credit report is exactly as the name suggests—a report on an individual's creditworthiness. Credit reports have your identification, employment record, payment history, inquiries from other creditors, and certain public information, such as bankruptcies and tax liens. Consumers have the right to access their credit reports under the Fair Credit Reporting Act. The three major companies who track credit reports—Trans Union, Experian, and Equifax—are required under federal law to give consumers a free copy of their credit report once every 12 months upon request. Consumers can also pay a small fee to obtain a copy at other times. Federal law sets the maximum fee at $11.

Also, the Fair Credit Reporting Act provides that if a fraud alert is placed in a consumer's credit report, that consumer can have two free credit reports within the next 12 months.

Credit bills can easily sneak up on consumers, and with high interest rates and fees, many Americans can quickly find themselves buried in debt in a matter of months (*iStock*).

What is a **credit score**?

A credit score is a score—usually between 300 to 800—that determines how creditworthy a person is. Many factors go into this credit evaluation, such as payment history, amount of outstanding debt, recent credit applications, and income-to-debt ratio. A score above 700 is considered excellent, while a score below 500 is poor.

Can **consumers view** their credit **scores**?

Yes, a federal law known as the Fair and Accurate Credit Transactions Act of 2003 (FACTA) provides that consumers have free access to their credit reports and the revealing of their credit scores. Consumers can also receive their credit scores from companies, such as Experian, Trans Union, and Equifax.

What is the **Fair Credit Reporting Act**

The Fair Credit Reporting Act (FCRA) governs credit reports and the information included on such reports. The stated purpose of the FCRA is "to require that consumer reporting agencies adopt reasonable procedures for meeting the needs of commerce for consumer credit, personnel, insurance, and other information in a manner which is fair and equitable to the consumer, with regard to the confidentiality, accuracy, relevancy, and proper utilization of such information in accordance with the requirements of this title."

In general. Upon the request of a consumer for a credit score, a consumer reporting agency shall supply to the consumer a statement indicating that the information and credit scoring model may be different than the credit score that may be used by the lender, and a notice which shall include—

 (A) the current credit score of the consumer or the most recent credit score of the consumer that was previously calculated by the credit reporting agency for a purpose related to the extension of credit;

 (B) the range of possible credit scores under the model used;

 (C) all of the key factors that adversely affected the credit score of the consumer in the model used …

 (D) the date on which the credit score was created; and

 (E) the name of the person or entity that provided the credit score or credit file upon which the credit score was created.

What is the difference between a **secured** and **unsecured creditor**?

A secured creditor is one who has a security interest in the debtor's property, while an unsecured creditor has no security interest. For example, a person might borrow $20,000 from a local bank but would need to put down something as security or collateral in exchange for the $20,000. Once the debtor pays back the $20,000 principal

195

loan balance and the accompanying interest, then the debtor receives back the title to his property and there is no longer an active lien on his property. Many creditors, however, are unsecured. Credit card companies are unsecured creditors. This becomes important in bankruptcy law, as secured creditors get paid before unsecured creditors.

Recently a **creditor denied me credit** for what I believe was because of my race or gender. Do I have **any recourse**?

Possibly, you may have some recourse if the creditor discriminated against you because of your race or gender under the Equal Credit Opportunity Act (ECOA), a federal law passed in 1974 to prohibit such conduct. The law prohibits creditors from discriminating on the basis of "race, color, religion, national origin, sex or marital status or age."

A creditor can deny you credit because you have a bad credit history, but not because of the aforementioned factors.

How do you **prove credit discrimination**?

One way is to prove that a creditor intentionally discriminated against an applicant based on race or gender. If a credit applicant can show that a creditor treated him worse than a similarly situated person not of his race or gender, that is called disparate treatment discrimination. For example, if a creditor gives credit to a white male with a credit score of 570 but denies credit to a Latino male with a credit score of 610, that raises an inference that the creditor has engaged in disparate treatment discrimination.

There is another method of proving discrimination called disparate impact discrimination. Disparate impact refers to a facially neutral policy that works an adverse impact upon a particular group of people. For example, let's say that a creditor gives poorer credit terms across the board to all residents living within a certain zip code. Furthermore, that zip code is an area of town that is populated primarily by African-Americans. A group of African-Americans living within that zip code might have a good case of showing disparate impact discrimination. There have been many lawsuits against creditors based on poorer credit terms being extended to certain groups. However, it is difficult to prove such allegations and many of the lawsuits are dismissed without ever making it to trial.

Does the Equal Credit Opportunity Act (ECOA) prohibit credit discrimination based on sexual orientation?

No, the ECOA does not prohibit discrimination based on sexual orientation.

Can a consumer reporting agency send a credit report to prospective employers?

Yes, prospective employers can request applicants' credit reports. A section of the FCRA entitled "permissible purposes of consumer reports" provides that consumer reporting agencies can release credit reports to a person whom the agency reasonably believes "intends to use the information for employment purposes."

Can a credit report include bankruptcies, lawsuits, and arrests?

A credit report can include bankruptcy filings except that such reports may not include bankruptcies that are more than 10 years old. Credit reports also can include records of civil judgments, lawsuits, and arrest records provided they are not more than seven years old.

Do credit reports contain credit scores?

Yes, most credit reports will contain credit scores. They also will include information as to why a credit application was denied and possible reasons for why the credit score is low. For example, if you apply for a credit card or apply for a higher limit on your credit card and are denied, the credit reporting agency will send you correspondence explaining the reasons for the denial. Common reasons for the denial are too much existing debt and poor payment history.

197

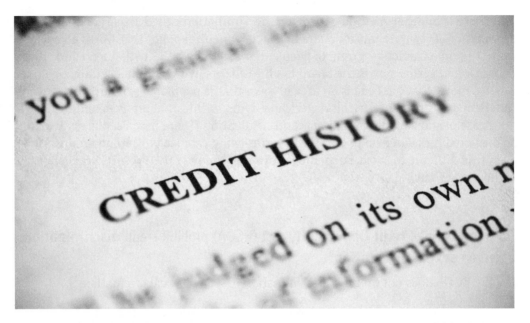

Many people don't know this, but you can check your credit history for free once a year. It is helpful to know your credit history before applying for a loan, as well as to make sure there are no irregularities that might indicate credit or identity theft (*iStock*).

If a **consumer disputes** information on his or her credit report must that be **included** in the **credit report**?

Yes, the FCRA requires that credit reporting agencies include the fact that a consumer disputes certain information on the credit report.

If there is an **error** on your **credit report**, what do **you do**?

You can start by contacting one of the three major consumer reporting agencies if you determined that information in your credit report is inaccurate or incomplete. You can contact the agencies as follows:

- Equifax: 1-800-685-1111, or www.equifax.com
- Experian: 1-888-397-3742, or www.experian.com
- TransUnion: 1-800-916-8800, or www.transunion.com

If a **credit reporting agency unfairly refuses** to correct a mistake, can you **sue**?

Yes, most courts have held that the Fair Credit Reporting Act (FCRA) enables individuals to sue. In the law, this is called a private right of action. In order to make a claim under the FCRA, a consumer must establish the following factors:

1. The inclusion of inaccurate information in the credit report;

2. the inaccuracy caused by the consumer reporting agency's failure to follow reasonable procedures to assure accuracy;

3. injury;

4. the injury caused by the inaccuracy of the credit report.

Can **companies purchase** copies of **credit reports**?

Yes, but the FCRA imposes requirements on those who purchase credit reports. The law provides:

A person may not procure a consumer report for purposes of reselling the report (or any information in the report) unless the person discloses to the consumer reporting agency that originally furnishes the report:

(A) the identity of the end-user of the report (or information); and

(B) each permissible purpose under section 604 [§ 1681b] for which the report is furnished to the end-user of the report (or information).

How **long** does **negative information** stay on my **credit report**?

Negative information does not stay on your credit report for life. Most information must be removed after seven years. However, records of bankruptcies can be reported for 10 years.

What is **credit insurance**?

Credit insurance is insurance bought that pays off the balance of a loan if you become disabled and cannot work to earn money to pay back the money you borrowed. There are different types of credit insurance, including credit life insurance, credit health insurance, and credit disability insurance. If a person does not have life insurance, credit insurance may be a good purchase, particularly the type that will pay off a loan in case of your death.

What is **identity theft**?

Identity theft, the fastest growing crime in America, refers to someone else committing fraud by using your account information or stealing your identity to make monetary purchases. There are different types of identity theft. For example, if someone steals your credit card or writes down your credit card number, they may commit fraud by using that card to make purchases.

At other times someone calls your credit card company with your credit card number and makes a change-of-address. They then have the statements billed to this new address and begin using your card in this manner. To help detect these unauthorized change of address requests, many financial institutions mail a change of address notification or confirmation to the original (old) address after they receive a change of address request. Make sure to read all notifications sent to you by your financial institutions carefully, and contact your financial institutions immediately if you believe any unauthorized or fraudulent activity may have occurred or been attempted regarding one of your accounts.

Perhaps the most common type of identity theft occurs when someone pretends to be you and opens up new accounts in your name. They may start credit card accounts, cell phone accounts, checking accounts and other accounts that are simply not yours.

How can you **protect yourself** from **identity thieves**?

You have to jealously guard your personally identifiable information. This includes your social security number, your credit card numbers, and your bank account numbers. Do not allow people untrammeled access to your personal computer, as that might become a classic gateway for the predatory identity thief. Realize that some identity thieves are relentless in their quest for other people's personally identifiable information. When you throw away credit card receipts and bank receipts, make sure that they are fully shredded. Some identity thieves even "dumpster dive" (actually physically go through other people's trash) to find key information.

Another tip is to ask why someone needs your social security number. Someone could be asking for an improper purpose. Another safety measure is to follow up if you don't receive a monthly bill from a creditor. While a natural impulse may be to not worry about receiving a bill, it could signify an attempted account takeover by an identity thief who has made a fraudulent change-of-address to take over your account.

Also, never keep your account passwords and pin numbers written down near your actual cards. That may be the ultimate *faux pas*. Don't make it easy for identity thieves.

What are some ways to **prevent identity theft**?

Some good tips include:

- If you lose your credit card, report it to the credit card company as soon as possible.
- Make sure your credit card information and any passwords for online sites are kept in a secure place.
- Never provide personal information over the phone or online unless you trust the business one hundred percent.
- Monitor your credit card reports closely to make sure there are no charges you did not authorize. If there are, contact your credit card company promptly.

- Do not put your social security number or other important personal information, such as a birth date or mother's maiden name, on checks, postcards, or envelopes.

- Use passwords that are not easy to guess and do not include your birth date, social security number, personal name, etc.

- Do not respond to emails allegedly from your bank, credit card company, or PayPal that ask you for your credit card information. They are almost always fraudulent.

- Install firewalls, anti-virus, and anti-spyware on your computer and keep these programs updated.

- Do not click on links on unsolicited emails.

- Although in some states it is illegal to print full credit card numbers on receipts, some businesses still do this. Always keep these receipts and destroy them when you no longer need them.

- Much identity theft is low-tech. Information can be stolen from mail boxes, so always pick up your mail as soon as possible, rather than leaving it in your mailbox. And don't leave your mail for pick up.

- Order a free copy of your credit report to check for anything unusual or unexpected. To order your free annual report from one or all the national consumer reporting companies, visit www.annualcreditreport.com, call toll-free 877-322-8228, or complete the Annual Credit Report Request Form and mail it to: Annual Credit Report Request Service, P.O. Box 105281, Atlanta, GA 30348-5281.

- Reduce the amount of unsolicited mail you receive by calling 1-888-5OPT-OUT. To receive less national advertising mail, you can pay one dollar to register for the Direct Marketing Association's Mail Preference Service. They can be reached at www.dmachoice.org, or P.O. Box 282, Carmel, NY 10512.

What is **phishing**?

Phishing refers to the fraudulent activity of sending an e-mail under false pretenses with the goal of obtaining bank account or credit card information from an unsuspecting consumer. The e-mails often falsely claim to be a financial institution, like your personal bank, but are really identity thieves in disguise. They ask for personally identifiable information that they would then use for nefarious purposes. The e-mails usually contain a link to a website. If the consumer clicks on the link in the e-mail, it takes them to a screen and asks for log-in information in the form of account numbers and passwords. Do not even open these e-mails and by all means do not provide account number information.

Some states have passed laws defining and prohibiting phishing. For example, Arkansas law defines phishing as "the use of electronic mail or other means to imitate

201

Computer hackers are people who try to gain access to personal or corporate information electronically for fraudulent purposes (*iStock*).

a legitimate company or business in order to entice the user into divulging passwords, credit card numbers, or other sensitive information for the purpose of committing theft or fraud."

How does the **Fair and Accurate Credit Transactions Act** (FACTA) help consumers **fight identity theft**?

The Fair and Accurate Credit Transactions Act (FACTA) helps consumers fight identity theft by allowing them to issue a one-call fraud alert to one of the three major credit reporting agencies. If one of the agencies receives such a fraud alert, it must then notify the other two major reporting agencies. This puts these agencies on notice that someone may be illegally accessing another person's credit.

What is a **credit freeze**?

A credit freeze is an action taken by a consumer to freeze activity on their accounts. Under a credit freeze, no one can take out any new credit in a consumer's name and no one can receive a credit report of the consumer without his or her specific authorization.

LOANS

What is **predatory lending**?

Predatory lending refers to lending that preys on those most vulnerable by providing credit but with steep costs. Predatory lending is marked by larger penalties for late payments, penalties for pre-payment, a repayment plan under which periodic payments cause the loan balance to rise instead of drop, and clauses that allow lenders to accelerate the amount of debt.

The Center for Responsible Lending (http://www.responsiblelending.org) has identified what it calls "eight signs" of predatory lending. They are:

1. Excessive fees

2. Prepayment penalties

3. Inflated interest rates from brokers

4. Steering and targeting

5. Adjustable interest rates that explode

6. Promises to fix problems with future refinancing

7. Not counting taxes and insurance

8. Repeated refinances that drain your resources.

What are **payday loans**?

Payday loans are high-interest, short-term loans in which the repayment period is generally conceived to arise on an individual's work payday, thus inspiring the name "payday loans." Unfortunately, payday loans are best known for the high interest rates charged on such loans. In payday loans, individuals promise to write a check in order to obtain immediate cash. For example, an individual agrees to write a $420 check in order to obtain $350. But, if the individual does not pay back the $420 in a timely fashion, then the interest rates often skyrocket and the individual falls further into spiraling debt. Many states have begun to regulate such payday loans. Some loans that often bear closer scrutiny are rent-to-own purchases, auto title loans, and income tax refund loans.

What are **home equity loans**?

Home equity loans are those in which a borrower uses equity in his or her home as collateral for a loan. Often consumers take out home equity loans to pay for college, make major renovations to a house or otherwise need a quick and sizeable infusion of cash to pay for expenses. The danger with a home equity loan is that—if unpaid—it could drive someone closer to foreclosure. In fact, the Federal Deposit Insurance Company (FDIC) has an online publication entitled "Putting Your Home on the Loan Line is a Risky Business."

What is a **reverse mortgage**?

A reverse mortgage, sometimes called a lifetime mortgage, is one in which the lender pays the homeowner the value of the equity in the home as a lump sum or regular payments, reducing the equity in the home. The obligation to repay the loan is deferred until the death of the homeowner or the home is sold. When the house is sold or the borrower moves, the borrower must repay the loan plus the accrued interest. Rarely do the reverse mortgages exceed the value of the home. Most reverse mortgages are age-dependent, requiring the homeowner to be at least 62 years of age. These loans—much like home equity loans—represent a difficult decision-making process and should not be entered into lightly.

203

DEBT COLLECTORS AND THE LAW

What is the **Fair Debt Collections Practices Act**?

The primary federal law regulating debt collectors is the Fair Debt Collections Practices Act. This law imposes obligations and standards of conduct upon those who collect debts. This 1977 law amended the Consumer Credit Protection Act to prohibit certain conduct by "debt collectors." The U.S. Congress noted the purpose of the law in its findings: "There is abundant evidence of the use of abusive, deceptive, and unfair debt collection practices by many debt collectors. Abusive debt collection practices contribute to the number of personal bankruptcies, to marital instability, to the loss of jobs, and to invasions of individual privacy."

Are there **limitations** when **debt collectors can call** consumers?

Yes, the Fair Debt Collection Practices Act provides that debt collectors cannot contact consumers "at any unusual time or place known or which should be known to be inconvenient to the consumer." It establishes as a default rule that debtors should confine their debt calls to between 8:00 AM and 9:00 PM. Debt collectors can call a person if they have "the prior consent of the consumer."

The debt collector also cannot contact a consumer at the person's place of employment "if the debt collector knows or has reason to know that the consumer's employer prohibits the consumer from receiving such communication." Debt collectors also should not contact a consumer if they know or have reason to know that the debtor is represented by an attorney with respect to that debt.

Debt collectors can only contact you in person with your specific permission, and they cannot harass you with phone calls at odd hours or use abusive language on the phone. A good option for avoiding debt collectors is to work closely with a financial advisor who can negotiate on your behalf (*iStock*).

What is considered **harassing behavior** under the **Fair Debt Collections Practices Act** (FDCPA)?

The law prohibits the "the threat of use of violence," "use of obscene or profane language," the publication of a list of consumers who refuse to pay debts, and repeated ringing of a consumer's telephone "with the intent to annoy, abuse, or harass any person at the called number." The law also prohibits telephone calls without disclosing the identity of the caller.

LegalSpeak: Congressional Findings for the Fair Debt Collection Practices Act § 802. Congressional findings and declaration of purpose:

(a) There is abundant evidence of the use of abusive, deceptive, and unfair debt collection practices by many debt collectors. Abusive debt collection practices contribute to the number of personal bankruptcies, to marital instability, to the loss of jobs, and to invasions of individual privacy.

(b) Existing laws and procedures for redressing these injuries are inadequate to protect consumers.

(c) Means other than misrepresentation or other abusive debt collection practices are available for the effective collection of debts.

(d) Abusive debt collection practices are carried on to a substantial extent in interstate commerce and through means and instrumentalities of such commerce. Even where abusive debt collection practices are purely intrastate in character, they nevertheless directly affect interstate commerce.

(e) It is the purpose of this title to eliminate abusive debt collection practices by debt collectors, to insure that those debt collectors who refrain from using abusive debt collection practices are not competitively disadvantaged, and to promote consistent State action to protect consumers against debt collection abuses."

What **other conduct** does the **FDCPA prohibit**?

It prohibits "false and misleading representations" by debt collectors. This includes false communications that an individual is an attorney, affiliated with the U.S. government, misstating the amount of a debt, falsely stating that a consumer committed a crime, or representing that nonpayment of a debt will result in the "arrest or imprisonment of any person." False and misleading speech by debt collectors also includes the use of a business name or company other than the true name of the debtor, the implication that a debt collector works with a credit reporting agency and "the use of any false representation or deceptive means to collect or attempt to collect any debt or to obtain information concerning a consumer."

The act also lists a host of "unfair practices," which include depositing or threatening to deposit a postdated check early, the collection of interest not provided for by law, communicating with debtors by postcards, and using any language or symbol other than the debt collector's address when communicating with a consumer by mail.

205

Can consumers **sue** for **violations** of the **FDCPA**?

Yes, the law provides for a "civil liability" section that includes consumers receiving damages. Consumers can receive actual damages and additional damages of up to $1,000. The law also allows consumers to sue under a class-action theory. Consumers can also recover reasonable attorney's fees if they prevail in such an action. The law provides that such actions must be brought in a federal district court within one year from the date of the violations.

BANKRUPTCY

What is **bankruptcy**?

Bankruptcy is a process in which an individual or company files a court action declaring that he or it is financially unable to pay off debts. During bankruptcy, a court liquidates a person or company's assets, discharges debt, and repays a portion back to creditors (if there are any available funds). Bankruptcy also provides for an orderly process for reorganizing businesses and distributing payments to creditors. Bankruptcy has its own set of federal courts, as nearly every one of the 94 federal judicial districts in the country has its own bankruptcy court.

What are the basic **types of bankruptcy**?

There are six different types of bankruptcy cases, but by far the two most common are Chapter 7 bankruptcy and Chapter 13 bankruptcy. The other forms are Chapter 9, Chapter 11, Chapter 12, and Chapter 15. The types are so-named after the chapters they fall under in the Bankruptcy Code.

Chapter 7—sometimes referred to as straight bankruptcy or liquidation bankruptcy—is the most commonly filed form of bankruptcy. Most individual consumers file Chapter 7 bankruptcy. This form is ideal for consumers with modest economic means, little in the way of assets, and high debts. In Chapter 7, most of the time a consumer's debts are discharged—meaning they are wiped away clean, giving the person a chance at a fresh start in life. More than 60 percent of all bankruptcy cases are filed under Chapter 7.

Chapter 13 is referred to as reorganization bankruptcy for individuals. In such a bankruptcy, individuals repay a portion of their debts over a three- to five-year period.

What must a consumer do **before filing bankruptcy**?

A consumer contemplating filing bankruptcy must undergo credit counseling within 180 days before filing for bankruptcy. This requirement was added as a result of the

Bankruptcy Abuse Prevention and Consumer Protection Act of 2005. The debtor must present the bankruptcy court with a certificate of completion from such counseling. The law requires that bankruptcy courts maintain a list of approved credit counselors in the area and the courts do review counselors to determine if they are appropriate places for consumers to receive such services.

When filing a bankruptcy petition, the consumer must include much information. These filings must include the following: a list of creditors; a listing of assets and liabilities, current income and payment obligations, statement of financial affairs, copies of all payment advances, statement of monthly net income, and a statement disclosing any expected future income in the coming year. These various forms can be obtained from the Bankruptcy Courts website at http://www.uscourts.gov/bkforms/index.html.

The consumer may also have to provide tax returns and photo identification. These various forms are referred to as "schedules," and consumers must take great pains to insure that the information is both accurate and complete. For example, completed schedules include Form 6 Schedules— Statistical Summary of Certain Liabilities and Related Data (28 U.S.C. § 159):

Schedule A: Real Property

Schedule B: Personal Property

Schedule C: Property Claimed as Exempt

Schedule D: Creditors Holding Secured Claims

Schedule E: Creditors Holding Unsecured Priority Claims

Schedule F: Creditors Holding Unsecured Nonpriority Claims

Schedule G: Executory Contracts and Unexpired Leases

Schedule H: Codebtors

Schedule I: Current Income of Individual Debtor(s)

Schedule J: Current Expenditures of Individual Debtors(s)

After a consumer files a bankruptcy petition, the court will notify the different creditors of the petition. The court will appoint a bankruptcy trustee, who will serve as the moderator and controller of the debtor's estate and assets.

What does it **cost** to file for **bankruptcy**?

As of this writing, debtors must pay a filing fee of $245, an administrative fee of $39, and a trustee surcharge fee of $15 for a total of $299 in fees. Debtors will pay this in addition to the fees they will pay their attorney. Failure to pay the required fees can result in dismissal of the bankruptcy petition. However, there is a form for debtors who wish to seek a waiver of the fee because of extreme financial hardship. The form is available at http://www.uscourts.gov/rules/BK_Forms_1207/B_003B_1207f.pdf.

What is a **bankruptcy trustee**?

A bankruptcy trustee is someone appointed by the Office of the United States Trustee (a branch of the Department of Justice) who makes sure that unsecured creditors are paid and ensures compliance with bankruptcy laws. Often bankruptcy trustees are local attorneys or others well versed in the bankruptcy process.

What is the **means test**?

The "means test"—a requirement of the 2005 Bankruptcy Abuse Prevention Act—requires that a debtor show whether he or she has sufficient means to avoid bankruptcy. This test compares a consumer's debts with their income to determine if they have sufficient means to avoid Chapter 7 bankruptcy. The consumer provides his or her current monthly income as compared with their regular debts.

Declaring bankruptcy should be a step taken only if one is completely without other options, and not just a convenient method to avoid paying back creditors (*iStock*).

Congress adopted this requirement in the law to prevent abusive filings by those seeking Chapter 7 discharges when they really could pay their creditors. Sometimes the application of the means test results in individuals having to file Chapter 13 instead of Chapter 7, which means they have to pay a greater portion of their debts back to creditors. The form for the means test is available at http://www.uscourts.gov/rules/BK_Forms_08_Official/B_022A_1208.pdf.

What are **exempt assets**?

Remember that in bankruptcy a consumer must list all of his or her assets. Fortunately, some of these assets are exempt from the process, meaning that the consumer gets to keep those assets and not fear that they will fall into the hands of creditors. Some of these exempt assets include: $20,200 in the consumer's home, jewelry with a value up to $1,325, $2,025 in books or tools of a consumer's trade, up to nearly $10,000 in household appliances and items, though there is a maximum of $585 per item, and money in an Individual Retirement Account (IRA). For a full listing of exempt assets, see 11 U.S.C. § 522.

Exempt assets mean that unsecured creditors cannot touch them. However, secured creditors who have a security interest may still be able to recover.

LegalSpeak: Text of the "341 Meeting" Provision in the Bankruptcy Code—11 U.S.C. § 341.

Meetings of creditors and equity security holders:

(a) Within a reasonable time after the order for relief in a case under this title, the United States trustee shall convene and preside at a meeting of creditors.

(b) The United States trustee may convene a meeting of any equity security holders.

(c) The court may not preside at, and may not attend, any meeting under this section including any final meeting of creditors. Notwithstanding any local court rule, provision of a State constitution, any otherwise applicable nonbankruptcy law, or any other requirement that representation at the meeting of creditors under subsection (a) be by an attorney, a creditor holding a consumer debt or any representative of the creditor (which may include an entity or an employee of an entity and may be a representative for more than 1 creditor) shall be permitted to appear at and participate in the meeting of creditors in a case under chapter 7 or 13, either alone or in conjunction with an attorney for the creditor. Nothing in this subsection shall be construed to require any creditor to be represented by an attorney at any meeting of creditors.

(d) Prior to the conclusion of the meeting of creditors or equity security holders, the trustee shall orally examine the debtor to ensure that the debtor in a case under chapter 7 of this title is aware of.

  (1) the potential consequences of seeking a discharge in bankruptcy, including the effects on credit history;

  (2) the debtor's ability to file a petition under a different chapter of this title;

  (3) the effect of receiving a discharge of debts under this title; and

  (4) the effect of reaffirming a debt, including the debtor's knowledge of the provisions of section 524(d) of this title.

(e) Notwithstanding subsections (a) and (b), the court, on the request of a party in interest and after notice and a hearing, for cause may order that the United States trustee not convene a meeting of creditors or equity security holders if the debtor has filed a plan as to which the debtor solicited acceptances prior to the commencement of the case."

Are there **exemptions** under **state laws**?

Yes, while most of bankruptcy law is federal, there are state-law aspects to bankruptcy as well. An example is that some states have specific exemptions that might provide greater protection for consumers. For example, some states have greater homestead exemptions than the $20,200 provided for under federal law. Florida and several other states have no limit on homestead exemptions, meaning that consumers in those states get to keep their homes free and clear.

Are all **debts dischargeable** under **Chapter 7**?

No, not all debts are dischargeable under Chapter 7 bankruptcy. Some of these that are usually nondischargeable are child support and alimony, most student loans, back taxes, debts for personal injuries, and court-imposed fines.

What is a **no-asset case**?

A no-asset case is one in which all of the debtor's property is exempt and there is nothing for the trustee to sell off and pay the creditors. Many Chapter 7 bankruptcy cases are no-asset cases.

Is there a way to **keep** certain **property** by working out a **deal** with **creditors**?

Consumers filing bankruptcy do have the option of seeking to reaffirm debts. Under the reaffirmation process, a consumer-debtor promises to pay the creditor a certain amount in exchange for keeping the property. If the debtor adheres to his or her promises, he or she gets to keep the property. Federal bankruptcy law requires creditors to post the following statements on a reaffirmation agreement:

- "Reaffirming a debt is a serious financial decision. The law requires you to take certain steps to make sure the decision is in your best interest. If these steps are not completed, the reaffirmation agreement is not effective, even though you have signed it."
- "You may rescind (cancel) your reaffirmation agreement at any time before the bankruptcy court enters a discharge order, or before the expiration of the 60-day period that begins on the date your reaffirmation is filed with the court, whichever occurs later."

What is a **341 meeting**?

A "341 meeting" is an initial meeting of creditors so-called because it is required under Section 341 of the Bankruptcy Code in a Chapter 7 case (see LegalSpeak, p. 209). The consumer-debtor also must attend the meeting. The bankruptcy trustee presides over the meeting and asks various questions of the consumer-debtor under oath regarding his financial affairs. Often creditors do not show up at these meetings.

Filing with bankruptcy begins with deciding between Chapter 13 and 7 based on your eligibility, finding an attorney, completing the paperwork, and working patiently with the court. This can be a long and complicated process (*iStock*).

CHAPTER 13

What is the **main difference** between **Chapter 13** and **Chapter 7**?

There are many differences, but probably the main difference is that in Chapter 13 you get to keep your property as long as you are adhering to the repayment plan. In other words, Chapter 13 is not a liquidation bankruptcy like Chapter 7, where much of the debtor's assets (if there are any) are liquidated. Consumers who file Chapter 13 pay their debtors out of their future income instead of their liquidated assets.

What are some **advantages** of filing **Chapter 13 versus** filing for **Chapter 7**?

There are many advantages to each form of bankruptcy. The Chapter 13 advantages are: the retention of most assets, it can be filed more frequently, and it is more likely that you will keep your home. Some Chapter 7 advantages are that the cases are quicker (months as opposed to years), the discharge of nearly all debts and it is a much better option for those with few assets. Often it is best to consult with an attorney well versed in bankruptcy law to determine the best option for consumers.

How does a **Chapter 13** case **begin**?

As with a Chapter 7 petition, a consumer must complete a credit counseling course within 180 days of filing a bankruptcy petition. The consumer must then fill out a

211

packet of forms similar to a Chapter 7 consumer. The difference is that the Chapter 13 consumer must come up with a workable plan to repay some of his or her debts over a three- to five-year period. The consumer must also include proof of paying income taxes and provide the most recently IRS tax return as well.

Chapter 13 petitioners must file their planned repayment schedule within 15 days of filing their petition. The repayment plan is based on the disposable income of the petitioner.

What **types of consumers must file** for Chapter 13?

Those consumers with higher incomes usually must opt for Chapter 13, because they don't pass the "means test." Those who have an income level higher than their state median income level generally must file for Chapter 13.

How **long** do **Chapter 13** cases last **compared to Chapter 7** cases?

Chapter 13 cases last much longer than Chapter 7 cases. The typical Chapter 7 cases lasts only about 4 to 6 months, while Chapter 13 cases last three to five years.

What **eligibility requirements** are there for **Chapter 13**?

A consumer-debtor must not have more than $336,900 in unsecured debt and have less than $1,010,650 in secured debt in order to file Chapter 13.

Do **prior bankruptcy filings affect eligibility** to file other bankruptcy petitions?

Yes, there are time limitations. An individual is ineligible for a Chapter 13 discharge if he or she has had a previous Chapter 13 case in the past two years or a Chapter 7 case in the past four years. You cannot file a Chapter 7 petition if you have had a previous Chapter 7 case in the past eight years.

What is **disposable income**?

Disposable income refers to whatever is left over from your total income after you have paid for taxes and reasonable and necessary living expenses, as determined on a monthly basis. This is arguably the most important calculation in Chapter 13 cases, as this determines how much money you will repay and how much money you will have for regular living expenses. The Bankruptcy Code defines "disposable income" as follows:

> For purposes of this subsection, the term "disposable income" means current monthly income received by the debtor (other than child support payments, foster care payments, or disability payments for a dependent child made in

accordance with applicable nonbankruptcy law to the extent reasonably necessary to be expended for such child) less amounts reasonably necessary to be expended....

EMPLOYMENT LAW

AT–WILL EMPLOYMENT

What legal doctrine still provides the baseline rule that employees have little protection in the employment relationship in the United States?

Many workers must accept the fact that they are "at-will" employees subject to the employment-at-will doctrine. This doctrine provides that either the employer or employee can end the employment relationship at will—even for a seemingly unfair reason. The Tennessee Supreme Court explained the doctrine in *Payne v. Western & Atlantic R. Co.* (1884): "All may dismiss their employees at will, be they many or few, for good cause, for no cause or even for cause morally wrong without being thereby guilty of legal wrong." Under the employment-at-will doctrine, an employer can dismiss an employee for a good reason, bad reason, or no reason at all. The reasoning behind the rule is that because an employee can leave the employment relationship at any time, the employer should have the same right to terminate the relationship at will. Unfortunately, the rule does not take into consideration the power disparity between most employers and employees. An employer often can easily replace an employee, while an employee often has a much more difficult time finding a comparable job.

Much of current employment law deals with whether various exceptions to the employment-at-will doctrine apply. For example, employers (with a certain number of employees) cannot fire workers for certain discriminatory reasons—because of the employees' race, sex, or religion. There also have developed many so-called public policy exceptions to the employment-at-will doctrine. Common public policy exceptions to the employment-at-will doctrine are that employers may not fire workers for serving on a jury, exposing illegal activities by the employer in the workplace, filing a workers' compensation claim, or having your wages garnished.

215

What broad **categories of workers** are **not subject** to the **employment-at-will** doctrine?

Workers who have an employment relationship governed by a contract called a collective bargaining agreement (CBA) generally are not subject to the employment-at-will doctrine. The CBA is a contract of the employment relationship between the workers, usually represented by a union, and the management of the employer. Workers under a CBA are not subject to the harsh rule of employment-at-will because a common goal for unions in their negotiations with management is to include a just-cause provision in the CBA, which is the governing contract that controls the parameters of the employment relationship. A just-cause clause provides that an employer shall not fire a worker except for just cause—a very good or justifiable reason.

Sometimes workers who do not work at a large plant with a collective bargaining agreement still are not subject to the employment-at-will doctrine because they have signed an employment contract. This means that a worker who has a valid employment contract is often not subject to the employment-at-will doctrine. Rather, the employee is subject to the terms and conditions of the signed contract. Most workers, however, are not protected by a specific contract. If there is not an agreement that serves as the guide to the employer-employee relationship, the default rule in many states is the employment-at-will doctrine.

Can the **employee handbook** that an employer hands out to you constitute a **valid contract** that binds the employer?

It depends. Courts in some states recognize a so-called "handbook exception" to employment at will, which means that the employer can create a contract by making certain promises and offers in the employee handbook. For example, some courts have determined that employee handbooks that make statements providing a form of job security for employees can alter the employment-at-will relationship. The Michigan Supreme Court first recognized the handbook exception to the employment-at-will doctrine in 1980.

Other states hold that an employee handbook cannot convert an at-will employment relationship into a contractual relationship. Many courts have determined that the employee handbook must set forth a clear promise which the employees view as an offer in order to be viewed as an enforceable contract. Many times employers will include a statement in the handbook which expressly disclaims the intention to create any sort of contract. Often these statements say that the employer reserves the right to unilaterally change any provisions in the handbook. Here is one such sample statement: "I UNDERSTAND THAT THIS HANDBOOK IS A GENERAL GUIDE AND THAT THE PROVISIONS OF THIS HANDBOOK DO NOT CONSTITUTE AN EMPLOYMENT AGREEMENT (CONTRACT) OR A GUARANTEE OF CONTINUED EMPLOYMENT."

For many Americans in a variety of jobs, employment-at-will agreements mean they can be terminated at any time for little or no reason (*iStock*).

How did the **employment-at-will doctrine originate** in the United States?

In England, the common rule was the so-called English rule, which provided that employment should be presumed for a year or through the respective season. This was a rule that provided a degree of protection to workers even when there was not the highest demand for labor. However, American employers in the late 1800s shifted focus to the at-will rule, perhaps as a way to complete in the growing industrial economy.

Many scholars trace the employment-at-will rule to a New York-based legal writer named Horace Gay Wood, who wrote in his treatise *Master and Servant* (1877): "[T]he rule is inflexible, that a general or indefinite hiring is *prima facie* a hiring at will, and if the servant seeks to make it out a yearly hiring, the burden is upon him to establish it by proof.... It is competent for either party to show what the mutual understanding of the parties was in reference to the matter; but unless their understanding was mutual that the service was to extend for a certain fixed and definite period, it is an indefinite hiring and is determinable at the will of either party." Wood's rule was that the burden was on the employee to show that the employment relationship was not governed by the employment-at-will relationship.

Wood's statement of the employment-at-will doctrine became the norm in laws throughout the states, as various state high courts cited Wood's treatise in adopting the doctrine. By the end of the 1930s, nearly every state had accepted the employment-at-will doctrine as the default rule in the employment setting.

LegalSpeak: *Rooney v. Tyson* (N.Y. 1998)

A sensible path to declare New York law starts with these two steps: (1) if the duration is definite, the at-will doctrine is inapplicable, on the other hand, (2) if the employment term is indefinite or undefined, the rebuttable at-will presumption is operative and other factors come into the equation....

When an agreement is silent as to duration, however, it is presumptively at-will, absent an express or implied limitation on an employer's otherwise unfettered ability to discharge an employee. Only when we discern no term of some definiteness or no express limitation does the analysis switch over to the rebuttable presumption line of cases. They embody the principle that an employment relationship is terminable upon even the whim of either the employer or the employee. The agreement in this case is not silent and manifestly provides a sufficiently limiting framework....

The range of the employment relationship, concededly created and actualized for several years in the framework of this Federal dispute, is established by the definable commencement and conclusion of Tyson's professional boxing career. Though the times are not precisely predictable and calculable to dates certain, they are legally and experientially limited and ascertainable by objective benchmarks.

What if an employer offers **lifetime** or **permanent employment**? Does the **employment-at-will** doctrine still **apply**?

Yes, in many jurisdictions the offer of permanent employment is considered to be for an indefinite term and the employment-at-will doctrine still applies. The offer of permanent employment is considered too indefinite to overcome the presumption that the employment-at-will doctrine applies.

However, sometimes courts will recognize seemingly lifetime contracts. For example, in a famous case involving former heavyweight boxing champion Mike Tyson and his former trainer Kevin Rooney, the New York Court of Appeals (the state's highest court) found that an oral statement to Rooney that he could train the boxer "as long as he fights professionally" was a contract for a definite time period even though there was of course no guarantee as to how long Tyson would fight. The court concluded that "an oral contract between a fight trainer and a professional boxer to train the boxer 'for as long as the boxer fights professionally' is a contract for a definite duration."

How does a **court determine** a public policy **exception** to the at-will doctrine?

Different state courts apply different rules to determine when there are public policy exceptions to the at-will doctrine. Some states provide that public policy is evinced by the legislature. In these states, if there is a specific law or statute that provides an exception to the at-will doctrine, that suffices to establish public policy. For example, the states of Pennsylvania and Tennessee provide that public policy is shown by the legislature—the branch of government most attuned to setting policy. In other states, the courts develop public policy exceptions judicially. This means that the state supreme court (usually the name for the highest court in a state) establishes public policy exceptions to the employment-at-will doctrine.

What are some of the most **common types** of public policy **exceptions** to the **employment-at-will** doctrine?

In most states, employers may not fire or discriminate against employees for serving on jury duty, exposing criminality in the workplace, filing a workers' compensation claim, protecting others from physical danger, or refusing to take a polygraph test.

However, sometimes what seems like good public policy does not result in a favorable outcome for an employee. A good example is the case of *Green v. Winston Murphy Bryant* (1995) in Pennsylvania. The case involved the employee of a doctor's office who was terminated after she informed a physician that her physical injuries were the result of a severe beating she endured from her estranged husband. The doctor's office fired the woman, ostensibly because they feared the estranged husband might pose a danger to the office staff.

The woman sued, but a reviewing federal district court ruled that Green was an at-will employee who did not have a legal claim. Ms. Green argued that her dismissal violated two public policies protecting employee privacy rights and protecting victims of domestic violence. She pointed out that there was a Pennsylvania law that created a crime victim's compensation board that applied to domestic violence victims. However, the court pointed out that this law was a general criminal law that did not create a "protected employment class." The court concluded that "in the absence of any indication that Pennsylvania has established a clear mandate that crime victims generally, or spousal abuse victims specifically, are entitled to benefits or privileges beyond those enumerated in the laws, I must conclude that plaintiff's dismissal was not in violation of public policy."

What is the story of **Jason Little** and how the public policy exception to employment at will protected him from **physical assault**?

Jason Little worked as a clerk for a convenience store in Jackson, Tennessee. While on duty, Little noticed a man across the street assaulting a woman. Little grabbed a baseball bat from under the store counter, ran across the street and yelled at the man. Little's actions saved the woman from further harm.

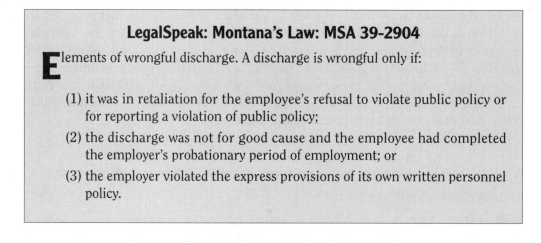

LegalSpeak: Montana's Law: MSA 39-2904

Elements of wrongful discharge. A discharge is wrongful only if:

(1) it was in retaliation for the employee's refusal to violate public policy or for reporting a violation of public policy;

(2) the discharge was not for good cause and the employee had completed the employer's probationary period of employment; or

(3) the employer violated the express provisions of its own written personnel policy.

Two days later the store fired Little for leaving store property to engage in a fight. The store claimed that it could not risk this sort of "liability." Little sued for wrongful termination, alleging he was subjected to a retaliatory discharge for protecting the safety of a third party. He cited a Tennessee statute providing that a person is justified in using or threatening to use physical force to protect another person.

The Tennessee Court of Appeals agreed with a trial court's refusal to dismiss Little's retaliatory discharge claim. "Here, Tennessee's public policy of placing a high priority on the sanctity of human life is clearly evinced in its statutes," the appeals court wrote in *Little v. Eastgate of Jackson* (2007). The appeals court believed that Tennessee law showed a clear public policy of encouraging people to act to protect people who are in "imminent danger of death or serious bodily harm."

What **state** passed a **law** that **repealed** the **employment at-will** doctrine?

Montana is the only state that has passed a law that eliminated the at-will employment doctrine. Montana had a statute that provided for at-will employment. However, in 1987 the Montana legislature passed law called the Wrongful Discharge from Employment Act (WDFEA). It established that for employers needed good cause to fire employees who have completed their probationary periods of employment.

The interesting part of this was that when the Montana legislature passed its wrongful discharge law, it did not repeal its prior statute providing for at-will employment. However, in *Whidden v. Nerison* (1999), the Montana Supreme Court ruled that the Montana legislature repealed the at-will statute by implication, writing: "[W]e hold … that the WDFEA has superseded and impliedly repealed the at-will act." The Montana high court also determined that the burden is on an employer to determine that an employee was discharged during a probationary period.

Anti-discrimination laws are designed to prevent employers from not hiring someone just because of his or her race, religion, gender, or national origin. A diverse workforce can actually benefit a business, as it can allow for a broader range of input from employees with various backgrounds and experiences (*iStock*).

EMPLOYMENT DISCRIMINATION

Can **employers** really **discriminate against employees** for any reason?

No, a major exception to the employment-at-will doctrine is employment discrimination law. There are a host of federal and state laws that limit certain employers (employers with a certain number of employees) from discriminating against workers for certain reasons, such as their race or sex.

What are some of the major **anti-discrimination laws** at the **federal** level?

There are several numerous federal anti-discrimination laws. The major federal anti-discrimination law is Title VII of the Civil Rights Act of 1964, which prohibits employers from discriminating against workers because of their race, color, national origin, religion, and gender. It makes it "an unlawful employment practice for an employer … to discriminate against any individual with respect to his compensation, terms, conditions, or privileges of employment, because of such individual's race, color, religion, sex, or national origin."

Passed during the Civil Rights Movement, Title VII remains the leading anti-discrimination law in employment. Title VII also prohibits employers from retaliating

221

against those employees who participate in Title VII proceedings or oppose employment practices that they reasonably believe are unlawful.

However, Title VII is not the only such statute. The Age Discrimination in Employment Act of 1967 (ADEA) prohibits employers from discriminating against workers who are a certain age (40 years of age or older). The Rehabilitation Act of 1973 and the Americans with Disabilities Act of 1990 (ADA) prohibit employers from discriminating against employees with disabilities. Still another anti-discrimination law is 42 U.S.C. 1981, which prohibits intentional racial discrimination in employment.

The Equal Pay Act provides that women and men receive equal pay for equal work.

Does my **state** also have **anti-discrimination laws** that protect me as an employee?

Yes, states also have laws that protect employees from unlawful discrimination. Many of these state laws are based on the federal laws. For example, Tennessee has an employment discrimination law known as the Tennessee Human Rights Act of 1978. That law was based on major federal anti-discrimination laws such as Title VII of the Civil Rights Act of 1964 and the Age Discrimination Act of 1967.

Your lawyer can give you guidance on whether to sue for employment discrimination under a federal law, state law or both. The lawyer can tell you, for instance, whether your state anti-discrimination law offers more or less protection than the federal law.

TITLE VII

What is **Title VII**?

Title VII is the seventh major section (or title) of the Civil Rights Act of 1964, a major piece of civil rights legislation enacted during the Civil Rights Movement as a way to provide greater protection to people.

Does **Title VII** apply to **all employees**?

No, Title VII applies to those employers in the public and private sectors who employ 15 or more full-time employees in 20 or more calendar weeks during the year or previous year. This means that an employer who has only 10 full-time employees is not subject to Title VII. Fortunately, many workers who are not covered by Title VII may be protected by a state anti-discrimination law. For example, the Tennessee Human Rights Act prohibits employers who employ eight or more full-time employees from discriminating on the basis of race, sex, religion, and other protected characteristics. Employees should consult with an attorney well-versed in both federal and state employment to determine what the best legal option available.

LegalSpeak: *McDonald v. Santa Fe Transportation Co.* (1976)

Title VII of the Civil Rights Act of 1964 prohibits the discharge of "any individual" because of "such individual's race," 703 (a) (1), 42 U.S.C. 2000e-2 (a) (1). Its terms are not limited to discrimination against members of any particular race. Thus, although we were not there confronted with racial discrimination against whites, we described the Act in Griggs v. Duke Power Co. (1971), as prohibiting "[d]iscriminatory preference for any [racial] group, minority or majority." Similarly the EEOC, whose interpretations are entitled to great deference, has consistently interpreted Title VII to proscribe racial discrimination in private employment against whites on the same terms as racial discrimination against nonwhites … This conclusion is in accord with uncontradicted legislative history to the effect that Title VII was intended to "cover white men and white women and all Americans," 110 Cong. Rec. 2578 (1964) (remarks of Rep. Celler), and create an "obligation not to discriminate against whites." We therefore hold today that Title VII prohibits racial discrimination against the white petitioners in this case upon the same standards as would be applicable were they Negroes [or] … white.

What **types of discrimination** does Title VII **prohibit**?

Title VII prohibits discrimination against an employee based on that employee's race, color, religion, sex, or national origin. Title VII also prohibits retaliating against employees who oppose such unlawful employment practices or who participate in Title VII proceedings in some capacity.

Does **Title VII protect** individuals of **all races**?

Yes, it does. The U.S. Supreme Court made this clear in *McDonald v. Santa Fe Transportation Co.* (1976) when it ruled that Title VII protected Caucasian employees in addition to African-American employees. While Title VII was passed during the Civil Rights Movement in large part because of rampant discrimination against African-Americans, the language applies to any employee based on race. The *McDonald v. Santa Fe* case involved three employees who were caught stealing company property. The employer retained an African-American employee but discharged the two Caucasian employees involved with the incident. The Court reversed the lower courts and reinstated the two employees' discrimination claims under Title VII.

Title VII **protects individuals** based on their **gender**, but does it protect people because of their **sexual orientation**?

No, Title VII does not cover employees from workplace discrimination based on sexual orientation. For many years, measures have been introduced into Congress to add sexu-

While U.S. citizens are protected under Title VII from discrimination because of their gender, the same courtesy does not yet apply to gay, lesbian, bisexual, or transgender people (*iStock*).

al orientation to the list of protected characteristics in Title VII, but none of the measures has passed. In November 2007, the House passed 235 to 198 the Employment Non-Discrimination Act of 2007, which would amend Title VII to add sexual orientation. However, the measure did not come up for a full vote in the Senate. President Barack Obama indicated his support for the Employment Non-Discrimination Act during his campaign.

Since Title VII does not protect employees from **discrimination** based on **sexual orientation** does that mean these employees have no protection?

Some employees have protection from employment discrimination based on sexual orientation under their respective state laws. In some states, the legislature has passed a law that prohibits discrimination against employees because of sexual orientation. In other states, public employees are protected from such discrimination. For example, in 2002 the Alaska governor signed an executive order prohibiting sexual orientation discrimination against state employees.

What **states** have **laws** that **prohibit discrimination** against employees (public and private) because of **sexual orientation**?

The states that prohibit such discrimination are: California, Colorado, Connecticut, Hawaii, Illinois, Maine, Maryland, Massachusetts, Minnesota, Nevada, New Hampshire, New Jersey, New Mexico, New York, Oregon, Rhode Island, Vermont, Washington, and Wisconsin.

Which **states prohibit** employment **discrimination** based on **sexual orientation** for **public employees** only?

These states are Alaska, Delaware, Indiana, Louisiana, Michigan, Montana, Ohio, and Pennsylvania.

Does **Title VII** apply to just **intentional discrimination**?

Title VII applies to more than just intentional discrimination—sometimes referred to as disparate treatment—treating people differently based on a protected class (race, sex,

> ## LegalSpeak: Legislative Proposal—
> ## Employment Non-Discrimination Act
>
> a) Employer Practices—It shall be an unlawful employment practice for an employer—
>
> (1) to fail or refuse to hire or to discharge any individual, or otherwise discriminate against any individual with respect to the compensation, terms, conditions, or privileges of employment of the individual, because of such individual's actual or perceived sexual orientation; or
>
> (2) to limit, segregate, or classify the employees or applicants for employment of the employer in any way that would deprive or tend to deprive any individual of employment or otherwise adversely affect the status of the individual as an employee, because of such individual's actual or perceived sexual orientation.

color, etc.). However, Title VII sometimes also prohibits even unintentional discrimination that works an adverse impact—called disparate impact—on certain classes of people.

What are the **two main types** or theories of **discrimination**?

The two legal terms used to describe types of discrimination are (1) disparate treatment and (2) disparate impact. Disparate treatment refers to an employer intentionally treating an employee differently based on race, gender, religion, disability, age, or some other protected category. For example, let's say that two employees—a male and a female—both commit the same offense of reading personal email excessively on company time. Then, the employer suspends the male employee but only issues a verbal warning to the female employee. The male employee may claim that he was subjected to disparate treatment based on sex. When employers apply their rules and regulations inconsistently to different employees, it raises the possibility that certain employees were subjected to disparate treatment discrimination.

Disparate impact discrimination is different. It refers to facially neutral employment policies that work an adverse impact on a protected class.

What is an **example** of an **employer policy** that would be considered **disparate impact**?

If an employer adopted a minimum height and weight requirement on police officers, that would work a disparate impact based on sex. If the employer says that all police officers must be at least five-feet, five-inches tall and weigh at least 140 pounds, more women than men would be excluded. Such a policy would work a disparate impact upon female workers and could constitute unlawful sex discrimination—even if the discrimination was not based upon bad intent.

When did the U.S. **Supreme Court** first **recognize** that Title VII **included disparate impact** claims?

The U.S. Supreme Court recognized that Title VII included disparate impact claims in its decision in *Griggs v. Duke Power* (1971; see LegalSpeak, p. 228). The case involved a claim by 13 African-American employees at Duke Power Co. who claimed that two requirements for transfer to a better division within in the company discriminated against them and others (they filed a class action suit on behalf of all African-American employees) on the basis of race. The employer—who years before had refused to hire African-Americans except for manual labor jobs—instituted two policies for transfer to the better divisions after the passage of Title VII. Any employee seeking transfer had to either have a high school education or have passed a general intelligence test.

Evidence in the case showed that neither requirement was imposed on white employees already within certain divisions. Evidence also established that neither requirement was substantially related to good job performance. For example, there were white employees who had no high school education or passed such an intelligence test who performed very well in these departments.

In oft-cited language, Chief Justice Warren Burger wrote: "The Act proscribes not only overt discrimination but also practices that are fair in form, but discriminatory in operation. The touchstone is business necessity. If an employment practice which operates to exclude Negroes cannot be shown to be related to job performance, the practice is prohibited."

An example of a "disparate impact" hiring policy would be requiring police officers to be of a certain height and weight that would discriminate agains women (*iStock*).

Who was **Griggs** in the *Griggs v. Duke Power* case?

Willie S. Griggs was the lead plaintiff in the *Griggs v. Duke Power* (1971; see Legal-Speak, p. 228) case and an employee of the Duke Power company plant. He was listed first in the initial lawsuit, which is why the famous case bears his name.

What if an employer has **multiple reasons** for taking adverse action against an employee—a **discriminatory reason** and a **lawful reason**?

Title VII provides that "an unlawful employment practice is established when the complaining party demonstrates that race, color, religion, sex, or national origin was a motivating factor for any employment practice, even though other factors also motivated the practice." This is sometimes referred to as a mixed-motive case. Under a mixed-motive case, an employer can try to show that it would have made the same employment decision absent the unlawful reason.

For example, let's say that an employee alleged she was fired for her sex. However, apparently there also was evidence that she had trouble getting along with her supervisor and other behavioral issues. This may qualify as a mixed-motive case. The employee must show that her sex was a motivating factor in the discharge decision. The employer must show that it would have made the same decision regarding the employee absent her sex—in other words that the employer would have fired her for her behavioral issues anyway. If the employer proves the same decision defense, it can prevent the plaintiff

227

LegalSpeak: *Griggs v. Duke Power* (1971)

The objective of Congress in the enactment of Title VII is plain from the language of the statute. It was to achieve equality of employment opportunities and remove barriers that have operated in the past to favor an identifiable group of white employees over other employees. Under the Act, practices, procedures, or tests neutral on their face, and even neutral in terms of intent, cannot be maintained if they operate to "freeze" the status quo of prior discriminatory employment practices....

Congress has now provided that tests or criteria for employment or promotion may not provide equality of opportunity merely in the sense of the fabled offer of milk to the stork and the fox. On the contrary, Congress has now required that the posture and condition of the job-seeker be taken into account. It has—to resort again to the fable—provided that the vessel in which the milk is proffered be one all seekers can use. The Act proscribes not only overt discrimination but also practices that are fair in form, but discriminatory in operation. The touchstone is business necessity. If an employment practice which operates to exclude Negroes cannot be shown to be related to job performance, the practice is prohibited.

from collecting damages. However, the plaintiff may still be able to obtain attorneys' fees and injunctive relief (an order prohibiting the employer from doing something).

The U.S. Supreme Court recognized mixed-motive claims for discrimination in Title VII in the gender discrimination case of *Price Waterhouse v. Hopkins* (1989; see LegalSpeak, p. 229). Ann Hopkins sued Price Waterhouse after she did not make partner at the accounting firm. Hopkins introduced evidence of gender stereotyping in the workplace. However, the employer said that Hopkins was too brusque and had personality issues that motivated the decision in part. The question before the U.S. Supreme Court was how to deal with cases in which an employer had both a permissible and impermissible motive—a mixed-motive case.

Under a mixed-motive claim, a plaintiff must show that an illegitimate motive (gender discrimination) played a role in the employer's decision against the employee. If the employee meets this burden, the employer must then show that it would have made the same decision against the employee regardless of the bad motive.

How does an employee file a claim under Title VII or other federal employment law?

An individual who believes they have been the victim of discrimination in the workforce must file a claim with the federal agency called the Equal Employment Opportu-

LegalSpeak: *Price Waterhouse v. Hopkins* (1989)

But-for causation is a hypothetical construct. In determining whether a particular factor was a but-for cause of a given event, we begin by assuming that that factor was present at the time of the event, and then ask whether, even if that factor had been absent, the event nevertheless would have transpired in the same way. The present, active tense of the operative verbs of 703(a)(1) ("to fail or refuse"), in contrast, turns our attention to the actual moment of the event in question, the adverse employment decision. The critical inquiry, the one commanded by the words of 703(a)(1), is whether gender was a factor in the employment decision at the moment it was made. Moreover, since we know that the words "because of" do not mean "solely because of," we also know that Title VII meant to condemn even those decisions based on a mixture of legitimate and illegitimate considerations. When, therefore, an employer considers both gender and legitimate factors at the time of making a decision, that decision was "because of" sex and the other, legitimate considerations—even if we may say later, in the context of litigation, that the decision would have been the same if gender had not been taken into account....

We have, in short, been here before. Each time, we have concluded that the plaintiff who shows that an impermissible motive played a motivating part in an adverse employment decision has thereby placed upon the defendant the burden to show that it would have made the same decision in the absence of the unlawful motive. Our decision today treads this well-worn path....

Finally, an employer may not meet its burden in such a case by merely showing that at the time of the decision it was motivated only in part by a legitimate reason. The very premise of a mixed-motives case is that a legitimate reason was present, and indeed, in this case, Price Waterhouse already has made this showing by convincing Judge Gesell that Hopkins' interpersonal problems were a legitimate concern. The employer instead must show that its legitimate reason, standing alone, would have induced it to make the same decision.

nity Commission (EEOC). This is called a "charge of discrimination." A person—called the charging party—files such a charge at the nearest EEOC office. Many states have multiple local or field offices. For example, in the state of Florida there is an EEOC office in Miami and Tampa.

In the charge, the charging party must include his or her name, address and phone number, the employer's name and address, and must also explain the charge of discrimination—the factual basis for the charge—and the date. The so-called "Charge Form" will contain a section entitled "Cause of Discrimination" and will list boxes next to race, age, color, disability, sex, religion, national origin, retaliation or other. The charging party must check all boxes that possibly apply. If not, that could prevent the raising of the claim later down the road.

For more information check out the EEOC's website at http://www.eeoc.gov/charge/overview_charge_filing.html.

What are the **time limits** for **filing** an Equal Employment Opportunity Commission **(EEOC) charge**?

A person must file an EEOC charge within 180 days of the alleged discriminatory event. This can be extended to 300 days in some states. However, most states follow the federal 180-day rule. Carefully check this and make sure that you timely file a claim. If you do not file a claim with the EEOC, then you lose your right to sue under federal anti-discrimination laws.

This may be another advantage of filing a claim under a state anti-discrimination law. For example, employees in Tennessee can bypass the administrative charging process and file a claim under the Tennessee Human Rights Act directly in court. Once again, this shows the advantage of having a good attorney who can help guide you through these important decisions.

What happens once an **employee files** a charge of **discrimination**?

Once an employee or former employee files a charge, the EEOC then conducts an investigation. The EEOC does not have the resources to conduct full-blown investigations in every case. They often focus on charges the agency thinks are particularly egregious or those in which a broad class of employees are involved (class action suits). The EEOC will perform some level of investigation , which can include interviewing witnesses, visiting employer sites, requesting employment documents and other actions. The EEOC will then tell its findings to both the charging party and the employer.

What if the **EEOC finds** there has been **discrimination**?

The EEOC will inform the charging party and the employer of its findings. It will attempt to reach conciliation with the employer to remedy the situation. If the conciliation is not successful, the EEOC may initial legal action on its own on behalf of the employee or it may issue a right-to-sue letter to the employee.

What is a **right-to-sue letter**?

A right-to-sue letter is a letter from the EEOC to the employee that complained of discrimination in an EEOC charge. The letter informs the employee that the EEOC has decided not to pursue the matter further and informs the employee that they can now file a lawsuit against the employer.

Gender discrimination in the workplace often stems from preconceived stereotypes about what is "men's work" and what is "women's work." Fortunately, there are legal steps you can take to protect yourself (*iStock*).

What if the EEOC **does not find** there has been **discrimination**?

If the EEOC does not find reasonable cause of discrimination, that does not end the matter. The EEOC will issue a right-to-sue letter to the charging party, which then means that the charging party has 90 days (from the issuance of the letter) to file suit in federal or state court. When the EEOC sends a right-to-sue letter to an employee, it does not necessarily mean that the employer did not think the employee was discriminated against; rather, it could simply mean that the EEOC has chosen to focus its attention and litigation resources on larger class-action type cases where an employer has discriminated against a whole bunch of people instead of just one employee.

Does the **EEOC's finding** of **no discrimination prevent** a **subsequent** court proceeding?

No, the U.S. Supreme Court made clear in *McDonnell Douglas v. Green* (1973) that the EEOC's finding of no reasonable cause for discrimination does not prevent a subsequent employment discrimination lawsuit. Similarly, courts have determined that an EEOC finding of reasonable cause of discrimination does not mean that a plaintiff-employee has established a basic claim of discrimination.

The U.S. Supreme Court ruled in *Chandler v. Roudebush* (1976) that prior EEOC administrative findings may be admitted as evidence under the federal rules of evidence. Trial judges generally have the discretion to determine the admissibility of such administrative agency findings. Remember that the existence of discrimination still depends upon the facts of particular cases, not upon the EEOC's findings. Some courts have determined that EEOC findings have limited probative value.

How does a **court determine** whether an employee suffers **discrimination**?

In some cases an employee may put forth direct evidence that he or she suffered discrimination in the workplace. However, most employers do not come right out and state: "We fired you or demoted you or refused to promote you because of your race or sex." In many disputed cases, the employee contends that the reason he or she was discharged was a discriminatory reason, while the employer contends that the reason was because the employee was a bad employee. The law must come up with some way to analyze the actual reason for the adverse employment action suffered by the employee.

Rather, employees must put forth circumstantial evidence of discrimination. The common method of analyzing such cases comes from the U.S. Supreme Court's decision in *McDonnell Douglas v. Green* (1973)—called the McDonnell Douglas framework. The three-part framework consists of (1) the employee must establish a *prima facie*, or basic, case of employment discrimination; (2) the employer must then come back with a legitimate, nondiscriminatory reason for the adverse employment action; and (3) the employee must then show that the employer's stated reasons for its actions were pretexual or false.

Under the *McDonnell Douglas* framework, how does an **employee establish** a *prima facie* **case** of discrimination?

Under the *McDonnell Douglas* framework, the employee has the initial burden (called a burden of production) to show that there is sufficient evidence for a jury to conclude that the employee suffered discrimination. The employee must show the following:

(1) The employee was in a protected class;
(2) The employee was qualified for the job or was meeting the legitimate business expectations of the job;
(3) The employee suffered an adverse employment action; and
(4) The employer treated the employee worse than similarly-situated individuals outside the employee's protected class.

What was the *McDonnell Douglas* case **about**?

In *McDonnell Douglas v. Green* (1973) a large manufacturing company (McDonnell Douglas) laid off much of its workforce, including Percy Green, an African-American

> ## LegalSpeak: *McDonnell Douglas v. Green* (1973)
>
> The complainant in a Title VII trial must carry the initial burden under the statute of establishing a *prima facie* case of racial discrimination. This may be done by showing (i) that he belongs to a racial minority; (ii) that he applied and was qualified for a job for which the employer was seeking applicants; (iii) that, despite his qualifications, he was rejected; and (iv) that, after his rejection, the position remained open and the employer continued to seek applicants from persons of complainant's qualifications.

civil rights activist. During the layoff period, Green had protested what he believed to be discriminatory hiring practices of his employer by helping to engage in a stall-in, where protestors would take their cars and then stall them on the road leading into the employer's business.

McDonnell Douglas then began a rehiring of many workers. Green applied for reinstatement but was denied. He sued, alleging that McDonnell Douglas failed to rehire him because of his civil rights activism and his race. The lower courts rejected his claim. However, the U.S. Supreme Court said that the lower courts failed to give him a chance to prove that the company's reasons for not rehiring him—participation in illegal acts of disruption—were pretextual or false. The importance of the case is the allocation of proof that the Court established for Title VII plaintiffs and defendants.

What happened to **Percy Green** after *McDonnell Douglas v. Green*?

Green eventually lost his case on remand because the federal trial court ruled that the evidence showed that Green was rejected for hire not because of his race but because of his illegal activities. He earned a B.A. from St. Louis University and a master's from Washington University. He continued to work as an activist and has been arrested more than 100 times in protests.

What is a **protected class**?

A protected class refers to groups of people who are protected from discrimination. Protected classes include such terms as race, sex, religion, color, national origin, age, and disability. This is often the easiest prong to establish under the McDonnell Douglas test. However, sometimes courts rule that people do not fit within a protected class. For example, several courts have ruled that transsexuals are not a protected class under Title VII because under Title VII sex discrimination means it is "unlawful to discriminate against women because they are women and men because they are men."

233

How should and **employer determine** if an **employee** is **qualified**?

An employee must show that he or she was a decent employee. This may be done by showing that he or she generally received positive job performance reviews until a specific time during their time in the workplace. The employee may also be able to point to whether the employee is performing as well as other employees.

It is illegal to discriminate against any "protected class," of people, including those of a different race, religion, age, national origin, sex, or disability (*iStock*).

What is an **adverse employment action**?

An adverse employment action is an action taken by an employer that results in a significant change in the employee's status in the workplace. Examples of adverse employment actions include: discharges (firings), refusals to hire, promotion denials, demotions, reassignments with significantly different responsibilities, or a decision causing a significant change in benefits.

Would a **negative performance evaluation** constitute an adverse employment action?

In general, a negative performance evaluation does not constitute an adverse employment action unless the evaluation has an adverse impact on an employee's wages or salary. Thus, to characterize a negative performance evaluation as an adverse employment action, the plaintiff must point to a tangible employment action that she alleges she suffered, or is in jeopardy of suffering, because of the downgraded evaluation.

If an **employee presents** a *prima facie* (or basic) case of **discrimination**, what must the **employer show**?

If an employee establishes a threshold showing of discrimination, then the employer must present a legitimate nondiscriminatory reason for the discharge. Examples of legitimate, nondiscriminatory reasons for discharge include that the employee was often tardy to work, showed insubordination to a superior, did not meet performance evaluation standards or violated other company policies. Often, a discrimination claim—if it goes to a jury—rests on whether the jury believes that the employee was subject to an adverse employment action for a discriminatory reason or for a legitimate reason.

> ## LegalSpeak: Title VII 42 U.S.C. Section 2000e-2(m)
>
> (m) Impermissible consideration of race, color, religion, sex, or national origin in employment practices. Except as otherwise provided in this title [42 USCS §§ 2000e et seq.], an unlawful employment practice is established when the complaining party demonstrates that race, color, religion, sex, or national origin was a motivating factor for any employment practice, even though other factors also motivated the practice.

If an employer does present a **legitimate, nondiscriminatory reason** for the **discharge** then what must the **employee do** to **prove** his or her **case**?

If the employer presents a seemingly plausible and legal reason for its action against the employee, the employee must show that the employer's actual stated reasons were pretextual or false. For example, if an employer says that it fired an employee because of her excessive tardiness, the employee may be able to show that other employees who were tardier than she were not disciplined. Or the employee may be able to show that the tardiness claim by the employer was simply not the actual reason for the discharge.

Does **Title VII apply** to **harassing behavior** on the part of employers?

Yes, Title VII prohibits much racial, sexual, or religious harassment in the employment relationship. Title VII protects employees from such harassment if such harassment is unwelcome and is severe or pervasive. The "severe and pervasive" requirement means that the harassment must be more than an occasional bad comment but generally must occur enough that it makes it much more difficult for an employee to do his or her job. As several courts have written, Title VII is "not a general civility code." In legal parlance, it must alter the terms and conditions of the workplace.

The U.S. Supreme Court also has distinguished between harassment committed by a co-employee and harassment committed by a supervisor. If the harassment is committed by a co-employee, the employer is liable if the employer knew or should have known of the harassing behavior. If the harassment was committed by a supervisory employee and the employee was discharged or suffers another similar type of tangible employment action, then the employer may be strictly liable.

If a **supervisor commented** on an employee's **physical anatomy** a few times and made several **sexual jokes** in her presence, is that **sexual harassment**?

Possibly, but remember that the plaintiff-employee must be able to show that the harassment was "severe and pervasive" and that it unreasonably altered the terms and

235

Harassment at work is not always between the sexes. Title VII protects you from being harassed by people of your own gender, as well (*iStock*).

conditions of the workplace. A court might find that the conditions were too sporadic and not severe enough to impose liability.

Can employers assert **any defense** to **supervisory harassment**?

It depends on whether the employers have a defense if the harassment by a supervisory employee led to a tangible employment action being taken against the employee. In other words, if the employee had to quit because of the harassing conditions, the employer probably would have no defense, because there was a tangible employment action—a constructive discharge.

However, if the harassment does not end up in a tangible employment action, then an employer can assert an affirmative defense by showing two things: (1) that employer took prompt remedial action to ensure no further harassment; and (2) that the employee failed to take advantage of any existing anti-harassment policy or procedures put in place by the employer.

Does **Title VII protect** employees who are **harassed** by members of the same sex?

Yes, the U.S. Supreme Court ruled in *Oncale v. Sundowner Offshore Services* (1998; see LegalSpeak, p. 238) that Title VII also prohibits discrimination based on sex that

> **LegalSpeak:**
> **U.S. Supreme Court in *Faragher v. City of Boca Raton* (1998)**
>
> When no tangible employment action is taken, a defending employer may raise an affirmative defense to liability or damages, subject to proof by a preponderance of the evidence, see Fed. Rule. Civ. Proc. 8(c). The defense comprises two necessary elements: (a) that the employer exercised reasonable care to prevent and correct promptly any sexually harassing behavior, and (b) that the plaintiff employee unreasonably failed to take advantage of any preventive or corrective opportunities provided by the employer or to avoid harm otherwise. While proof that an employer had promulgated an antiharassment policy with complaint procedure is not necessary in every instance as a matter of law, the need for a stated policy suitable to the employment circumstances may appropriately be addressed in any case when litigating the first element of the defense. And while proof that an employee failed to fulfill the corresponding obligation of reasonable care to avoid harm is not limited to showing an unreasonable failure to use any complaint procedure provided by the employer, a demonstration of such failure will normally suffice to satisfy the employer's burden under the second element of the defense. No affirmative defense is available, however, when the supervisor's harassment culminates in a tangible employment action, such as discharge, demotion, or undesirable reassignment.

includes same-sex sexual harassment. Joseph Oncale alleged that he was sexually harassed by several male co-workers, including one who threatened to rape him. His complaints to supervisors went ignored and he sued under Title VII.

Does **Title VII** prohibit **discrimination** against **transsexuals**?

The courts are divided on this question. Transsexuals who have sued for unlawful sex discrimination generally advance two claims. First, they argue that they have been literally discriminated against because of their sex in violation of Title VII. Second, they argue that they have been subject to impermissible "sex stereotyping" by employers in violation of Title VII. This "sex stereotyping" claim arose from the U.S. Supreme Court's famous decision in *Price Waterhouse v. Hopkins* (1989) in which the Court ruled that a woman denied a promotion to partner because she did not supposedly conform to recognized gender stereotypes did present a claim of unlawful sex discrimination.

Many courts have rejected the first argument—that transsexuals are a protected class—but have accepted the second argument—that an employer can violate Title VII by imposing sexual stereotypes upon a transsexual.

237

Admittedly, this is a very difficult area of the law and once again shows the necessity of a skilled attorney to litigate these matters competently.

RELIGIOUS DISCRIMINATION

Title VII also prohibits religious discrimination by covered employers. What is the law's definition of religion?

Title VII provides for a broad definition of what constitutes religion. The statute provides: "The term 'religion' includes all aspects of religious observance and practice, as well as belief, unless an employer demonstrates that he is unable to reasonably accommodate to an employee's religious observance or practice without undue hardship on the conduct of the employer's business."

How does an employee prove a claim of religious discrimination?

The employee first must establish a *prima facie*, or basic, claim of religious discrimination. This consists of three elements. First, the employee must show that he holds a sincere religious belief or practice that conflicts with an employer's work policy. Second, the employee must establish that he or she has informed the employer about the conflict between the employee's religion and the employer practice. Third, the employee must show that he or she was discharged or disciplined because of this conflict.

If the employee establishes a *prima facie* claim, what must the employer do?

The employer must show that it cannot reasonably accommodate the employee's religious practice without working an undue hardship on the employer's business. In this case, the burden is on the employer to show that the accommodation was unreasonable—that it would constitute an undue hardship.

A classic example would be where an employee's Sabbath day for his religion falls on a Saturday. In other words, the employee's religious practices preclude him from working on Saturdays. The employer, however, insists that the employee work on Saturdays. Depending on the particular facts at that place of employment, a court might find that the employer would have to reasonably accommodate the employee's request and simply place the employee on shifts on other days and not require the employee to work on Saturdays.

What is an **example** of a **discrimination case involving religion** in which it was ruled that the **employer did not accommodate** the employee adequately?

In *EEOC v. Texas Hydraulics*, 583 F.Supp. 2d 904 (M.D. Tenn. 2008), an employee worked at a plant, but the employee's religious beliefs prevented him from working on

Saturday—the Sabbath day of his religion. For many years in the workplace this was not a problem. However, the employer's business demands increased and the employer required the employee to work on Saturdays. After the employee failed to work on several Saturdays, he was terminated. The employee filed a claim of religious discrimination under Title VII. The employer later filed a motion for summary judgment, contending that the employee's claim should be dismissed.

A reviewing federal district court refused to dismiss the employee's claim and determined that there was evidence that the employer failed to reasonably accommodate the employee's religious beliefs. According to the court, the employer could have:

- Initiated a voluntary shift exchange with this employee and other employees.

- Posted a notice asking other employees to work for the employee on Saturday.

In the American workplace, employers are supposed to make any reasonable accommodations necessary for employees when it comes to religious practices, such as allowing those of the Jewish faith to observe the Sabbath (*iStock*).

239

• Modified or changed the employee's job so that he would not have to work nearly as many Saturday shifts.

Under the facts of this particular case, the reviewing federal district court determined that the employer did not make a good enough attempt at accommodating the employee's religious practices.

RETALIATION

What does **Title VII** say about **retaliation**?

Title VII prohibits employers from retaliating against employees who oppose an unlawful employment practice or who participate in an employment discrimination proceeding. This means that if an employee complains about sexual harassment in the workplace, the employer cannot retaliate against that employee by demoting them or subjecting them to some other sort of adverse employment action. It also means that an employer cannot take adverse action against an employee if that employee gives a deposition in a co-employee's discrimination suit.

Does Title VII's **retaliation clause protect** an **employee** who **participates** not in a court proceeding or EEOC investigation but in an **employer's internal investigation** of sexual harassment?

Yes, the United States Supreme Court ruled in *Crawford v. Metropolitan Government of Nashville* (2009) that Title VII's protection against retaliation extends to a worker who speaks out against discrimination when questioned during an employer's internal investigation. Some lower courts had ruled that the anti-retaliation clause of Title VII did not extend to cover employees during internal investigations.

The Court explained that there is "reason to doubt that a person can 'oppose' by responding to someone else's question just as surely as by provoking the discussion, and nothing in the statute requires a freakish rule protecting an employee who reports discrimination on her own initiative but not one who reports the same discrimination in the same words when her boss asks a question."

If an employee files both a **sex or race discrimination** claim and a **retaliation claim**, can the retaliation **claim survive** even if the underlying sex or race claim is **dismissed**?

Yes, an employee's retaliation claim can stand on its own merits—even if the underlying discrimination claim fails. For example, let's say a waitress alleges that her manager sexu-

> ## LegalSpeak: Title VII's Anti-Retaliation Provision
>
> It shall be an unlawful employment practice for an employer to discriminate against any of his employees ... because he has **opposed** any practice made an unlawful employment practice by this subchapter, or because he has made a charge, testified, assisted, or **participated** in any manner in an investigation, proceeding or hearing under this subchapter.

ally harassed her. She complains about the harassment to management and then receives less desirable work shifts and other retaliatory actions. The waitress' retaliation claim would be strong even if her underlying sexual harassment claim was rejected by the court.

How does an employee **prove retaliation**?

It can be difficult for an employee to prove unlawful retaliation by an employer. However, one factor that is important is the closeness in time (in legal terms called "temporal proximity") between the employee's complaint of discrimination and the adverse employment action. For example, let's say an employee complains about sexual harassment and then the employer terminates her only one month later. That closeness in time may be enough to prove unlawful retaliation. It certainly seems to create an inference of unlawful retaliation. On the other hand, if there is a time gap between the protected conduct (complaining about discrimination) and the adverse employment action, then the employee must come up with some other type of evidence of retaliation.

What sorts of **employer actions** can constitute **unlawful retaliation**?

This is a great question but employers can come up with a variety of methods of retaliating against an employee short of discharging that employee. The U.S. Supreme Court in *Burlington Northern v. White* (2006; see LegalSpeak, p. 242) determined that employers retaliate against employees under Title VII if the employer engages in conduct that is materially adverse to an employee or engages in conduct that would deter a reasonable employee from complaining about retaliatory conduct.

AGE DISCRIMINATION

What **federal law prohibits** employment **discrimination** based on **age**?

In 1967, Congress passed the Age Discrimination in Employment Act (ADEA), which prohibits discrimination based on age for all employers (public and private) who employ at least 20 full-time employees.

LegalSpeak: *Burlington Northern v. White* (2006)

We conclude that the anti-retaliation provision does not confine the actions and harms it forbids to those that are related to employment or occur at the workplace [i.e., employers can retaliate against employees in a variety of ways—some of which donít take place at work]. We also conclude that the provision covers those (and only those) employer actions that would have been materially adverse to a reasonable employee or job applicant [this means that retaliation consists of real harm to an employee, not just petty slights or minor things]. In the present context that means that the employer's actions must be harmful to the point that they could well dissuade a reasonable worker from making or supporting a charge of discrimination....

The anti-retaliation provision protects an individual not from all retaliation, but from retaliation that produces an injury or harm. As we have explained, the Courts of Appeals have used differing language to describe the level of seriousness to which this harm must rise before it becomes actionable retaliation. We agree with the formulation set forth by the Seventh and the District of Columbia Circuits. In our view, a plaintiff must show that a reasonable employee would have found the challenged action materially adverse, which in this context means it well might have "dissuaded a reasonable worker from making or supporting a charge of discrimination."

We speak of *material* adversity because we believe it is important to separate significant from trivial harms. Title VII, we have said, does not set forth "a general civility code for the American workplace." ... An employee's decision to report discriminatory behavior cannot immunize that employee from those petty slights or minor annoyances that often take place at work and that all employees experience.... The anti-retaliation provision seeks to prevent employer interference with "unfettered access" to Title VII's remedial mechanisms. It does so by prohibiting employer actions that are likely "to deter victims of discrimination from complaining to the EEOC," the courts, and their employers. And normally petty slights, minor annoyances, and simple lack of good manners will not create such deterrence." ...

We phrase the standard in general terms because the significance of any given act of retaliation will often depend upon the particular circumstances. Context matters.

How old must an employee be to qualify for protection under the ADEA?

The ADEA only provides protections to employees who are at least 40 years of age. This means that if an employer fires a 38-year-old employee and replaces him with a 18-year-old employee, the employer has not violated the ADEA.

What if an employer **fires** one **employee** who is **65** and **replaces him or her** with someone who is **47**. Does this constitute age discrimination since both employees are over 40?

Yes, it can constitute age discrimination, because the U.S. Supreme Court ruled in *O'Connor v. Consolidated Coin Caterers, Inc.* (1996) that an employer can violate the ADEA by firing an older worker in the protected class (over 40) and replaced him or her with a younger worker in the protected class. The court reinstated the ADEA claim of a 56-year-old worker who was fired and replaced by a 40-year-old employee.

In the age-discrimination context, such an inference cannot be drawn from the replacement of one worker with another worker insignificantly younger. Because the ADEA prohibits discrimination on the basis of age and not class membership, the fact that a replacement is substantially

Firing someone just because they are getting up in years is against the law. Employers sometimes try to do this anyway, though, to avoid paying retirement and other benefits (*iStock*).

younger than the plaintiff is a far more reliable indicator of age discrimination than is the fact that the plaintiff was replaced by someone outside the protected class.

Can a **younger person** in the protected class **sue** for **age discrimination**?

No, the U.S. Supreme Court has made clear in *General Dynamics v. Cline* (2004) that the ADEA does not sanction so-called reverse age discrimination claims. In *Cline* the Court considered whether a retirement plan that treated older workers in the protected class better than younger workers amounted to age discrimination. The Supreme Court said no, reasoning that "the ADEA was concerned to protect a relatively old worker from discrimination that works to the advantage of the relatively young." The Court concluded: "We see the text, structure, purpose, and history of the ADEA, along with its relationship to other federal statutes, as showing that the statute does not mean to stop an employer from favoring an older employee over a younger one."

Can **young people**—even those under 40—sue for **age discrimination** under **state laws**?

Most state laws have followed the example of the ADEA and limit protection to those employees who are at least 40 years. However, some state laws do not have an age barrier. For example, Minnesota's age discrimination law provides protection to any employee over the age of majority (18) who is the victim of age discrimination. Minnesota law "prohibits using a person's age as a basis for a decision if the person is over the age of majority."

My supervisor made comments like "you're too old for the job." Is that evidence of age discrimination?

Yes, it is evidence of age discrimination and could be enough to take a case to the jury. It may not be enough to establish a claim under the ADEA as some courts say that stray comments here and there do not suffice to establish a claim. But, that evidence could be "smoking gun" evidence in other cases. It certainly helps an age discrimination case to have this type of evidence.

Can an employer establish mandatory retirement limits?

Generally, no, an employer cannot establish a mandatory retirement age—at least in the vast majority of professions. However, employers can set a retirement age of 65 for high-ranking executives provided that those executives receive a certain amount in pension benefits ($44,000). Federal regulations provide that this exemption only applies to employees who are "employed in a bona fide executive or higher policymaking position."

Does it violate the ADEA for an employer to provide a date of birth question on an employment application?

No, federal regulations interpreting and implementing the ADEA provide: "A request on the part of an employer for information such as 'Date of Birth' or 'State Age' on an employ-

> ## LegalSpeak: *Gross v. FBL* (2009)
>
> Justice Clarence Thomas (majority): "Our inquiry therefore must focus on the text of the ADEA to decide whether it authorizes a mixed-motives age discrimination claim. It does not.... Thus, the ordinary meaning of the ADEA's requirement that an employer took adverse action "because of" age is that age was the "reason" that the employer decided to act.... even if *Price Waterhouse* was doctrinally sound, the problems associated with its application have eliminated any perceivable benefit to extending its framework to ADEA claims."
>
> Justice John Paul Stevens (dissent): "The Age Discrimination in Employment Act of 1967(ADEA), 29 U. S. C. §621 et seq., makes it unlawful for an employer to discriminate against any employee 'because of' that individual's age, §623(a). The most natural reading of this statutory text prohibits adverse employment actions motivated in whole or in part by the age of the employee."

ment application form is not, in itself, a violation of the Act." However, such questions will be "closely scrutinized" to assure that the purpose of the questioning is permissible.

Are mixed-motive claims cognizable under the ADEA as they are under Title VII?

No, the U.S. Supreme Court rejected mixed-motive claims under the ADEA in its recent decision in *Gross v. FBL* (2009). Writing for the Court, Justice Clarence Thomas reasoned: "This Court has never held that this burden-shifting framework applies to ADEA claims. And, we decline to do so now."

DISABILITY DISCRIMINATION

What major laws prohibit discrimination based on disability or handicap?

The two major laws are the Rehabilitation Act of 1973 and the Americans with Disabilities Act of 1990. The Rehabilitation Act of 1973 only extends to the federal government and protects only workers in the federal sector. The Americans with Disabilities Act of 1990 (ADA) applies to all employees—both in the private and public sector—provided that their employer has 15 or more full-time employees for the calendar year. The Rehabilitation Act uses the term "handicap," while the ADA uses the term "disability."

How is a disability defined within the Americans with Disabilities Act (ADA)?

There are three parts to the definition of a disability in the ADA. The first is that a disability is as an impairment that substantially limits one or more major life activities.

245

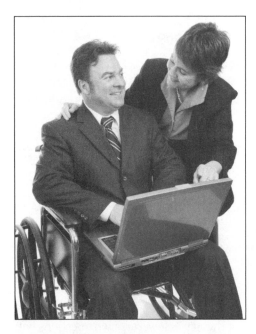

Under the Americans with Disabilities Act, employers cannot discriminate against disabled people and must accommodate any reasonable request that does not cause the employer undue hardship in return (*iStock*).

The second is that a disability is one in which there is a record of an employee having such an impairment. The third part of the definition is that the person is "regarded" as having a disability.

What exactly does the **ADA prohibit**?

The ADA applies to more than the employment sector, but Title I of the ADA covers employment. It prohibits employers from discriminating against qualified individuals with a disability with regard to "job application procedures, the hiring, advancement, or discharge of employees, employee compensation, job training, and other terms, conditions, and privileges of employment."

What are some **examples of disabilities** under the ADA?

There are an almost innumerable number of disabilities recognized by the ADA. They can include virtually any physical or mental impairment as long as it is substantially limiting of a major life activity. Examples of commonly litigated disabilities include cancer, back injuries, depression, diabetes, asthma, heart conditions, and carpal tunnel syndrome.

Are **mental conditions** cognizable under the ADA?

Yes, the ADA's primary definition of a disability says "any physical or mental impairment" that substantially limits a major life activity.

The ADA mentions a "qualified individual with a disability." What is such a "**qualified individual**"?

The ADA defines a qualified individual as "an individual who, with or without reasonable accommodation, can perform the essential functions of the employment position that such individual holds or desires. For the purposes of this subchapter, consideration shall be given to the employer's judgment as to what functions of a job are essential, and if an employer has prepared a written description before advertising or interviewing applicants for the job, this description shall be considered evidence of the essential functions of the job."

LegalSpeak: Findings of Congress in the ADA

a) Findings.—The Congress finds that—

(1) physical or mental disabilities in no way diminish a person's right to fully participate in all aspects of society, yet many people with physical or mental disabilities have been precluded from doing so because of discrimination; others who have a record of a disability or are regarded as having a disability also have been subjected to discrimination;

(2) historically, society has tended to isolate and segregate individuals with disabilities, and, despite some improvements, such forms of discrimination against individuals with disabilities continue to be a serious and pervasive social problem;

(3) discrimination against individuals with disabilities persists in such critical areas as employment, housing, public accommodations, education, transportation, communication, recreation, institutionalization, health services, voting, and access to public services;

(4) unlike individuals who have experienced discrimination on the basis of race, color, sex, national origin, religion, or age, individuals who have experienced discrimination on the basis of disability have often had no legal recourse to redress such discrimination;

(5) individuals with disabilities continually encounter various forms of discrimination, including outright intentional exclusion, the discriminatory effects of architectural, transportation, and communication barriers, overprotective rules and policies, failure to make modifications to existing facilities and practices, exclusionary qualification standards and criteria, segregation, and relegation to lesser services, programs, activities, benefits, jobs, or other opportunities;

(6) census data, national polls, and other studies have documented that people with disabilities, as a group, occupy an inferior status in our society, and are severely disadvantaged socially, vocationally, economically, and educationally;

(7) the Nation's proper goals regarding individuals with disabilities are to assure equality of opportunity, full participation, independent living, and economic self-sufficiency for such individuals; and

(8) the continuing existence of unfair and unnecessary discrimination and prejudice denies people with disabilities the opportunity to compete on an equal basis and to pursue those opportunities for which our free society is justifiably famous, and costs the United States billions of dollars in unnecessary expenses resulting from dependency and nonproductivity.

There are two key terms in this definition—"essential functions" and "reasonable accommodation." This basically means that the employee must be able to perform the key functions of the job either with or without a reasonable accommodation from the employer.

What is a **"reasonable accommodation"** in the ADA?

The ADA provides that a reasonable accommodation may include:

(A) making existing facilities used by employees readily accessible to and usable by individuals with disabilities; and

(B) job restructuring, part-time or modified work schedules, reassignment to a vacant position, acquisition or modification of equipment or devices, appropriate adjustment or modifications of examinations, training materials or policies, the provision of qualified readers or interpreters, and other similar accommodations for individuals with disabilities.

For example, the EEOC provides an example of a cashier in a store who has the disease lupus, which makes her more prone to fatigue. The employer could provide a reasonable accommodation to this employee by giving her a stool to allow her to sit, instead of stand, while performing her cashier duties. Another example of a reasonable accommodation would be an employee who has a physical disability may request a parking permit to be able to park closer to work that some of her colleagues. This would be considered a reasonable accommodation.

The law requires employers to make reasonable accommodations for people with physical disabilities (*iStock*).

Are there **limitations** as to what are **reasonable accommodations**?

Yes, an employee request is not considered a reasonable accommodation if it results in an "undue hardship" on the employer. An undue hardship could be a request that is financially prohibitive or an accommodation that would be too extensive or disruptive of existing work conditions.

How does a **court handle** the issue of **reasonable accommodations** and **undue hardships**?

A court requires that an employee bear the burden of showing that he or she requested a reasonable accommodation

LegalSpeak: *U.S. Airways v. Barnett* (2002)

Justice Steven Breyer (majority): "In our view, the seniority system will prevail in the run of cases. As we interpret the statute, to show that a requested accommodation conflicts with the rules of a seniority system is ordinarily to show that the accommodation is not 'reasonable.' Hence such a showing will entitle an employer/defendant to summary judgment on the question—unless there is more. The plaintiff remains free to present evidence of special circumstances that make "reasonable" a seniority rule exception in the particular case."

Justice Antonin Scalia (dissenting): "The principal defect of today's opinion, however, goes well beyond the uncertainty it produces regarding the relationship between the ADA and the infinite variety of seniority systems. The conclusion that any seniority system can ever be overridden is merely one consequence of a mistaken interpretation of the ADA that makes all employment rules and practices—even those which (like a seniority system) pose no *distinctive* obstacle to the disabled—subject to suspension when that is (in a court's view) a 'reasonable' means of enabling a disabled employee to keep his job. That is a far cry from what I believe the accommodation provision of the ADA requires: the suspension (within reason) of those employment rules and practices *that the employee's disability prevents him from observing.*"

Justice David Souter (dissenting): "Because a unilaterally-imposed seniority system enjoys no special protection under the ADA, a consideration of facts peculiar to this very case is needed to gauge whether Barnett has carried the burden of showing his proposed accommodation to be a 'reasonable' one despite the policy in force at US Airways. The majority describes this as a burden to show the accommodation is 'plausible' or 'feasible,' *ante*, at 10, and I believe Barnett has met it."

from the employer and that the request was objectively reasonable. This is not an onerous burden, as the employee must show only that the costs of the accommodation do not clearly outweigh the benefits. This qualifies to establish that the request is, at least at first glance, reasonable.

If the employee meets this initial burden, then the courts require the employer to show that the request is unreasonable and imposes an undue hardship on the employer.

What does the court do if a **reasonable accommodation conflicts** with a **seniority system**?

In *U.S. Airways v. Barnett* (2002), the U.S. Supreme Court reasoned that normally a seniority system would trump most requests for reasonable accommodations, because such accommodations would be unreasonable when forcing a worker with seniority to give up his job to accommodate someone with less seniority.

Can an employer **refuse to hire** an employee whose **disability** would present a **health risk** to himself or others?

Yes, an employer does not violate the ADA if the employer refuses to hire an employee who poses a direct to others or himself on the job. In *Chevron U.S.A. v. Echazabal* (2002), the U.S. Supreme Court unanimously ruled that an employer did not violate the ADA when it refused to hire a former employee whose disability (hepatitis and liver problems) would be exacerbated by exposure to toxins in the workplace. The Court reasoned that the direct-threat defense articulated in federal regulations should also extend to workers who posed a danger to themselves. The Court did say that the direct-threat defense must be based on reasoned medical judgment and should not used as a guise to discriminate against disabled workers who don't truly pose a threat at all.

The Supreme Court ruled, in a case involving extremely nearsighted airline pilots, that if an otherwise disabling condition could be corrected so an employee could perform his or her duties, then the employer could not discriminate against said employee (*iStock*).

Does the ADA prohibit **disability-based harassment** in the workplace?

Yes, employees can sue for disability-based harassment under the Rehabilitation Act (if they are federal employees) and the ADA. To prevail on a disability harassment claim, an employee must show: (1) that he or she is disabled within the meaning of the law; (2) that he or she was subjected to a hostile workplace environment; and (3) that hostility was directed at the employee because of his or her disability.

How did Congress **change the ADA** in 2008?

Congress passed the ADA Amendments Act of 2008 to broaden the scope of the law's protection. The United States Supreme Court had narrowed the law's protections in a couple of its rulings: *Sutton v. United Airlines* (1999) and *Toyota Motor Manufacturing v. Williams* (2002). In *Sutton*, the Court had ruled that if a

> ## LegalSpeak: *Chevron U.S.A. v. Echazabal* (2002)
>
> The direct threat defense must be "based on a reasonable medical judgment that relies on the most current medical knowledge and/or the best available objective evidence," and upon an expressly "individualized assessment of the individual's present ability to safely perform the essential functions of the job," reached after considering, among other things, the imminence of the risk and the severity of the harm portended. 29 CFR § 1630.2(r) (2001). The EEOC was certainly acting within the reasonable zone when it saw a difference between rejecting workplace paternalism and ignoring specific and documented risks to the employee himself, even if the employee would take his chances for the sake of getting a job.

disability could be corrected or mitigated, that prevented the condition from being considered a true disability that substantially limited an employee. The case involved two airline pilots who were very near-sighted.

In *Williams* the Court ruled that a disability had to be substantially limiting by severely restricting a major life activity that was of central importance to a person's daily life—not something that simply prevent them from performing certain tasks on the job.

The ADA Amendments Act of 2008 was introduced in order, as the sponsor of the legislation said, "to restore the protections" of the original ADA.

Are there **other laws** that allowed **injured** employees to receive **time off** from work?

Yes, the Family and Medical Leave Act of 1993 (FMLA) entitles a worker up to 12 weeks of work leave for a serious health condition that makes the employee unable to perform the functions of his or her job. FMLA leave is either unpaid or paid at the employer's discretion.

For what **other reasons** can an employee take **FMLA leave**?

FMLA leave is also available when a parent needs to take care of a newborn child, recent placement of an adopted child in the employee's home, or to care for an immediate family member (spouse, child or parent) who has a serious health condition.

What employers are obligated to follow the FMLA?

Employers who employ 50 or more full-time employees are subject to the FMLA. Additionally, a worker must have been employed for at least a year and worked at least 1,250 hours for that employer during the preceding 12 months to qualify for FMLA leave.

251

What happens to an **employee's job** when he or she **returns** from FMLA **leave**?

The FMLA requires that the employer restore the employee to his or her original job status upon the employee's return from FMLA leave.

If your **employer** is **not covered** by the FMLA, are there any **state laws** that could help?

There may be, depending on the state. Remember that many employees will not be covered by the FMLA, because they work for employers who employ less than 50 full-time workers.

What is the **Lily Ledbetter Act**?

The Lily Ledbetter Fair Pay Act is a federal law passed by Congress in 2009 as a legislative response to the U.S. Supreme Court's decision in *Ledbetter v. Goodyear Tire & Rubber* (2007), which did not allow workers to sue for race or gender discrimination under Title VII for pay discrimination if the employee did not file suit within 180 days of the discriminatory act.

LegalSpeak: ADA Amendments Act of 2008

Findings—Congress finds that—

(1) in enacting the Americans with Disabilities Act of 1990 (ADA), Congress intended that the Act "provide a clear and comprehensive national mandate for the elimination of discrimination against individuals with disabilities" and provide broad coverage;

(2) in enacting the ADA, Congress recognized that physical and mental disabilities in no way diminish a person's right to fully participate in all aspects of society, but that people with physical or mental disabilities are frequently precluded from doing so because of prejudice, antiquated attitudes, or the failure to remove societal and institutional barriers;

(3) while Congress expected that the definition of disability under the ADA would be interpreted consistently with how courts had applied the definition of a handicapped individual under the Rehabilitation Act of 1973, that expectation has not been fulfilled;

(4) the holdings of the Supreme Court in *Sutton v. United Air Lines, Inc.*, 527 U.S. 471 (1999) and its companion cases have narrowed the broad scope of protection intended to be afforded by the ADA, thus eliminating protection for many individuals whom Congress intended to protect;

(5) the holding of the Supreme Court in *Toyota Motor Manufacturing, Kentucky, Inc. v. Williams*, 534 U.S. 184 (2002) further narrowed the broad scope of protection intended to be afforded by the ADA;

(6) as a result of these Supreme Court cases, lower courts have incorrectly found in individual cases that people with a range of substantially limiting impairments are not people with disabilities;

(7) in particular, the Supreme Court, in the case of *Toyota Motor Manufacturing, Kentucky, Inc. v. Williams*, 534 U.S. 184 (2002), interpreted the term "substantially limits" to require a greater degree of limitation than was intended by Congress; and

(8) Congress finds that the current Equal Employment Opportunity Commission ADA regulations defining the term "substantially limits" as "significantly restricted" are inconsistent with congressional intent, by expressing too high a standard.

Lily Ledbetter was the plaintiff in the case, who sued for discrimination after she found out that she received less pay than male counterparts. However, the Court ruled that many of her claims were time-barred.

EMPLOYEE COMPENSATION

What is the major **federal law regulating compensation** for employees?

The major federal law regulating wages for employees is the Fair Labor Standards Act (FLSA), passed by Congress in 1938 as part of the New Deal legislation. The purpose was to establish a minimum wage below which employers could not pay employees. The law also dealt with overtime pay and the regulation of child labor. The FLSA applies to states but states are free to pass legislation that provides even greater protections to employees than the federal law. When a state law conflicts with FLSA, the employer must provide the employee with the benefits of the law that provides greater protection. In other words, the FLSA sets a floor, not a ceiling.

What does **FLSA** say about **overtime pay**?

FLSA requires employers to pay at least time and a half wages (1.5 times the normal rate of pay) when a worker labors more than 40 hours in a week. However, not all employees are covered under the overtime pay provisions. In other words, many employees—for example professionals—are not subject to the overtime pay provision. For more information about overtime pay, review the Department of Labor's "Fact Sheet" about overtime pay under FLSA at http://www.dol.gov/esa/whd/regs/compliance/whdfs23.pdf.

The Fair Labor Standards Act established a minimum wage in 1938, so that low-skilled laborer could better earn a livable income (*iStock*).

What is the **minimum wage** required by the FLSA?

Beginning on July 24, 2009, the minimum wage was raised to $7.25 per hour. The previous rate was $6.55 per hour. See the U.S. Department of Labor's website at http://www.dol.gov/esa/whd/flsa/ for updates on FLSA pay.

History of Minimum Wage*

Year	Wage	Year	Wage
1938	$0.25	1978	$2.65
1939	$0.30	1979	$2.90
1945	$0.45	1980	$3.10
1956	$0.75	1981	$3.35
1961	$1.15	1990	$3.80
1963	$1.25	1991	$4.25
1967	$1.40	1996	$4.75
1968	$1.60	1997	$5.15
1974	$2.00	2007	$5.85
1975	$2.10	2008	$6.55
1976	$2.30	2009	$7.25

*Source: Department of Labor at http://www.dol.gov/esa/minwage/chart.htm.

Do all **states** have **separate laws** dealing with **minimum wages**?

No, five states have no state law mandating minimum wages. These states are Louisiana, Alabama, Mississippi, Tennessee, and South Carolina.

What **state** has the **highest minimum wage** law?

Washington has the highest minimum wage law at $8.55 per hour. Oregon has the next highest minimum wage law at $8.40 per hour. California, Illinois, Massachusetts, Vermont, and Connecticut have the next highest minimum wage laws, providing for at least $8.00 per hour. However, the Connecticut and Illinois laws already provide for an increase to $8.25 in 2010.

What are some of the **exceptions** to the **overtime pay** requirement?

Some exceptions to the overtime pay provision are executives, administrative employees, professionals and outside sales persons. Executives—those employees with managerial responsibilities—must be paid on a salary basis. Executives are determined more by their actual job duties than their official job title. Administrative employees include those who are treasurers, public relation directors, human resources employees and personnel directors. Administrative employees regularly exercise discretion and independent judgment in their jobs.

Professionals are those who have advanced knowledge or learning. They often have advanced educational degrees in their areas of expertise. Educators, architects and attorneys, for example, fall within the professional exemption to the overtime pay requirements. Outside sales persons must regularly work outside the employer's main place of business.

Do **blue collar workers** who have great **expertise** in their respective jobs fall under the **professional overtime exemption** under FLSA?

No, federal regulations provide that the professional exemption does not apply to "manual laborers" and "blue collar" workers who engage in repetitive tasks with their "hands, physical skill and energy." The regulation in question further provides that such blue collar workers "gain the skills and knowledge required for performance of their routine manual and physical work through apprenticeships and on-the-job training, not through the prolonged course of specialized intellectual instruction required for exempt learned professional employees such as medical doctors, architects and archeologists."

Do **computer programmers** and computer **system analysts** qualify as professionals and **exempt** from FLSA's **overtime provisions**?

It depends on the nature of the computer programmer's job and whether he or she fits under a 1996 amendment to FLSA specifically addressing computer programmers. It depends on whether the employee's primary duties related to "the application of systems analysis techniques and procedures" and whether they make at least $27.63 an hour.

In an **FLSA case**, who has the **burden of proof** to show that an **employee is exempt** from the **overtime** pay benefit?

Employers have the burden of proof to prove by clear and convincing evidence that an employee fits into an exemption, relieving the employer of having to pay

If a blue collar worker is considered particularly skilled in his or her trade, he or she is still considered a manual labor and, thus, does not qualify for the professional overtime exemption (*iStock*).

257

overtime. For example, if an employer claims that an executive secretary fits within a FLSA exemption, the employer must show that the employee performed managerial and administrative duties, as opposed to mostly clerical duties. If an employee performs primarily clerical duties and secretarial work, a jury may find that the employee was entitled to overtime pay.

What is the "taxicab exemption"?

It is, as the name suggests, an exemption under the overtime provisions of FLSA for taxicab drivers.

What is a "Belo" contract?

A Belo contract refers to a contract in which an employer offers a guaranteed weekly salary to an employee who works irregular hours. It comes from the United States Supreme Court decision *Walling v. A.H. Belo Corp.* (1942), which upheld an employer's attempt to comply with the letter and spirit of the FLSA by providing payments to workers who labored an irregular number of hours each week.

What about employees **receiving tips** and how they are treated under **FLSA**?

Tipped employees are those who regularly earn more $30 per month in tips. Under the FLSA, employers only need to guarantee $2.13 per hour to tipped employees. If the employee's tips and $2.13 per hour do not add up to the minimum wage under FLSA, then the employer must make up the difference. For more information on tipping and FLSA, see the Department of Labor's Fact Sheet on the subject at http://www.dol.gov/esa/whd/regs/compliance/whdfs15.pdf.

Much litigation currently occurs in American courts regarding tipped employees. Much of the litigation centers on the legality of various tipping pool arrangements that force tipped employees to share their tips with other workers, including some who do not deal directly with customers. In some cases, the courts have ruled that such tip sharing agreements violate the FLSA.

What is the **key factor** in determining whether **employees** may be **included** in a valid **tip pool**?

The key factor in determining whether certain employees can be included in a valid tip pool is their level of interaction with customers. For example, a federal district court in Florida recently ruled that card dealers could not be forced to share tips with cardroom floor supervisors who did not interact much with customers in the gaming establishment (see LegalSpeak, p. 262).

LegalSpeak:
Computer Systems Analyst Exemption in FLSA—29 U.S.C. 213

(17) any employee who is a computer systems analyst, computer programmer, software engineer, or other similarly skilled worker, whose primary duty is—

(A) the application of systems analysis techniques and procedures, including consulting with users, to determine hardware, software, or system functional specifications;

(B) the design, development, documentation, analysis, creation, testing, or modification of computer systems or programs, including prototypes, based on and related to user or system design specifications;

(C) the design, documentation, testing, creation, or modification of computer programs related to machine operating systems; or

(D) a combination of duties described in subparagraphs (A), (B), and (C) the performance of which requires the same level of skills, and who, in the case of an employee who is compensated on an hourly basis, is compensated at a rate of not less than $27.63 an hour.

LegalSpeak: Belo Contract Provision in the FLSA

Employment necessitating irregular hours of work

No employer shall be deemed to have violated subsection (a) of this section by employing any employee for a workweek in excess of the maximum workweek applicable to such employee under subsection (a) of this section if such employee is employed pursuant to a bona fide individual contract, or pursuant to an agreement made as a result of collective bargaining by representatives of employees, if the duties of such employee necessitate irregular hours of work, and the contract or agreement (1) specifies a regular rate of pay of not less than the minimum hourly rate provided in subsection (a) or (b) of section 206 of this title (whichever may be applicable) and compensation at not less than one and one-half times such rate for all hours worked in excess of such maximum workweek, and (2) provides a weekly guarantee of pay for not more than sixty hours based on the rates so specified.

WORKERS' COMPENSATION LAW

What is the **purpose** of **workers' compensation**?

Workers' compensation is designed to provide an expedited manner for employees injured on the job to recover money and receive medical benefits for injuries that they suffer on the job. Before the advent of workers compensation laws in the early part of the twentieth century, employees would have to sue their employers in order to receive compensation for injuries on the job. This led to a situation in which workers often could not work because of their injury and received no medical coverage from their employers for the injuries. Workers compensation laws provide an avenue in which employees receive quicker benefits in exchange for not suing their employers in court.

Of course, sometimes employees could not recover in tort against their employers because the work-related injuries were the fault of the employee more so than the employer. Usually negligence is not an issue in workers compensation. As long as the injury is sufficiently work-related, then the employee can recover workers compensation benefits.

LegalSpeak: *Walling v. A.H. Belo Corp.* (1942)

The problem presented by this case is difficult—difficult because we are asked to provide a rigid definition of "regular rate" when Congress has failed to provide one. Presumably Congress refrained from attempting such a definition because the employment relationships to which the Act would apply were so various and unpredictable. And that which it was unwise for Congress to do, this Court should not do. When employer and employees have agreed upon an arrangement which has proven mutually satisfactory, we should not upset it and approve an inflexible and artificial interpretation of the Act which finds no support in its text and which as a practical matter eliminates the possibility of steady income to employees with irregular hours. Where the question is as close as this one, it is well to follow the Congressional lead and to afford the fullest possible scope to agreements among the individuals who are actually affected. This policy is based upon a common-sense recognition of the special problems confronting employer and employee in businesses where the work hours fluctuate from week to week and from day to day. Many such employees value the security of a regular weekly income. They want to operate on a family budget, to make commitments for payments on homes and automobiles and insurance. Congress has said nothing to prevent this desirable objective. This Court should not.

Why is **workers' compensation considered** a form of **compromise**?

It is a compromise because the employee gives up the opportunity to sue for large damage awards in a tort case in exchange for the quicker (usually) benefits of workers compensation. The employer receives the benefit of knowing that the workers compensation claim is the exclusive and only remedy for the employee. Thus, the employer knows that it will not face the specter of large damage awards.

What **entity handles** worker compensation **claims**?

The employee does not file a worker compensation claim in a court, such as is done with a traditional civil law contract or tort claim. Instead, an employee files a worker compensation claim before an administrative board. If the employee loses administratively, then the employee can appeal to a court.

What is considered a **work-related injury**?

An employee's injury is covered by workers' compensation if the injury arises out of employment and is in the course of the employment relationship. If the injury meets

261

these two criteria—(1) arising out of and (2) in the course of—then the employee can receive worker compensation benefits even if the employer was not negligent.

When does an injury arise out of and in the course of employment?

An injury arises out of the employment relationship if the cause of the injury is causually related (arose out of) the workplace environment. The injury occurs "in the course of" employment when it occurred during the performance of work-related duties. In many instances, it is clear that an injury is work-related enough to be covered by workers compensation. For example, if you fall and injure your leg at work that injury arose out of the employment relationship and constitutes a compensable injury.

However, let's say that you are at work and suddenly have a lot of back pain. Is the back pain caused by your job or is the back pain caused by activities you have done outside of the work environment, such as helping a friend move furniture to new lodgings?

What if you **suffer a heart attack** due to **stress** on the **job**? Are you compensable under workers compensation?

It depends. In some jurisdictions the question would be whether the heart attack was brought about by physical exertion or strain on the job as opposed to one brought about from mental stress or an emotional issue. If the heart attack is brought on by undue physical exertion on job, that would be compensable. If the heart attack was brought on by mental stress, the question would be whether there was an abnormal or unusual event at work that brought on the heart attack.

For example, one Tennessee court determined that there was a compensable injury under workers' compensation for the family of a security guard who suffered a

Workers can receive compensation for a work-related injury even if the employer was not negligent in the incident (*iStock*).

263

LegalSpeak: *Cunningham v. Shelton Security Service* (Tenn. 2001)

The rule is different, however, when the heart attack is caused by a mental or emotional stimulus rather than physical exertion or strain. In such cases, "it is obvious that in order to recover when there is no physical exertion, but there is emotional stress, worry, shock, or tension, the heart attack must be immediately precipitated by a specific acute or sudden stressful event rather than generalized employment conditions." Thus, if the heart attack is caused by a mental or emotional stimulus rather than physical exertion or strain, there must be a "climactic event or series of incidents of an unusual or abnormal nature" if a recovery is to be permitted. Id. Although "excessive and unexpected mental anxiety, stress, tension or worry attributable to the employment can cause injury sufficient to justify an award of benefits," the ordinary stress of one's occupation does not because "emotional stress, to some degree, accompanies the performance of any contract of employment." In other words, "normal ups and downs are part of any employment relationship, and as we have said on many previous occasions, do not justify finding an 'accidental injury' for purposes of worker[s'] compensation law." Accordingly, the rule is settled in this jurisdiction that physical or mental injuries caused by worry, anxiety, or emotional stress of a general nature or ordinary stress associated with the worker's occupation are not compensable. The injury must have resulted from an incident of abnormal and unusual stressful proportions, rather than the day-to-day mental stresses and tensions which workers in that field are occasionally subjected.

With these principles in mind, we review the record in the present case to determine whether the employee's death arose out of his employment. We note first that there was no physical exertion or strain involved in precipitating his heart failure. Instead, the mental stress or tension associated with confronting the suspected shoplifters caused the heart failure, at least according to some of the medical proof. Applying the law as just described, the trial court concluded

heart attack and died on his job shortly after confronting several would-be shoplifters who threatened him. The court reasoned that the injury arose out of the employment relationship because the heart attack was precipitated by the unusually volatile confrontation between the security guard and the would-be shoplifters.

What does the **employee receive** in workers's compensation **benefits**?

Normally, the employee receives medical coverage for the work-related injury and the employee receives a portion of his or her wages while the employee recovers and cannot work. Generally the employee receives a portion of their average weekly wage for a

the employee's death was not compensable because he was not confronted with circumstances of an unusual or abnormal nature given his work as a security guard. As the record reflects, verbal confrontations occurred at least once a week at the store, and it was common for the employee to "go out and yell at these people." However, the record also reflects that the individuals chased off by the employee threatened to return and kill him. We believe that this additional circumstance makes a difference and is sufficient to warrant the conclusion that the employee's death did not result from generalized employment conditions, but from something beyond the norm, even for a security guard. Accordingly, we find that the evidence preponderates against the trial court's finding that the employee's death did not arise out of his employment.

The reason, simply put, is that the employee has met the burden of establishing that his heart failure was caused by a mental or emotional stimulus of an unusual or abnormal nature, beyond what is typically encountered by one in the employee's position. We thus reiterate the rule again in this case that if the cause or stimulus of the heart attack is mental or emotional in nature, such as stress, fright, tension, shock, anxiety, or worry, there must be a specific, climatic event or series of incidents of an unusual or abnormal nature if the claimant is to be permitted a recovery, but no recovery is permitted for the ordinary mental stresses and tensions of one's occupation because "emotional stress, to some degree, accompanies the performance of any contract of employment." If the rule were otherwise, workers' compensation coverage would become as broad as general health and accident insurance, which it is not.

We conclude that the evidence preponderates against the trial court's finding that the employee's death did not arise out of his employment. Accordingly, we agree with the Panel that the trial court erred in dismissing the case and that the case must be remanded for further proceedings.

period of time. In most states the employee receives 66 percent, or two-thirds, of their average weekly wage during the pendency of their time away from work recovering from the compensable injury. Keep in mind that worker compensation laws vary considerably from state to state.

What if an employee suffers a **permanent disability**?

If an employee suffers a permanent disability from a work-related illness the employee generally will receive a lump sum payment that is designed to give at least some redress to the employee not only for the present but also for future expenses. Often it is very important to have an attorney to negotiate the best settlement possible in such a situation.

Are there **time limits** and **notice requirements** on **filing** worker compensation **claims**?

Yes, there are both time limits and notice requirements for those employees who have suffered a compensable injury. The employee must give notice to the employer and then must file the workers compensation claim within 30 days in most states.

Can an **employer fire** an employee for **filing** a workers' compensation claim?

They can but that would be unlawful. Most state high courts have explained that if an employer fires an employee for filing a worker compensation claim, then the employee can file a tort claim for retaliatory discharge. There have been many court decisions providing that employees can recover punitive damages (see chapter on Personal Injury Law) if their employer fired them for filing a legitimate workers compensation claim.

OTHER EMPLOYMENT LAW CONSIDERATIONS

Are employment **discrimination awards taxable**?

Yes, much of the awards are taxable. Employees must pay taxes on any type of damages for lost wages and also for any type of noneconomic damages, such as pain and suffering. Section 104(a)(2) of the Internal Revenue Code provides an exclusion from gross income for damage awards received on account of physical injury or physical sickness. Any awards that do not fit under this exclusion are included in taxable income, which means that the employee or former employee must pay taxes on the award.

This also means that sometimes damages for emotional distress are taxable if they are not connected to a physical injury or sickness. You want to make sure to discuss this issue carefully with your attorney, because a lot of the time awards from employment discrimination cases are taxable and that factor needs to be taken into account carefully.

Must employers give employees **time off** for **lunch** and for **rest periods**?

Yes, states have different laws that provide that employers must provide time for lunch and a couple rest periods for employees who work a full day. For example, Nevada provides that employers must provide its eight-hour-a-day workers with a 30-minute lunch period and at least two 10-minute rest periods.

Must an **employer** do anything to **accommodate employees** who wish to **breast feed** their children?

Many states have laws regarding rest or break time for employees who wish to breast feed or express breast milk for supplying their children later in the day. For example, an Oklahoma law provides: "An employer may provide reasonable unpaid break time each day to an employee who needs to breast-feed or express breast milk for her child to maintain milk supply and comfort. The break time, if possible, shall run concurrently with any break time, paid or unpaid, already provided to the employee. An employer is not required to provide break time under this section if to

Many Americans choose to work through their lunch breaks, but the law stipulates that employers cannot require them to do so (*iStock*).

do so would create an undue hardship on the operations of the employer." Mississippi's law is more blunt: "No employer shall prohibit an employee from expressing breast milk during any meal period or other break period provided by the employer."

If you are **fired** from your job can you obtain **unemployment benefits** coverage?

It depends. In many jurisdictions, workers who lose their job can apply for—and often receive—unemployment benefits coverage for a certain period of time. However, there is usually an exception for workers who engaged in so-called "willful misconduct." There are also exceptions for those who willingly leave jobs and for those who are principally self-employed (own their own business). Thus, if you are fired from your job due to a typical reduction-in-force or because of a general layoff, you likely can receive unemployment benefit coverage for a period of time. However, if you were fired for stealing employer property, then you are unlikely to receive unemployment benefit coverage.

How does the **unemployment benefits process** work?

If a worker is involuntarily let go from employment, he or she is eligible to apply for unemployment benefits. If you willingly leave a job, then you are not entitled to such benefits. The worker then applies with the state department of labor. That administrative entity then makes a determination as to whether the employee is entitled to unemployment benefits. The employer is given an opportunity to contest the employee's application for benefits.

267

After the administrative decision approving or denying benefits, then either the employee or the employer can appeal that finding to a court of law for a determination.

Can your employer **require you** to take a **drug test**?

In most states, yes, an employer can require employees to take drug tests. Some public employees (those who work for the government) may be able to assert a Fourth Amendment claim (against unreasonable searches and seizures) because a drug test is an invasive process. However, private employees do not have the benefit of asserting a Fourth Amendment claim.

Many states have passed drug-testing laws for employees and provide certain circumstances under which employees can be drug tested. Many state laws provide that employees can be tested when they are job applicants, when they have been involved in an accident (called post-accident drug testing) and when there is reasonable suspicion to conduct a drug test. Other states also allow employers to engage in random drug testing.

However, some states do not allow random drug testing for most employees. For example, Minnesota law prohibits employers from imposing random drug or alcohol tests on employees unless the employees are in "safety sensitive positions" or they are employed as professional athletes pursuant to a collective bargaining agreement. Virginia law prohibits random drug testing of employee unless there is a requirement to do so under some type of federal regulation. Thus, the state laws vary quite a bit on this controversial issue.

Many employees have asserted that drug testing invades their privacy rights, but many courts have not found those claims meritorious and upheld the state laws that allow such testing. Consult with your attorney to see if there are any grounds to contest an employer drug test.

What if you **test positive** for drugs, but you really believe that the **test was wrong**? Is there any **recourse**?

There may be some recourse, as some state laws require that an employer require a confirmatory test—a second test to ensure the accuracy of the first test which is often referred to as an initial, screening test. Additionally, some state laws allow the employee to obtain access to the test sample and, at the employee's own expense, pay for their own testing by a reputable testing company. Once again this area of law differs quite dramatically from state to state.

Can your **employer read** your **email** at work?

In most cases, yes, your employer can read your work email on your work computer. Most employers have employment policies that state that email is for work usage.

> ## N.R.S. 608.019 Periods for Meals and Rest
>
> 1. An employer shall not employ an employee for a continuous period of 8 hours without permitting the employee to have a meal period of at least one-half hour. No period of less than 30 minutes interrupts a continuous period of work for the purposes of this subsection.
> 2. Every employer shall authorize and permit all his employees to take rest periods, which, insofar as practicable, shall be in the middle of each work period. The duration of the rest periods shall be based on the total hours worked daily at the rate of 10 minutes for each 4 hours or major fraction thereof. Rest periods need not be authorized however for employees whose total daily work time is less than 3 and one-half hours. Authorized "rest period" shall be counted as hours worked, for which there shall be no deduction from wages....

Additionally, the employer owns the computers and the server upon which those emails are transmitted. Most reviewing courts have determined that employees do not have a reasonable expectation of privacy in emails.

If the employer cracked into an employer's private email—say a Yahoo or Google email account at work—that might present a different story. However, the problem is that employees are supposed to be doing company work on company time rather than surfing the Internet, playing computer games or sending messages to "friends" over a social networking site.

Can your **employer force** you to take a **polygraph** test?

A federal law known as the Employee Polygraph Protection Act establishes some strict limits on employers' imposing a requirement on employees to take polygraph or lie-detector tests. There are some exceptions, as government employees can be subjected to such examinations. Furthermore, the law contains an "ongoing investigation" exception which means that an employer can require an employee to participate in a polygraph if there is an investigation regarding embezzlement or theft at the employer's place of business and the employee had access to the property in question and the employer has reasonable suspicion that the employee had involvement in the embezzlement or theft.

Many states have laws on the books that limit and restrict the use of polygraphs as well. Your attorney should be able to tell you whether your employer is in compliance with federal and state law regarding a polygraph or requested polygraph.

FAMILY LAW

What types of **issues** are **covered** by **family law,** or the law of domestic relations?

This area encompasses all aspects of intra-familial life, including but not limited to marriage, divorce, child custody, child support, child visitation, adoption, paternity, and surrogacy. Most state law codes contain a separate section or sections—called a title or titles—that deal exclusively with family law. For example, there is a separate title (Title 25) in Arizona called "Marital and Domestic Relations." Tennessee has a separate title (Title 36) called "Domestic Relations." Often attorneys will specialize in particular aspects of family law given the complexity and depth of the subject.

Family law interacts with many other areas of law, including contracts, torts, crimes, and other areas. Marriage itself is a civil contract between two parties (in nearly every state between one man and one woman). Both parties must consent to the marriage just as with any other type of contract. Sometimes parties will enter into contractual arrangements before marriage referred to as prenuptial agreements. Sometimes parties to a marriage will allege criminal and/or tortious (wrongful) conduct committed by their partner.

MARRIAGE

How is **marriage defined** by the law?

Marriage is a civil contract or union between two persons (in nearly all U.S. jurisdictions between one man and one woman) who live together and share their lives together (at least until a dissolution). Ideally, the two people share deep emotional and physical bonds that allow them to survive and even thrive during the hardships

Although most marriages are performed in religious settings, certain legal actions must be taken for the parties to be considered married partners by the state (*iStock.com*).

of life. Unfortunately, we know that a large number of marriages dissolve and end up in divorce.

How can people be married?

Most people are married through a ceremony performed by a religious figure or a secular figure authorized by the state to perform marriages. Many people are married in churches or chapels by a minister of one of the person's church. Others are married at the local courthouse by a judge or justice of the peace. Still others are married by a family friend who has the authority as a lay person to perform marriages. These unions are referred to as ceremonial marriages, because the institution or process of marriage is performed through a ceremony.

The parties to a marriage must provide their names, addresses, ages and social security numbers to obtain a marriage license from a county clerk. Other states require applicants to also disclose their places of birth and their current occupations. Those applicants who have been previously married may have to disclose information about those prior marriages. The applicants must swear that the provided information is true in most states. The clerk then gives the parties the license, which they provide to the person performing the marriage ceremony. In fact, in a few states (South Carolina is an example) a person who performs a marriage ceremony without receiving a valid marriage license from the parties can be punished and fined.

What is a common-law marriage?

In some states, parties can form a common-law marriage, meaning that the state recognizes the persons as legally married even though they have not performed a ceremonial marriage. Instead, the parties live together for a period of years and hold themselves out to be married.

How much does a marriage license cost?

This varies from state to state. In Delaware, marriage licenses are only $10. In Alaska, the legislature designates the registrar to set the fee for a marriage certificate, which is only $20. In Hawaii, a state statute provides that the cost of a marriage license is $60. In Tennessee, the cost is more than $90.

Must you take a **blood test** before getting married?

It used to be that many states required such blood tests. Now, only Montana still requires a blood test for females for rubella (see LegalSpeak, p. 274). The marriage applicants can decline the blood test only if they file an informed consent form acknowledging an understanding of rubella information and declining the immunity testing. Rubella, often called German measles, can cause a wide variety of problems if a mother is infected with the disease during pregnancy.

What is a **covenant marriage**?

A covenant marriage is a distinct type of marriage—available in only a few states—in which the parties agree that marriage is a lifelong bond between them. These individuals willingly enter authorized pre-marital counseling and agree that grounds for divorce for them will be more limited for them. A party can obtain a divorce in a covenant marriage only when there has been a complete and total breach of the marriage agreement—such as adultery or the commission of a felony. What this means is that parties who enter into a covenant marriage will not be able to be divorced simply on the basis of irreconcilable differences.

What **states** allow **covenant marriages**?

Louisiana became the first state to provide for this type of marriage in 1997. Arizona passed its law in 1998 and then Arkansas passed its law allowing covenant marriages in 2001 (Arkansas law A.C.A. 9-11-803(a)(1) states: "A covenant marriage is a marriage entered into by 1 male and 1 female who understand and agree that the marriage between them is a lifelong relationship.") Bills authorizing covenant marriages have been introduced in several other states but have not yet passed.

Can parties who enter into a regular marriage **change** or convert that **marriage** into a **covenant marriage**?

Parties can do so in the state of Arizona, which provides that parties to an existing marriage simply must sign and file the statement of covenant marriage, which reads:

> We solemnly declare that marriage is a covenant between a man and a woman who agree to live together as husband and wife for as long as they both live. We have chosen each other carefully and have received premarital counseling on the nature, purposes and responsibilities of marriage. We understand that a covenant marriage is for life. If we experience marital difficulties, we commit ourselves to take all reasonable efforts to preserve our marriage, including marital counseling.

With full knowledge of what this commitment means, we do declare that our marriage will be bound by Arizona law on covenant marriages and we promise to love, honor and care for one another as husband and wife for the rest of our lives.

What does the law say about **limiting marriages** between **family members**?

Incest is forbidden under state laws. Many state laws specifically spell out and forbid a person from marrying certain relatives. For example, Maryland law forbids a man from marrying his grandmother, mother, daughter, sister, or granddaughter. Maryland law forbids a woman from marrying her grandfather, father, son, brother, or grandson.

Can **cousins** legally **marry**?

In most states first cousins cannot marry. However, in some states it is allowed. For example, Tennessee law does not forbid first cousins to marry. In Ohio the parties must be no nearer than second cousins. Arizona law provides that first cousins cannot

requirement for a blood test for rubella immunity. Informed consent must be recorded on a form provided by the department and must be signed by both applicants. The informed consent form must include:

(a) the reasons for undergoing a blood test for rubella immunity;

(b) the information that the results would provide about the woman's rubella antibody status;

(c) the risks associated with remaining uninformed of the rubella antibody status, including the potential risks posed to a fetus, particularly in the first trimester of pregnancy; and

(d) contact information indicating where applicants may obtain additional information regarding rubella and rubella immunity testing.

(3) A person who by law is able to obtain a marriage license in this state is also able to give consent to any examinations, tests, or waivers required or allowed by this section. In submitting the blood specimen to the laboratory, the physician or other person authorized to issue a medical certificate shall designate that it is a premarital test.

Many states have rules that require testing of pregnant women for HIV, but that such requirements apply to pregnant women, not simply those who are married.

marry unless both parties are over the age of 65 and it is proven that at least one of the parties is incapable of reproducing.

Courts will generally allow parties who are first cousins to remain married even if they reside in a state that does not allow such marriages. For example, in *Mason v. Mason* (2002), an Indiana appeals court refused to grant a man who had legally married his first cousin in Tennessee a divorce in Indiana. The court wrote that "as a matter of comity (legal reciprocity), Indiana can choose to recognize Tennessee marriages between first cousins, even though such a marriage could not be validly contracted between residents of Indiana."

What **states** still recognize **common-law marriages**?

The states of Alabama, Colorado, Idaho, Iowa, Kansas, Montana, Rhode Island, South Carolina, Texas, and Utah still recognize common-law marriages. The District of Columbia also recognizes common-law marriages. Georgia recognizes existing common-law marriages that were entered into before January 1, 1997.

In many states a couple can be considered married, even without a ceremony and a marriage license, if they live together as husband and wife for a specified number of years (*iStock.com*).

In common-law marriages, if the parties reside together for a certain number of years (often seven) and hold themselves out as a married couple, then they will have a valid, common-law marriage.

What are **civil unions**?

Civil unions are a recognized category of relationship between two persons that provides many of the benefits of marriage. It represents a separate legal category that allows persons of the same sex to enter into a protected and recognized legal relationship that accords benefits to its parties. Vermont became the first state to pass a civil union law in 2000.

What are the **differences** between **civil unions** and **marriages**?

The biggest difference is that marriage has been a recognized legal institution for hundreds of years in the United States (and around the world), while civil unions are a relatively recent phenomenon. Civil unions provide for benefits in the state that recognizes such unions, but those benefits may not be recognized elsewhere. Perhaps the primary difference is that many advocating for equal treatment for gays and lesbians assert that civil unions accord a second-class legal status than marriage. For example, the group Gay and Lesbian Advocates and Defenders (GLAD) writes that "marriages are far more likely to be respected by others than newly minted 'civil unions.'"

At what **age** can a person **legally marry**?

In most states there is an age limit for marriage. For example, in Ohio a male must be 18 years of age and a female must be at least 16 years of age. In many states a minor party must obtain the consent of their parent or guardian before marriage.

In many states the age of consent for marriage is 18 years of age. Parties under the age of 18 can marry only if they prove that they have the consent of their parents or legal guardian. For example, the State of West Virginia provides:

48-2-301. Age of consent for marriage; exception:

(a) The age of consent for marriage for both the male and the female is eighteen years of age. A person under the age of eighteen lacks the capacity to contract a marriage without the consent required by this section.

(b) The clerk of the county commission may issue a marriage license to an applicant who is under the age of eighteen but sixteen years of age or older if the clerk obtains a valid written **consent** from the applicant's parents or legal guardian.

(c) Upon order of a circuit judge, the clerk of the county commission may issue a marriage license to an applicant who is under the age of sixteen, if the clerk obtains a valid written consent from the applicant's parents or legal guardian. A circuit judge of the county in which the application for a marriage license is filed may order the clerk of the county commission to issue a license to an applicant under the age of sixteen if, in the court's discretion, the issuance of a license is in the best interest of the applicant and if consent is given by the parents or guardian.

Alaska's law is similar but limits marriage to those who are 14 years of age or older. And those under the age of 16 have to prove consent after a court hearing.

Can parties of the **same sex marry**?

In the vast majority of states, parties of the same sex are legally forbidden to marry each other. Many states have a specific law or constitutional amendment proscribing such marriages. However, same-sex persons can marry in the states of Connecticut, Maine, Massachusetts, New Hampshire, Vermont, and Iowa. As of December 2009, the District of Columbia appeared close to allowing such marriages as well.

Same-sex marriages are still prohibited in most U.S. states, with laws sometimes even written into state constitutions to ban gay marriage (*iStock.com*).

LegalSpeak: Iowa Supreme Court in *Varnum v. Brien* (2009)

So, today, this court again faces an important issue that hinges on our definition of equal protection. This issue comes to us with the same importance as our landmark cases of the past. The same-sex-marriage debate waged in this case is part of a strong national dialogue centered on a fundamental, deep-seated, traditional institution that has excluded, by state action, a particular class of Iowans. This class of people asks a simple and direct question: How can a state premised on the constitutional principle of equal protection justify exclusion of a class of Iowans from civil marriage? ...

Therefore, with respect to the subject and purposes of Iowa's marriage laws, we find that the plaintiffs are similarly situated compared to heterosexual persons. Plaintiffs are in committed and loving relationships, many raising families, just like heterosexual couples. Moreover, official recognition of their status provides an institutional basis for defining their fundamental relational rights and responsibilities, just as it does for heterosexual couples. Society benefits, for example, from providing same-sex couples a stable framework within which to raise their children and the power to make health care and end-of-life decisions for loved ones, just as it does when that framework is provided for opposite-sex couples.

In short, for purposes of Iowa's marriage laws, which are designed to bring a sense of order to the legal relationships of committed couples and their families in myriad ways, plaintiffs are similarly situated in every important respect, but for their sexual orientation. As indicated above, this distinction cannot defeat the application of equal protection analysis through the application of the similarly situated concept because, under this circular approach, all distinctions would evade equal protection review. Therefore, with respect to the government's purpose of "providing an institutional basis for defining the fundamental relational rights and responsibilities of persons," same-sex couples are similarly situated to opposite-sex couples.

New York recognizes same-sex marriages from other states but does not allow them to be performed within its borders. Several other states—mainly in the northeastern region of the country—permit civil unions between persons of the same sex. In November 2008, Connecticut passed a law allowing civil unions between members of the same sex. In 2009, the Iowa Supreme Court legalized gay marriage. In April 2009, Vermont passed a law legalizing gay marriage. In May 2009, the Maine legislature passed a law allowing gay marriages. In June 2009, the New Hampshire legislature also passed a law allowing such marriages.

The California Supreme Court also legalized gay marriage in 2008, but then the state constitution was amended to prohibit such marriages.

> ## LegalSpeak:
> ## California Supreme Court in *In Re Marriage Cases* (2008)
>
> **F**urther, entry into a formal, officially recognized family relationship provides an individual with the opportunity to become a part of one's partner's family, providing a wider and often critical network of economic and emotional security.... The opportunity of a couple to establish an officially recognized family of their own not only grants access to an extended family but also permits the couple to join the broader family social structure that is a significant feature of community life. Moreover, the opportunity to publicly and officially express one's love for and long-term commitment to another person by establishing a family together with that person also is an important element of self-expression that can give special meaning to one's life. Finally, of course, the ability to have children and raise them with a loved one who can share the joys and challenges of that endeavor is without doubt a most valuable component of oneís liberty and personal autonomy....
>
> In light of the fundamental nature of the substantive rights embodied in the right to marry—and their central importance to an individual's opportunity to live a happy, meaningful, and satisfying life as a full member of society the California Constitution properly must be interpreted to guarantee this basic civil right to *all* individuals and couples, without regard to their sexual orientation.

What do various **state constitutions** or **statutes** say about **same-sex marriages**?

The majority of states prohibit same-sex marriages either by statute or in their state constitution—or both. The following is a compilation of these statutory and/or state constitutional provisions.

State	Provision
Alabama	Ala. Code 1975 § 30-1-19

Definition: Marriage is inherently a unique relationship between a man and a woman. As a matter of public policy, this state has a special interest in encouraging, supporting, and protecting the unique relationship in order to promote, among other goals, the stability and welfare of society and its children. A marriage contracted between individuals of the same sex is invalid in this state.

Alaska	AS § 25.05.013

Definition: A marriage entered into by persons of the same sex ... is void in this state....

Arizona	25-101(c)

Definition: Marriage between persons of the same sex is void and prohibited.

279

State	Provision

Arkansas — Arkansas Constitution, Amendment 83, § 1

Definition: Marriage consists only of the union of one man and one woman.

Arkansas — Arkansas Statute A.C.A. 9-11-208

Definition: (a) It shall be the declared public policy of the State of Arkansas to recognize the marital union only of man and woman. No license shall be issued to persons to marry another person of the same sex and no same-sex marriage shall be recognized as entitled to the benefits of marriage. (b) Marriages between persons of the same sex are prohibited in this state. Any marriage entered into by persons of the same sex, when a marriage license is issued by another state or by a foreign jurisdiction, shall be void in Arkansas, and any contractual or other rights granted by virtue of that license, including its termination, shall be unenforceable in the Arkansas courts.

California — Cal. Fam. Code § 308.5

Definition: Only marriage between a man and a woman is valid or recognized in California [a court decision in 2008 rendered this statute unconstitutional on equal protection grounds].

Colorado — Colorado Statute C.R.S.A. § 14-2-104.

Definition: Formalities (1) Except as otherwise provided in subsection (3) of this section, a marriage is valid in this state if: (a) It is licensed, solemnized, and registered as provided in this part 1; and (b) It is only between one man and one woman.

Delaware — Delaware Statute 13 Del. C. § 101(a)

Definition: A marriage is prohibited and void ... between persons of the same gender.

Florida — F.S.A. § 308.5

Definition: Marriages between persons of the same sex entered into in any jurisdiction ... are not recognized for any purpose in this state.

Georgia — Georgia Constitution, Article I, § 4

Definition: (a) This state shall recognize as marriage only the union of man and woman. Marriages between persons of the same sex are prohibited in this state. (b) No union between persons of the same sex shall be recognized by this state as entitled to the benefits of marriage. This state shall not give effect to any public act, record, or judicial proceeding of any other state or jurisdiction respecting a relationship between persons of the same sex that is treated as a marriage under the laws of such other state or jurisdiction. The courts of this state shall have no jurisdiction to grant a divorce or separate maintenance with respect to any such relationship or otherwise to consider or rule on any of the parties' respective rights arising as a result of or in connection with such relationship.

Georgia — Georgia Statute—Ga. Code Ann. § 19-3-3.1

Definition: (a) It is declared to be the public policy of this state to recognize the union only of one man and woman. Marriages between members of the same sex are prohibited in this state.

State	Provision

Hawaii   HRS § 572—1

Definition: In order to make valid the marriage contract, which shall be only between a man and a woman....

Illinois   750 ILCS 5/213.1

Definition: A marriage between 2 individuals of the same sex is contrary to the public policy of this state.

Indiana   Indiana Statute 31-11-1-6

Definition: Only a female may marry a male. Only a male may marry a female. A marriage between persons of the same gender is void in Indiana even if the marriage is lawful in the place where it is solemnized.

Kansas   Kansas Statute—K.S.A. 23-101

Definition: The marriage contract is to be considered in law as a civil contract between two parties who are of opposite sex. All other marriages are declared to be contrary to the public policy of this state and are void. The consent of the parties is essential. The marriage ceremony may be regarded either as a civil ceremony or as a religious sacrament, but the marriage relation shall only be entered into, maintained or abrogated as provided by law.

Kentucky   Kentucky Statute K.R.S. 402.005

Definition: Definition of marriage As used and recognized in the law of the Commonwealth, "marriage" refers only to the civil status, condition, or relation of one (1) man and one (1) woman united in law for life, for the discharge to each other and the community of the duties legally incumbent upon those whose association is founded on the distinction of sex.

Louisiana   La. C.C. Art. 86

Definition: Marriage is a legal relationship between a man and a woman that is created by civil contract. The relationship and the contract are subject to special rules prescribed by law.

Louisiana   La. C.C. Art. 3520(B)

Definition: A purported marriage between persons of the same sex violates a strong public policy of the state of Louisiana and such a marriage contracted in another state shall not be recognized in this state for any purpose, including the assertion of any right or claim as a result of the purported marriage.

Maryland   Md. FAMILY LAW Code Ann. § 2-201

Definition: Only a marriage between a man and a woman is valid in this state.

Michigan   Mich. Constitution Art. I, § 25

Definition: To secure and preserve the benefits of marriage for our society and for future generations of children, the union of one man and one woman in marriage shall be the only agreement recognized as a marriage or similar union for any purpose.

State	Provision

Michigan   M.C.L.A. § 551.1.

Definition: Marriage between same sex, invalidity: Marriage is inherently a unique relationship between a man and a woman. As a matter of public policy, this state has a special interest in encouraging, supporting, and protecting that unique relationship in order to promote, among other goals, the stability and welfare of society and its children. A marriage contracted between individuals of the same sex is invalid in this state.

Minnesota   Minnesota Statute M.S.A. § 517.01

Definition: Marriage, so far as its validity in law is concerned, is a civil contract between a man and a woman, to which the consent of the parties, capable in law of contracting, is essential. Lawful marriage may be contracted only between persons of the opposite sex and only when a license has been obtained as provided by law and when the marriage is contracted in the presence of two witnesses and solemnized by one authorized, or whom one or both of the parties in good faith believe to be authorized, so to do. Marriages subsequent to April 26, 1941, not so contracted shall be null and void.

Missouri   Missouri Constitution: Art. I, § 33

Definition: That to be valid and recognized in this state, a marriage shall exist only between a man and a woman.

Missouri   Missouri Statute 451.022

Definition: Marriage, public policy, validity—marriage licenses, issued, when 1. It is the public policy of this state to recognize marriage only between a man and a woman. 2. Any purported marriage not between a man and a woman is invalid. 3. No recorder shall issue a marriage license, except to a man and a woman. 4. A marriage between persons of the same sex will not be recognized for any purpose in this state even when valid where contracted.

Nebraska   Nebraska Constitution, Art. I, § 29

Definition: Only marriage between a man and a woman shall be valid or recognized in Nebraska. The uniting of two persons of the same sex in a civil union, domestic partnership, or other similar same-sex relationship shall not be valid or recognized in Nebraska.

New York   Domestic Relations Law

Definition: No particular form or ceremony is required when a marriage is solemnized as herein provided by a clergyman or magistrate, but the parties must solemnly declare in the presence of a clergyman or magistrate and the attending witness or witnesses that they take each other as husband and wife. In every case, at least one witness beside the clergyman or magistrate must be present at the ceremony.

North Dakota   North Dakota Constitution Art. 11, § 28

Definition: Marriage consists only of the legal union between a man and a woman. No other domestic union, however denominated, may be recognized as a marriage or given the same or substantially equivalent legal effect.

State	Provision

North Dakota   North Dakota Statute, NDCC 14-03-01

Definition: Marriage is a personal relation arising out of a civil contract between one man and one woman to which the consent of the parties is essential. The marriage relation may be entered into, maintained, annulled, or dissolved only as provided by law. A spouse refers only to a person of the opposite sex who is a husband or a wife.

Oregon   Oregon Statute 106.010

Definition: Marriage contract; age of parties—"Marriage is a civil contract entered into in person by males at least 17 years of age and females at least 17 years of age, who are otherwise capable, and solemnized in accordance with ORS 106.150.

South Dakota   South Dakota Constitution, Article 21, § 9

Definition: Only marriage between a man and a woman shall be valid or recognized in South Dakota. The uniting of two or more persons in a civil union, domestic partnership, or other quasi-marital relationship shall not be valid or recognized in South Dakota.

Tennessee   T.C.A. 36-3-113(b)

Definition: The legal union in matrimony of only one (1) man and one (1) woman shall be the only recognized marriage in this state.

Utah   U.C.A. 30-1-8.

Definition: (1) A marriage license may be issued by the county clerk to a man and a woman only after an application has been filed in his office, requiring the following information: (a) the full names of the man and the woman, including the maiden name of the woman....

Washington   RCWA 26.04.020. Prohibited marriages:

Definition: Marriages in the following cases are prohibited ... when the parties are persons other than a male and a female.

Wisconsin   Constitution, Article 13, § 13

Definition: Only a marriage between one man and one woman shall be valid or recognized as a marriage in this state. A legal status identical or substantially similar to that of marriage for unmarried individuals shall not be valid or recognized in this state.

When did the law allow **interracial marriages**?

In the twentieth century, more and more states allowed interracial marriages. In 1967 the United States Supreme Court ruled in *Loving v. Virginia* that a Virginia state law banning interracial marriages violated the equal protection clause of the fourteenth amendment. At the time of the *Loving* decision, more than a dozen states still had laws banning interracial marriages.

Chief Justice Earl Warren said in *Loving*:

Allowing people of different races to marry did not begin to gain acceptance in the United States until the second half of the twentieth century. Today, it is a common practice (*iStock.com*).

There is patently no legitimate overriding purpose independent of invidious racial discrimination which justifies this classification. The fact that Virginia prohibits only interracial marriages involving white persons demonstrates that the racial classifications must stand on their own justification, as measures designed to maintain White Supremacy. We have consistently denied the constitutionality of measures which restrict the rights of citizens on account of race. There can be no doubt that restricting the freedom to marry solely because of racial classifications violates the central meaning of the Equal Protection Clause.

Can a person have **multiple spouses**?

No, bigamy (or polygamy) is criminalized in every state in the union. Even individuals who have a sincere religious belief in polygamy cannot legally engage in such a practice. The U.S. Supreme Court rejected a First Amendment-based religious freedom defense to a bigamy charge in *Reynolds v. United States* (1878). The Court reasoned that if it granted George Reynolds a religious-based exemption from polygamy, it would make him a law unto himself.

Who can **perform marriages**?

In most states, persons authorized to marry are members of the clergy and judges. Arizona allows "duly licensed or ordained clergymen" and various judges or justices of the peace to perform marriages.

Is a **marriage** in a **foreign country recognized** as valid in the United States?

Generally, yes—marriages in foreign countries are recognized as valid in the United States unless the marriage would violate clear public policy in the states (such as polygamy).

PRE–MARITAL AGREEMENTS

Are **prenuptial** agreements, or **pre-marital agreements**, valid?

Yes, in general, prenuptial, or antenuptial, agreements are valid. The theory is that each party willingly entered into the agreement and, as such, are contractually bound. However, if a court determines that a party did not willingly enter into the prenuptial agreement or the agreement was based on fraud, then the agreement will not be enforceable. For example, a party can contest a prenuptial agreement if he or she did not receive full and frank knowledge of all available assets of the other person. Likewise, a party can try to contest the validity of such an agreement if the agreement is too one-sided or unfair as to be considered unconscionable under state law.

What can parties **contract** to in a **pre-marital agreement**?

Those who are entering into marriage may enter into a contract with regard to virtually any matter regarding their rights and obligations, including disposition of proper-

What is the Uniform Premarital Agreement Act?

Twenty-six (26) states have adopted the Uniform Premarital Agreement Act, a model piece of legislation that was drafted in 1983. It defines such agreements and explains when such agreements are not enforceable.

Section 6 of the Model Act provides that such acts are not enforceable if one party did not enter into the contract voluntarily, the contract was unconscionable, one party did not receive full and fair disclosure of applicable assets, Another section of the law provides that the agreement cannot be modified or revoked without the written consent of both parties.

The following states have adopted a version based upon this model act: Arizona, Arkansas, California, Connecticut, Delaware, Hawaii, Idaho, Illinois, Indiana, Iowa, Kansas, Maine, Montana, Nebraska, Nevada, New Jersey, New Mexico, North Carolina, North Dakota, Oregon, Rhode Island, South Dakota, Texas, Utah, Virginia, and Wisconsin

ty, spousal support or alimony, life insurance policies and other financial arrangements. However, the parties cannot contract away the right to child support. For example, Arkansas law provides: "The right of a child to support may not be adversely affected by a pre-marital agreement."

Can you be **liable** for the **debts** your **spouse** acquired **prior to marriage**?

In most states, a spouse is not liable for the pre-marital (or antenuptial) debts of his or her spouse. Most states specifically provide for such in a law. For example, Arkansas law provides: "In all marriages solemnized after February 1, 1899, neither spouse shall be held liable for the antenuptial debts of the other, except by virtue of a written contract."

DIVORCE

How can a marriage be **annulled**?

If a marriage is annulled, it is declared a legal nullity, meaning that it never existed. Grounds for annulment vary from state to state, as it does for most areas of domestic relations laws. Common examples include when a party lacked the capacity to consent to marriage through mental infirmity or when one party was under the influence of alcohol or drugs. A marriage can be annulled if one party obtained consent from the other party through force or fraud. A marriage also can be annulled if one party lacks the physical ability to consummate the marriage (have sexual relations) and the other party did not know of this problem. A marriage also can be annulled if one party was under the age of consent as defined by applicable state law.

What are typical **grounds for divorce**?

Grounds for divorce vary from state to state. Common grounds for divorce include the failure of either party to consummate the marriage, imprisonment of one party, abandonment (desertion), bigamy, adultery, cruel and inhumane treatment, conviction of a felony or infamous crime, incurable mental illness, drug addiction, and attempted murder. Many states allow divorces under a catch-all category called "irreconcilable differences."

What are **"irreconcilable differences"**?

This is a widely used term and catch-all category in state codes to describe grounds for divorce where the parties simply cannot function as a marital unit any longer. For example, California law defines it as "those grounds which are determined by the court to be substantial reasons for not continuing the marriage and which make it

About half of all marriage end in divorce in the United States for a number of reason, ranging from unfaithfulness to desertion, mental illness, drug addiction, and criminal behavior (*iStock*).

appear that the marriage should be dissolved." Maine uses the term "irreconcilable marital differences."

Are there **differences** between **irreconcilable differences** and **other grounds** for divorce?

Yes, in certain states there is a difference between irreconcilable differences and other common grounds for divorce. For example, Maine law provides that if one party to the marriage alleges such differences and the other party denies them, then the judge may order the parties to marital counseling. Mississippi law provides that "no divorce shall be granted on the ground of irreconcilable differences where there has been a contest or denial." North Dakota law defines irreconcilable differences as "those grounds which are determined by the court to be substantial reasons for not continuing the marriage and which make it appear that the marriage should be dissolved."

If your **spouse leaves** and doesn't come back, is that grounds for divorce?

Yes, in most states abandonment constitutes a valid reason for divorce. In many states, such as Alabama, a party can legally claim abandonment if his or her spouse has left the family home for a period of one year before the filing of the petition for divorce. Connecticut law provides that grounds for divorce exist if there has been "willful desertion for one year with total neglect of duty."

287

What types of **crimes** committed by a spouse give the other spouse **grounds for divorce**?

It depends on individual state laws. In Georgia, any crime of moral turpitude in which a party is sentenced to two years or longer suffices as grounds for divorce. West Virginia law provides that any felony conviction can constitute a valid ground for divorce. Connecticut provides that life imprisonment or a sentence for "the commission of any infamous crime involving a violation of conjugal duty and punishable by imprisonment for a period in excess of one year" provides valid grounds for divorce.

What is **condonation**?

Condonation refers to forgiveness of a marital offense. It is the act of one spouse in forgiving another spouse of misconduct during the duration of the marriage. Usually, condonation was used as a defense when adultery was the alleged grounds for divorce. Condonation is no longer a valid defense in many jurisdictions.

What is **recrimination**?

Recrimination is a defense to a divorce action that says that a party is not entitled to a divorce if he or she has also committed the same offense as the other spouse. Sometimes, one party will file for divorce and the other party will then allege that the petitioning party also committed the same marital offense. This is the defense of recrimination.

Can persons **separate without** filing for a **divorce**?

In many states, yes, parties to a marriage can enter into a legal order of separation. This is often—but not always—a precursor to a full-blown divorce.

Can you file for **divorce** in a **state** that is **not the state** in which you were **married**?

A person does not have to file for divorce in the state in which they originally were married—unless both parties still reside in that state. However, persons can't file for divorce in any state of their choosing. Generally, a party can take up residence in a state before he or she can file for divorce in that state. Some states have residency requirements before a party can file for divorce in that state. A few require a person to reside in a state for at least six months in a state before filing for divorce there.

Are **divorces no-fault** or **fault-based**?

It depends upon individual state law. Some states allow both fault divorce and no-fault divorce. In other words, a party may petition for divorce, alleging fault on their spouse. A prime example is adultery. If one party committed adultery, the other party can petition for a divorce on fault grounds. However, another common ground for divorce is "irreconcilable differences,"—a legal term that covers situations when two people simply feel that they have grown apart. That often would be a no-fault ground for divorce.

If a couple owns a home, how does the court determine who gets the house if they desire a divorce? Several factors are considered by the courts in doing so (*iStock*).

The question becomes whether a party's faulty conduct may limit his or her recovery in the divorce. Again, this depends upon the laws of individual states. Some states allow fault-based divorces in which one party's recovery of marital property may be limited by their own culpable conduct. Other states, such as Tennessee, are no-fault states, meaning that the distribution of marital property generally is done without attribution of fault.

How does a **court determine** whether **property** is marital/community property or separate property?

Generally speaking, property acquired during the course of a party's marriage is considered marital property, meaning that it is subject to an equitable division by the courts. Property that a party had before entering into marriage may well be considered separate, non-marital property. Courts do not have the power to apportion separate, non-marital property. In many states, if one party inherits money from her parents, that property also would be considered separate property.

How can a **spouse ensure** that **property** remains **separate**?

In some states a spouse can actually go to the recorder's office in the county in which he or she resides and file a record or schedule of his or her separate property. This creates a presumption that such property is, and was at the time of the filing, separate property of that filing spouse. Again, one must check his or her individual state law to see if such an option exists.

Can **separate property** be **converted** to **marital property** during the course of a marriage?

It can depending upon the particular circumstances. If a party clearly intended to convert separate property into marital property, then it becomes marital property. Wisconsin law defines a category called "mixed property," describing when separate property commingles or mixes together with marital property.

How does a court determine how to **apportion marital property**?

This varies from state to state. Law in many states provide a great deal of discretion to trial courts to apportion marital property, as it deems just. Many states provide a list of factors that a court considers in making its decision. For example, Missouri law (Mo. Rev. Stat. § 452.330.1 [2008]) provides that courts should consider the following five factors in apportioning marital property:

(1) The economic circumstances of each spouse at the time the division of property is to become effective, including the desirability of awarding the family home or the right to live therein for reasonable periods to the spouse having custody of any children;

(2) The contribution of each spouse to the acquisition of the marital property, including the contribution of a spouse as homemaker;

(3) The value of the nonmarital property set apart to each spouse;

(4) The conduct of the parties during the marriage; and

(5) Custodial arrangements for minor children.

In some states, courts start with a presumption that the marital property should be distributed relatively equally. But, then the parties can rebut that presumption by presenting evidence of marital fault or substantial contributions by one spouse. For example, Indiana law (Ind. Code Ann. § 31-15-7-5 [2008]) provides as follows:

The court shall presume that an equal division of the marital property between the parties is just and reasonable. However, this presumption may be rebutted by a party who presents relevant evidence, including evidence concerning the following factors, that an equal division would not be just and reasonable:

(1) The contribution of each spouse to the acquisition of the property, regardless of whether the contribution was income producing.

(2) The extent to which the property was acquired by each spouse:

(A) before the marriage; or

(B) through inheritance or gift.

(3) The economic circumstances of each spouse at the time the disposition of the property is to become effective, including the desirability of awarding the family residence or the right to dwell in the family residence for such periods as the court considers just to the spouse having custody of any children.

(4) The conduct of the parties during the marriage as related to the disposition or dissipation of their property.

(5) The earnings or earning ability of the parties as related to:

(A) a final division of property; and

(B) a final determination of the property rights of the parties.

Is a party's **retirement account** considered **marital** or **separate property**?

This depends on individual state law. In some states it depends on whether the retirement account accrued before the parties's marriage. Another pertinent factor is whether both parties contributed to the appreciation of the asset.

ALIMONY

What is **alimony**?

Alimony refers to the support of one spouse by the other while the parties are going through divorce proceedings and also after the parties are divorced. Traditionally, courts may require the spouse that makes more money to provide alimony to the spouse that makes less money. Often, a party will file a motion, seeking interim or *pendente lite* support. The main goal of alimony is to give the supported spouse relatively the same level of maintenance or support that they enjoyed the duration of the marriage.

LegalSpeak: Tennessee v. New Jersey State Laws on Alimony

Tennessee law provides for the following factors:

(1) The relative earning capacity, obligations, needs, and financial resources of each party, including income from pension, profit sharing or retirement plans and all other sources;

(2) The relative education and training of each party, the ability and opportunity of each party to secure such education and training, and the necessity of a party to secure further education and training to improve such party's earning capacity to a reasonable level;

(3) The duration of the marriage;

(4) The age and mental condition of each party;

(5) The physical condition of each party; including, but not limited to, physical disability or incapacity due to a chronic debilitating disease;

(6) The extent to which it would be undesirable for a party to seek employment outside the home because such party will be custodian of a minor child of the marriage;

(7) The separate assets of each party, both real and personal, tangible and intangible;

(8) The provisions made with regard to the marital property as defined in § 36-4-121;

(9) The standard of living of the parties established during the marriage;

(10) The extent to which each party has made such tangible and intangible contributions to the marriage as monetary and homemaker contributions, and tangible and intangible contributions by a party to the education, training or increased earning power of the other party;

(11) The relative fault of the parties in cases where the court, in its discretion, deems it appropriate to do so; and

What are the different **types of alimony**?

There are different types of alimony, and states use different terminology to describe different types of alimony. These include permanent alimony, limited duration alimony, reimbursement alimony, rehabilitative alimony, alimony *in solido*, alimony in gross, alimony in future, periodic alimony, and transitional alimony.

New Jersey recognizes rehabilitative, reimbursement, limited duration, and permanent alimony. Often courts will award *pendente lite* or temporary support to maintain a spouse between the time of separation and eventual divorce. The other types of

(12) Such other factors, including the tax consequences to each party, as are necessary to consider the equities between the parties.

New Jersey, NJSA 2A:34–23(b)(1)–(13) considers many of the same factors:

(1) The actual need and ability of the parties to pay;

(2) The duration of the marriage;

(3) The age, physical and emotional health of the parties;

(4) The standard of living established in the marriage and the likelihood that each party can maintain a reasonably comparable standard of living;

(5) The earning capacities, educational levels, vocational skills, and employability of the parties;

(6) The length of absence from the job market of the party seeking maintenance;

(7) The parental responsibilities for the children;

(8) The time and expense necessary to acquire sufficient education or training to enable the party seeking maintenance to find appropriate employment …;

(9) The history of the financial or non-financial contributions to the marriage by each party …;

(10) The equitable distribution of property ordered and any payments on equitable distribution, directly or indirectly, out of current income, to the extent this consideration is reasonable, just and fair;

(11) The income available to either party through investment[s] …;

(12) The tax treatment and consequences to both parties of any alimony award …; and

(13) Any other factors which the court may deem just.

alimony are for a given period of time ranging from a couple years to virtually permanent support.

What are the **factors** a court considers in deciding whether and **how much** to award in **alimony**?

Again, this can vary depending upon respective state law. The two most important factors in most states are the need of the lower-earning spouse and the ability of the higher-earning spouse to pay such spousal support.

293

Judges often award alimony if one spouse earns signicantly more than the other and/or has considerably more valuable assets (*iStock*).

What happens if your **former spouse** to whom you are paying **alimony remarries**?

Most states provide that if a person receiving alimony remarries, then the obligation to pay alimony terminates. For example, Alabama law provides that a decree for alimony "shall be modified by the court to provide for the termination of such alimony upon petition of a party to the decree and proof that the spouse receiving such alimony has remarried or that such spouse is living openly or cohabiting with a member of the opposite sex."

CHILD CUSTODY

What is **child custody**?

Child custody refers to the legal process of determining what parent or legal guardian assumes custody or control over a minor child. Generally, a party to a marriage who has filed for a legal separation or divorce will file a petition for custody. Courts determine which parent or guardian to which to award custody.

What different **types of child custody** are there?

There are two basic types of custody—sole custody and joint custody. Sole custody means that one parent has legal custody of the child. Joint custody means that the parents share legal custody of the child. Some state laws—such as Arizona—divide joint custody into "joint legal custody" and "joint physical custody."

Other states use different names for custody, such as legal custody, partial custody and shared custody. For example, Pennsylvania law defines legal custody, as the "legal right to make major decisions affecting the best interest of a minor child, including, but not limited to, medical, religious and educational decisions."

How do courts determine **custody** for a **child**?

Most states laws provide that a court is to award custody based on the "best interests" of the child. State laws allow a court to consider numerous factors to determine the best interests of the child. Many states begin with a presumption that it is best for the child to maintain continuous contact of some sort with each parent.

The parent who does not receive legal or primary custody usually will have reasonable visitation rights. This may include every other weekend, some holidays, and time in the summer.

Perhaps the most painful part of divorce involves the issue of child custody. Children are often the unintended victims when a marriage ends, and the law can only do so much to find a solution (*iStock*).

Does the **race** of the parent or child have a legitimate **role** in **custody** determinations?

Many courts hold that race cannot be the determinative factor in a child-custody case. Several courts have held that race can play a role in a custody determination. Other courts hold that race cannot be considered in a child custody determination.

In *Palmore v. Sidoti* (1984; see LegalSpeak, p. 297) the U.S. Supreme Court reversed a change in custody award to a father after the mother cohabitated with a man of another race. The trial court determined that the mother's interracial cohabitation would subject her child to peer pressures and stigma at school. The U.S. Supreme Court determined that the trial court's obsession with race violated the Fourteenth Amendment of the Constitution. "Private biases may be outside the reach of the law, but the law cannot, directly or indirectly, give them effect," the Court wrote.

Other courts have determined that race can play in a factor in racial classifications. *In Re Marriage of Gambla and Woodson* (Ill. 2006; see LegalSpeak, p. 298), an

A. The court shall determine custody, either originally or on petition for modification, in accordance with the best interests of the child. The court shall consider all relevant factors, including:

1. The wishes of the child's parent or parents as to custody.

2. The wishes of the child as to the custodian.

3. The interaction and interrelationship of the child with the child's parent or parents, the child's siblings and any other person who may significantly affect the child's best interest.

4. The child's adjustment to home, school and community.

5. The mental and physical health of all individuals involved.

6. Which parent is more likely to allow the child frequent and meaningful continuing contact with the other parent.

7. Whether one parent, both parents or neither parent has provided primary care of the child.

8. The nature and extent of coercion or duress used by a parent in obtaining an agreement regarding custody.

9. Whether a parent has complied with chapter 3, article 5 of this title.

10. Whether either parent was convicted of an act of false reporting of child abuse or neglect....

B. In a contested custody case, the court shall make specific findings on the record about all relevant factors and the reasons for which the decision is in the best interests of the child.

Illinois appeals court allowed race to be a determinative factor in awarding custody of a couple's biracial child to the African-American mother instead of the Caucasian father. "Indeed, it appears that so long as race is not the sole consideration for custody decisions, it is not an unconstitutional consideration," the state high court wrote.

Can a **parent** have **child custody** if he or she has **committed a crime**?

Some states prohibit or limit parents's custody if they have committed certain sex or violent crimes. For example, Arizona prohibits a parent from having custody or even unsupervised parental time if he or she is a convicted sex offender or a murderer of a former spouse—unless the court makes written findings that the parent poses no significant risk to the child.

LegalSpeak: *Palmore v. Sidoti* (1984)

It would ignore reality to suggest that racial and ethnic prejudices do not exist or that all manifestations of those prejudices have been eliminated. There is a risk that a child living with a stepparent of a different race may be subject to a variety of pressures and stresses not present if the child were living with parents of the same racial or ethnic origin.

The question, however, is whether the reality of private biases and the possible injury they might inflict are permissible considerations for removal of an infant child from the custody of its natural mother. We have little difficulty concluding that they are not. The Constitution cannot control such prejudices but neither can it tolerate them. Private biases may be outside the reach of the law, but the law cannot, directly or indirectly, give them effect....

This is by no means the first time that acknowledged racial prejudice has been invoked to justify racial classifications. ...

Whatever problems racially mixed households may pose for children in 1984 can no more support a denial of constitutional rights than could the stresses that residential integration was thought to entail in 1917. The effects of racial prejudice, however real, cannot justify a racial classification removing an infant child from the custody of its natural mother found to be an appropriate person to have such custody.

Pennsylvania law requires courts to give consideration to the fact that any parent, seeking custody or visitation, has been convicted of homicide, kidnapping, rape, unlawful restraint, prostitution, sexual abuse, indecent exposure or indecent assault. Thus, criminal conduct can have a negative impact on a parent's future custody.

Some states prohibit a court from awarding custody to a parent who has committed murder.

Can a parent with custody **move out of state** with a **child without permission** of the other parent?

Similar to many family law issues, this depends upon individual state law. Most states have statutes that specifically address the question of the custodial parent's relocation. In many states, the custodial parent must provide a certain notice to the noncustodial parent and then the noncustodial parent has a right to object.

West Virginia's statute provides that the custodial parent "should be allowed to relocate with the child so long as that parent shows that the relocation is in good faith for

297

LegalSpeak:
In Re Marriage of Gambla and Woodson (III. App. 2006)

Judge Gilleran Johnson (majority): "The Supreme Court determined that the custody award was unconstitutional, not because the trial court considered race, but because the trial court considered solely race. ... Volumes of cases from other jurisdictions have interpreted Palsmore as not prohibiting the consideration of race in matters of child custody. ... In this case, Kira's racial status did play a role in the trial court's decision to award custody to Kimberly. However, contrary to the dissent's contention, it was not the sole factor."

Judge Robert McLaren (dissenting): "Despite this court's weak protest to the contrary, the remarks in the trial court's letter of opinion show that the court's decision for custody improperly hinged on the sole factor of race: that only an African-American person can properly raise a biracial child in this society. An award of custody based solely on race is impermissible, as an improper exercise of a trial court's discretion. The United States Supreme Court has also specifically rejected the consideration of racial biases, or the effects of racial prejudice and classifications, in child custody matters as a violation of the equal protection clause of the United States Constitution. Thus, the trial court here erroneously used race as its basis for awarding custody."

a legitimate purpose and to a location that is reasonable in light of the purpose." Nevada law also provides that the custodial parent must give notice to the noncustodial parent and that failure to give proper notice can be a factor in the court's ultimate custody determination. In many states the primary custodial parent can relocate the child only if he or she provides advance written notice of approximately two months to the other parent. The other parent can then file a petition with the court seeking to block the relocation. Many state laws then require the court to determine whether relocation is in the best interests of the child. This is a multi-factor test that takes into account many factors. In most states the burden is on the parent seeking relocation to show to the court's satisfaction that the relocation does further the best interests of the child. In other states, the child—if of sufficient age—can object to the relocation and the courts will give that factor great consideration.

In those states that examine the relocation of a parent under a "best interests of the child" analysis, what are the factors that courts consider?

States have different factors that they use to determine the best interests of the child. Some common factors include: whether the relocation will improve the quality of life for the primary custodial parent and the child; whether the motivation for the move is legitimate or done in bad faith to frustrate the visitation rights of the other parent; whether the relocation will allow each parent a realistic amount of time to be a parent; whether the relocation will have a positive or negative impact on the child's stability; and whether the primary custodial parent is likely to comply with visitation requests from the other parent. Again, these factors can vary quite a bit from state to state. It is important to consult good legal counsel if confronted with this legally and emotionally difficult situation.

Child custody can become particularly problematic if one of the parents needs to move far away from the other spouse. In such cases, the courts consider what to do in the best interest of the children (*iStock*).

What is **supervised visitation**?

Supervised visitation means that a parent can have visitation but it must be supervised by a person approved of by the court. It can be either a counselor, other family member or another person designated by a court order. Usually, supervised visitation is required for a parent when there is a concern of abuse, neglect, or past criminal behavior that would caution against the awarding of unsupervised visitation. For example, Maryland law provides: "If it is in the best interest of the child, the court may approve a supervised visitation arrangement that assures the safety and the physiological, psychological, and emotional well-being of the child."

Can a court **require parents** to attend **counseling** sessions before awarding **custody**?

In some states, courts can require parents to attend counseling sessions before awarding custody. Courts may also require the counselors to submit reports of the progress (or lack thereof) of the counseling sessions regarding custody arrangements.

Can courts **modify custody** arrangements?

Yes, and courts frequently do so depending upon changed circumstances amongst the parents. In order for a court to change custody, in most states the court must find that there has been a "material change in circumstances." This means that, for example, a custodial parent has taken up residence with a known drug abuser. That could constitute a "material change in circumstances" that could allow the noncustodial parent the right to regain custody.

The Washington nonparental visitation statute is breathtakingly broad. According to the statute's text, "*[a]ny person* may petition the court for visitation rights at any time," and the court may grant such visitation rights whenever "visitation may serve *the best interest of the child*." §26.10.160(3) (emphases added). That language effectively permits any third party seeking visitation to subject any decision by a parent concerning visitation of the parent's children to state-court review. Once the visitation petition has been filed in court and the matter is placed before a judge, a parent's decision that visitation would not be in the child's best interest is accorded no deference. Section 26.10.160(3) contains no requirement that a court accord the parent's decision any presumption of validity or any weight whatsoever. Instead, the Washington statute places the best-interest determination solely in the hands of the judge. Should the judge disagree with the parent's estimation of the child's best interests, the judge's view necessarily prevails. Thus, in practical effect, in the State of Washington a court can disregard and overturn any decision by a fit custodial parent concerning visitation whenever a third party affected by the decision files a visitation petition, based solely on the judge's determination of the child's best interests.

What if one **parent refuses** another parent's **visitation rights**?

If one parent denies another parent's visitation rights, a court can require additional visitation time, impose further conditions to prevent future violations, and assess costs and attorney fees against the parent who thwarts reasonable visitation rights.

Can **grandparents** have **visitation rights**?

Many states have grandparent visitation statutes that provide for reasonable visitation by grandparents. However, the U.S. Supreme Court has ruled that a court cannot require grandparent visitation upon the objection of parents who are considered fit.

CHILD SUPPORT

Can a court **require** a parent to pay **child support**?

Yes, a court can require the noncustodial parent (the parent without primary or legal custody) to provide reasonable child support—including medical expenses. Before child support can be imposed on a person, there must be an establishment of parenthood. In most instances, a mother seeks to establish paternity of the alleged father of her child. Once paternity is established—usually by testing—then child support can be imposed upon the so-called father.

How does a **court determine** the **amount** of **child support**?

States have child support guidelines that provide for a requisite degree of support that depends upon the income of the parent who must pay child support and the number of children. Under the Maryland child support guidelines, if a noncustodial parent (who has been ordered to pay child support) makes $5,000 a month and has one child, he or she must pay $670 a month in child support.

Court-ordered child support is not optional, and parents who do not pay can find themselves in jail (*iStock*).

Many states' child support guidelines are accessible on the Internet. For example, Tennessee's rules are available at http://www.tennessee.gov/sos/rules/1240/ 1240-02/1240-02-04.20080815.pdf. To learn more about child support guidelines, see the website http://www.supportguidelines.com/.

What happens if a person **refuses** to **pay child support**?

If a person continues to refuse to pay child support, he or she can be found guilty of criminal contempt and placed in jail. Some states refer to the crime as "criminal nonsupport." The penalties can be serious. Alaska law provides that a person can be sentenced to a Class A felony for criminal nonsupport. Tennessee law provides that a person can be jailed in a county workhouse for up to six months for failure to comply with support obligations.

Can courts **modify child support** obligations?

Yes, a party can petition the court for a change in child support obligations provided that they can show a material change in circumstances. For example, if a custodial parent learns that the other parent who provides child support recently obtained a new job that pays much more money, the custodial parent can petition for an increase in child support. Likewise, if a person ordered to pay child support makes less money and the court determines such a loss in income is not his or her fault, the court might order a reduction in child support.

PATERNITY

If you are a **pregnant** and **unmarried** woman, and the **father refuses** to **acknowledge paternity**, what can you do?

Hopefully (assuming the person is not abusive or otherwise a danger) you can convince the boyfriend to acknowledge paternity. He can do this by signing an acknowledgement of paternity at the child's birth. This means that the boyfriend admits that he is the child's father. If the boyfriend denies paternity or is not responsive, you can serve that boyfriend with notice of paternity and financial responsibility. You can do this by contacting a local office of child support enforcement. The agency will work with you in helping to establish paternity. The agency will initiate court proceedings on your behalf that require the boyfriend to submit to a paternity test. If the test determines he is the father of the child, then the agency can initiate action to help you obtain child support.

If you think you are the **father** of a child, but you are **not married** and the **mother refuses** to let you **see the baby**, is there anything you can do?

If the mother of the child will recognize that you are the baby's father, then you and she can sign an "acknowledgement of paternity" which takes care of the issue. If the mother will not recognize you as the baby's father, then you will have to file suit in court to establish paternity. You would file suit in court, contending that you are the father. You would seek a paternity test that will determine whether you are the baby's father. Once your paternity has been established, then you can exercise your rights to visitation as the baby's father. Admittedly, this process can be a difficult one, particularly without the cooperation of the child's mother.

ADOPTION

What is **adoption**?

Adoption is a legal process in which a person or persons become the legal parents or guardians of a child who is not their birth child. Once the adoption process is complete, the adoptive parents are the full and legal parents of that child—just as if they were the birth parents.

What **methods of adoptions** are there?

There are agency adoptions and private adoptions. Agency adoptions involve either a public or private adoption that is licensed by the state. A private adoption involves the parties themselves handling the adoption process. People wishing to adopt contact a lawyer who then facilitates the adoption process. Court approval is needed for private adoptions as well as agency adoptions.

Who must **consent** to an **adoption**?

The adopted child (if over a certain age— 14 in several states), the adoptee's mother and the adoptee's father or putative (presumed) father if the putative father has made efforts to be included in the putative father registry.

Can a **minor birth mother consent** to an adoption?

Many states require a minor mother to have a guardian *ad litem* appointed by the court before she can give proper consent to an adoption.

After going to an adoption agency, a hopeful parent must also get the approval of a judge to finalize the process (*iStock*).

Do **birth parents** always have to **consent** to an adoption?

Most of the time they do, but their consent is not required or needed if such birth parents have been deemed unfit by a court. States have child protection acts which are designed to remove children from unfit and unsafe parents.

Can birth **mothers withdraw consent** to an adoption?

In most states birth mothers can withdraw their consent to an adoption though there are fairly strict time limits. For example, in the state of Alaska a birth mother cannot withdraw her consent after there has been a court decree authorizing the adoption. A birth mother can withdraw her consent up to 10 days after giving it.

What information does an **adoption agency consider** when **determining** whether to place a child with prospective **adoptive parents**?

The agencies will conduct an investigation of the prospective adoptive parents, which can include a background check for past criminal history and possible past child abuse. In most states the agency will prepare a report and study for approval by the court that will determine whether the adoption is in the best interest of the child and that placement with the prospective adoptive parents is in the best interest of the child.

What is the **court** or judge's **role** in the **adoption process**?

The judge has to approve of the adoption. This means that the judge must determine that the adoption fits the best interest of the children. Some states have laws specifically authorizing judges to interview adoptees to determine their attitudes about the pending adoption.

What is a **foreign adoption**?

A foreign or international adoption is where a person or persons have adopted a child from a foreign country. Generally, the prospective adoptive parents must comply with the laws and procedures of the foreign country. Still, an American judge has to give final approval to the adoption though usually that is a mere formality, which simply requires the judge to sign a petition acknowledging the foreign adoption.

Can **adoption agencies consider** the **race** of the adoptive parents or children when **making decisions**?

In most states the racial preferences of adopting parents can be taken into consideration and honored. However, many state laws specifically prohibit an adoptive agency from denying or delaying an adoption based on the race of the adoptive parents or the adoptee. For example, Arizona law provides: "Notwithstanding any law to the contrary, the division, an agency, or the court shall not deny or delay a placement or an adoption certification based on the race, the color or the national origin of the adoptive parent or the child."

Can **prospective adoptive parents advertise** that they wish to adopt a child?

It depends on individual state law. The trend is that more states do allow prospective adoptive parents to advertise their interest in adopting a child.

What **expenses** do **adoptive parents pay** to the birth mother?

That depends but most states allow prospective adoptive parents to pay the birth mother's medical expenses and other costs during the pregnancy period. However, the adoptive parents cannot pay a flat sum to a birth mother to relinquish her rights to the child.

What **age restrictions** are imposed on prospective **adoptive parents**?

Some states provide that prospective adoptive parents be a certain amount older than the minor children they seek to adopt. For example, California law provides that a non-familial adoptive parent must be at least 10 years older than the minor child he or she seeks to adopt. Most states require that adoptive persons be at least 21 years of age.

Does a **biological father** have the **right to notification** that his child may be placed for adoption by the child's mother?

Yes, the laws of many states may require that biological fathers be notified of the adoption of his child. Biological fathers may be placed in a putative father registry. A putative father is defined as the alleged or reputed father of a child born out of wedlock. Such notice in many states can be by registered or certified mail, personal service.

Can **stepparents adopt** their spouse's (biological) children?

Yes, stepparent adoptions are recognized by state laws. Generally, a stepparent can adopt his or her spouse's children as long as they have resided with the minor child for a certain period of time. For example, Alabama's adoption scheme requires stepparents to reside with the children for one year before approving such adoptions.

Are **adoption records private**?

Yes, most adoption records are confidential. Many state laws allow such records to be accessed by an adoptee (once they turn 18), the birth parents of the adoptees, and biological siblings of the adoptee.

PERSONAL INJURY LAW

What is a **tort**?

A tort is a civil wrong not based on contract law that results when a defendant engages in socially unreasonable conduct that harms another person. Generally, in tort claims the suing party (called the plaintiff) asks for monetary damages from the defendant (sometimes called the tortfeasor or person who committed the tort) to compensate him or her for the harm he or she has suffered. If you punch someone in the face, you have committed the tort of battery. If you drive your car recklessly and hit another vehicle, you have committed the tort of negligence. If you write false things on the Internet that harm another person's reputation, you have committed the tort of defamation. If you take pictures of a person changing clothes in a restroom, you have committed the tort of invasion of privacy.

Where does the **word "tort"** come from?

Most scholars trace it to the Latin word "tortus," which means twisted. If you think about it, that makes sense because tort law is concerned with socially unreasonable conduct or conduct twisted from the norm.

What **types of cases** are examples of **tort** cases?

Most automobile accidents are tort cases. So-called slip and fall cases are tort cases. Nearly all personal injury cases are tort cases of some sort. Libel cases are tort cases. Products liability and medical malpractice cases are tort cases. When you hear a lawyer advertise herself as handling personal injury cases, that means she deals in tort law.

A case involving an auto accident falls under the classification of "tort" law (*iStock*).

How does **tort law differ** from criminal law?

Tort law differs from criminal law in several ways. Tort law is a form of civil law instead of criminal law. Criminal law serves the purpose of society at large, as criminal suits are brought by prosecutors on behalf of the state or the federal government. Tort suits generally are filed by private parties.

The fundamental purpose of criminal law is to punish those individuals who commit crimes. In contrast, the basic purpose of tort law is to compensate individuals for the harm that they have suffered.

Another major difference between tort and criminal law concerns the burden of proof. Criminal cases require the prosecution to prove its case by a very high standard called beyond a reasonable doubt. This requires almost absolute certainty by the jury (or judge) that the criminal defendant committed the unlawful act for which he is charged. Tort suits require the plaintiff to prove his case by preponderance of the evidence, which means more likely than not.

Can the **same conduct** form the basis for **both** a **crime** and a **tort**?

Absolutely. If you punch another person in the face, you can be charged with criminal assault and battery by the state or local government. Likewise, the victim (the person you punched) also can sue you for damages in court in a tort action. A famous example concerns the two trials involving former football great Orenthal James (O.J.)

Simpson. In 1995, a jury acquitted Simpson for the murders of his former wife, Nicole Brown Simpson, and her companion Ronald Goldman.

However, the families of the victims then sued Simpson for the tort action of wrongful death. They prevailed in civil court—perhaps because of the lower standard of proof—and won a substantial monetary judgment against Simpson. The difference was that the civil tort suit led to a monetary judgment but no prison sentence.

How does **tort law differ** from **contract** law?

Tort and contract law are both forms of civil law, but they differ. Tort law imposes duties on everyone in society to act in a socially reasonable manner. Contract law imposes duties only on individuals who sign a contract. Similarly, tort law imposes obligations on everyone to act reasonably, while contract law imposes obligations on the parties who sign the contract.

Another major difference between these two forms of civil law concern the time period in which a person has to file a lawsuit—called a statute of limitations. In many states the standard time frame to file a tort lawsuit is one or two years, while the period for a suit based on contract is longer. Remember to check the law in your respective state for information on the applicable statute of limitations.

What are the basic **types of torts**?

Torts are divided into three general categories: (1) intentional torts, (2) torts of negligence, and (3) strict liability torts. The three types differ based on the intent of the defendant or tortfeasor (the person who allegedly commits a tort). Intentional torts occur when a tortfeasor acts knowing that a certain result will occur or with substantial certainty that a harmful result will occur. Negligent acts occur when you act carelessly or recklessly enough to cause harm to another.

For example, if you intentionally ram your car into the rear of your friend's car, you have committed the intentional tort of battery. However, if you accidentally run into the rear of your friend's car, you were negligent. You did not intend to harm your friend's property, but you acted carelessly enough to be liable in tort for your negligent or faulty conduct.

Strict liability applies in tort law in special circumstances when a defendant does not intend harm (as in many intentional tort situations) or when a defendant is negligent. Strict liability applies when a defendant engages in certain dangerous activities, such as the storing of flammable liquids or the transportation of toxic materials. Strict liability often applies for harm caused by a person's trespassing animal. Again, you should check your applicable state law to determine when strict liability applies in tort law.

309

LegalSpeak: *Hackbart v. Cincinnati Bengals* (10th Cir. 1979)

The general customs of football do not approve the intentional punching or striking of others. That this is prohibited was supported by the testimony of all of the witnesses. They testified that the intentional striking of a player in the face or from the rear is prohibited by the playing rules as well as the general customs of the game. Punching or hitting with the arms is prohibited. Undoubtedly these restraints are intended to establish reasonable boundaries so that one football player cannot intentionally inflict a serious injury on another. Therefore, the notion is not correct that all reason has been abandoned, whereby the only possible remedy for the person who has been the victim of an unlawful blow is retaliation.

What are some **examples** of **intentional torts**?

Examples of intentional torts against a person include assault, battery, intentional infliction of emotional distress, and false imprisonment. Intentional torts against property include trespass to chattels, trespass to land, and conversion.

A common intentional tort is battery, defined as the intentional infliction of a harmful or offensive contact. If person A punches person B in the mouth, A has committed battery. If A throws a water balloon and water lands on B, A has committed battery. If A kisses B without B's consent, then A may have committed battery.

What was the famous **plate-snatching case**?

The 1960s case of Emmett E. Fisher shows that the tort of battery can include offensive contacts that are not necessarily physically harmful. Fisher, an African-American man, worked as a mathematician at an agency of the National Aeronautics and Space Agency (NASA). An electronics company had invited Fisher to attend a meeting held at the Carrousel Motor Hotel. The hotel contained a restaurant called the Brass Ring, which served the luncheon for the meeting Fisher attended.

Fisher entered the Brass Ring and grabbed a plate for lunch. The manager of the Brass Ring snatched the plate from Fisher and shouted that negroes could not be served in the club. Fisher sued the hotel for battery, seeking compensatory and punitive damages for the humiliation he suffered as a result of the manager's conduct. A jury awarded Fisher $400 in compensatory damages and $500 in punitive damages. However, a Texas appeals court reversed, finding that there was no battery because there was no direct physical contact.

On appeal, the Texas Supreme Court reversed in *Fisher v. Carrousel Motor Hotel*, 424 S.W.2d 627 (Tex. 1967). The Texas high court reasoned that the tort of battery consisted of offensive contacts, as well as physically harmful contacts. The court explained:

> Under the facts of this case, we have no difficulty in holding that the intentional grabbing of plaintiff's plate constituted a battery. The intentional snatching of an object from one's hand is as clearly an offensive invasion of his person as would be an actual contact with the body....

> Personal indignity is the essence of an action for battery; and consequently, the defendant is liable not only for the contacts which do actual physical harm, but also for those which are offensive and insulting. We hold, therefore, that plaintiff was entitled to actual damages for mental suffering due to the willful battery, even in the absence of any physical injury.

The Texas high court reinstated the jury's damage award of $900 and, more importantly, established a leading tort-law precedent.

Can an **injury** in a **sports** contest constitute a **battery**?

Most injuries in sports contests—even if caused by direct contact from an opposed player—would not constitute a battery. The theory is that a sport participant consents to performing in sporting events and, therefore, assumes the risk of injury when playing. However, if a participant intentionally engages in egregious conduct that flouts the rules of the sport, then he or she can be liable for battery.

For example, a federal district court refused to dismiss a lawsuit by former Denver Broncos defensive back Dale Hackbart, who was struck with a forearm to the head by Cincinnati Bengals running back Charles Clark, while Hackbart was kneeling on the ground.

Are **punching** and **kicking** the **only** acts that are regarded as **battery**?

No, battery is when someone acts intending to cause any harmful or offensive contact with another person. This would include spitting, throwing, and hitting

When playing contact sports, it is expected that injuries will occur. However, egregiously violent behavior may be grounds for charges of assault and battery (*iStock*).

someone with a water balloon or other object, kissing someone without their consent, or touching them in an inappropriate or unwelcome way.

Does a person have a **tort claim** if they are **wrongfully detained** for **shoplifting** in a major department store?

Perhaps; the person might have a tort claim for false imprisonment, depending on the particular factual circumstances. False imprisonment is an intentional tort that occurs when one person intentionally confines another person against his or her will. Many states, however, have shopkeepers' privilege laws, which give merchants immunity from civil liability if they reasonably detain persons for a reasonable amount of time and if they have a reasonable belief that the person may be shoplifting. Much of this will depend on the wording of the state's shopkeeper privilege law.

For example, Arizona's laws provides:

A merchant, or a merchant's agent or employee, with reasonable cause, may detain on the premises in a reasonable manner and for a reasonable time any person who is suspected of shoplifting as prescribed in subsection A of this section for questioning or summoning a law enforcement officer.

Ohio's law reads similarly:

A merchant, or an employee or agent of a merchant, who has probable cause to believe that items offered for sale by a mercantile establishment have been unlawfully taken by a person, may, for the purposes set forth in division (C) of this section, detain the person in a reasonable manner for a reasonable length of time within the mercantile establishment or its immediate vicinity.

Both these laws require the merchants or the merchant's employees to have some sort of reasonable belief ("reasonable cause" in Arizona and "probable cause" in Ohio) that the person is a shoplifter. Both laws also require that store employees detain the person for a reasonable amount of time.

What is **intentional infliction** of **emotional distress**?

Intentional infliction of emotional distress, sometimes called outrageous conduct, refers to intentional or reckless conduct of an extreme and outrageous nature that causes another person to suffer severe emotional distress. The conduct complained of must be beyond the pale of decency such that it would cause a reasonable person to exclaim: "That's an outrage" or "That's outrageous."

For example, the Washington Supreme Court in 2003 upheld a $60,000 jury verdict for intentional infliction of emotional distress in favor of a woman whose former live-in male friend continually harassed her with hundreds of phone calls after the relationship ended. Even though the woman had obtained an order of protection, the man continued a nonstop barrage of phone calls. The man called the woman 640 times at home, 100 times at work and called the homes of several men with whom he thought the woman was having a relationship. He also threatened to kill the woman. The Washington Supreme Court reasoned that this deplorable crossed the line into outrageousness sufficient to justify the jury's verdict.

Another example of outrageous conduct to a reviewing court occurred after a car accident in Georgia. The plaintiff contacted the insurance company of the other driver who was at fault during the accident. The claims examiner allegedly began using a torrent of bad language and racial slurs toward the African-American plaintiff. The court found that the "abusive and obscene" language used by the claims examiner sufficed to constitute intentional infliction of emotional distress.

What is a famous intentional infliction of **emotional distress case** involving *Hustler Magazine*?

In 1983, pornography publisher Larry Flynt lampooned the Reverend Jerry Falwell in his *Hustler Magazine*. Hustler wrote a fake advertisement based on actual Campari Liquor ads, featuring celebrities talking about their "first times"—the first time they tasted Campari liquor with the obvious double entendre of their first sexual experience.

The Hustler piece entitled "Jerry Falwell talks about his first time" said that Falwell's first time was with his mother in an outhouse. The ad did not contain a disclaimer in small language at the bottom of the page that read: "ad parody—not to be taken seriously." The ad outraged Falwell, the president of the Moral Majority and a nationally known televangelist. Falwell sued Flynt in federal court under three tort theories—invasion of privacy, defamation, and intentional infliction of emotional distress.

The judge threw out the invasion of privacy claim, but the lawsuit proceeded on the libel and infliction of emotional distress claims. A federal jury rejected the libel claim but awarded Falwell $200,000 on the intentional infliction of emotional distress claims. A federal appeals court affirmed the jury verdict, setting the stage for the United States Supreme Court.

In February 1988, the U.S. Supreme Court issued its decision in *Hustler Magazine v. Falwell*, 485 U.S. 46 (1988), ruling that Falwell could not establish intentional infliction of emotional distress because the ad could not be interpreted as stating actual facts about Jerry Falwell. In his opinion for the Court, Chief Justice William H. Rehnquist compared the *Hustler* ad to political cartoons satirizing a broad range of public officials. Rehnquist warned the outrageousness was too subjective a standard when imposing liability on speech about public figures such as Jerry Falwell.

Rehnquist wrote: "'Outrageousness' in the area of political and social discourse has an inherent subjectiveness about it which would allow a jury to impose liability on the basis of the jurors' tastes or views, or perhaps on the basis of their dislike of a particular expression. An 'outrageousness' standard thus runs afoul of our longstanding refusal to allow damages to be awarded because the speech in question may have an adverse emotional impact on the audience."

The famous battle between Larry Flynt and Jerry Falwell shows that there is a high constitutional bar to establishing an intentional infliction of emotional distress claim against a person for their speech about public affairs, public officials or public figures.

What are some **other examples** of intentional **infliction** of **emotional distress**?

Some examples of conduct held to constitute intentional infliction of emotional distress by courts are: subjecting an employee to sexual harassment over a long period of time; detaining a potential car buyer for four hours of extreme pressure accompanied with misrepresentations; humiliating an employee by demoting them from company vice-president to the position of janitor; planting company checks on an employee to make it appear falsely that the person was stealing from the company; refusing to release the body of a widow's husband because she decided to seek services from another funeral home; and accusing a customer of shoplifting and then pummeling the person.

If you are attacked, you have the right to defend yourself without fear of being found guilty of assault if you are justified in your actions. Laws about using deadly force can vary from state to state, however (*iStock*).

Is there a **tort** that you can use or **sue under** if someone files **false criminal charges** against you?

Yes, the tort of malicious prosecution may provide you with redress if someone files false criminal charges against you. If a tortfeasor files false criminal charges, has no probable cause and acted out an improper motive, then the tortfeasor has committed the tort of malicious prosecution.

Unfortunately, some parents will file false legal actions against their former spouse in order to obtain an advantage in the child custody arena. The difficulty for someone suing for malicious prosecution is they have to show that the other person acted without probable cause. The person also has to prevail in the underlying criminal action. This means that if someone files false criminal charges against you but you plead guilty to avoid the hassle of going to trial, you forfeit your right to sue for malicious prosecution.

What are some **defenses** to **intentional torts**?

Some applicable defenses to intentional torts are consent, self-defense, necessity, and statute of limitations. For example, let's say a boxer knocks out his opponent with a vicious uppercut, the fallen boxer cannot file a tort suit for battery because he has voluntarily consented to the punches. However, former world heavyweight boxing champion Evander Holyfield may have had a good tort case against former opponent (and former champion) Mike Tyson when they fought their second bout. In that infamous bout, Tyson bit Holyfield's ear twice. Holyfield consented to punches in the boxing ring but not the ear bites.

Self-defense is another interesting defense. The general rule is that a person has a privilege to use reasonable force to defend him or herself. Questions arise whether a defendant used reasonable force under the circumstances to protect his home or property. People have been sued because they shot and killed intruders or thieves. State laws differ on the availability of the scope of self-defense, particularly the use of deadly force. Some states allow the use of deadly force to protect property, not just a person's life.

NEGLIGENCE

What is **negligence** and what are the **elements** of a **negligence claim**?

Negligence refers to a common type of tort claim in which the plaintiff alleges that a defendant acted carelessly or unreasonably and harmed the plaintiff. If a person is negligent, that person is at fault. In other words, if person A fails to follow a yield sign and plows her car into the vehicle of person B, B may sue A for negligence. The theory is that A operated her motor vehicle in a negligent, or faulty, fashion. It doesn't matter that A did not mean to harm B. What matters is whether A was at fault and unreasonable in the operation of her motor vehicle and caused harm to B.

Similarly, if a business cleans its floors with slippery substances and does not clean up the floor and warn its customers of the dangerous condition, the business is negligent. The theory is that it is socially unreasonable for the business owner to place its customers in harm's way.

The elements of a negligence claim are (1) duty; (2) breach of duty; (3) causation; and (4) damages. Duty means that a person owes a duty to other people to act in a socially reasonable manner. Breach of duty occurs when the defendant fails to act reasonably under the circumstances, or fails to act like a reasonable person under the circumstances. Causation means that the defendant's conduct caused the harm suffered by the plaintiff. Damages refer to the requirement that the plaintiff suffers some type of actual harm.

What is a **"reasonable person"**?

A reasonable person refers to a fictional person who conforms his or her conduct to the applicable standards of care in society. In other words, a reasonable person is a person who does not act negligently and serves as a guide in determining whether defendants in tort cases adhered to a reasonableness standard.

The Restatement of Torts (2d) § 283, comment b provides in part:

> Negligence is a departure from a standard of conduct demanded by the community for the protection of others against unreasonable risk.... In dealing with this problem the law has made use of the standard of a hypothetical "reasonable man." Sometimes this person is called a reasonable man of ordinary prudence, or an ordinarily prudent man, or a man of average prudence, or a man of reasonable sense exercising ordinary care. It is evident that all such phrases are intended to mean very much the same thing. The actor is required to do what this ideal individual would do in his place.

The reasonable person standard is an objective standard that provides a comparison between the defendant and the ideal person who is acting reasonably. Factors important in determining reasonableness sometimes include the defendant's profession, custom, age, whether the defendant violated a statute or law, and physical characteristics of the defendant. For example, a blind person is not held to the same standard of care as people who have their eyesight.

Are **children** held to the same **standard of care** as adults?

No, children are held to the standard of care of a reasonable person their age. The rule provided by Restatement of Torts (2d) § 283A is: "If the actor is a child, the standard of conduct to which he must conform to avoid being negligent is that of a reasonable person of like age, intelligence, and experience under the like circumstances."

Children can be held to an adult standard of care if they are engaging in an adult activity, such as operating a motor vehicle or flying an airplane.

In many states children under seven years old are not capable of negligence or cannot be sued for negligence. However, this is not uniform in all states. Consult your state's judicial decisions and/or statutes to determine at what age a child and his parents can be sued for the negligent actions of a young child.

What is **negligence *per se*?**

Negligence *per se* is a doctrine that provides that if a person is negligent while violating a related law or regulation, the person is negligent, or a presumption is created that the person is negligent. Negligence *per se* allows a plaintiff to prove the breach of duty element in a negligence case.

For example, let's say that there is a car accident between car A and car B. A sues B for negligence. A is able to prove that B was driving 20 miles over the speed limit. The fact that B exceeded the speeding law—a safety regulation—probably establishes that B was negligent *per se*.

What is *res ipsa loquitur*?

This Latin term literally means "the thing speaks for itself." In legal parlance, it refers to a doctrine that helps a plaintiff show that a defendant was negligent when the injury-causing instrument was under the control of the defendant and it is probable that the negligence resulted from the defendant. As a Connecticut court wrote, "*res ipsa loquitur* is a method to prove negligence as opposed to being a separate tort in and of itself."

Res ipsa loquitur applies when the rational explanation for the plaintiff's injuries was because of the defendant's negligence. The doctrine is an exception to the general rule that negligence cannot be presumed from the mere occurrence of an accident and injury. A Nebraska appeals court applied the doctrine when a property owner sued after a high voltage line maintained by a local power district fell onto their property and started a fire. The court noted that "powerlines do not normally fall without fault on behalf of the company that maintains them and that *res ipsa loquitur* is applied in the absence of a substantial, significant, or probable explanation." (See LegalSpeak, p. 316).

What are the **two types of causation** in tort cases?

The two types of causation are actual or factual causation and proximate or legal causation. Actual cause refers to whether the defendant's conduct was the actual, factual cause of the plaintiff's harm. Take the example of a man with a sore leg who enters a department store and slips on the slick floor. The man claims that he injured his leg in his fall. However, the store may claim that his leg was injured already and the fall did not add to his condition at all.

The second type of causation is legal or proximate cause. This type of causation limits a defendant's liability to the reasonably foreseeable injuries caused by his tortious conduct. In other words, let's say a man falls in the department store. The man suffers a knee injury and has to be transported by an ambulance to a local hospital. However, a careless driver then pulls out in front of the ambulance driver and causes a bad accident that kills the man who is a passenger-patient in the ambulance. It is not reasonably foreseeable that a wet floor would lead to a patron being killed in an ambulance.

What was the case of *Palsgraf v. Long Island Railroad Company* concerning proximate causation?

The most famous case on the meaning of proximate causation resulted from an unfortunate incident on a Long Island Railroad station. Two men attempted to board a train as it was leaving the Queens' Jamaica Station.

Palsgraf v. Long Island Railroad Co., 162 N.E. 99 (N.Y. 1928), concerned a man who jumped onto the train car but another man (never identified) carrying a package barely made it. One guard on the car pulled the man up, while another guard ran and pushed the man from behind. This dislodged the man's package, which fell upon the rails. The package—covered by newspaper—contained fireworks. The fireworks exploded and knocked down some scales that struck a 43-year-old woman named Helen Palsgraf at the other end of the platform.

Palsgraf sued the railroad company for negligence. A trial court awarded her $6,000. An appeals court affirmed the award. However, the New York Court of Appeals (the state's highest court) reversed 4 to 3 in a majority opinion by Benjamin Cardozo, who would later serve on the United States Supreme Court.

Cardozo reasoned that there was no proximate causation because injury to Mrs. Palsgraf was not reasonably foreseeable by the train station. "Nothing in the situation gave notice the falling package had in it the potency of peril to persons thus removed,"

Slip-and-fall accidents can easily lead to lawsuits, but injuries may not always be the fault of the company or individual being sued (*iStock*).

he wrote. "Here, by concession, there was nothing in the situation to suggest to the most cautious mind that the parcel wrapped in newspaper would spread wreckage through the station."

Judge William S. Andrews wrote a dissenting opinion, believing that the duty owed by the railroad station extended beyond those within a certain radius or zone of danger. "Every one owes to the world at large the duty of refraining from those acts that may unreasonably threaten the safety of others," he wrote. Andrews noted that the negligent act by the railroad employee that knocked the package was a "substantial factor in producing the result." He also pointed out that "there was no remoteness in time" and that "injury in some form was most probable."

Can a **business be liable** for **injuries caused** to its patrons by **third parties**?

Yes, though the outcome is fact-intensive and may—like much of tort law—vary from state to state. The general rule—provided for in the Restatement of Torts (Second)—is that businesses can be liable for third-party criminal attacks that are reasonably foreseeable if the business owner takes little or no security precautions.

For example, let's say that a shopping mall experiences a rash of crime, including robberies and assaults of its patrons. The mall fails to provide increased lighting or for an extra security guard to patrol the mall parking lots. A jury may find that the mall

LegalSpeak: *Delgado v. Trax Bar & Grill* (Cal. 2005)

Even when proprietors such as those described above have no duty under Ann M. and Sharon P. to provide a security guard or undertake other similarly burdensome preventative measures, the proprietor is not necessarily insulated from liability under the special relationship doctrine. A proprietor that has no duty under Ann M. and Sharon P. to hire a security guard or to undertake other similarly burdensome preventative measures still owes a duty of due care to a patron or invitee by virtue of the special relationship, and there are circumstances (apart from the failure to provide a security guard or undertake other similarly burdensome preventative measures) that may give rise to liability based upon the proprietor's special relationship....

Moreover, as especially relevant to the present case, California decisions long have recognized, under the special relationship doctrine, that a proprietor who serves intoxicating drinks to customers for consumption on the premises must "exercis[e] reasonable care to protect his patrons from injury at the hands of fellow guests", and that such a duty "arises ... when one or more of the following circumstances exists: (1) A tavern keeper allowed a person on the premises who has a known propensity for fighting; (2) the tavern keeper allowed a person to remain on the premises whose conduct had become obstreperous and aggressive to such a degree the tavern keeper knew or ought to have known he endangered others; (3) the tavern keeper had been warned of danger from an obstreperous patron and failed to take suitable measures for the protection of others; (4) the tavern keeper failed to stop a fight as soon as possible after it started; (5) the tavern keeper failed to provide a staff adequate to police the premises; and (6) the tavern keeper tolerated disorderly conditions."

owner's refusal to provide increased security measures crosses the line into negligent behavior, particularly when the mall owner knew about the prior incidents of crime.

However, the shopping mall owner will contend that the criminal act of the third party was a superseding, intervening cause that broke the chain of causation. This may be a difficult argument for the mall owner to advance if it can be established that the mall owner knew of existing crime on the premises.

The answer also could depend on whether a court finds that there is a special relationship to protect patrons or customers. The California Supreme Court ruled that there was a special relationship and potential premise liability when a patron warned a bouncer about impending trouble from people in and near the bar. The patron was later beaten severely right outside the bar. On that set of facts, the California high

LegalSpeak: *Rucshner v. ADT Security Systems* (Wash. App. 2009)

To prove negligent hiring, the plaintiff must demonstrate that (1) the employer knew or, in the exercise of ordinary care, should have known of the employee's unfitness at the time of hiring; and (2) the negligently hired employee proximately caused the plaintiff's injury....

Rucshner argues that PSP's agreement with ADT created a duty to customers such as MH, which PSP breached by failing to conduct Robinson's criminal background check and drug screening. We agree....

Rucshner also argues that PSP negligently hired Robinson because it knew, or should have known, that employing Robinson without conducting a criminal background check posed a risk of harm to its customers. We have already held that a genuine issue of material fact exists as to PSP's contractual duty to perform criminal background checks on its employees. Nevertheless, we also reach Rucshner's causation argument to point out that a genuine issue of material fact also exists on the issue of foreseeability of harm of the type that Robinson caused here.

court found there was a duty of care owed to the patron and that it was reasonably foreseeable that this attack could happen.

Can an **employer** be held **negligent** if it retains or hires an **employee** who is **dangerous** to the public?

Yes, if a state recognizes the torts of negligent hiring or negligent retention. Negligent hiring means that an employer negligently hired an employee that it knew or should have known through reasonable diligence present a risk to the public. For example, let's say that a trucking company hires a new driver who then drives drunk and injures some motorists. If a reasonable investigation by the employer would have revealed past convictions for drunk driving, the injured motorists would have a good case against the trucking company for negligent hiring.

Similarly, let's say that a private security firm receives a complaint that one of its officers sexually harassed a woman at a job site. The company fails to properly discipline this employee. If a few months later, this same employee allegedly sexually assaults another person, then the security firm may be liable for negligent retention. The theory behind negligent retention is that the employer should have known that this particular employee presented a risk to the public and should have terminated his employment earlier.

A company could also face liability for negligence if it fails to conduct any criminal background check at all, particularly if the company claims that it does conduct such background checks. For example, a Washington appeals court in 2009 refused to dismiss a claim against a security services dealer after one of its employees raped a 14-year-old girl whose family was a customer. The appeals court focused on the fact that that the company—which contracted with the larger security company that it conducted background checks on its employees—failed to perform a criminal background check on its employee, who had numerous convictions.

What if some **unexpected event** causes **damage** to a plaintiff **after** a defendant's **negligent act**?

The law refers to these as superseding or intervening causes. In some states the terms are different. In other states the terms may be used more as synonyms. The point is that a superseding cause is an event, which occurs after the defendant's original negligent act, that breaks the chain of causation.

For example, let's say Driver A negligently rear-ends Driver B, causing injury to Driver B. An emergency crew comes to pick up Driver B to take her to the hospital for evaluation. As medical personnel take Driver B from the ambulance, a lightning bolt strikes the stretcher and kills Driver B. The lightning strike would qualify as a superseding cause that breaks the chain of causation from Driver A's negligent driving.

Many times such intervening causes are called Acts of God. One recent example occurred in Louisiana when the owner of a building alleged that the company that leased his building had negligently attached a sign to the top of his building. During Hurricane Katrina, the sign smashed into the building and caused significant damage. The owner of the building sued the company that leased his building, contending that the improper attachment of the sign caused the damage. A Louisiana appeals court disagreed in *Duboue v. CBS Outdoor* (La.App. 2008; see LegalSpeak above), finding that the damage from Hurricane Katrina was an act of God that broke the chain of causation.

Can a **"Good Samaritan"** be held **liable** if he or she **acts negligently** even though they are trying to help?

"Good Samaritan" laws are designed to provide protection to those who render emergency aid to people in distress. The idea behind the statute is that someone should not be sued if they are trying to do a good deed and help someone even when there is no legal duty to help another. The policy reason behind good Samaritan laws is that without such laws, some people may avoid helping others for fear of being sued.

These laws vary from state to state, but most provide protection from ordinary negligence. The good Samaritan must be really, really negligent (called "gross negligence") in order to be liable. Tennessee's good Samaritan law provides protection to those who render emergency aid unless those individuals act with gross negligence. Texas law provides protection to those who in "good faith administer emergency care" unless they are "willfully or wantonly negligent."

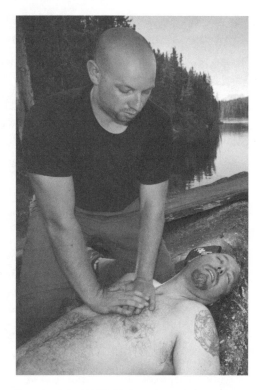

You cannot be held liable for trying to help someone, even if your efforts to save them fail (*iStock*).

Where does the **term "good Samaritan"** come from?

The term comes from the Bible and specifically a parable from the gospel of Luke. In that parable, Jesus relates the story of a Samaritan who stopped to assist a Jewish man who was badly beaten and needed food. The parable stands for the basic principles that people should be good neighbors, treat each other civilly and do not refuse to help someone simply because they belong to a different race, religion, or nationality.

If you **fall** on a **slippery floor** in a store, can you **sue** for negligence?

Yes, you can sue for negligence in a type of case that is known as a "slip and fall." Generally, a plaintiff must show either that there was a foreign substance on the floor that caused the plaintiff harm or that the substance on the floor was on the floor long enough so that store employees knew or should have known of its existence. This explains why in many stores there will be a sign warning of slick spots—to prevent people from falling and hurting themselves and also to prevent "slip and fall" lawsuits. The doctrine of *res ipsa loquitur* does not apply in slip and fall cases.

What happens if **both parties** (plaintiff and defendant) are **negligent**?

In the vast majority of states a plaintiff can recover damages for a negligence action against a defendant as long as a jury determines that the plaintiff was less negligent than the defendant. Most states have adopted comparative negligence either through a statute passed by the legislature or through judicial decisions (called the common law).

Comparative negligence means that a jury compares the negligence of the defendant to the negligence of the plaintiff. It also means that the plaintiff receives a reduced amount of damages calculated by the percentage of the plaintiff's own negligence. For example, let's say that Driver A and Driver B are involved in a car accident that occurred after B wrongfully pulled out in front of Driver A. However, Driver A was speeding and the jury determines that A's speeding contributed to the accident. The jury determines that A suffered $20,000 in damages but that A was 20% negligent.

LegalSpeak: A Comparative Negligence State—Kansas' Comparative Negligence Law: K.S.A. § 60-258a. Comparative Negligence

(a) The contributory negligence of any party in a civil action shall not bar such party or such party's legal representative from recovering damages for negligence resulting in death, personal injury, property damage or economic loss, if such party's negligence was less than the causal negligence of the party or parties against whom claim for recovery is made, but the award of damages to any party in such action shall be diminished in proportion to the amount of negligence attributed to such party. If any such party is claiming damages for a decedent's wrongful death, the negligence of the decedent, if any, shall be imputed to such party.

(b) Where the comparative negligence of the parties in any such action is an issue, the jury shall return special verdicts, or in the absence of a jury, the court shall make special findings, determining the percentage of negligence attributable to each of the parties, and determining the total amount of damages sustained by each of the claimants, and the entry of judgment shall be made by the court. No general verdict shall be returned by the jury.

(c) On motion of any party against whom a claim is asserted for negligence resulting in death, personal injury, property damage or economic loss, any other person whose causal negligence is claimed to have contributed to such death, personal injury, property damage or economic loss, shall be joined as an additional party to the action.

(d) Where the comparative negligence of the parties in any action is an issue and recovery is allowed against more than one party, each such party shall be liable for that portion of the total dollar amount awarded as damages to any claimant in the proportion that the amount of such party's causal negligence bears to the amount of the causal negligence attributed to all parties against whom such recovery is allowed.

(e) The provisions of this section shall be applicable to actions pursuant to this chapter and to actions commenced pursuant to the code of civil procedure for limited actions.

This means that A would receive $20,000 minus 20 percent of $20,000, which is $4,000, leaving a total recovery of $16,000.

Most states have a form of comparative fault. A few states, such as Alabama, still retain the older model of contributory negligence. Under this system, a plaintiff cannot prevail if it is shown that he or she contributed to the injury or harm with his or her own negligence. Contributory negligence has been criticized as an all-or-nothing system that denied many deserving plaintiffs of compensation.

What are the **different forms** of **comparative negligence**?

The two different forms of comparative negligence are: (1) pure comparative negligence; and (2) modified comparative negligence. In a pure comparative negligence system, a plaintiff can recover damages even if he or she is 80 percent at fault. In other words, the plaintiff can recover damages no matter what his or her percentage of fault, as long as it is less than 100 percent.

In a modified comparative negligence system, some states apply a 50 percent rule and some apply a 51 percent rule. In a 50 percent rule, a plaintiff can recover as long as his or her negligence is less than 50 percent of the fault. In a 51 percent rule, a plaintiff must be 49 percent or less at fault in order to recover.

Who determines the percentages of fault of the parties?

The jury determines the percentage of fault of each party. The jury verdict form will contain blanks for the jury to apportion fault. The judge generally cannot alter the jury's percentages of a fault.

Why is **comparative fault** considered **fairer** than **contributory negligence**?

Contributory negligence was considered harsh in some instances because it was an all-or-nothing rule. Sometimes a deserving plaintiff would be denied recovery—even though he or she was far less negligent than the defendant—because the jury or judge determined that the plaintiff was also a little bit negligent. In comparative negligence, a party is only responsible for his or her percentage of the total fault, which seems to be a much fairer and equitable system.

Which **states** still do have **contributory negligence**?

Alabama, Maryland, North Carolina, Virginia, and the District of Columbia still follow a system of contributory negligence.

What is the **duty** to **mitigate damages**?

Mitigation of damages is a required element of tort law, as well as contract law. It means that a plaintiff has an obligation to lessen or reduce their damages if they can. For example, let's say that a person has his or her arm broken during a fall on a slippery floor in a department store. The person may well have a good case of negligence against the store.

However, if the person refuses to receive medical treatment and the arm worsens, the duty to mitigate may lessen the amount of recovery. Let's say that a person loses her job as a result of the negligence of another person. The person cannot simply sit at home for more than three months and expect to receive lost wages for that amount of time. The duty to mitigate damages would require the person to seek other employment more quickly.

What types of **damages** are most **common** in **tort cases**?

The standard type of damages available in a tort case is compensatory damages, which are designed to compensate the plaintiff for the harm that she suffered as a result of the tortfeasor's unreasonable conduct. Compensatory damages would include the medical bills incurred by the plaintiff, lost wages, pain and suffering, and other damages the plaintiff can prove that she incurred as a result of the defendant's conduct.

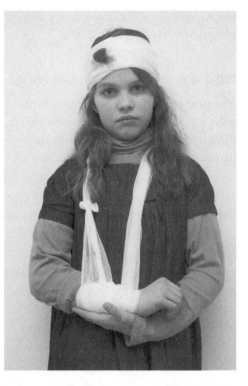

In tort cases, the law tries to compensate plaintiffs for their pain and suffering, as well as lost wages or other damages (*iStock*).

The other types of damages available in tort cases are nominal and punitive damages. Nominal damages are negligible damages or damages in name only. Juries sometimes will award only nominal damages if the plaintiff technically has proven her case but is not able to show any real harm. However, punitive (sometimes called exemplary) damages present a much different picture. Juries impose punitive damages to punish the wrongdoer and send a message that such conduct will not be tolerated. Punitive damages are based in part on the wealth of the defendant.

Why are **punitive damage** awards considered **controversial**?

Punitive damages are controversial to some because many fear that a "runaway" jury can get carried away and impose an astronomical figure on a defendant that represents a windfall to a plaintiff. The fundamental purpose of tort law is to compensate the plaintiff for the harm he or she has suffered, not to provide plaintiffs with large punitive damage awards. On the other hand, supporters of the tort system respond that without large punitive damage awards available, wealthy corporate defendants

327

would simply figure damage to potential plaintiffs as a cost of doing business and not modify their tortious behavior.

What was the McDonald's **hot coffee case**?

The poster child case for tort reform is the McDonald's restaurant hot coffee case in which a jury in New Mexico awarded 2.7 million dollars in punitive damages against McDonald's for serving very hot coffee to an elderly woman. Many viewed the case as a prime example of a jury system and a tort-law system that were out of control.

The facts present a different story. 79-year-old Stella Liebeck drove through a McDonald's drive-thru lane in Albuquerque, New Mexico. She ordered coffee. When she stopped to add sugar and cream to the coffee, it spilled on her. She suffered several third-degree burns, had skin-graft surgeries and stayed in the hospital for more than a week.

She asked McDonald's to pay for her hospital bills of about $11,000. McDonald's refused to pay. She then contacted a Houston attorney Morgan Reed, who made a request for $80,000 for medical expenses and pain and suffering. McDonald's offered $800.

Liebeck then sued. The case proceeded to a jury which heard evidence that McDonald's had more than 700 complaints of burns from its hot coffee, which reached temperatures of up to 190 degrees. McDonald's, however, ignored these complaints and refused to lower the temperature of its coffee.

A jury awarded Liebeck $200,000 in compensatory damages. The jury also found Liebeck 20 percent at fault so that reduced her compensatory damage award down to $160,000. The jury also awarded Liebeck $2.7 million dollars in punitive damages, but the trial judge reduced that award down to $480,000.

The parties later settled the case for an undisclosed amount. After the case, McDonald's has a prominent sign at its stores warning customers that its coffee and hot tea are "VERY HOT!"

What are some examples of **frivolous lawsuits**?

Once the whole story was revealed, many believed that the Stella Liebeck hot coffee lawsuit was not frivolous. She suffered severe burns, requiring skin graft surgery. However, other lawsuits do seem to border on the ridiculous and could qualify as frivolous, or lacking merit.

Proponents of tort reform often cite examples of frivolous lawsuits as a reason to curtail the tort law system. Some of the more unusual examples include:

- A man sued a strip club in Florida, claiming that an exotic dancer's large breasts gave him whiplash during a lap dance.

LegalSpeak: *Hodges v. S.C. Toof Co.* (Tenn. 1992)

In a trial where punitive damages are sought, the court, upon motion of defendant, shall bifurcate the trial. During the first phase, the factfinder shall determine (1) liability for, and the amount of, compensatory damages and (2) liability for punitive damages in accordance with the standards announced above. During this phase, evidence of a defendant's financial affairs, financial condition, or net worth is not admissible.

If the factfinder finds a defendant liable for punitive damages, the amount of such damages shall then be determined in an immediate, separate proceeding. During this second phase, the factfinder shall consider, to the extent relevant, at least the following:

(1) The defendant's financial affairs, financial condition, and net worth;

(2) The nature and reprehensibility of defendant's wrongdoing, for example

    (A) The impact of defendant's conduct on the plaintiff, or

    (B) The relationship of defendant to plaintiff;

(3) The defendant's awareness of the amount of harm being caused and defendant's motivation in causing the harm;

(4) The duration of defendant's misconduct and whether defendant attempted to conceal the conduct;

(5) The expense plaintiff has borne in the attempt to recover the losses;

(6) Whether defendant profited from the activity, and if defendant did profit, whether the punitive award should be in excess of the profit in order to deter similar future behavior;

(7) Whether, and the extent to which, defendant has been subjected to previous punitive damage awards based upon the same wrongful act;

(8) Whether, once the misconduct became known to defendant, defendant took remedial action or attempted to make amends by offering a prompt and fair settlement for actual harm caused; and

(9) Any other circumstances shown by the evidence that bear on determining the proper amount of the punitive award.

• A prisoner in Colorado sued prison officials after he injured himself during an escape attempt. His rationale was that prison officials were negligent in making it too easy for inmates to attempt to escape.

• A judge in New York is suing for more than $1 million dollars he slipped and fell on a courthouse floor.

• An administrative law judge in the District of Columbia sued a dry cleaners for more than $50 million for allegedly losing his clothes.

What is the **role** of **punitive damages** in **bifurcated tort cases**?

A bifurcated tort case is one in which there are two separate phases. The first part is the liability phase in which the jury must determine whether the defendant is liable (legally responsible), the amount of compensatory damages, and answering yes or no on the question of punitive damages. The second phase of the tort suit then asks the jury to debate on the amount of punitive damages.

What **factors** does a court **consider** in determining the **amount** of **punitive damages**?

Most courts will consider the factual context, the egregiousness of the conduct, and the financial wealth of the defendant.

Are there **limits** to **punitive damage awards**?

Yes, the United States Supreme Court has held that the Due Process Clause of the Fourteenth Amendment—"no state shall deprive a person of life, liberty or property without due process of law"—imposes limitations on punitive damage awards. The Due Process Clause prohibits awards that are grossly excessive, because such awards fail to provide fair notice to a defendant of the penalty he or she might have to face. The Due Process Clause also prohibits states from punishing defendants for injuries caused to persons not before the court (persons who are not litigants or parties to the litigation).

For example, in *BMW v. Gore* (1994) the U.S. Supreme Court ruled that a $2 million dollar punitive damage award against a car manufacturer for failing to disclose that a BMW had been repainted was grossly excessive when the actual damages to the plaintiff were only $4,000. "Elementary notions of fairness enshrined in our constitutional jurisprudence dictate that a person receive fair notice not only of the conduct that will subject him to punishment, but also of the severity of the penalty that a State may impose," the Court wrote.

In *Philip Morris USA v. Williams* (2007), the U.S. Supreme Court reversed a jury's $79.5 million punitive damage verdict against a cigarette manufacturer for negligence and deceit (two torts). The Court reasoned that the Due Process Clause prohibits the award of punitive damages against a defendant based upon injuries to persons who are "strangers to the litigation."

Can **states cap** punitive damage **awards**?

Yes, state legislatures can pass laws that limit the amount of punitive damages. Several states have such a statute that provides that punitive damages are limited to a cer-

> # LegalSpeak:
> ## U.S. Supreme Court in *Philip Morris USA v. Williams* (2007)
>
> In our view, the Constitution's Due Process Clause forbids a State to use a punitive damages award to punish a defendant for injury that it inflicts upon nonparties or those whom they directly represent, i.e., injury that it inflicts upon those who are, essentially, strangers to the litigation. For one thing, the Due Process Clause prohibits a State from punishing an individual without first providing that individual with "an opportunity to present every available defense." Yet a defendant threatened with punishment for injuring a nonparty victim has no opportunity to defend against the charge, by showing, for example in a case such as this, that the other victim was not entitled to damages because he or she knew that smoking was dangerous or did not rely upon the defendant's statements to the contrary....
>
> Finally, we can find no authority supporting the use of punitive damages awards for the purpose of punishing a defendant for harming others. We have said that it may be appropriate to consider the reasonableness of a punitive damages award in light of the potential harm the defendant's conduct could have caused. But we have made clear that the potential harm at issue was harm potentially caused the plaintiff.

tain fixed amount or within a certain percentage of compensatory damages. For example, North Carolina's law provides that punitive damages are limited to $250,000, or three times the amount of compensatory damages, whichever is greater.

North Carolina General Statutes Annotated (N.C.G.S.A.) § 1D-25 provides:

(a) In all actions seeking an award of punitive damages, the trier of fact shall determine the amount of punitive damages separately from the amount of compensation for all other damages.

(b) Punitive damages awarded against a defendant shall not exceed three times the amount of compensatory damages or two hundred fifty thousand dollars ($250,000), whichever is greater. If a trier of fact returns a verdict for punitive damages in excess of the maximum amount specified under this subsection, the trial court shall reduce the award and enter judgment for punitive damages in the maximum amount.

(c) The provisions of subsection (b) of this section shall not be made known to the trier of fact through any means, including voir dire, the introduction into evidence, argument, or instructions to the jury.

This means that if a jury awards $50,000 in compensatory damages, then the maximum amount of punitive damages is the capped limit of $250,000. However, if a jury

331

Punitive damages can be capped by state law; tort reform efforts are designed to limit how much plaintiffs can receive in compensation (*iStock*).

awarded $500,000, then the maximum amount of punitive damages would $1.5 million (three times the compensatory damage award).

What is **tort reform**?

Tort reform refers to a movement designed to limit damages and exposure in a wide variety of tort suits. Much of tort reform focuses on limiting damages in products liability and medical malpractice cases. Many tort reform proponents also emphasize—as mentioned earlier in the text—the danger of large punitive damage awards.

Tort reform proponents warn about the high costs that lawsuits and damage awards have on the creation of products, small businesses, and rising medical costs. Tort reform advocates claim that there has been a litigation explosion filled with frivolous lawsuits that drives up the costs of doing business for everyone, which ultimately leads to increased costs placed upon consumers. The issue has even come up during presidential campaigning, as candidates have sparred about issues surrounding health care reform and medical malpractice.

What is the difference between a **lump-sum** settlement and a **structured settlement**?

The difference between a lump-sum settlement and a structured settlement centers on when the plaintiff receives the monies from the tortfeasor or the tortfeasor's insurance company. A plaintiff who receives all of her money in one payment up front has received a lump-sum settlement. A plaintiff who receives periodic payments stretched out over a period of years has received a structured settlement.

Are **awards** in tort cases **taxable**?

It depends upon the nature of the award. The Internal Revenue Service provides that compensatory damages for personal physical injuries are not taxable whether received in a lump sum or in installment payments over a period of time. Damages for emotional distress are not taxable if they are received for an underlying physical injury or sickness. However, if the emotional distress damages are not due to a physical sickness or illness then those damages are taxable.

Other forms of damages that are taxable include: interest on any award, compensation for lost wages and lost profits, and punitive damages in most cases even if the award relates to a physical sickness. For further information on this admittedly difficult subject, see Internal Revenue Service, "Publication No. 525—Taxable and Nontaxable Income," at http://www.irs.gov/pub/irs-pdf/p525.pdf.

What is **vicarious liability**?

Vicarious liability means that one party or entity is (vicariously) liable for the negligence committed by another. When applied in the employer-employee context, the term is called respondeat superior, which is Latin for "let the superior answer." This doctrine applies to employers who are responsible for most torts committed by their employees.

For example, if you are driving down the road and a truck driver employed by Ace Trucking Company negligently hits your car, you can sue not only the truck driver but also Ace Trucking Company. The general rule is that employers are vicariously liable for the tortious acts of their employees. If you shop in a department store and an employee at the department store starts cursing at you and falsley accuses you of shoplifting without reasonable or probable cause, you can sue not only the employee individually but also the department store.

Employers generally are not liable for the torts of independent contractors. Thus, an important legal question in many tort cases is whether an alleged tortfeasor is an employee or an independent contractor. Take the example of a newspaper delivery person who negligently hits another vehicle. The question becomes whether the newspaper company can be sued for the tortious action of the delivery person. If the delivery person is an employee, then the newspaper publisher may be liable. If the delivery person is only an independent contractor, the newspaper publisher may not be liable.

What is a **"frolic and detour"**?

"Frolic and detour" refers to the action of an employee/agent in which the employee advances his own personal business rather than engaging in work for his employer. The concept is important in tort law, because if an employee is engaging in a "frolic and detour," the employer is not vicariously liable for the negligent acts committed by the employee during this time period.

What is the concept of **deep pockets**?

"Deep pockets" is an important principle in tort law and refers to the principle that a plaintiff hopes to be able to recover damages from a party who has the ability to pay a court judgment. Recall that the primary purpose of tort law is to compensate an injured party for the damages that he or she has suffered. A party with deep pockets has the financial ability to pay in a tort case. Take the example of the newspaper delivery person who hits your car, causing significant property damage to your car and personal injury to you. You hope you can sue the newspaper that employed the delivery person, because the newspaper publisher probably has "deep pockets," while the delivery person may not be able to pay any judgment or settlement.

PROFESSIONAL NEGLIGENCE

What is **professional negligence**?

Professional negligence refers to negligence claims against professionals such as medical doctors, dentists, accountants, and lawyers.

What is **medical malpractice**?

Medical malpractice claims are a highly visible form of professional negligence claims. If a medical provider provides faulty medical care that results in harm to a patient, that medical provider may well be liable for medical malpractice.

What are **examples** of **professional negligence** claims?

Let's say a patient goes into the hospital to have part of his right leg amputated, but, due to an error, the doctor amputates the wrong leg. That appears to be a prime case of negligence. Other cases are more difficult to prove, as when a physician fails to diagnose a form of cancer. The case is more difficult because it is far less obvious that the physician failed to adhere to a reasonable standard of care for physicians. Many professional negligence claims require the plaintiff to produce expert testimony showing that the defendant professional violated the applicable standard of care.

In cases involving medical malpractice, it is frequently essential to have expert testimonials during the trial (*iStock*).

Is **expert testimony required** in **medical malpractice** cases?

Yes, expert testimony is required in the vast majority of medical malpractice cases. Physicians are held to the standard of care of similar physicians generally in their locale. This means that a radiologist in Nebraska is held to the standard of

334

care for radiologists in that area of the country—not the prevailing standard at John Hopkins Medical Center in Baltimore.

However, some egregious examples of malpractice do not require expert testimony because a layperson can tell that there has been malpractice. This is sometimes called the "common knowledge" exception for cases of extreme and obvious malpractice. Examples include failing to remove a surgical instrument from a patient's body following a procedure or amputating the wrong arm or leg.

Different states also have special rules regarding expert witnesses in medical malpractice cases. For example, Tennessee has something called the "contiguous state" rule. This means that an expert must be licensed from Tennessee or a state that is contiguous (a state that borders) to Tennessee.

What is the **standard of care** for a **physician**?

It depends upon particular state law and the type of physician at issue. For example, a neurosurgeon is held to the standard of care of a reasonable neurosurgeon, not a general surgeon. This means that specialists are often held to more rigorous standards of care than generalists. The other difference between different state laws is that some states hold physicians to a national standard of care, while other state law holds physicians to a local standard of care.

What is an **example** of **attorney malpractice**?

Let's say that you were injured in an auto accident after another driver exceeded the speed limit and crossed into your lane of traffic. Clearly, the other driver was negligent in failing to operate her motor vehicle in a safe manner. However, the other driver's insurance company refuses to give you a fair amount of money to repair your vehicle. You contact an attorney and ask him or her to handle the matter. The attorney contacts the other insurance company but then forgets to preserve your claim by failing to file a lawsuit within the requisite one year statute of limitations. This means that you can no longer sue the other driver for negligence, because the statute of limitations has run or expired on your claim. However, you have a very good case against your attorney for missing the statute of limitations.

Are all attorney or **legal malpractice claims** based on **negligence** law?

No, legal malpractice law can occur based on contract law and breach of fiduciary duty. Remember that you sign a contract with an attorney when you enter into an attorney-client relationship. If the attorney violates the terms of that contract, he or she can be liable for breach of contract.

Also, an attorney owes a client a duty of loyalty and a duty of confidentiality. This imposes a special duty—called a fiduciary duty—upon the attorney. If the attorney violates either of those duties, then the attorney may be on the hook for a malpractice claim for breach of fiduciary duty.

What are **statutes of limitations**?

Statutes of limitations—often referred to as limitations of actions—refer to the required time periods to sue in a case. Most personal injury tort suits have a one-year statute of limitations. This means that a plaintiff must file suit within that one-year window or forfeit their legal rights forever. Note that not all states have the same statute of limitations. It can vary dramatically from state to state.

What is the **discovery rule** and how does it impact statutes of limitations in tort cases?

The discovery rule is a rule that often operates as an exception to a statute of limitations. For instance, let's say that an attorney performs legal services negligently upon a client three years earlier and the statute of limitations for an attorney malpractice case is one year from the date of the negligence. However, the person does not reasonably discover the attorney's negligence for three years. By strict operation of the statute of limitations, the client cannot sue the attorney because the statute of limitations has passed or expired.

The discovery rule imposes a limitation on the statute of limitations. It provides that the statute does not begin tolling, or running, until the client reasonably discovered or should have discovered the underlying negligent or harmful act.

What is a **statute of repose**?

A statute of repose is a special type of statute of limitations that imposes an absolute bar on liability after a certain period of time. Statutes of repose are passed in order to provide defendants—often manufacturers of products—a sense of protection after a certain point in time.

The difference between a statute of limitation and statute of repose is that a statute of limitation does not accrue, or start to run, until the plaintiff reasonably discovers the underlying problem. A statute of repose, which is longer, begins to run immediately upon the creation of the product or the delivery of services.

For example, let's say that the manufacturer of a swimming pool designed a pool in 1999. In 2010, a young swimmer jumped off the diving board and hit his head on the bottom of the sloping-downward pool. The tragic injury was caused by a design defect in the pool—that the slope of the pool in the deeper end should have been steeper so as to prevent any type of injury. However, the state has a 10-year statute of repose for design defects in product liability cases. The statute of repose in this instance may well bar the lawsuit.

OTHER TORTS

What is **defamation**?

Defamation refers to the publication or speaking of a false statement of fact about another person that harms that person's reputation. Defamation seeks to compensate an individual for reputational harm. Defamation is sometimes referred to as libel or slander. The general rule is that libel constitutes written defamation, while slander constitutes oral defamation. For example, if person A yells to a crowd that person B a "sex offender," that would be slander. If newspaper A writes that person B is a "sex offender," that would be libel.

What are the **required elements** of a **defamation claim**?

The necessary elements of a defamation claim are identification, publication, defamatory meaning, falsity, a statement of fact, and damages. Identification means that the plaintiff must show that the publication was about or "of and concerning" the plaintiff. Most of the time this is an easy requirement for defamation plaintiffs. If a publication says that "David Hudson, the author of *The Handy Law Answer Book*, is a sex offender," the identification requirement has been met easily.

Telling a lie about someone is one element of a defamation claim (*iStock*).

However, what if a work of fiction contains several identifying characteristics similar to a real person? The real person may file a defamation action, claiming that many people would reasonably understand the fictional character to be based on him. Believe it or not, many defamation suits have been filed against publishers of works of fiction.

Publication means that the defamatory information has been conveyed to two or more people. This element is usually easily satisfied.

The language in question must be capable of having a defamatory meaning. Some language that you think may be fine may actually be defamatory. One publication found this out when it included a review of an attorney that called that attorney "an ambulance chaser." A reviewing federal court determined that the term "ambulance chaser" was defamatory, because ambulance chasing involved direct solicitation of clients in violation of attorney professional rules of conduct. In essence, by calling an attorney "an ambulance chaser," the publication said that the attorney violated rules of professional conduct.

Falsity is another requirement, as truth is a defense to a defamation action. If person A says that person B "is a sex offender," B cannot recover if he really is a sex offender. The final requirement is damages. A person generally has to show that the defamatory statements caused them some type of harm.

What if an **editorial writer** uses **strong language** to describe a person?

This is a difficult question to answer, as editorial writers have more leeway in using figurative language than, say, a reporter writing a straight news story. If an editorial writer describes a very tough school board member as a "Nazi" and it is clear from the story that the writer uses the term to describe their arbitrary and tough personality rather than actual membership in the Nazi party, the writer may have a defense to a defamation claim.

LegalSpeak: Libel Proof Plaintiff Case—
Davis v. The Tennessean (Tenn.App. 2001)

This case involved a plaintiff who was convicted of murder and sentenced to 99 years in prison for his participation in an armed robbery. However, the plaintiff was not the triggerman in the armed robbery. A prominent newspaper inaccurately printed that the plaintiff was the triggerman. The man then sued the newspaper for libel. The Court explained:

> However, "the basis for an action for defamation, whether it be slander or libel, is that the defamation has resulted in an injury to the person's character and reputation." To be actionable, the allegedly defamatory statement must "constitute a serious threat to the plaintiff's reputation." Damages from false or inaccurate statements cannot be presumed; actual damage must be sustained and proved.

> It is from these general principles establishing that the gravamen of a libel claim is injury to reputation that the concept of "libel proof" parties has arisen. This doctrine essentially holds that "a notorious person is without a 'good name' and therefore may not recover for injury to it." Robert D. Sack, Sack on Defamation: Libel, Slander and Related Problems, 35 (Cum.Supp.1998).

> If the purpose of defamation law is to guard against harm to reputation, a person without reputation has nothing for the law of defamation to protect. Whether for this reason, or because courts wish to rid their dockets of and spare defendants from nuisance suits by people with nothing legitimate to gain from such litigation, some courts have held that there are persons so notorious that they have no reputation on which to base a defamation claim. Their suits are necessarily frivolous. They are said to be "libel-proof."…

> Although Mr. Davis alleges he suffered unjustified humiliation because of the publication, he does not allege his public reputation has been injured. We conclude he cannot show such injury because, at the time of the publication, he was serving a ninety-nine year sentence for aiding and abetting the murder which is the subject of the article and his complaint. He participated in the crime which resulted in the murder. His character reputation with the public was established and could not be harmed by inaccurate attribution to him of conduct which was part of the crime in which he participated. His continued incarceration for a long time after the publication renders actual damage, with regard to his standing in the community, as a result of the article unlikely.

What are **common defenses** to **defamation** claims?

The best defense is truth. Other defenses may include a privilege (legislators have a privilege when they speak on the legislative floor), fair report, rhetorical hyperbole, libel-proof plaintiff doctrine, or a retraction statute. The fair report privilege generally applies to a defendant who reports on the deliberations of a public body, such as a city council meeting. Rhetorical hyperbole applies to certain language in certain contents (editorial/opinion column), when it is understood by the readers to be figurative language not to be interpreted literally. The libel-proof plaintiff doctrine applies to a person who has no good reputation to protect.

What is a **public figure** and why is that important to **defamation law**?

Plaintiffs in defamation cases have different burdens of proof depending on their status. If a plaintiff is considered to be a public official or a public figure, he or she must prove that the defendant acted with actual malice, which means that the defendant acted knowing the statement in question was false or acted in reckless disregard as to whether the statement was true or false.

However, if a plaintiff suing for defamation is only a private figure, then he or she generally must prove only negligence or fault.

The rationale behind the public official or public figure rationale is two-fold. First, the thinking is that public officials and public figures can more easily counter false statements about them than can private figures. For example, if a tabloid newspaper defames Tom Cruise, he and his public relations people can call a press conference and refute the allegations. However, if someone defames David Hudson, the author of this book, it would be much more difficult for him to counter false allegations.

The second rationale for the different treatment of public and private figures concerns accepting the aspects of fame. Famous people must expect that with fame and public acclaim will come some negative aspects as well.

Another rationale—perhaps even more strongly rooted in the law—is that people should have a strong First Amendment (freedom of expression) right to speak about public issues and that punishing them for every single error would chill free expression. This reasoning led the U.S. Supreme Court to adopt the public official rule in defamation cases in *New York Times Co. v. Sullivan* (1964).

What are **examples** of **public officials** and public **figures**?

Public officials generally refer to those individuals who hold office, such as political figures. A president, governor, mayor, senator or representative would certainly qualify as a public official.

LegalSpeak: *Time v. Firestone* (1975)

Respondent did not assume any role of especial prominence in the affairs of society, other than perhaps Palm Beach society, and she did not thrust herself to the forefront of any particular public controversy in order to influence the resolution of the issues involved in it....

Dissolution of a marriage through judicial proceedings is not the sort of "public controversy" referred to in Gertz, even though the marital difficulties of extremely wealthy individuals may be of interest to some portion of the reading public. Nor did respondent freely choose to publicize issues as to the propriety of her married life. She was compelled to go to court by the State in order to obtain legal release from the bonds of matrimony. We have said that in such an instance "[r]esort to the judicial process ... is no more voluntary in a realistic sense than that of the defendant called upon to defend his interests in court.

Public figures refer to those individuals who are people in the public eye and have achieved fame or notoriety. For example, sports stars, movie stars, entertainers, and national broadcasters would qualify as public figures.

The law also recognizes so-called "limited purpose" public figures—persons who have not achieved pervasive fame enough to be all-purpose public figures, but who are public figures for a particular issue or controversy. This is a difficult area of the law, as many persons may become well known in connection with a particular contentious issue but are not considered public figures. In *Time v. Firestone* (1975; see LegalSpeak above), the U.S. Supreme Court reasoned that the former wife of a man in one of the country's wealthiest families was not a limited purpose public figure.

What happened in *New York Times Co. v. Sullivan*?

In this 1964 case, *The New York Times* printed an editorial advertisement submitted by the Committee to Defend Dr. Martin Luther King Jr. The advertisement spoke about civil rights abuses in the state of Alabama, specifically in the city of Montgomery, Alabama. Some of the statements in the advertisement were false and the commissioner in charge of the police in Montgomery, a Mr. L.B. Sullivan, sued for defamation. He prevailed before the Alabama state courts, but the U.S. Supreme Court reversed. The court decided:

Thus we consider this case against the background of a profound national commitment to the principle that debate on public issues should be uninhibited, robust, and wide-open, and that it may well include vehement, caustic, and sometimes unpleasantly sharp attacks on government and public officials ... erroneous statement is inevitable in free debate, and that it must be protected if the freedoms of expression are to have the "breathing space" that they need ... to survive....

The interest of the public here outweighs the interest of appellant or any other individual. The protection of the public requires not merely discussion, but information. Political conduct and views which some respectable people approve, and others condemn, are constantly imputed to Congressmen. Errors of fact, particularly in regard to a man's mental states and processes, are inevitable.... Whatever is added to the field of libel is taken from the field of free debate....

The constitutional guarantees require, we think, a federal rule that prohibits a public official from recovering damages for a defamatory falsehood relating to his official conduct unless he proves that the statement was made with "actual malice"—that is, with knowledge that it was false or with reckless disregard of whether it was false or not....

We hold today that the Constitution delimits a State's power to award damages for libel in actions brought by public officials against critics of their official conduct. Since this is such an action, the rule requiring proof of actual malice is applicable.

What **tort protects** a person from being **photographed** in the **bathroom**?

The tort of invasion of privacy likely would apply in this situation. Invasion of privacy refers to a collection of causes of actions designed to protect a person's "right to be let alone." Born in the late nineteenth century, this tort actually consists of four different types: (1) intrusion, (2) public disclosure of private facts, (3) false light, and (4) appropriation.

Intrusion applies when a tortfeasor unreasonably intrudes on a person's physical privacy by following them, photographing them, or opening their private mail. Public disclosure of private facts occurs when a person discloses material of a person's personal private life that is not of legitimate concern to the public. This tort differs from defamation, because the tortfeasor can be sued for the disclosure of even true information. False light refers to placing a person in a false light in a manner that would be highly offensive to a reasonable person. Let's say a television program ran a program on the problems of street prostitution and featured stock footage of a woman walking down the street. That woman may have a claim for false light, claiming that the placement of the footage falsely implied she was a prostitute. The final type of invasion of privacy is appropriation, which refers to the use of a plaintiff's name or likeness for financial gain without permission.

How did the **invasion of privacy** tort **originate**?

Invasion of privacy has a very unusual beginning—a law review article. Boston lawyer Samuel Warren became upset that some of the local press reported about the conduct of Warren's wife at Beacon Hill parties. Warren believed that the press should not be allowed to write about such private matters. He asked his law partner and former Harvard law classmate Louis Brandeis (a future United States Supreme Court Justice) to draft an article arguing for a right of privacy.

Brandeis and Warren published their article "A Right to Privacy" in the 1890 edition of the *Harvard Law Review*. They argued that the law should protect a person's right to be let alone. They warned:

> Instantaneous photographs and newspaper enterprise have invaded the sacred precincts of private and domestic life; and numerous mech-

Photographing people in the bathroom is a gross invasion of privacy under tort law (*iStock*).

> anical devices threaten to make good the prediction that "what is whispered in the closet shall be proclaimed from the house-tops."… Of the desirability — indeed of the necessity — of some such protection, there can, it is believed, be no doubt. The press is overstepping in every direction the obvious bounds of propriety and of decency. Gossip is no longer the resource of the idle and of the vicious, but has become a trade, which is pursued with industry as well as effrontery. To satisfy a prurient taste the details of sexual relations are spread broadcast in the columns of the daily papers. To occupy the indolent, column upon column is filled with idle gossip, which can only be procured by intrusion upon the domestic circle. The intensity and complexity of life, attendant upon advancing civilization, have rendered necessary some retreat from the world, and man, under the refining influence of culture, has become more sensitive to publicity, so that solitude and privacy have become more essential to the individual.

Courts at first were reluctant, fearing that there would be too many frivolous lawsuits of dubious character. However, gradually the courts began to recognize invasion of privacy. Today nearly every state recognizes all four privacy sub-torts in its common law.

The paparazzi are often despised by celebrities because they intrude on personal lives. Sometimes, these actions can reach the point of being considered illegal, despite laws protecting freedom of the press (*iStock*).

What is a **famous tort case** of involving **intrusion**?

The paparazzi are susceptible to tort claims of intrusion if they harass and stalk the celebrities they are seeking to photograph. A famous case of intrusion involved paparazzo Ron Galella, who relentlessly pursued former First Lady Jacqueline Onassis (Kennedy) and her children. He followed son John Jr. on his bicycle and interrupted daughter Caroline while she played tennis. Once, he got very close to a boat carrying Jackie O. in another boat to snap pictures. A federal court (*Galella v. Onassis*, 487 F.2d 986 [2d. Cir. 1974]) issued an injunction, ordering Galella from staying a certain distance away from Jackie O. and her children.

A reviewing federal appeals court upheld the order and finding of an invasion of privacy. "When weighed against the de minimis public importance of the daily activities of the defendant, Galella's constant surveillance, his obtrusive and intruding presence, was unwarranted and unreasonable," the court wrote. "If there were any doubt in our minds, Galella's inexcusable conduct toward defendant's minor children would resolve it."

What if the **press reports** on the **sex life** of a **famous politician**? Is that invasion of privacy?

A court might well find that such information is newsworthy, as opposed to the privacy sub-tort of public disclosure of private facts. The privacy claim of public

> ## LegalSpeak: Rejecting False Light: *Cain v. Hearst Corp.* (Tex. 1994)
>
> **W**e reject the false light invasion of privacy tort for two reasons: 1) it largely duplicates other rights of recovery, particularly defamation; and 2) it lacks many of the procedural limitations that accompany actions for defamation, thus unacceptably increasing the tension that already exists between free speech constitutional guarantees and tort law....
>
> If we were to recognize a false light tort in Texas, it would largely duplicate several existing causes of action, particularly defamation. As we observed ... some of the right of privacy interests have been afforded protection under such traditional theories as libel and slander, wrongful search and seizure, eavesdropping and wiretapping, and other similar invasions into the private business and personal affairs of an individual. Recovery for defamation requires the communication of a false statement....
>
> Furthermore, the elements of damages that have been recognized in false light actions are similar to those awarded for defamation.... The false light cases considered by Texas courts of appeals, were all brought, or could have been brought, under another legal theory.

disclosure of private facts does not apply to information that would be of legitimate concern to the public. The pressing question in public disclosure of private-facts cases is whether the information is newsworthy or of legitimate concern to the public.

Newsworthiness is evaluated by an examination of several factors, including the social value of the disclosed material, the depth of intrusion into personal life, and the extent to which the person is already in public view. Even Louis Brandeis and Samuel Warren in their famous law review article (mentioned on p. 343) wrote in 1890: "The right to privacy does not prohibit any publication of matter which is of public or general interest."

What is an **example** of **false light** invasion of privacy?

An example of false light invasion of privacy would encompass conduct by a news agency that uses stock footage of a photo of a person to accompany a news story that the person is not connected to in any fashion. For example, let's say that a news station runs a segment on the problems of street prostitution. In the opening segment, the station runs a segment of a woman walking down the street in a short skirt. However, the woman is not a prostitute at all. That may present a case for false light invasion of privacy.

Do **all states** recognize the **different** sub-torts of **invasion of privacy**?

No, a few states do not recognize the tort of false-light invasion of privacy, believing that it is too similar to the tort of defamation. For example, the Texas Supreme Court wrote in 1994: "False light remains the least-recognized and most controversial aspect of invasion of privacy." Consult with an attorney to determine whether a false light invasion of privacy claim exists in your state.

What is the **tort of nuisance**?

Nuisance is a tort that protects a person's right to enjoyment of his or land from substantial interference. Often nuisances involve conduct that occurs near a plaintiff's land but does not involve an actual physical trespass. Let's say a person constantly hears a barrage of loud music from his neighbor. The neighbor may have committed the tort of nuisance if the music is loud enough that it unreasonably interferes with the neighbor's enjoyment of his property.

Nuisances are divided into public nuisances and private nuisances. A public nuisance involves harm to the public at large. A house of prostitution or a crack house (used as a place for the sale of illegal drugs) may constitute public nuisances.

The city of Chicago and Cook County, Illinois, filed a nuisance action against several gun manufacturers, distributors, and dealers, contending that their production, distribution, and sale of handguns in a community harmed by gun violence created a public nuisance. However, the Illinois Supreme Court rejected the claim, finding that the handgun violence was caused by the superseding, intervening causes of third parties (actual criminals) rather than the companies associated with the creation, sale, and distribution of guns.

PRODUCTS LIABILITY

What is **products liability**?

Products liability refers to the area of tort law holding manufacturers, sellers, and suppliers of products liable for injuries caused by their products. Products liability actions arise when a product is defective and causes injury or harm to a user or consumer of that product. Products liability actions can be brought under a variety of legal theories, including negligence, strict liability, and breach of warranty.

What is **breach of warranty**?

Warranty claims are a hybrid of tort and contract law in which a manufacturer or seller makes claims or warranties that a product will perform to a certain level. An express warranty means that a seller represents that a product contains or possesses certain qualities. For example, let's say a manufacturer of a fiberglass door claims that the door is shatterproof. This means that the manufacturer represents that the door will not shatter.

Implied warranties—which are more based on contract law—are those that are implied in the sale of a product without express statements about the product. For example, a warrant of merchantability means that a product is fit for the ordinary purposes for which it is sold.

State law varies as to whether most warranty claims are based on contract law, tort law, or a combination of both.

Why would it be **fair** to impose **strict liability** on the **manufacturer** of a product?

One theory behind allowing strict liability as a basis for recovery in products liability law is that consumers need protection from harm and need compensation for injuries. Thus, the thinking is that risk should be allocated to manufacturers who are better able to absorb the costs and bear the risks associated with the injuries than consumers. A related theory is that manufacturers and sellers are able to incorporate the cost of liability and injuries into the creation of the product itself. Another theory is that many modern products are sophisticated and the average consumer will not be able to prove that a manufacturer was negligent in the creation of the product. Thus, strict liability will allow more consumers to recover damages in tort actions.

What types of **problems** cause **product liability** actions?

Most product liability cases arise because of manufacturing defects, design defects, and failure to warn consumers of possible harm. A manufacturing defect means that a single product was produced in a faulty manner that makes it prone to cause injury. For instance, let's say a manufacturer produces 1,000 lawn mowers and 998 operate perfectly. However, in the building process, two lawn mowers were not put together properly. Those two lawn mowers have a manufacturing defect.

A design defect is different. This means that the product itself is flawed in its creation. A lawn mower with a design defect means that all such mowers have the potential to cause harm because of an inherent flaw in the creation of the product. Take the example of a swimming pool that places the diving board near a sloping floor that is not deep enough for divers. This design defect means that a certain number of divers will hit their heads on the pool floor when they dive into the pool.

The last type of defect results from a failure to warn consumers of possible harm that can result from foreseeable misuse of the product.

347

What was the **Ford Pinto** problem?

In 1968, Lee Iacocca suggested that Ford Motor Company introduce a subcompact car into the marketplace. The result was the Ford Pinto. The cars seemed fine at first, but later it was determined that a defect in the fuel delivery system made it more likely that the cars would explode upon certain rear-end impacts. Several people died in accidents when they were rear-ended in their Pinto vehicles. Ford chose not to adopt a new design, figuring that the new design would cost more than the occasional damages they would have to pay out in tort cases from family members of deceased drivers. Ford executives knew of potential danger because of test crash studies they had done when building the new car.

Several juries across the country imposed hefty damage awards against Ford as a result of these accidents. A jury in California (*Grimshaw v. Ford Motor Co.*, 119 Cal.App.3d 757, 174 Cal.Rptr. 348 [1981]) imposed millions of dollars in damages against Ford for the death of a woman from fatal burns after her 1972 Pinto was rear-ended. In upholding the award of punitive damages, a California appeals court explained:

> Through the results of the crash tests Ford knew that the Pinto's fuel tank and rear structure would expose consumers to serious injury or death in a 20 to 30 mile-per-hour collision. There was evidence that Ford could have corrected the hazardous design defects at minimal cost but decided to defer correction of the shortcomings by engaging in a cost-benefit analysis balancing human lives and limbs against corporate profits. Ford's institutional mentality was shown to be one of callous indifference to public safety. There was substantial evidence that Ford's conduct constituted "conscious disregard" of the probability of injury to members of the consuming public.

APPENDIX A
Explanation of Case and Statute Citations

How are **legal authorities** identified?

Legal authorities—judicial opinions, statutes, regulations, ordinances, and others— are identified by legal citations. When a lawyer cites or mentions a legal authority in a document filed before a court, he or she must provide the legal citation. The citation enables the court, other attorneys, and legal researches to identify and locate the legal authority.

Remember that the legal system relies on precedent or past legal authority. Judges care what courts have ruled in the past so that their rulings comport with existing law.

What is a **judicial opinion**?

A judicial opinion is a written document in which a judge or panel of judges explain the reasons for their rulings. Another way to describe a judicial opinion is as a written resolution of legal issues. Judicial opinions are important, as they serve as a guide—as precedent—for future decisions. For example, an opinion by the U.S. Supreme Court is very important because it serves as a guide to all other courts in the country, both state and federal. Lower courts view U.S. Supreme Court decisions as mandatory authority to follow.

Where are **judicial opinions located**?

Judicial opinions are located in sets of books called reporters. Most appellate court opinions are also available online. For example, U.S. Supreme Court opinions are located in the United States Reporters—a legal reporter published by the U.S. government—and also in the Supreme Court Reporter and the Lawyers Edition, reporters published by private publishing companies. U.S. Supreme Court opinions are also accessible in different locations online. Courts have their own individual websites, which are good places to find recent judicial opinions (see Appendix C).

What is a **citation** for a **judicial opinion**?

An example of a citation for a judicial opinion is *Miranda v. Arizona,* 384 U.S. 466 (1966). This citation consists of the name of the case and the reporter in which the case can be found. More specifically, a case citation includes:

- The name of the case

- The volume number of the reporter in which the case opinion appears

- The abbreviation for the reporter in which the case appears

- The beginning page number on which the judicial opinion begins

- In parentheses, the abbreviation for the court that decided the case if not apparent from the reporter and the year the case was decided

For example, the case name is *Miranda v. Arizona*. The case if found at volume 384 of the United States Reports beginning at page 466. The U.S. Supreme Court released this opinion in 1966. Another way to say it is—pick up volume 466 of the U.S. Reports, turn to page 466 and you will find the case *Miranda v. Arizona*.

Can you explain the **elements** of a **lower court citation**?

Yes, let's take the example of *McIntyre v. Ballentine*, 833 S.W.2d 52 (Tenn. 1992)—a famous decision in Tennessee where the state's high court adopted a system of comparative negligence (see the chapter on personal injury law for a discussion of comparative negligence).

Let's break down the elements of the legal citation:

Citation Element	Example
Name of case:	McIntyre v. Ballentine
Volume number of reporter:	833
Reporter where case found:	Southwestern Reporter, abbreviated as S.W.2d (S.W. for Southwestern Reporter, 2d. for 2nd series)
Beginning page # of opinion:	52
Court info and year:	Tenn. stands for Tennessee Supreme Court, and 1992 is the year the case was decided.

How does a person keep track of all the **abbreviations** and **requirements** for **legal citations**?

Good question. Lawyers are required to take a legal research and writing class, or classes, in law school. Instructors devote a course that often takes the entire school year to teach students the basics of legal research and writing. There are books that explain the rules for legal citation, including *The Bluebook: A Uniform System of*

Citation. It is called the *Bluebook* because it has a blue cover. As it says on its website, http://thelegalbluebook.com, the *Bluebook* "continues to provide a systematic method by which members of the profession communicate important information to one another about the sources and legal authorities upon which they rely in their work."

The *Bluebook* is not the only legal citation book. Two other popular legal citation books include: *The University of Chicago Manual of Legal Citation*—often called the maroon book because of its maroon cover—and Mary M. Prince's *Bieber Dictionary of Legal Citations: A Reference Guide for Attorneys, Legal Secretaries, Paralegals and Law Students.*

How do you **cite** a **statute or law**?

Statutes are cited differently than cases. Federal statutes or laws consist of three primary elements: (1) a title number; (2) abbreviation for the federal code; and (3) the section number. For example, 42 U.S.C. § 1983 is an important federal civil rights statute; 42 refers to the title (Public Health and Welfare) of the U.S. Code where this statute is found; U.S.C. stands for United States Code (where federal laws are codified or arranged); and 1983 refers to a section number.

What are **titles**?

Statutory codes are topical compilations of statutes or laws. The United States Code, which contains a topical arrangement of federal laws, is divided into 50 basic titles. For example, title 2 is Congress; title 5 is Government Organization and Employees; title 11 is bankruptcy; and title 28 is Judiciary and Judicial Procedure. Thus, if you know that you are looking for a bankruptcy law, you would know that this particular law is found in Title 11 of the United States Code.

What do we mean by an **annotated code**?

Annotated codes are important because they contain not only the text of the various laws (in the code) but they also provide annotations that give information about different legal sources that mention or cite different laws. For example, if you look up 42 U.S.C. § 1983 in the United States Code Annotated, you will find pages upon pages of citations to various judicial opinions that cite, mention, or explain the reach of this particular law. In other words, an annotated code allows a legal researcher to find both an applicable statute and perhaps some citations to cases that explain that statute or law.

How much **legal information** is available **online** now?

Quite a bit of legal information is available online. You can access the text of all U.S. Supreme Court opinions, for example. You can also find most appellate court decisions—state and federal—after a certain date. But you still cannot find many older lower court decisions online. Also, the vast majority of state and federal trial court opinions are still not available online for free. Most lawyers subscribe to an electronic database service—the two biggest are Westlaw and Lexis/Nexis—that provides access to nearly all legal authorities.

The Constitution
of the United States

We the People of the United States, in Order to form a more perfect Union, establish Justice, insure domestic Tranquility, provide for the common defence, promote the general Welfare, and secure the Blessings of Liberty to ourselves and our Posterity, do ordain and establish this Constitution for the United States of America.

ARTICLE I.

SECTION 1. All legislative Powers herein granted shall be vested in a Congress of the United States, which shall consist of a Senate and House of Representatives.

SECTION 2. The House of Representatives shall be composed of Members chosen every second Year by the People of the several States, and the Electors in each State shall have the Qualifications requisite for Electors of the most numerous Branch of the State Legislature.

No Person shall be a Representative who shall not have attained to the Age of twenty five Years, and been seven Years a Citizen of the United States, and who shall not, when elected, be an Inhabitant of that State in which he shall be chosen.

Representatives and direct Taxes shall be apportioned among the several States which may be included within this Union, according to their respective Numbers, which shall be determined by adding to the whole Number of free Persons, including those bound to Service for a Term of Years, and excluding Indians not taxed, three fifths of all other Persons.

The actual Enumeration shall be made within three Years after the first Meeting of the Congress of the United States, and within every subsequent Term of ten Years, in such Manner as they shall by Law direct. The Number of Representatives shall not exceed one for every thirty Thousand, but each State shall have at Least one Representative; and until such enumeration shall be made, the State of New Hampshire shall be entitled to chuse three, Massachusetts eight, Rhode Island and Providence Plantations one, Connecticut five, New York six, New Jersey four, Pennsylvania eight,

Delaware one, Maryland six, Virginia ten, North Carolina five, South Carolina five and Georgia three.

When vacancies happen in the Representation from any State, the Executive Authority thereof shall issue Writs of Election to fill such Vacancies.

The House of Representatives shall chuse their Speaker and other Officers; and shall have the sole Power of Impeachment.

SECTION 3. The Senate of the United States shall be composed of two Senators from each State, chosen by the Legislature thereof, for six Years; and each Senator shall have one Vote.

Immediately after they shall be assembled in Consequence of the first Election, they shall be divided as equally as may be into three Classes. The Seats of the Senators of the first Class shall be vacated at the Expiration of the second Year, of the second Class at the Expiration of the fourth Year, and of the third Class at the Expiration of the sixth Year, so that one third may be chosen every second Year; and if Vacancies happen by Resignation, or otherwise, during the Recess of the Legislature of any State, the Executive thereof may make temporary Appointments until the next Meeting of the Legislature, which shall then fill such Vacancies.

No person shall be a Senator who shall not have attained to the Age of thirty Years, and been nine Years a Citizen of the United States, and who shall not, when elected, be an Inhabitant of that State for which he shall be chosen.

The Vice President of the United States shall be President of the Senate, but shall have no Vote, unless they be equally divided.

The Senate shall chuse their other Officers, and also a President pro tempore, in the absence of the Vice President, or when he shall exercise the Office of President of the United States.

The Senate shall have the sole Power to try all Impeachments. When sitting for that Purpose, they shall be on Oath or Affirmation. When the President of the United States is tried, the Chief Justice shall preside: And no Person shall be convicted without the Concurrence of two thirds of the Members present.

Judgment in Cases of Impeachment shall not extend further than to removal from Office, and disqualification to hold and enjoy any Office of honor, Trust or Profit under the United States: but the Party convicted shall nevertheless be liable and subject to Indictment, Trial, Judgment and Punishment, according to Law.

SECTION 4. The Times, Places and Manner of holding Elections for Senators and Representatives, shall be prescribed in each State by the Legislature thereof; but the Congress may at any time by Law make or alter such Regulations, except as to the Place of Chusing Senators.

The Congress shall assemble at least once in every Year, and such Meeting shall be on the first Monday in December, unless they shall by Law appoint a different Day.

SECTION 5. Each House shall be the Judge of the Elections, Returns and Qualifications of its own Members, and a Majority of each shall constitute a Quorum to do Business; but a smaller number may adjourn from day to day, and may be authorized to compel the Attendance of absent Members, in such Manner, and under such Penalties as each House may provide.

Each House may determine the Rules of its Proceedings, punish its Members for disorderly Behavior, and, with the Concurrence of two-thirds, expel a Member.

Each House shall keep a Journal of its Proceedings, and from time to time publish the same, excepting such Parts as may in their Judgment require Secrecy; and the Yeas and Nays of the Members of either House on any question shall, at the Desire of one fifth of those Present, be entered on the Journal.

Neither House, during the Session of Congress, shall, without the Consent of the other, adjourn for more than three days, nor to any other Place than that in which the two Houses shall be sitting.

SECTION 6. The Senators and Representatives shall receive a Compensation for their Services, to be ascertained by Law, and paid out of the Treasury of the United States. They shall in all Cases, except Treason, Felony and Breach of the Peace, be privileged from Arrest during their Attendance at the Session of their respective Houses, and in going to and returning from the same; and for any Speech or Debate in either House, they shall not be questioned in any other Place.

No Senator or Representative shall, during the Time for which he was elected, be appointed to any civil Office under the Authority of the United States which shall have been created, or the Emoluments whereof shall have been increased during such time; and no Person holding any Office under the United States, shall be a Member of either House during his Continuance in Office.

SECTION 7. All bills for raising Revenue shall originate in the House of Representatives; but the Senate may propose or concur with Amendments as on other bills.

Every Bill which shall have passed the House of Representatives and the Senate, shall, before it become a Law, be presented to the President of the United States; If he approve he shall sign it, but if not he shall return it, with his Objections to that House in which it shall have originated, who shall enter the Objections at large on their Journal, and proceed to reconsider it. If after such Reconsideration two thirds of that House shall agree to pass the Bill, it shall be sent, together with the Objections, to the other House, by which it shall likewise be reconsidered, and if approved by two thirds of that House, it shall become a Law. But in all such Cases the Votes of both Houses shall be determined by Yeas and Nays, and the Names of the Persons voting for and against the Bill shall be entered on the Journal of each House respectively. If any Bill shall not be returned by the President within ten Days (Sundays excepted) after it shall have been presented to him, the Same shall be a Law, in like Manner as if he had signed it, unless the Congress by their Adjournment prevent its Return, in which Case it shall not be a Law.

355

Every Order, Resolution, or Vote to which the Concurrence of the Senate and House of Representatives may be necessary (except on a question of Adjournment) shall be presented to the President of the United States; and before the Same shall take Effect, shall be approved by him, or being disapproved by him, shall be repassed by two thirds of the Senate and House of Representatives, according to the Rules and Limitations prescribed in the Case of a Bill.

SECTION 8. The Congress shall have Power To lay and collect Taxes, Duties, Imposts and Excises, to pay the Debts and provide for the common Defence and general Welfare of the United States; but all Duties, Imposts and Excises shall be uniform throughout the United States;

To borrow money on the credit of the United States;

To regulate Commerce with foreign Nations, and among the several States, and with the Indian Tribes;

To establish an uniform Rule of Naturalization, and uniform Laws on the subject of Bankruptcies throughout the United States;

To coin Money, regulate the Value thereof, and of foreign Coin, and fix the Standard of Weights and Measures;

To provide for the Punishment of counterfeiting the Securities and current Coin of the United States;

To establish Post Offices and Post Roads;

To promote the Progress of Science and useful Arts, by securing for limited Times to Authors and Inventors the exclusive Right to their respective Writings and Discoveries;

To constitute Tribunals inferior to the supreme Court;

To define and punish Piracies and Felonies committed on the high Seas, and Offenses against the Law of Nations;

To declare War, grant Letters of Marque and Reprisal, and make Rules concerning Captures on Land and Water;

To raise and support Armies, but no Appropriation of Money to that Use shall be for a longer Term than two Years;

To provide and maintain a Navy;

To make Rules for the Government and Regulation of the land and naval Forces;

To provide for calling forth the Militia to execute the Laws of the Union, suppress Insurrections and repel Invasions;

To provide for organizing, arming, and disciplining the Militia, and for governing such Part of them as may be employed in the Service of the United States, reserving to the States respectively, the Appointment of the Officers, and the Authority of training the Militia according to the discipline prescribed by Congress;

To exercise exclusive Legislation in all Cases whatsoever, over such District (not exceeding ten Miles square) as may, by Cession of particular States, and the acceptance of Congress, become the Seat of the Government of the United States, and to exercise like Authority over all Places purchased by the Consent of the Legislature of the State in which the same shall be, for the Erection of Forts, Magazines, Arsenals, dock-Yards, and other needful Buildings; And

To make all Laws which shall be necessary and proper for carrying into Execution the foregoing Powers, and all other Powers vested by this Constitution in the Government of the United States, or in any Department or Officer thereof.

SECTION 9. The Migration or Importation of such Persons as any of the States now existing shall think proper to admit, shall not be prohibited by the Congress prior to the Year one thousand eight hundred and eight, but a tax or duty may be imposed on such Importation, not exceeding ten dollars for each Person.

The privilege of the Writ of Habeas Corpus shall not be suspended, unless when in Cases of Rebellion or Invasion the public Safety may require it.

No Bill of Attainder or *ex post facto* Law shall be passed. No capitation, or other direct, Tax shall be laid, unless in Proportion to the Census or Enumeration herein before directed to be taken.

No Tax or Duty shall be laid on Articles exported from any State.

No Preference shall be given by any Regulation of Commerce or Revenue to the Ports of one State over those of another: nor shall Vessels bound to, or from, one State, be obliged to enter, clear, or pay Duties in another.

No Money shall be drawn from the Treasury, but in Consequence of Appropriations made by Law; and a regular Statement and Account of the Receipts and Expenditures of all public Money shall be published from time to time.

No Title of Nobility shall be granted by the United States: And no Person holding any Office of Profit or Trust under them, shall, without the Consent of the Congress, accept of any present, Emolument, Office, or Title, of any kind whatever, from any King, Prince or foreign State.

SECTION 10. No State shall enter into any Treaty, Alliance, or Confederation; grant Letters of Marque and Reprisal; coin Money; emit Bills of Credit; make any Thing but gold and silver Coin a Tender in Payment of Debts; pass any Bill of Attainder, *ex post facto* Law, or Law impairing the Obligation of Contracts, or grant any Title of Nobility.

No State shall, without the Consent of the Congress, lay any Imposts or Duties on Imports or Exports, except what may be absolutely necessary for executing its inspection Laws: and the net Produce of all Duties and Imposts, laid by any State on Imports or Exports, shall be for the Use of the Treasury of the United States; and all such Laws shall be subject to the Revision and Controul of the Congress.

No State shall, without the Consent of Congress, lay any duty of Tonnage, keep Troops, or Ships of War in time of Peace, enter into any Agreement or Compact with another State, or with a foreign Power, or engage in War, unless actually invaded, or in such imminent Danger as will not admit of delay.

ARTICLE II.

SECTION 1. The executive Power shall be vested in a President of the United States of America. He shall hold his Office during the Term of four Years, and, together with the Vice-President chosen for the same Term, be elected, as follows:

Each State shall appoint, in such Manner as the Legislature thereof may direct, a Number of Electors, equal to the whole Number of Senators and Representatives to which the State may be entitled in the Congress: but no Senator or Representative, or Person holding an Office of Trust or Profit under the United States, shall be appointed an Elector.

The Electors shall meet in their respective States, and vote by Ballot for two persons, of whom one at least shall not lie an Inhabitant of the same State with themselves. And they shall make a List of all the Persons voted for, and of the Number of Votes for each; which List they shall sign and certify, and transmit sealed to the Seat of the Government of the United States, directed to the President of the Senate. The President of the Senate shall, in the Presence of the Senate and House of Representatives, open all the Certificates, and the Votes shall then be counted. The Person having the greatest Number of Votes shall be the President, if such Number be a Majority of the whole Number of Electors appointed; and if there be more than one who have such Majority, and have an equal Number of Votes, then the House of Representatives shall immediately chuse by Ballot one of them for President; and if no Person have a Majority, then from the five highest on the List the said House shall in like Manner chuse the President. But in chusing the President, the Votes shall be taken by States, the Representation from each State having one Vote; a quorum for this Purpose shall consist of a Member or Members from two-thirds of the States, and a Majority of all the States shall be necessary to a Choice. In every Case, after the Choice of the President, the Person having the greatest Number of Votes of the Electors shall be the Vice President. But if there should remain two or more who have equal Votes, the Senate shall chuse from them by Ballot the Vice President.

The Congress may determine the Time of chusing the Electors, and the Day on which they shall give their Votes; which Day shall be the same throughout the United States.

No person except a natural born Citizen, or a Citizen of the United States, at the time of the Adoption of this Constitution, shall be eligible to the Office of President; neither shall any Person be eligible to that Office who shall not have attained to the Age of thirty-five Years, and been fourteen Years a Resident within the United States.

In Case of the Removal of the President from Office, or of his Death, Resignation, or Inability to discharge the Powers and Duties of the said Office, the same shall devolve on the Vice President, and the Congress may by Law provide for the Case of Removal, Death, Resignation or Inability, both of the President and Vice President, declaring what Officer shall then act as President, and such Officer shall act accordingly, until the Disability be removed, or a President shall be elected.

The President shall, at stated Times, receive for his Services, a Compensation, which shall neither be increased nor diminished during the Period for which he shall have been elected, and he shall not receive within that Period any other Emolument from the United States, or any of them.

Before he enter on the Execution of his Office, he shall take the following Oath or Affirmation: "I do solemnly swear (or affirm) that I will faithfully execute the Office of President of the United States, and will to the best of my Ability, preserve, protect and defend the Constitution of the United States."

SECTION 2. The President shall be Commander in Chief of the Army and Navy of the United States, and of the Militia of the several States, when called into the actual Service of the United States; he may require the Opinion, in writing, of the principal Officer in each of the executive Departments, upon any subject relating to the Duties of their respective Offices, and he shall have Power to Grant Reprieves and Pardons for Offenses against the United States, except in Cases of Impeachment.

He shall have Power, by and with the Advice and Consent of the Senate, to make Treaties, provided two thirds of the Senators present concur; and he shall nominate, and by and with the Advice and Consent of the Senate, shall appoint Ambassadors, other public Ministers and Consuls, Judges of the supreme Court, and all other Officers of the United States, whose Appointments are not herein otherwise provided for, and which shall be established by Law: but the Congress may by Law vest the Appointment of such inferior Officers, as they think proper, in the President alone, in the Courts of Law, or in the Heads of Departments.

The President shall have Power to fill up all Vacancies that may happen during the Recess of the Senate, by granting Commissions which shall expire at the End of their next Session.

SECTION 3. He shall from time to time give to the Congress Information of the State of the Union, and recommend to their Consideration such Measures as he shall judge necessary and expedient; he may, on extraordinary Occasions, convene both Houses, or either of them, and in Case of Disagreement between them, with Respect to the Time of Adjournment, he may adjourn them to such Time as he shall think proper; he shall receive Ambassadors and other public Ministers; he shall take Care that the Laws be faithfully executed, and shall Commission all the Officers of the United States.

SECTION 4. The President, Vice President and all civil Officers of the United States, shall be removed from Office on Impeachment for, and Conviction of, Treason, Bribery, or other high Crimes and Misdemeanors.

359

ARTICLE III.

SECTION 1. The judicial Power of the United States, shall be vested in one supreme Court, and in such inferior Courts as the Congress may from time to time ordain and establish. The Judges, both of the supreme and inferior Courts, shall hold their Offices during good Behavior, and shall, at stated Times, receive for their Services a Compensation which shall not be diminished during their Continuance in Office.

SECTION 2. The judicial Power shall extend to all Cases, in Law and Equity, arising under this Constitution, the Laws of the United States, and Treaties made, or which shall be made, under their Authority; to all Cases affecting Ambassadors, other public Ministers and Consuls; to all Cases of admiralty and maritime Jurisdiction; to Controversies to which the United States shall be a Party; to Controversies between two or more States; between a State and Citizens of another State; between Citizens of different States; between Citizens of the same State claiming Lands under Grants of different States, and between a State, or the Citizens thereof, and foreign States, Citizens or Subjects.

In all Cases affecting Ambassadors, other public Ministers and Consuls, and those in which a State shall be Party, the supreme Court shall have original Jurisdiction. In all the other Cases before mentioned, the supreme Court shall have appellate Jurisdiction, both as to Law and Fact, with such Exceptions, and under such Regulations as the Congress shall make.

Trial of all Crimes, except in Cases of Impeachment, shall be by Jury; and such Trial shall be held in the State where the said Crimes shall have been committed; but when not committed within any State, the Trial shall be at such Place or Places as the Congress may by Law have directed.

SECTION 3. Treason against the United States, shall consist only in levying War against them, or in adhering to their Enemies, giving them Aid and Comfort. No Person shall be convicted of Treason unless on the Testimony of two Witnesses to the same overt Act, or on Confession in open Court.

The Congress shall have power to declare the Punishment of Treason, but no Attainder of Treason shall work Corruption of Blood, or Forfeiture except during the Life of the Person attainted.

ARTICLE IV.

SECTION 1. Full Faith and Credit shall be given in each State to the public Acts, Records, and judicial Proceedings of every other State. And the Congress may by general Laws prescribe the Manner in which such Acts, Records and Proceedings shall be proved, and the Effect thereof.

SECTION 2. The Citizens of each State shall be entitled to all Privileges and Immunities of Citizens in the several States.

A Person charged in any State with Treason, Felony, or other Crime, who shall flee from Justice, and be found in another State, shall on demand of the executive Authority of the State from which he fled, be delivered up, to be removed to the State having Jurisdiction of the Crime.

No Person held to Service or Labour in one State, under the Laws thereof, escaping into another, shall, in Consequence of any Law or Regulation therein, be discharged from such Service or Labour, But shall be delivered up on Claim of the Party to whom such Service or Labour may be due.

SECTION 3. New States may be admitted by the Congress into this Union; but no new States shall be formed or erected within the Jurisdiction of any other State; nor any State be formed by the Junction of two or more States, or parts of States, without the Consent of the Legislatures of the States concerned as well as of the Congress.

The Congress shall have Power to dispose of and make all needful Rules and Regulations respecting the Territory or other Property belonging to the United States; and nothing in this Constitution shall be so construed as to Prejudice any Claims of the United States, or of any particular State.

SECTION 4. The United States shall guarantee to every State in this Union a Republican Form of Government, and shall protect each of them against Invasion; and on Application of the Legislature, or of the Executive (when the Legislature cannot be convened) against domestic Violence.

ARTICLE V.

The Congress, whenever two thirds of both Houses shall deem it necessary, shall propose

Amendments to this Constitution, or, on the Application of the Legislatures of two thirds of the several States, shall call a Convention for proposing Amendments, which, in either Case, shall be valid to all Intents and Purposes, as part of this Constitution, when ratified by the Legislatures of three fourths of the several States, or by Conventions in three fourths thereof, as the one or the other Mode of Ratification may be proposed by the Congress; Provided that no Amendment which may be made prior to the Year One thousand eight hundred and eight shall in any Manner affect the first and fourth Clauses in the Ninth Section of the first Article; and that no State, without its Consent, shall be deprived of its equal Suffrage in the Senate.

ARTICLE VI.

All Debts contracted and Engagements entered into, before the Adoption of this Constitution, shall be as valid against the United States under this Constitution, as under the Confederation.

This Constitution, and the Laws of the United States which shall be made in Pursuance thereof; and all Treaties made, or which shall be made, under the Authority of the United States, shall be the supreme Law of the Land; and the Judges in every State shall be bound thereby, any Thing in the Constitution or Laws of any State to the Contrary notwithstanding.

The Senators and Representatives before mentioned, and the Members of the several State Legislatures, and all executive and judicial Officers, both of the United States and of the several States, shall be bound by Oath or Affirmation, to support this Constitution; but no religious Test shall ever be required as a Qualification to any Office or public Trust under the United States.

ARTICLE VII.

The Ratification of the Conventions of nine States, shall be sufficient for the Establishment of this Constitution between the States so ratifying the Same.

DONE in Convention by the Unanimous Consent of the States present the Seventeenth Day of September in the Year of our Lord one thousand seven hundred and Eighty seven and of the Independence of the United States of America the Twelfth. In Witness whereof We have hereunto subscribed our Names.

Go. Washington
President and deputy from Virginia

New Hampshire
John Langdon
Nicholas Gilman

Massachusetts
Nathaniel Gorham
Rufus King

Connecticut
Wm Saml Johnson
Roger Sherman

New York
Alexander Hamilton

New Jersey
Wil Livingston
David Brearley
Wm Paterson
Jona. Dayton

Pennsylvania
B Franklin
Thomas Mifflin
Robt Morris
Geo. Clymer
Thos FitzSimons
Jared Ingersoll
James Wilson
Gouv Morris

Delaware
Geo. Read
Gunning Bedford jun
John Dickinson
Richard Bassett
Jaco. Broom

Maryland
James McHenry
Dan of St Tho Jenifer
Danl Carroll

Virginia
John Blair
James Madison Jr.

North Carolina
Wm Blount
Richd Dobbs Spaight
Hu Williamson

South Carolina
J. Rutledge

Charles Cotesworth Pinckney
Charles Pinckney
Pierce Butler

Georgia
William Few
Abr Baldwin

Attest: William Jackson, Secretary

AMENDMENT I.

Congress shall make no law respecting an establishment of religion, or prohibiting the free exercise thereof; or abridging the freedom of speech, or of the press; or the right of the people peaceably to assemble, and to petition the Government for a redress of grievances.

AMENDMENT II.

A well regulated Militia, being necessary to the security of a free State, the right of the people to keep and bear Arms, shall not be infringed.

AMENDMENT III.

No Soldier shall, in time of peace be quartered in any house, without the consent of the Owner, nor in time of war, but in a manner to be prescribed by law.

AMENDMENT IV.

The right of the people to be secure in their persons, houses, papers, and effects, against unreasonable searches and seizures, shall not be violated, and no Warrants shall issue, but upon probable cause, supported by Oath or affirmation, and particularly describing the place to be searched, and the persons or things to be seized.

AMENDMENT V.

No person shall be held to answer for a capital, or otherwise infamous crime, unless on a presentment or indictment of a Grand Jury, except in cases arising in the land or naval forces, or in the Militia, when in actual service in time of War or public danger; nor shall any person be subject for the same offense to be twice put in jeopardy of life or limb; nor shall be compelled in any criminal case to be a witness against himself, nor be deprived of life, liberty, or property, without due process of law; nor shall private property be taken for public use, without just compensation.

AMENDMENT VI.

In all criminal prosecutions, the accused shall enjoy the right to a speedy and public trial, by an impartial jury of the State and district wherein the crime shall have been committed, which district shall have been previously ascertained by law, and to be informed of the nature and cause of the accusation; to be confronted with the witnesses against him; to have compulsory process for obtaining witnesses in his favor, and to have the Assistance of Counsel for his defence.

AMENDMENT VII.

In Suits at common law, where the value in controversy shall exceed twenty dollars, the right of trial by jury shall be preserved, and no fact tried by a jury, shall be otherwise re-examined in any Court of the United States, than according to the rules of the common law.

AMENDMENT VIII.

Excessive bail shall not be required, nor excessive fines imposed, nor cruel and unusual punishments inflicted.

AMENDMENT IX.

The enumeration in the Constitution, of certain rights, shall not be construed to deny or disparage others retained by the people.

AMENDMENT X.

The powers not delegated to the United States by the Constitution, nor prohibited by it to the States, are reserved to the States espectively, or to the people.

AMENDMENT XI.

The Judicial power of the United States shall not be construed to extend to any suit in law or equity, commenced or prosecuted against one of the United States by Citizens of another State, or by Citizens or Subjects of any Foreign State.

AMENDMENT XII.

The Electors shall meet in their respective states, and vote by ballot for President and Vice-President, one of whom, at least, shall not be an inhabitant of the same state with themselves; they shall name in their ballots the person voted for as President, and in distinct ballots the person voted for as Vice-President, and they shall make distinct lists of all persons voted for as President, and of all persons voted for as Vice-President and of the number of votes for each, which lists they shall sign and certify, and transmit sealed to the seat of the government of the United States, directed to the President of the Senate;

The President of the Senate shall, in the presence of the Senate and House of Representatives, open all the certificates and the votes shall then be counted;

The person having the greatest Number of votes for President, shall be the President, if such number be a majority of the whole number of Electors appointed; and if no person have such majority, then from the persons having the highest numbers not exceeding three on the list of those voted for as President, the House of Representatives shall choose immediately, by ballot, the President. But in choosing the President, the votes shall be taken by states, the representation from each state having one vote; a quorum for this purpose shall consist of a member or members from two-thirds of the states, and a majority of all the states shall be necessary to a choice. And if the House of Representatives shall not choose a President whenever the right of choice shall devolve upon them, before the fourth day of March next following, then the Vice-President shall act as President, as in the case of the death or other constitutional disability of the President.

The person having the greatest number of votes as Vice-President, shall be the Vice-President, if such number be a majority of the whole number of Electors appointed, and if no person have a majority, then from the two highest numbers on the list, the Senate shall choose the Vice-President; a quorum for the purpose shall consist of two-thirds of the whole number of Senators, and a majority of the whole number shall be necessary to a choice. But no person constitutionally ineligible to the office of President shall be eligible to that of Vice-President of the United States.

AMENDMENT XIII.

1. Neither slavery nor involuntary servitude, except as a punishment for crime whereof the party shall have been duly convicted, shall exist within the United States, or any place subject to their jurisdiction.

2. Congress shall have power to enforce this article by appropriate legislation.

AMENDMENT XIV.

1. All persons born or naturalized in the United States, and subject to the jurisdiction thereof, are citizens of the United States and of the State wherein they reside. No State shall make or enforce any law which shall abridge the privileges or immunities of citizens of the United States; nor shall any State deprive any person of life, liberty, or property, without due process of law; nor deny to any person within its jurisdiction the equal protection of the laws.

2. Representatives shall be apportioned among the several States according to their respective numbers, counting the whole number of persons in each State, excluding Indians not taxed. But when the right to vote at any election for the choice of electors for President and Vice-President of the United States, Representatives in Congress, the Executive and Judicial officers of a State, or the members of the Legislature thereof, is

denied to any of the male inhabitants of such State, being twenty-one years of age, and citizens of the United States, or in any way abridged, except for participation in rebellion, or other crime, the basis of representation therein shall be reduced in the proportion which the number of such male citizens shall bear to the whole number of male citizens twenty-one years of age in such State.

3. No person shall be a Senator or Representative in Congress, or elector of President and Vice-President, or hold any office, civil or military, under the United States, or under any State, who, having previously taken an oath, as a member of Congress, or as an officer of the United States, or as a member of any State legislature, or as an executive or judicial officer of any State, to support the Constitution of the United States, shall have engaged in insurrection or rebellion against the same, or given aid or comfort to the enemies thereof. But Congress may by a vote of two-thirds of each House, remove such disability.

4. The validity of the public debt of the United States, authorized by law, including debts incurred for payment of pensions and bounties for services in suppressing insurrection or rebellion, shall not be questioned. But neither the United States nor any State shall assume or pay any debt or obligation incurred in aid of insurrection or rebellion against the United States, or any claim for the loss or emancipation of any slave; but all such debts, obligations and claims shall be held illegal and void.

5. The Congress shall have power to enforce, by appropriate legislation, the provisions of this article.

AMENDMENT XV.

1. The right of citizens of the United States to vote shall not be denied or abridged by the United States or by any State on account of race, color, or previous condition of servitude.

2. The Congress shall have power to enforce this article by appropriate legislation.

AMENDMENT XVI.

The Congress shall have power to lay and collect taxes on incomes, from whatever source derived, without apportionment among the several States, and without regard to any census or enumeration.

AMENDMENT XVII.

The Senate of the United States shall be composed of two Senators from each State, elected by the people thereof, for six years; and each Senator shall have one vote. The electors in each State shall have the qualifications requisite for electors of the most numerous branch of the State legislatures.

When vacancies happen in the representation of any State in the Senate, the executive authority of such State shall issue writs of election to fill such vacancies: Provided, That the legislature of any State may empower the executive thereof to make temporary appointments until the people fill the vacancies by election as the legislature may direct.

This Amendment shall not be so construed as to affect the election or term of any Senator chosen before it becomes valid as part of the Constitution.

AMENDMENT XVIII.

1. After one year from the ratification of this article the manufacture, sale, or transportation of intoxicating liquors within, the importation thereof into, or the exportation thereof from the United States and all territory subject to the jurisdiction thereof for beverage purposes is hereby prohibited.

2. The Congress and the several States shall have concurrent power to enforce this article by appropriate legislation.

3. This article shall be inoperative unless it shall have been ratified as an Amendment to the Constitution by the legislatures of the several States, as provided in the Constitution, within seven years from the date of the submission hereof to the States by the Congress.

AMENDMENT XIX.

The right of citizens of the United States to vote shall not be denied or abridged by the United States or by any State on account of sex.

Congress shall have power to enforce this article by appropriate legislation.

AMENDMENT XX.

1. The terms of the President and Vice President shall end at noon on the 20th day of January, and the terms of Senators and Representatives at noon on the 3d day of January, of the years in which such terms would have ended if this article had not been ratified; and the terms of their successors shall then begin.

2. The Congress shall assemble at least once in every year, and such meeting shall begin at noon on the 3d day of January, unless they shall by law appoint a different day.

3. If, at the time fixed for the beginning of the term of the President, the President elect shall have died, the Vice President elect shall become President. If a President shall not have been chosen before the time fixed for the beginning of his term, or if the President elect shall have failed to qualify, then the Vice President elect shall act as

President until a President shall have qualified; and the Congress may by law provide for the case wherein neither a President elect nor a Vice President elect shall have qualified, declaring who shall then act as President, or the manner in which one who is to act shall be selected, and such person shall act accordingly until a President or Vice President shall have qualified.

4. The Congress may by law provide for the case of the death of any of the persons from whom the House of Representatives may choose a President whenever the right of choice shall have devolved upon them, and for the case of the death of any of the persons from whom the Senate may choose a Vice President whenever the right of choice shall have devolved upon them.

5. Sections 1 and 2 shall take effect on the 15th day of October following the ratification of this article.

6. This article shall be inoperative unless it shall have been ratified as an Amendment to the Constitution by the legislatures of three-fourths of the several States within seven years from the date of its submission.

AMENDMENT XXI.

1. The eighteenth article of Amendment to the Constitution of the United States is hereby repealed.

2. The transportation or importation into any State, Territory, or possession of the United States for delivery or use therein of intoxicating liquors, in violation of the laws thereof, is hereby prohibited.

3. The article shall be inoperative unless it shall have been ratified as an Amendment to the Constitution by conventions in the several States, as provided in the Constitution, within seven years from the date of the submission hereof to the States by the Congress.

AMENDMENT XXII.

1. No person shall be elected to the office of the President more than twice, and no person who has held the office of President, or acted as President, for more than two years of a term to which some other person was elected President shall be elected to the office of the President more than once. But this Article shall not apply to any person holding the office of President, when this Article was proposed by the Congress, and shall not prevent any person who may be holding the office of President, or acting as President, during the term within which this Article becomes operative from holding the office of President or acting as President during the remainder of such term.

2. This article shall be inoperative unless it shall have been ratified as an Amendment to the Constitution by the legislatures of three-fourths of the several States within seven years from the date of its submission to the States by the Congress.

AMENDMENT XXIII.

1. The District constituting the seat of Government of the United States shall appoint in such manner as the Congress may direct: A number of electors of President and Vice President equal to the whole number of Senators and Representatives in Congress to which the District would be entitled if it were a State, but in no event more than the least populous State; they shall be in addition to those appointed by the States, but they shall be considered, for the purposes of the election of President and Vice President, to be electors

appointed by a State; and they shall meet in the District and perform such duties as provided by the twelfth article of Amendment.

2. The Congress shall have power to enforce this article by appropriate legislation.

AMENDMENT XXIV.

1. The right of citizens of the United States to vote in any primary or other election for President or Vice President, for electors for President or Vice President, or for Senator or Representative in Congress, shall not be denied or abridged by the United States or any State by reason of failure to pay any poll tax or other tax.

2. The Congress shall have power to enforce this article by appropriate legislation.

AMENDMENT XXV.

1. In case of the removal of the President from office or of his death or resignation, the Vice President shall become President.

2. Whenever there is a vacancy in the office of the Vice President, the President shall nominate a Vice President who shall take office upon confirmation by a majority vote of both Houses of Congress.

3. Whenever the President transmits to the President pro tempore of the Senate and the Speaker of the House of Representatives his written declaration that he is unable to discharge the powers and duties of his office, and until he transmits to them a written declaration to the contrary, such powers and duties shall be discharged by the Vice President as Acting President.

4. Whenever the Vice President and a majority of either the principal officers of the executive departments or of such other body as Congress may by law provide, transmit to the President pro tempore of the Senate and the Speaker of the House of Representatives their written declaration that the President is unable to discharge the powers and duties of his office, the Vice President shall immediately assume the powers and duties of the office as Acting President.

Thereafter, when the President transmits to the President pro tempore of the Senate and the Speaker of the House of Representatives his written declaration that no inability exists, he shall resume the powers and duties of his office unless the Vice President and a majority of either the principal officers of the executive department or of such other body as Congress may by law provide, transmit within four days to the President pro tempore of the Senate and the Speaker of the House of Representatives their written declaration that the President is unable to discharge the powers and duties of his office. Thereupon Congress shall decide the issue, assembling within forty eight hours for that purpose if not in session. If the Congress, within twenty one days after receipt of the latter written declaration, or, if Congress is not in session, within twenty one days after Congress is required to assemble, determines by two thirds vote of both Houses that the President is unable to discharge the powers and duties of his office, the Vice President shall continue to discharge the same as Acting President; otherwise, the President shall resume the powers and duties of his office.

AMENDMENT XXVI.

1. The right of citizens of the United States, who are eighteen years of age or older, to vote shall not be denied or abridged by the United States or by any State on account of age.

2. The Congress shall have power to enforce this article by appropriate legislation.

AMENDMENT XXVII.

No law, varying the compensation for the services of the Senators and Representatives, shall take effect, until an election of Representatives shall have intervened.

APPENDIX C
Online Resources

The U.S. Constitution (See also Appendix B)
http://www.usconstitution.net/const.html

State Constitutions

Alabama
http://www.legislature.state.al.us/Codeofalabama/constitution/1901/constitution1901_toc.htm

Alaska
http://ltgov.alaska.gov/services/constitution.php

Arizona
http://www.azleg.gov/Constitution.asp

Arkansas
http://www.sos.arkansas.gov/ar-constitution/arconst/arconst.htm

California
http://www.leginfo.ca.gov/const.html

Colorado
http://www.colorado.gov/cs/Satellite/CO-Portal/CXP/1178305752117

Connecticut
http://www.cslib.org/constitutionalAmends/constitution.htm

Delaware
http://www.delcode.state.de.us/constitution/index.htm

Florida
http://www.leg.state.fl.us/statutes/index.cfm?mode=constitution&submenu=3&tab=statutes

Georgia
http://sos.georgia.gov/ELECTIONS/constitution_2007.pdf

Hawaii
http://hawaii.gov/lrb/con/

371

Idaho
http://www.legislature.idaho.gov/idstat/IC/Title003.htm

Illinois
http://www.ilga.gov/commission/lrb/conmain.htm

Indiana
http://www.in.gov/legislative/ic/code/const/

Iowa
http://www.legis.state.ia.us/Constitution.html

Kansas
http://www.kslib.info/constitution/index.html

Kentucky
http://www.lrc.ky.gov/Legresou/Constitu/intro.htm

Louisiana
http://senate.legis.state.la.us/documents/Constitution/

Maine
http://www.maine.gov/legis/const/

Maryland
http://www.msa.md.gov/msa/mdmanual/43const/html/const.html

Massachusetts
http://www.mass.gov/legis/const.htm

Michigan
http://www.legislature.mi.gov/documents/publications/Constitution.pdf

Minnesota
http://www.house.leg.state.mn.us/cco/rules/mncon/preamble.htm

Mississippi
http://www.sos.state.ms.us/pubs/constitution/constitution.asp

Missouri
http://www.moga.mo.gov/const/moconstn.htm

Montana
http://leg.mt.gov/css/Laws%20and%20Constitution/Current%20Constitution.asp

Nebraska
http://www.neded.org/files/research/stathand/parttwo/nebconst.html

Nevada
http://www.leg.state.nv.us/Const/NVConst.html

New Hampshire
http://www.nh.gov/constitution/constitution.html

New Jersey
http://www.njleg.state.nj.us/lawsconstitution/constitution.asp

New Mexico
http://www.sos.state.nm.us/pdf/2007nmconst.pdf

New York
http://www.dos.state.ny.us/info/constitution.htm

North Carolina
http://www.ncleg.net/Legislation/constitution/ncconstitution.html

North Dakota
http://www.legis.nd.gov/information/statutes/const-laws.html

Ohio
http://www.legislature.state.oh.us/constitution.cfm

Oklahoma
http://oklegal.onenet.net/okcon/index.html

Oregon
http://www.leg.state.or.us/orcons/

Pennsylvania
http://sites.state.pa.us/PA_Constitution.html

Rhode Island
http://www.rilin.state.ri.us/gen_assembly/riconstitution/riconst.html

South Carolina
http://www.scstatehouse.gov/scconstitution/scconst.htm

South Dakota
http://legis.state.sd.us/statutes/Constitution.aspx

Tennessee
http://www.state.tn.us/sos/bluebook/05-06/46-tnconst.pdf

Texas
http://tarlton.law.utexas.edu/constitutions/text/1876index.html

Utah
http://www.le.state.ut.us/~code/const/const.htm

Vermont
http://www.leg.state.vt.us/statutes/const2.htm

Virginia
http://legis.state.va.us/laws/search/constitution.htm

Washington
http://www.secstate.wa.gov/history/constitution.aspx

West Virginia
http://www.wvculture.org/HISTORY/statehood/constitution.html

Wisconsin
http://www.legis.state.wi.us/rsb/2wiscon.html

Wyoming
http://legisweb.state.wy.us/statutes/constitution.aspx?file=titles/title97/title97.htm

Federal Courts

U.S. Supreme Court
http://www.supremecourtus.gov/

Federal Courts of Appeals

1st Circuit
http://www.ca1.uscourts.gov/

2nd Circuit
http://www.ca2.uscourts.gov/

3rd Circuit
http://www.ca3.uscourts.gov/

4th Circuit
http://www.ca4.uscourts.gov/

5th Circuit
http://www.ca5.uscourts.gov/

6th Circuit
http://www.ca6.uscourts.gov/

7th Circuit
http://www.ca7.uscourts.gov/

8th Circuit
http://www.ca8.uscourts.gov/

9th Circuit
http://www.ca9.uscourts.gov/

10th Circuit
http://www.ca10.uscourts.gov/

11th Circuit
http://www.ca11.uscourts.gov/

D.C. Circuit
http://www.cadc.uscourts.gov/internet/home.nsf
Federal Circuit
http://www.cafc.uscourts.gov/

The best source for access to various U.S. Courts is the U.S. Courts site at http://www.us courts.gov/courtlinks/

State Courts

Each state has a website devoted to its judicial branches. Below are the names (note that the states use different names for their court systems) and links to these websites.

Alabama Judicial System
http://www.judicial.state.al.us/

Alaska Court System
http://courts.alaska.gov/

Arizona Judicial Branch
http://www.supreme.state.az.us/

Arkansas Judiciary
http://courts.state.ar.us/

California Judicial Branch
http://www.courtinfo.ca.gov/

Colorado State Judicial Branch
http://www.courts.state.co.us/

Connecticut Judicial Branch
http://www.jud.ct.gov/

Delaware State Courts
http://courts.delaware.gov/

Florida State Courts
http://www.flcourts.org/

Georgia — Judicial Branch of Georgia
http://www.georgiacourts.org/

Hawaii State Judiciary
http://www.courts.state.hi.us/

Idaho State Judiciary
http://www.isc.idaho.gov/

Illinois Courts
http://www.state.il.us/court/

Indiana Courts
http://www.in.gov/judiciary/

Iowa Judicial Branch
http://www.iowacourts.gov/

Kansas Judicial Branch
http://www.kscourts.org/

Kentucky Court of Justice
http://courts.ky.gov/

Louisiana Government — Judicial Branch
http://la.gov/Government/Judicial_Branch/

Maine Judicial Branch
http://www.courts.state.me.us/

Maryland Judiciary
http://www.courts.state.md.us/

Massachusetts Judicial Branch
http://www.mass.gov/courts/

Michigan Judicial Branch
http://courts.michigan.gov/supremecourt/index.htm

Minnesota Judicial Branch
http://www.mncourts.gov/default.aspx

Mississippi Judiciary
http://www.mississippi.gov/ms_sub_sub_template.jsp?Category_ID=13

Missouri Courts
https://www.courts.mo.gov/casenet/base/welcome.do

Montana Judicial Branch
http://courts.mt.gov/default.mcpx

Nebraska Judicial Branch
http://www.supremecourt.ne.gov/

Nevada Judiciary
http://www.nevadajudiciary.us/

New Hampshire Judicial Branch
http://www.courts.state.nh.us/

New Jersey Courts Online
http://www.judiciary.state.nj.us/

New Mexico Courts
http://www.nmcourts.com

New York State Unified Court System
http://www.courts.state.ny.us/

North Carolina Judicial Branch
http://www.nccourts.org/

North Dakota Courts
http://www.ndcourts.com/court/courts.htm

Ohio Judicial Branch
http://www.legislature.state.oh.us/judicial.cfm

Oklahoma Judicial Branch
http://www.ok.gov/section.php?sec_id=1

Oregon Courts
http://courts.oregon.gov/OJD/

Pennsylvania — Unified Judicial System of Pennsylvania
http://www.courts.state.pa.us/default.htm

Rhode Island Judiciary
http://www.courts.ri.gov/

South Carolina Judicial Department
http://www.judicial.state.sc.us/

South Dakota Unified Judicial System
http://www.sdjudicial.com/

Tennessee Court System
http://www.tsc.state.tn.us/

Texas Court System
http://www.courts.state.tx.us/

Utah State Courts
http://www.utcourts.gov/

Vermont Judiciary
http://www.vermontjudiciary.org/default.aspx

Virginia Judicial System
http://www.courts.state.va.us/

Washington Courts
http://www.courts.wa.gov/

West Virginia Judiciary System
http://www.state.wv.us/wvsca/wvsystem.htm

Wisconsin Court System
http://www.wicourts.gov/

Wyoming Judicial Branch
http://www.courts.state.wy.us/

Credit and Bankruptcy Resources

Bankruptcy Basics
http://www.uscourts.gov/bankruptcycourts/bankruptcybasics.html

Bankruptcy Lawyers Blog
http://blog.startfreshtoday.com/

Bankruptcy Litigation Blog
http://www.bankruptcylitigationblog.com/

Federal Trade Commission Credit Guide
http://www.ftc.gov/credit

Federal Trade Commission's Fair Debt Collection Act Links
http://www.ftc.gov/os/statutes/fdcpajump.shtm

Federal Trade Commission on Identity Theft
http://www.ftc.gov/bcp/menus/consumer/data/idt.shtm

Total Bankruptcy
http://www.totalbankruptcy.com/blog/

U.S. Bankruptcy Courts
http://www.uscourts.gov/bankruptcycourts.html

Criminal Law Resources

Bureau of Justice Statistics
http://www.ojp.usdoj.gov/bjs/

Criminal Justice Section of the American Bar Association
http://www.abanet.org/crimjust/home.html

CrimProf Blog
http://lawprofessors.typepad.com/crimprof_blog/

Findlaw's Criminal Law Center
http://criminal.findlaw.com/

National Association of Criminal Defense Lawyers
http://www.criminaljustice.org/public.nsf/freeform/publicwelcome?opendocument

National Criminal Justice Reference Service
http://www.ncjrs.gov/

National Institute of Justice
http://www.ojp.usdoj.gov/nij/

Not Guilty: A Texas Criminal Law Blog
http://hwlawfirm.blogspot.com/

Simple Justice: A New York Criminal Law Blog
http://blog.simplejustice.us/

United States Sentencing Commission
http://www.ussc.gov/guidelin.htm

Employment Law Resources

Age Discrimination Lawyers
http://www.agediscriminationlawyers.com/

Americans with Disabilities Act
http://www.ada.gov/pubs/ada.htm

Americans with Disabilities Act Resource Center
http://www.ncsconline.org/D_KIS/ADAResources.htm

Disability Rights Advocates
http://www.dralegal.org/

Equal Employment Opportunity Commission (EEOC)
http://www.eeoc.gov/

EEOC on Age Discrimination in Employment Act
http://www.eeoc.gov/policy/adea.html

EEOC Regulations
http://www.eeoc.gov/policy/regs/index.html

EEOC's Facts about Sexual Harassment
http://www.eeoc.gov/facts/fs-sex.html

National Employment Lawyers Association
http://www.nela.org/NELA/

Title VII of the Civil Rights Act of 1964
http://www4.law.cornell.edu/uscode/42/2000e.html

U.S. Department of Justice — Civil Rights Division (Employment Litigation Section)
http://www.justice.gov/crt/emp/faq.php

U.S. Department of Labor
http://www.dol.gov/

U.S. Department of Labor on Age Discrimination
http://www.dol.gov/dol/topic/discrimination/agedisc.htm

Workplace Prof Blog
http://lawprofessors.typepad.com/laborprof_blog/

Family Law Sources

ABA Center on Children and the Law
http://www.abanet.org/child/home.html

ABA's Family Law Quarterly
http://www.abanet.org/family/familylaw/tables.html

Adoption Resources
http://www.adoptionresources.org/

Child Custody Law Firms
http://www.childcustodylawfirms.com/

Child Custody Resource
http://www.custodysource.com/

DadsDivorce.com
http://www.dadsdivorce.com/

Divorce and Family Law Blog (Cavers)
http://divorce.caverslaw.com/

Divorce Source
http://www.divorcesource.com/

Divorce Support
http://www.divorcesupport.com/

Family Law Center (Findlaw)
http://family.findlaw.com/

Family Law Prof Blog
http://lawprofessors.typepad.com/family_law/

New York Divorce Report
http://divorce.clementlaw.com/

Support Guidelines
http://www.supportguidelines.com/

Direct Link to Child upport Guidelines
http://www.supportguidelines.com/links.html

Personal Injury/Torts

Accident and Injury Lawyer Blog
http://www.accidentinjurylawyerblog.com/2009/06/personal_injury_links.html

379

American Tort Reform Association (ATRA)
http://www.atra.org

Judicial Hellholes (publication by ATRA)
http://www.atra.org/reports/hellholes/report.pdf

Findlaw on Tort Law
http://www.findlaw.com/01topics/22tort/index.html

Findlaw's Accident and Injury Center
http://injury.findlaw.com/

LawInfo on Torts
http://www.lawinfo.com/Torts.html

Medical Malpractice Attorney Source
http://www.medical-malpractice-attorney-source.com/

TortsProfBlog
http://lawprofessors.typepad.com/tortsprof/

ToxLaw.com
http://www.toxlaw.com/

Glossary

Additur—The process in which a trial judge adds to a jury's award of damages. In a tort suit, a plaintiff may file a motion with the court, seeking an increase in damages. This is called an additur. In many jurisdictions, the court can suggest an additur to the defendant, which means that the defendant has a choice of accepting the additur or having to go through another trial against the plaintiff.

Adverse employment action—An action by an employer that has serious and significant impact on an employee's job. Adverse employment actions include discharges, suspensions, reduction in pay, and transfers to jobs with fewer responsibilities.

Aggravating circumstances—Factors in the sentencing phase of a death penalty case that support a death sentence for a defendant. Examples of aggravating factors include murder committed for monetary gain and murder committed in a particularly heinous manner.

Alienation of affections—A little-used tort (abolished now in the vast majority of states) that provides that a person can be liable to a husband or wife if he or she causes that spouse's partner to lose affection for the spouse. Jilted spouses sometimes asserted this tort claim against the person with whom their partner or former partner had an affair.

Alimony—The requirement that a party provide support—temporary or permanent—to his or her former spouse. Alimony is often required in a dissolved marriage in which one party earns substantially more than the other party.

Alternative dispute resolution—Alternative dispute resolution (ADR) refers to a process of resolving legal disputes aside from the traditional method of resolution by a court of law. Arbitration and mediation are the two most common forms of ADR.

Amici Curiae—Latin for "friends of the court." It refers to an interested organization or individual who files court papers (called amicus briefs) on behalf of one party or another in litigation.

Amicus brief—A brief filed in a case not by one of the parties or litigants but by an interested party known by the Latin term "amicus," which means "friend." They are also known as friend of the court briefs.

Appellant—The party or litigant who appeals an adverse verdict to an intermediate appeals court. For example, if a plaintiff loses at trial and appeals, he or she is known as the appellant.

Appellate advocacy—The practice of law before appellate courts, including arguing questions of law before panels of judges or justices.

Appellee—The party or litigant opposite the appellant. Appellees generally defend the judgment of lower courts because they prevailed before them.

Arbitration—A type of alternative dispute resolution in which the parties do not go to court but instead have their case or dispute heard before a neutral arbitrator who then renders a judgment that is normally binding on the parties. Some collective bargaining agreements call for claims to be submitted to an arbitrator.

Arraignment—An initial court hearing in a criminal case in which a judge informs a defendant of the criminal charges and often asks for an initial plea.

Assistance of counsel—The Sixth Amendment right to assistance of counsel means that a person charged with a crime must have an attorney provided for them if he or she does not have the financial means to acquire legal help.

Attractive nuisance—This refers to a condition on a person's property that is likely to attract children to trespass there. Traditionally, a person has not been obligated to protect trespassers from injury. However, the attractive nuisance doctrine imposes a duty on landowners to take extra precautions (such as warning signs or fences) to ensure that children are not enticed to come onto a property and injure themselves. The attractive nuisance doctrine can come into play, for instance, if a landowner has a swimming pool on his land and does not take any precautions to limit access by trespassing minors.

Bad faith—Bad faith means that a person or company has acted in an improper, often fraudulent, manner. The term is typically used in contract law to show that a party has engaged in very poor conduct against the terms or spirit of a contract. It is also used in employment law to show that a party has acted in a very negative manner.

Bail—The money or security that a defendant puts up in order to avoid immediate incarceration pending trial. The paying of bail money is supposed to ensure that the defendant will appear for later court dates. Generally, the more serious a crime the higher a judge will set bail.

Bankruptcy—A legal process that allows a person or company to start over financially by either discharging or reducing his or her debts. When we say a person is bankrupt that means the person does not have the means to repay creditors and qualifies for some type of legal relief.

Bar examination—A difficult test that law school graduates take in order to become licensed to practice law.

Battery—The intentional or offensive contact upon one person by another. This conduct can constitute a crime or a tort—or both. It is similar to the related concept of assault. In fact, some jurisdictions refer to the crime of "assault and battery." The difference between the two is that the tort of assault requires a plaintiff to actually apprehend an offensive or harmful contact, while battery simply requires the actual contact.

Bench trial—A trial without a jury. In bench trials the judge serves as both judge and jury.

Best interests of a child—This is a standard used in family law to determine the custody of a child. The judge will consider a variety of factors to determine who should be the primary custodial parent of the child. The standard is also used in other family law matters such as child visitation and adoption.

Beyond a reasonable doubt—A stringent legal standard imposed upon the prosecution in criminal cases. The prosecution must prove beyond a reasonable doubt—a very strong certainty—that the defendant committed the crime. Theoretically, many defendants may receive not guilty verdicts in a case, not because the jury thinks they are actually innocent of the crime but because the jury felt that the prosecution did not prove the case beyond a reasonable doubt.

Bifurcate—Bifurcate means to divide in two. In legal matters, this means that a judge has decided to divide certain legal issues into two parts. For example, in many personal injury cases, the first phase of the trial deals with liability and compensatory damages, while the second phase deals with punitive damages. In criminal law, the first phase refers to guilt or innocence and the second phase refers to sentencing.

Bigamy—Marriage to two people. Bigamy is outlawed in the United States and is grounds for divorce.

Brady violation—A Brady violation means that the prosecution has failed to turn over evidence (called exculpatory evidence) that might tend to show that a defendant did not commit the crime in question. The term comes from the U.S. Supreme Court decision *Brady v. Maryland* (1963).

Breach of contract—This means that a term or terms of a legal and binding contract have not been met. When someone breaches a contract, he or she has violated or not adhered to the terms of a contract.

Brief—A misnamed legal document (because it is often up to 20 to 50 pages in length) in which a litigant advances arguments and description of the facts in a case. There are both trial briefs and appellate briefs, as designated by the court, in which the documents are filed.

Burden of proof—The duty imposed upon a litigant to make a certain showing to maintain a claim or defense in legal proceedings. When the law says that a party has the burden of proof, it means that the onus, or burden, is upon that party to put forth some evidence supporting their position.

383

Case law—The law developed by courts in their judicial decisions or opinions. Case law forms the basis of common law.

Cause of action—A legal claim or theory advanced by one party in a lawsuit against another.

Change of venue—This refers to a process or determination by a judge that a trial needs to take place in a different location (or venue) for fairness concerns.

Citation—Citation has several meanings. One refers to a written document that holds a person in violation of a law or regulation. It also refers to the abbreviation or notation for a legal authority, such as a case, statute, administrative regulation, or secondary source.

Civil procedure—The body of law that governs how a case is to take place within the confines of the civil justice system. It regulates the filing of complaints, answers, discovery requests, motions to dismiss, motions for summary judgments, and other documents filed in cases.

Code of Federal Regulations—This publication contains the regulations passed by various federal administrative agencies. For example, rules from the Federal Communication Commission and the Federal Trade Commission are included in this book.

Comparative negligence—Comparative negligence means that the parties' negligent acts are compared and assigned percentages of fault. In such a system, a plaintiff's recovery is reduced by the percentage of his or her own fault.

Compensatory damages—Damages awarded to compensate a person for the harm that he or she has suffered. In a personal injury suit, the plaintiff often seeks compensatory damages for medical bills, loss of wages, pain and suffering, and other similar damages. They are different from nominal or punitive damages.

Compulsory Process Clause—The Sixth Amendment right to compulsory process means that a defendant can have the Court issue subpoenas to ensure that witnesses can be compelled to come to court and give testimony. Without this clause, many defendants would not be able to mount an effective defense.

Concurring opinion—An opinion that agrees with the final result of the majority, or main, opinion but does not necessarily agree with its reasoning.

Confrontation Clause—The Sixth Amendment provides that a defendant has the right "to be confronted with the witnesses against him." This means that a defendant, through his or her attorney, generally has the right to cross-examine witnesses, and if there is no chance for cross-examination, the evidence or statements may not be admitted into evidence and used against the defendant.

Consecutive sentences—When a defendant must serve his or her full sentence for one offense, after which he or she will then begin to serve a sentence for another crime.

Contemporary community standards—The practice of judging whether material is obscene or not by determining how the community views such sexually explicit or otherwise offensive material.

Contingency fee—An arrangement in which an attorney's fee is contingent upon a client's recovery. The standard contingency fee for a personal injury case is one-third of the recovery. In other words, the lawyer receives 33.33% of the award or settlement to the client.

Continuance—An action by a judge to move (or continue) a deadline in a case.

Continuing tort violation—A situation in which a series of individual acts by an employer or agent of an employer violates the rights of an employee. The continuing tort doctrine, or continuing violation theory, provides that the statute of limitations does not start running until the last act.

Contributory negligence—A system of negligence in which a plaintiff cannot recover damages if he or she is found to have contributed to the underlying accident. In other words, if the jury finds that the plaintiff contributed to his or her injuries, ordinarily he or she is barred from recovery.

Court-appointed attorney—An attorney appointed by the court to represent a criminal defendant or other litigant.

Creditor—The person or entity to whom a debtor owes money.

Cross examination—The process in which an attorney questions the other side's witnesses in a trial—civil or criminal. Cross-examination is supposed to serve as a crucible of truth in the sense

that a jury can better determine whether witnesses are telling the truth.

Cruel and unusual punishment—This language from the Eighth Amendment to the U.S. Constitution refers to punishment that is disproportionate to the crime committed and that violates contemporary standards of decency.

Custodial interrogation—The process in which a suspect is questioned by law enforcement officers while under the custody and care of those officials. Officers are supposed to give defendants their Miranda rights before interrogating them.

Defendant—The party or litigant who has been sued by the plaintiff or complaining party.

Defense attorney—The lawyer who represents a defendant during a criminal trial. More generally, it refers to the lawyer who represents a defendant in any type of case.

De minimus—A Latin term meaning "minimal" or "very small." The term is used in many different types of law, including contract law, employment law, and criminal law. For example, in employment law an employee can sue for discrimination if there has been a material change in circumstances in his or her job, not simply *de minimus* inconveniences or small changes in responsibilities.

Deposition—The sworn testimony of a party or witness conducted during the discovery phase of a lawsuit. Attorneys often compare the deposition and trial

385

testimonies of a witness during trial to see if they can uncover inconsistencies.

Dicta—*Dicta,* or *orbiter dicta,* refers to language in a court opinion that is not the essential holding or ruling of the case. If a lawyer wants to de-emphasize aspects of a court's decision, he or she will refer to that language as mere *dicta.*

Direct examination—The process in which an attorney conducts initial questioning of his or her witness. After the attorney finishes the direct examination of the witness, then the other side's attorney can conduct cross-examination of that witness.

Disbarment—The most severe form of professional discipline for an attorney which results in the loss of a law license for a period of years—often five years. The attorney then has to make a showing that he or she has been rehabilitated and complies with other conditions to receive his or her license back.

Discovery—The part of a lawsuit in which each side attempts to find out more information from the other side through a variety of tools, such as depositions, interrogatories, requests for production of documents, and requests for admissions.

Dissenting opinion—A dissenting opinion is one in which a judge disagrees with the result of the court's main opinion.

Diversion—An alternative "punishment" for a criminal defendant who is able to avoid prison time and instead engages in certain activities designed to foster rehabilitation. Diversion is usually available only for minor criminal offenses, such as misdemeanor drug possession.

Double jeopardy—The Fifth Amendment right to be free from double jeopardy means that a person must not face criminal prosecution after an acquittal or a conviction. It also means that the government may not charge a person with a crime that consists of the same evidence as a previous charge.

Due process—This freedom found in the Fifth and Fourteenth Amendments guarantees fundamental fairness under the law.

Equal Protection Clause—This clause in the Fourteenth Amendment requires that similarly situated persons receive the same basic personal rights and protection under the law.

Establishment Clause—This part of the First Amendment provides that "Congress shall make no law respecting an establishment of religion." It provides for a degree of separation between Church and State. Judges, scholars, and members of the community disagree vehemently over the reach and meaning of this clause.

Exclusionary rule—This rule provides that when law enforcement officials violate the Fourth Amendment rights of a person by engaging in an unconstitutional search or seizure, the court will invoke the exclusionary rule and exclude the evidence obtained from the unconstitutional search.

Exculpatory evidence—Evidence that shows that the defendant may be innocent of the charged crime. The U.S.

Supreme Court ruled in *Brady v. Maryland* (1963) that prosecutors are required to turn over exculpatory evidence to the attorneys for criminal defendants. If prosecutors refuse to turn over exculpatory evidence, then this is often referred to as a *Brady* violation.

Ex parte—A Latin term that means "by one party." Sometimes courts will issue "*ex parte* orders," which means that the court will issue a ruling requiring only one party to be present in court. Sometimes the term is used in a negative sense to refer to improper communications by one party with the court or judge without the presence of the other side.

Expert testimony—Testimony by an individual who is deemed by the court to be an expert in a particular field. Some tort cases require expert testimony to establish proof of fault.

Federalism—The distribution of power between the national, central (or federal) government, and the various state governments. The U.S. Constitution divides power between the federal and state governments.

Felony—A criminal offense in which the punishment is at least one year in prison. It is a serious offense in contrast to a misdemeanor. There are legal repercussions for those convicted of felonies, including the loss of several common privileges of citizenship (such as handgun ownership and voting).

For-cause challenges—These challenges are filed by attorneys against prospective jurors because they show or evince an obvious bias that they cannot decide a case impartially.

Force majeure—This French term means "superior force." It refers to a doctrine in contract law that relieves a party from liability if a party cannot fulfill its obligations due to some unforeseeable event, such as an act of God, or war, or a strike.

Fourteenth Amendment—This amendment, ratified in 1868 during Reconstruction, ensures the right of people to due process and equal protection. It is also the vehicle through which various freedoms found in the U.S. Bill of Rights are extended to protect people from infringements by state and local governmental actors.

Free exercise clause—This part of the First Amendment—"nor prohibit the free exercise thereof"—provides that the government shall not violate a person's right to practice his or her religious faith, or the right to believe in no religion at all. The clause provides absolute protection for freedom of belief, but not for conduct that may violate a general public health, safety, or welfare law.

Friend of the court brief—See "Amicus brief."

Grand jury—A large body of citizens (usually about 23) who serve as an initial screening mechanism in criminal cases to determine whether a prosecutor may indict a particular defendant of a crime.

Guardian *ad litem*—A guardian appointed by a court to represent the interests of someone (often a child).

Habeas corpus—A Latin term meaning "you have the body." It refers to a written document ordering prison officials to produce an inmate before the court and, if granted, to release that inmate from custody. Known as the "great writ," *habeas corpus* refers to a federal court action in which an inmate alleges that his conviction violated his or her constitutional rights.

Harmless error—An error committed during a criminal trial that does not impact the overall fairness of the proceeding. In other words, a criminal defendant seeks to show prejudicial, rather than harmless, error to overturn his conviction.

Impartial jury—The Sixth Amendment right to an impartial jury means that a trial jury must be selected from a reasonable cross-section of the community. It means, for example, that the cross-section must not exclude certain persons based on race, gender, or income.

Independent contractor—A person who has been hired to perform a job but who does not qualify as an employee because the employer does not maintain the right to control the details of a contractor's time and manner of the job. The distinction between an employee and independent contractor is very important in legal circles because an employer is generally liable for the torts committed by employees but not for those committed by independent contractors.

Indictment—A formal charge issued by a grand jury in finding that there is enough evidence that a defendant committed a crime for the case to move forward.

In loco parentis—This Latin term means "in place of a parent." It is used in legal circles to give nonparents the responsibility and control over children that ordinarily a child would have. It is sometimes used in school law to mean that school officials have the ability to act in a child's best interests when his or her parents are not present.

In solido—Latin term meaning that parties to a contract or parties to a certain action are held together. In law, sometimes it is said that parties are held liable *in solido* for the damages they cause.

Intentional infliction of emotional distress—This tort occurs when one person engages in outrageous conduct that is beyond the pale of a decent society and that causes another person severe emotional distress. Telling someone that his or her spouse died in an accident—knowing this not to be true—could constitute intentional infliction of emotional distress, for example.

Invitee—A legal term used to describe someone who enters another's land upon the landowner's request. The term is used in tort cases in which the question becomes whether a landowner or premise owner is liable for injuries suffered by the invitee on the landowner's property. Generally, a landowner must exercise ordinary care in protecting an invitee unless there is a so-called "special relationship" that heightens the duty of the landowner (such as the innkeeper-guest relationship).

Irreconcilable differences—A common justification for divorce, particularly when the parties engage in a no-fault divorce. It means that the parties cannot reconcile and the marriage relationship cannot be repaired without alleging specific fault on one or other of the parties. Nearly all states recognize this as a justification for divorce.

Judicial activism—This loaded term refers to a charge that a court or judge exceeds a proper judicial role and decides cases that are better left to the legislature. Often, critics use the label to refer to any court decision with which they disagree. Judicial activism is the opposite of judicial restraint.

Judicial restraint—This concept refers to the practice of judges to decide cases narrowly and to act cautiously to ensure not overstepping into the role of legislators.

Judicial review—The ability of courts to review actions by the legislative and executive branches and determine whether such actions are constitutional or not.

Jurisdiction—This refers to the ability or power of a court to hear a case. If a court has jurisdiction to hear a case, it means that the court has the power to decide the matter. Jurisdiction also generally refers to a geographical location for legal purposes.

Jury instructions—A set of guidelines or instructions read to jurors by the presiding judge. The jury instructions explain the law and related concepts that may be foreign to a layperson not familiar with the legal system.

Jury nullification—The practice of a jury going against the—or nullifying—the law to render a verdict against the evidence in a case. Jury nullification most often describes the practice of a jury to render a "not guilty" verdict in a case where a defendant clearly appears guilty. The jury may have thought that the law was unfair or may have simply acted arbitrarily.

Law clerk—An individual—often a recent law school graduate—who assists a judge in preparing background information about a case and sometimes writes draft opinions. Most U.S. Supreme Court justices employ four law clerks every year. Most law clerks only serve one or two years, while some justices will employ a career clerk.

Leading question—A leading question is one in which an attorney suggests the answer to a witness in his or her question. Leading questions are prohibited, and often you will see attorneys file objections based on the other sides' attorneys asking such questions.

Malpractice—Professional negligence. There are many forms of malpractice, including accountant malpractice, attorney malpractice, medical malpractice, and dental malpractice.

Mediation—A form of alternative dispute resolution in which parties bring their complaints to a third party (the mediator) who helps to hopefully resolve the situation. Mediators are frequently used in some states in family law and juvenile cases.

Medical malpractice—The failure of a medical professional to conform to the prevailing standard of care, resulting in harm to a patient. Most of the time a plaintiff must present expert testimony showing that a physician or other health care professional failed to conform to the necessary standard of care.

Mens rea—This Latin term meaning "guilty mind" refers to the necessary criminal intent of a defendant. To convict a defendant of a crime, a prosecutor must often establish that the defendant possesses the *mens rea* of purposely or knowingly engaging in criminal conduct.

Miller test—The primary test or legal rule used by courts to determine whether sexually oriented material crosses the line and constitutes legal obscenity. Under the *Miller* test—named after the U.S. Supreme Court's decision in *Miller v. California* (1973)—material must appeal predominately to the prurient (morbid or shameful) interest in sex, describe sexual material in a patently offensive way, and have no serious literary, artistic, political, or scientific value.

Miranda rights—Procedural safeguards and warnings that must be given by law enforcement to individuals they place in custody. The U.S. Supreme Court imposed these requirements in *Miranda v. Arizona* (1966) to reduce the problem of coerced confessions in criminal cases.

Misdemeanor—A lower level criminal offense that generally results in a fine or imprisonment for less than a year. Common misdemeanor offenses include simple assault, possession of small amounts of marijuana, traffic violations, and public drunkenness. A misdemeanor is a less serious offense than a felony.

Mistrial—This occurs when a judge orders that a trial must end because of some prejudicial error that affects the underlying fairness and impartiality of the proceedings. If a mistrial occurs, then often a second trial will be conducted at a later date.

Mitigating circumstances—Factors that suggest that a criminal defendant or litigant should receive less punishment than he or she might ordinarily deserve. Mitigating circumstances are important in a wide variety of legal cases, such as capital punishment and lawyer discipline cases. The fact that someone does not have a prior criminal record is a common mitigating factor.

Mitigation of damages—This duty provides that a person who sues another and claims damages must take some steps to lessen the impact of the harmful conduct. For example, if an employer unlawfully fires an employee, the employee must attempt to mitigate damages by seeking another job rather than simply stay at home and do nothing.

Mixed motive—This refers to a type of case in employment discrimination law in which an employer acted with both legitimate and illegitimate motives. A plaintiff must show that the employer's illegitimate motive played a substantial role in the unlawful employment action.

Model Penal Code—This code, developed by the American Law Institute, seeks to provide a comprehensive overview of criminal law. It offers model statutes for various types of crimes, defenses, and other relevant criminal concepts. Most states have adopted much of the Model Penal Code in their own legal codes.

Motion to compel—A motion filed in court by an attorney to force the other side to answer requests for information during discovery—the time in a case when each side seeks to uncover information from the other side. If a party refuses to respond in a timely fashion to a discovery request (such as interrogatories), the other party may file a motion to compel with the court.

Motion to reconsider—A motion filed by the losing party in a case asking the court or judge to reconsider the ruling of the judge or jury. A losing party often will file a motion to reconsider before filing an appeal to a higher court.

Mug shot—The photograph of a defendant during the booking process in which the arrested person is taken to the police station for processing.

Negligence—Negligence refers to fault and is one of the three major categories of tort suits. A negligence claim consists of (1) duty, (2) breach of duty, (3) causation, and (4) damages.

Negligence *per se*—This doctrine applies when someone violates a statute and is presumed to be negligent. For example, if you are driving 15 miles over the speed limit and hit someone, the law would say that you are negligent *per se*.

Nominal damages—Small damage awards that amount to damages in name only. Sometimes juries award nominal damages when they believe that plaintiffs have proven their cases but have not shown much evidence of actual harm.

Obscenity—Obscenity refers to an unprotected category of expression dealing in sexually explicit material that appeals to a morbid interest in sex, is patently offensive, and has no serious literary, artistic, political, or scientific value.

Opening statement—The introduction of a case to a jury by an attorney. In the opening statement, the attorney seeks to advance the client's theory of the case and create a favorable impression with the jury.

Palimony—A type of alimony or support that is given by one party to another in an unmarried relationship. When palimony is awarded, the unmarried couple generally has lived together for a long period of time.

Paralegal—A non-lawyer who performs routine legal tasks (often document management of discovery materials) and usually has achieved some level of legal education. A good paralegal can be invaluable to a lawyer.

Pendente lite—Latin for "while the matter is pending." It refers to a court order that applies while a matter is still under litigation. Its most common usage occurs in family law in which a party seeks *pendent lite* child support while the divorce and child custody matters are under litigation.

Peremptory challenges—These challenges are those filed by attorneys against a prospective juror because the attorney does not believe the person would make a good juror for his or her client. They are distinguished from for-cause challenges. The U.S. Supreme Court has placed limitations on the exercise of peremptory challenges, ruling that they

391

cannot be used in a racial or gender discriminatory manner.

Petitioner—The party that appeals (or petitions) the higher court to review a decision by a lower court. The party that appeals to the U.S. Supreme Court for review of a lower court decision is called the petitioner.

Petit jury—A petit jury, as opposed to a grand jury, is a trial jury normally comprised of 12 jurors. Not all states require petit juries to consist of 12 members.

Plurality opinion—An opinion that has not earned the votes of a majority of the court, but that has earned the votes of multiple judges or justices on a court.

Precedent—This term refers to the fact that a legal authority has lasting power and influence beyond simply the resolution of the particular issues and parties in the case itself. Past court decisions serve as precedent for future court decisions.

Preponderance of the evidence—This standard, used in most civil law cases, provides that something more than likely happened. It is a lower standard than either the clear and convincing evidence and beyond a reasonable doubt standards.

Presumption of innocence—This fundamental principle of American law means that a defendant accused of a crime is presumed innocent and the prosecution has the burden of proving beyond a reasonable doubt that the defendant committed the crime.

Prima facie—This Latin term literally means "at first face." In legal terms it means basic. In employment law, an

employee suing her employer for discrimination initially must establish a *prima facie* case of discrimination, which then shifts the burden to the employer to advance a legitimate reason for its action against the employee.

Probable cause—Probable cause means that there is a reasonably substantial basis that a crime took place. Probable cause means much more than a mere hunch; there has to be some articulable basis to suspect that a crime took place or contraband is at a location. The Fourth Amendment provides that no warrants shall issue unless the police show to a magistrate's satisfaction that there was probable cause for the search.

Pro bono—*Pro bono*, or *pro bono publico*, means "for the good of the public." It refers to legal services that are done by a lawyer free of charge. The ABA recommends that lawyers engage in a certain number of *pro bono* hours of service.

Pro se—A Latin term that signifies that a litigant represents himself or herself in court.

Prosecutorial discretion—Prosecutorial discretion refers to the ability of a prosecutor to decide whether to press charges and what type of charges to initiate.

Public defender—A public defender is a lawyer paid or funded by the government who provides legal assistance and legal services to indigent criminal defendants. Public defender systems arose across the country as a result of the U.S. Supreme Court's decision in *Gideon v. Wainwright* (1963), providing that state court defendants charged with felonies must have a lawyer appointed for them if they cannot afford an attorney.

Punitive damages—These damages punish the tortfeasor or wrongdoer as opposed to compensating a plaintiff for actual harm suffered. Some advocates of tort reform argue for limiting or eliminating punitive damages, contending that they provide a windfall for plaintiffs and their attorneys.

Rap sheet—A rap sheet refers to a defendant's arrest and conviction record that is maintained by a criminal justice agency.

Reasonable doubt—See "Beyond a reasonable doubt."

Record—The record in a case refers to the transcript of the official proceedings of a court hearing, trial, or other judicial proceeding. The record also includes the evidence and various transcripts in a case.

Remittitur—An action by a court to reduce the amount of damages in a civil case. In a tort case, for example, the defendant may petition the court to remit, or reduce, the amount of damages awarded by a jury. Sometimes a trial judge may grant a remittitur, and sometimes an appellate court may grant a remittitur.

Res ipsa loquitur—This Latin phrase means "the thing speaks for itself." It is a doctrine in tort law that provides that negligence is the only rational explanation for why harm befell a plaintiff.

Search warrant—This paper signed by a judge or magistrate authorizes a law enforcement official to search a particular area or place for particular pieces of contraband.

Settlement—A process in which parties to a legal dispute agree to resolve their differences (sometimes by one party paying money to another) rather than continue with the lawsuit.

Speedy trial—The Sixth Amendment right to a speedy trial means that there must not be unreasonable delay between the initial charging of a criminal defendant and further proceedings in the case.

Statute of limitation—A time period in which a plaintiff has to file suit. In many states, a plaintiff has a one-year statute of limitation for personal injury tort suits. This means that the plaintiff must file suit within a year of the accident or incident or else lose the right to sue forever.

Stop and frisk—A brief stop and patdown of a person by a police officer to make sure that individual is not carrying weapons.

Strict scrutiny—The highest standard of review in constitutional law cases. It means that the government must advance a compelling governmental interest in a most narrowly tailored manner, often in the least-restrictive way possible.

Structured settlement—A settlement that is structured or framed over a period of time for which one party pays another money to settle and resolve a lawsuit.

Tortfeasor—An individual who commits a tort. In other words, if person A invades the privacy of person B, person A is a tortfeasor because he or she has committed the tort of invasion of privacy.

393

Tort reform—A movement to curtail frivolous lawsuits, reduce the amount of punitive damages, and otherwise cut down on the litigiousness of the American judicial system. Tort reform advocates often highlight certain lawsuits that they think seek excessive damages and have little merit.

Trial attorney—An attorney who is a litigator, who regularly appears in courtrooms to try cases before judges and juries.

Venire—Venire refers to the panel of prospective persons from which attorneys and the court draw from to form a jury to hear a case.

Voir dire—This is an old French term meaning "to see and to speak." It refers to the process of selecting and sitting a jury in a case.

Wobbler—A crime that can be charged or prosecuted as either a misdemeanor or a felony.

Workers compensation—A system in which employees receive a portion of their wages and receive medical coverage for work-related injuries in exchange for not suing their employer.

Writ of certiorari—An order from the U.S. Supreme Court indicating that it agrees to hear a case appealed from a lower court. A litigant who loses in a lower court and seeks Supreme Court review files a petition for writ of certiorari.

Year and a day rule—The year and a day rule was a common law rule that held that a person could not be charged with murder if his or her victim died more than a year (a year and a day) after the original attack or assault. Nearly all jurisdictions have abolished the year and a day rule.

Zoning—The practice of land-use regulation that provides for the proper location of certain types of businesses or residences on certain areas of land. Oftentimes this area of law is referred to as land-use zoning. An example of a zoning law is one that might prohibit adult entertainment establishments from locating within certain distances of a school or playground or church.

Index

Note: (ill.) indicates photos and illustrations.

E

Easterbrook, Frank, 106
Eddings v. Oklahoma, 77
editorials, 338
Edmund v. Florida, 77
EEOC v. Texas Hydraulics, 239–40
Eighth Amendment
  cruel and unusual punishment, 73, 96
  death penalty, 73–81
  three-strikes law, 81–82
electoral college, 30
Ellsworth, Oliver, 5, 89, 100
email at work, 268–69
Emancipation Proclamation, 31
eminent domain, 67
emotional distress, 312–14
employee handbook, 216
Employee Polygraph Protection Act, 269
employment-at-will doctrine
  collective bargaining agreement (CBA), 216
  definition, 215
  employee handbook, 216
  lifetime employment, 218
  origin of, 217
  permanent employment, 218
  physical assault, 219–20
  public policy exception, 218–20
  repeal of, 220
employment compensation. *See* Fair Labor Standards Act
employment discrimination. *See* Title VII of the Civil Rights Act of 1964
employment law. *See also* Age Discrimination in Employment Act of 1967; Americans with Disabilities Act of 1990; employment-at-will doctrine; Fair Labor Standards Act; Title VII of the Civil Rights Act of 1964; workers' compensation

anti-discrimination laws, 221–22
breast feeding, 267
discrimination, 221–22
drug test, 268
email at work, 268–69
Family and Medical Leave Act of 1993, 251–52
Lily Ledbetter Act, 252, 254
lunch/rest periods, 266, 269
polygraph test, 269
taxable employment discrimination awards, 266
unemployment benefits, 267–68
unemployment benefits coverage when fired, 267
Employment Non-Discrimination Act of 2007, 224, 225
endorsement test, 41–42
Engel v. Vitale, 44–45
English, George W., 93
Equal Credit Opportunity Act (ECOA), 196, 197
Equal Employment Opportunity Commission, 228–32
Equal Pay Act, 222
equal protection clause, 86
equal protection violation, 87
Establishment Clause
  school prayer, 44–45
  Ten Commandments and government property, 43–44
  Van Orden v. Perry, 42
  violation of, 41
Evarts, William, 104–5
Evarts Act, 104–5
Ewing, Gary, 81
Ewing v. California, 81–82, 146
Ex Parte Quirin, 94
ex post facto laws, 25–26, 39, 40
excessive bail, 151–52
exclusionary rule, 61, 96

executive branch
  Clinton v. City of New York, 31, 32
  composition of, 29–30
  executive orders, 31–32
  impeachment, 32–33
  presidential elections, 30
  presidential powers, 30–31
executive orders, 31–32
exempt assets, 208
expert testimony, 334–35, 336
expert witnesses, 140–41

F

factual causation, 318
Fair and Accurate Credit Transactions Act, 195, 202
Fair Credit Billing Act, 194
Fair Credit Reporting Act, 194, 195, 197
Fair Debt Collections Practices Act, 204–6
Fair Employment Practice, 32
Fair Labor Standards Act
  Belo contract, 258, 259
  blue collar workers, 257
  computer programmers, 257
  definition, 254–55
  exemption law, 256
  minimum wage, 255–56
  overtime exemptions, 256–58
  overtime pay, 255
  taxicab exemption, 258
  tips, 258, 262
false criminal charges, 314–15
false light invasion of privacy, 345, 346
Falwell, Jerry, 313–14
fame, 340
Family and Medical Leave Act of 1993, 251–52
family courts, 115

404

pro bono, 126, 127

pro hac vice status, 121

probable cause, 58, 59–60

procedural due process, 66, 86–87

products liability
    breach of warranty, 346–47
    definition of, 346
    Ford Pinto, 348
    problems resulting in, 347
    strict liability, 347

professional negligence. *See also* negligence
    discovery rule, 336–37
    examples of, 334
    expert testimony, 334–35, 336
    legal malpractice, 335–36
    medical malpractice, 334–35
    statute of repose, 337
    statutes of limitations, 336–37

protected class, 233

proximate causation, 318–19

public defender, 128, 129

public employees, 51, 53, 54

public figure and defamation, 340–41

public hearings, 24

public interest law firm, 126

public officials, 340–41

public policy exception, 218–20

public school students, 53–55

public trial, 69

"Publius," 9

punitive damages, 327–28, 329, 330–32

pure comparative negligence, 326

Q

qualified immunity, 60

"qualified individual with a disability," 246, 248

R

race
    in adoption, 304
    in employment, 223

racial discrimination, 24, 26–27, 233

Randolph, Edmund, 5, 6, 12

rap music, 48

Read, George, 5

reaffirmation, 210

Reagan, Ronald, 91, 106

reasonable accommodation, 248–50

reasonable doubt, 144–45

"reasonable person," 316–17

rebuttal argument, 174

record, 183

recrimination, 288

Redding, Savana, 59, 60

Redding v. Sanford Unified School District, 59

Reed, Morgan, 328

Rehabilitation Act of 1973, 222, 245

Rehnquist, William
    appointment, 94
    as chief justice, 90
    Furman v. Georgia, 75
    Hustler Magazine v. Falwell, 313–14
    lack of judicial experience, 92
    Santa Fe Independent School District v. Doe, 47
    tenure of, 91
    Van Orden v. Perry, 42
    Wallace v. Jaffree, 47

religious discrimination, 238–40

remarriage, 294

reprimand, 132

requests for admissions, 135

requests for examinations, 135

requests for production of documents, 135

res ipsa loquitur, 316, 317–18

restaurants, 26

retainer, 125

retaliation, 240–41

retirement account, 291

reversal, 184

reverse age discrimination, 243

reverse mortgage, 203

Reynolds, George, 41, 284

Reynolds v. United States, 41, 284

rhetorical hyperbole, 340

Rhode Island
    common-law marriage, 275
    endorsement test, 41–42
    Good Samaritan laws, 324
    high court, 114
    opening trial statements, 173
    pre-marital agreement, 285
    sexual discrimination ban, 224

Richmond Newspapers v. Virginia, 69

right to bear arms, 55

right to counsel, 96, 153–54

right to privacy, 82, 83

right-to-sue letter, 230

Ring v. Arizona, 80

Ritter, Halsted L., 93

Roberts, John G., Jr.
    as chief justice, 90
    pre-Supreme Court, 91

Roberts v. Louisiana, 76

Robinson v. California, 96

Romano v. Oklahoma, 80

Rooney, Kevin, 218

Rooney v. Tyson, 218

Roper v. Simmons, 74, 80, 81, 111, 188–89

Roth v. United States, 48

Rucshner v. ADT Security Systems, 321

Rule 10, 100

rule of four, 97

rules of civil procedure, 136–37, 138

Rutgers, Elizabeth, 34

Rutgers v. Waddington, 34

Rutledge, John, 5, 89